THE DEAD OF WINTER

THE DEAD OF WINTER

HOW BATTLEFIELD INVESTIGATORS,
WWII VETERANS, AND FORENSIC
SCIENTISTS SOLVED THE MYSTERY
OF THE BULGE'S LOST SOLDIERS

BILL WARNOCK

Chamberlain Bros.
a member of
Penguin Group (USA) Inc.
New York
2005

CHAMBERLAIN BROS.
Published by the Penguin Group
Penguin Group (USA) Inc., 375 Hudson Street, New York, New York 10014, USA
Penguin Group (Canada), 90 Eglinton Avenue East, Suite 700, Toronto, Ontario M4P 2Y3,
Canada (a division of Pearson Penguin Canada Inc.)
Penguin Books Ltd, 80 Strand, London WC2R 0RL, England
Penguin Ireland, 25 St Stephen's Green, Dublin 2, Ireland (a division of Penguin Books Ltd)
Penguin Group (Australia), 250 Camberwell Road, Camberwell, Victoria 3124, Australia
(a division of Pearson Australia Group Pty Ltd)
Penguin Books India Pvt Ltd, 11 Community Centre, Panchsheel Park, New Delhi–110 017, India
Penguin Group (NZ), Cnr Airborne and Rosedale Roads, Albany, Auckland 1310, New
Zealand (a division of Pearson New Zealand Ltd)
Penguin Books (South Africa) (Pty) Ltd, 24 Sturdee Avenue, Rosebank, Johannesburg 2196,
South Africa

Penguin Books Ltd, Registered Offices: 80 Strand, London WC2R 0RL, England

Warnock, William C., date.
  The dead of winter: how battlefield investigators, WWII veterans, and forensic scientists
solved the mystery of the Bulge's lost soldiers / William C. Warnock.
    p. cm.
  ISBN 1-59609-085-5
  1. World War, 1939–1945—Missing in action—United States. 2. World War, 1939–1945—
Missing in action—Belgium. 3. World War, 1939–1945—Missing in action—Luxembourg.
4. Missing persons—Investigation—United States. 5. Ardennes, Battle of the, 1944–1945.
I. Title.
  D810.D4W37 2005   2005048484
  940.54'8—dc22

Printed in the United States of America
10 9 8 7 6 5 4 3 2 1

Book design by Mike Rivilis

CONTENTS

INTRODUCTION

I am a character in this book and also its author. Yet the book is hardly my story alone. It is the story of an entire team of unpaid volunteers in Belgium and the United States. Our group included young men as well as World War II veterans, and we joined forces to search for missing U.S. soldiers killed during the Battle of the Bulge. The team came into existence forty-five years after that epic struggle and began hunting for those lost servicemen in hopes of recovering their remains.

As founding member of the team, I served (and continue to serve) as its chief data analyst and archival researcher. Along with fellow team members in the United States, I endeavored to learn things not found in any book. My colleagues and I searched for keys to the past in government archives and private collections across America and in Europe. We interviewed countless eyewitnesses—living, breathing links to the past. All too often, the quest for clues revealed nothing helpful, but occasionally bits of wheat emerged from the mountain of chaff. Those kernels of information held the possibility of success—the possibility that a missing soldier might be reclaimed from the wilderness.

Team members in Belgium took that information and toiled to make success reality. They scoured former battlegrounds looking for unmarked grave sites. The Belgians persevered for years against long odds. Cold, blowing, drenching weather never stopped them. Weary to the bone and slathered with forest mud, they were happy being miserable, a strange paradox of recovery work. Their labor usually brought frustration and disappointment, but it also produced success.

This book recounts stories of success and failure, and it will also recount the lives of missing servicemen lost during the Bulge and how they met their tragic fates. The families of those men also are integral to the story. During and after the war, they grieved but had no remains to bury and scant answers to their questions. Regrettably, my teammates and I had no ability to create happy endings, but we succeeded in providing answers and the solace those answers brought. Our efforts afforded the families an opportunity to inter their lost loved ones in marked graves. We did that in the steadfast belief that all of America's war dead should be accounted for, no matter how many years have passed. In the words of President Calvin Coolidge, "The nation which forgets its defenders will itself be forgotten."

The young men who fell while carrying the weight of battle earned our grateful remembrance. And so we continue searching for those perished warriors who remain on bygone battlefields. Death took more from them than most. They patiently wait in faraway fields and forests, places where no memorials stand, places where no visitors leave flowers. May each man one day find his rightful quarters among the hallowed acres of marble crosses.

—b.w.

"The highest reward for a person's toil is not what they get for it, but what they become by it."
—*John Ruskin (1819–1900)*

Chapter 1
CREEPY CORNER

He dug down to a half-rotted overshoe and tugged it free from the black soil at the bottom of an old foxhole. The hair on the back of his neck prickled as he stared at the bottom of the hole. *"C'est occupé!"* he muttered in amazement. It was a grave. The clearing he had created revealed two human bones, the remains of a lower leg.

In the forest around the foxhole, spruce boughs shut out the sun, forcing twilight on the dig. The scent of freshly turned soil rose from the rich humus at the bottom of the hole. The digger knelt over it and scrabbled in the earth near the bones. One of his fingernails grazed something metal, and he grabbed a small, oblong artifact—a brass dog tag. He swelled with excitement, conscious that he stood on the threshold of something big. His partner shared the mood, leaning over to watch as the digger rubbed dirt and greenish oxidation from the tag to reveal the name Robert L. Muyres. The two men stared at each other and pondered the same question. Did the bones belong to the soldier named on the tag?

The date of the discovery was September 27, 1988. The digger, Jean-Louis Seel (surname pronounced "Sail"), and his partner, Jean-Philippe Speder, were natives of the French-speaking section of Belgium. Together, they had spent nine years searching for World War

II artifacts in the Ardennes region of their country and Germany. Among their many exploits, they had unearthed the lost graves of three German soldiers. But they had never found the remains of a U.S. serviceman, and they were unaware of anyone who had made such a find in recent decades. Numerous Germans had been found but no Americans. Apparently that was no longer true. The overshoe and dog tag found by Seel were both U.S. Army issue and 1940s vintage.

The events leading up to that discovery began three days prior on a Saturday morning. Speder and his wife, Sonia, had just returned from a vacation on the Mediterranean coast of Spain when Seel visited their home in Stavelot, Belgium. Speder later recalled, "He asked me if I was ready to make a 'reconnaissance patrol' on a new sector. My wife was dog tired from the trip, so I said, 'Let's go.'" The two relic hunters, equipped with metal detectors, hopped in their cars and drove east, toward Germany.

Just two weeks shy of his twenty-fifth birthday, Speder was a slender man, with rawboned features and blue eyes framed by gold-rimmed glasses. A sergeant in the Belgian Army Reserve, he was also the father of an eleven-month-old son. Besides being a part-time soldier, he worked full-time as a technician and troubleshooter at a water-treatment plant in the Belgian city of St. Vith. As for Seel, he was single, twenty-six years of age, solidly built, and a man of considerable vitality. He had served in the Belgian Army as a commando and now worked for the Belgian railway (SNCB) at a large marshaling yard near the town of Montzen. His friendship with Speder began when the two met as teenagers while attending a technical school where they studied electromechanics. At that time, Speder had already assembled a small collection of battlefield artifacts. He soon infected Seel with the relic-hunting bug.

By September 1988, the two diggers had amassed sizable collections and an abundance of field experience. They motored toward Germany, their destination Losheimergraben crossroads, which straddled the Belgian-German border. That junction had been the scene of heavy combat in December 1944, during the first two days of the Battle of the Bulge. Soldiers of the U.S. 99th Infantry Division defended the area against enemy troops of the 12.Volks-Grenadier-Division. After a fierce contest for the crossroads, the numerically superior Germans finally shook it free from the Americans (who were unable to recapture Losheimergraben until February 1945). Seel and Speder had searched that honor-soaked battleground several times, but only on the Belgian side.

This particular Saturday would be their first foray across the international boundary. They passed through the customs checkpoint at Losheimergraben, home to a contingent of Belgian and German border police. Several hundred yards away, Seel and Speder parked alongside Bundesstraße 265, a German highway that skirted the border. The two friends climbed out of their cars and slipped into the nearby woods clutching their metal detectors. The area lay within a German state forest and nature park, and it had become an unwelcome place for relic hunters, so Seel and Speder took care to remain out of sight. The woods around them consisted of spruce trees, many seventy feet tall and planted in perfectly straight rows. Their intermeshed branches shaded the forest floor except for small patches illuminated by shafts of light that filtered down from above. In that wilderness, a place more ethereal than wild, the two Belgians ambled along a brown-carpeted corridor that separated two rows of conifers. Seel and Speder soon came upon a line of old foxholes and began using their equipment. The ground teemed with metallic objects, everything from grenades to shell fragments and small-arms ammunition. Here and there, holes marred the forest floor where a ration can or chunk of shrapnel had been removed and tossed aside, indicating the presence of other searchers before them. In some places only an empty hole existed with no artifact resting nearby. Perhaps an object of value had been found there. One thing was certain; whoever made the holes had been untidy. Such behavior had helped make relic hunters unwelcome. Seel and Speder operated in a more discreet manner, filling in each hole they dug and erasing all evidence of their work.

Unable to canvass the entire area in one day, the duo returned on the following Tuesday, a crisp and clear autumn day. Clad in woolen sweaters and faded denims, they retraced their footsteps until they reached a new-growth section of the forest. The trees there were about fifteen feet high. As Seel surveyed the area, he noted numerous foxholes and larger entrenchments. They were still deep and apparently undisturbed. His attention then focused on a small, crumbling hole—a slit trench, almost completely filled in. Its shallowness distinguished it from every other hole, a seemingly insignificant fact to anyone who lacked Seel's keen eye.

He always looked for things that seemed out of place or inconsistent with their surroundings (a talent he had polished as a sniper with the commandos). When he passed his detector over the slit trench, he heard a shrill whine through his headphones. There was definitely something down there. He began using his hands and a lightweight mattock to dig through the layers of soil that separated past from present. The first object he uncovered was an aluminum cooking pan of U.S. manufacture. There were also K-ration cans, GI toothbrushes, and shaving razors. About that time, Speder approached the scene.

"Find anything?" he asked in French.

"It's full of stuff."

Speder stopped and took a seat next to the trench. He watched as his colleague continued downward until hitting the trench bottom. There he found the overshoe, dog tag, and leg bones. He handed the overshoe to Speder, who fished inside it and found a leather service shoe (size 9D), which held vestiges of a wool sock and more bones.

The Belgians felt certain they had located the grave of an American soldier—or at least part of one. Perhaps this was the resting place of Robert Muyres, the man identified on the dog tag. To ascertain the answer, they had to excavate the site. That first meant removing a young tree planted in the center of the hole. They severed its roots and wrenched it from the ground. Seel dragged the fallen timber away, far away. German forest rangers tended to regard unauthorized tree cutting as something tantamount to murder. With the tree out of their way, Seel and Speder delicately cleared the hole. After hours of labor, they reached the shattered remains of a skull and a bullet-pierced helmet. The unfortunate GI had apparently been killed by a head shot. Near the skull lay a pair of cervical vertebrae and two brass tags attached to a necklace, which had a St. Christopher medal affixed. Each tag had a rubber grommet around its outer edge—silencers. Infantrymen used these to prevent unwanted jingling sounds. The tags, corroded and dirt encrusted, were impossible to read.

Seel and Speder inventoried their discoveries on the forest floor beside the slit trench. They had over one hundred bones, all stained a drab earthen color from decades in the ground. The artifacts recovered with them included a mirror, plastic comb, cigarette lighter, leather wallet, PFC stripe, pocket-sized missal, St. Christopher medal, plastic prayer card, rosary beads, two Bakelite crucifixes, M1 helmet and liner, three dog tags, three coins, scraps of GI clothing, as well as footwear and leather-palmed gloves. A wool blanket covered the soldier's body. Above it, more U.S. artifacts: cookware, mess gear, shoelaces, eyeglasses, toothbrushes, shaving brushes, shaving razors, sulfadiazine tablets, goggle lenses, eating utensils, empty K-ration cans, water-purification tablets, shreds of a sleeping bag, cleaning tools for an M1 rifle, two rifle-grenade sights, three rifle-grenade launchers, three fragmentation grenades, .30- and .45-caliber ammunition, and a bayonet scabbard marked Guy Mathena. The jumble also included German items: a toothbrush, mess kit, pair of eyeglasses, bayonet frog and scabbard, 7.92-mm cartridges, three concussion grenades (Eierhandgranaten), and the moldering remains of a visored hat (Schirmmütze). In addition to being a grave, the slit trench had been a rubbish pit for the debris of battle.

Besides the dog tags and U.S. bayonet scabbard, the Belgians found three other American artifacts that denoted specific persons. The additional objects included two rubber stamps—S 8517 and B 5011—used for imprinting clothing and equipment with a laundry mark. The third object was a rotted hunk of cloth stamped S 8517. (Laundry marks were a form of identification derived from the first letter of a serviceman's surname and the last four digits of his serial number.)

As the sun dropped toward the western horizon, Seel and Speder finished the day's last task, defusing the grenades. The procedure took only a few seconds for each grenade, and it entailed three steps: unscrewing the fuse assembly, breaking off the detonator, and pouring out the powdered TNT charge. Shortly before sunset, Speder hustled back to his car and fetched a camera. The forest lacked sufficient light for photography, so the artifacts and bones had to be moved to a weedy clearing with enough ambient light to snap a few pictures. Afterward, Speder loaded the artifacts into his car trunk. Seel meanwhile placed the bones back in the slit trench and camouflaged the site. It was too risky to transport bones across the border. If the border police searched Speder's car, it would not bode well to have human remains stashed in the trunk. As it turned out, the police just waved the two Belgians through the Losheimergraben checkpoint.

That evening, at Speder's home, he and Seel scrubbed the two dog tags. The lower right corner of one tag revealed the letter C, which stood for Catholic. That suggested a decedent other than Robert

Muyres, a Protestant according to his tag. The Catholic religious artifacts also pointed toward someone other than Muyres. But who? Seel and Speder continued cleaning the tags until it was possible to read the name Alphonse M. Sito and the serial number 33728517. Here was the apparent answer. And it jibed with the laundry mark S 8517.

The next day was Jean-Philippe Speder's fourth wedding anniversary, and work still remained at the grave site. He promised his wife supper at an "unforgettable restaurant" if she excused his absence during the day. She readily accepted the arrangement. After a kiss good-bye, he was out the door and headed to the forest along with Seel and fellow artifact hunter, Jean-Michel Roth. The three men spread a plastic sheet beside the slit trench and arranged the bones on it. They spent most of the day sifting through the soil for anything they might have overlooked. Only one item turned up—a silk Christmas card about four inches square. It carried a holiday motif and four words: "To One I Love." The Belgians tried to imagine the woman who purchased it back in 1944. "We were very touched by it," Speder said. "We wondered if it had been mailed to Sito. And if so, what happened to the woman who sent it? Was she still alive?"

THERE WAS, OF COURSE, A LARGER QUESTION. What should be done with Sito's remains? Seel and Speder understood the procedure for handling the remains of a German soldier, but the process for an American was outside their experience. However, they knew where to turn for help. Seel telephoned William C. C. Cavanagh, a military historian and British expatriate who lived in the area. Cavanagh, an authority on the 99th Infantry Division and Battle of the Bulge events in eastern Belgium, spoke fluent French and was aware that Seel and Speder had recovered the remains of three German soldiers. He once made a request of the two diggers: "Call me if you ever find the grave of an American."

When that call finally came, Seel expressed one concern. If German police or forest rangers became involved, there could be trouble because Sito's remains were in a state forest. With that in mind, Cavanagh contacted Francis J. Duffy, a World War II veteran and superintendent of the Ardennes American Cemetery near Liège, Belgium. Duffy knew how to handle the matter. He rang the U.S. Army Memorial Affairs Activity–Europe and reported that two anonymous individuals had found the remains of a soldier believed to be Alphonse M. Sito. Duffy spoke with the head of Memorial Affairs, Michael C. Tocchetti, a funeral director and a civilian employee on the army payroll.

Tocchetti and his staff operated a mortuary at Frankfurt, Germany. Their facility was the central processing center for the bodies of Department of Defense personnel and their family members who died in Europe and neighboring countries. Most of the workload involved handling suicides, murders, cardiac failures, drug overdoses, and automobile accidents. There were also aircraft crashes. But at least once a year, staff members traveled to a bygone battlefield to recover World War II–era remains. These missions usually followed an accidental discovery, similar to the Alphonse Sito case.

After Duffy's call, Tocchetti checked microfiche records and confirmed that Sito's remains had never been recovered or positively identified. The head of Memorial Affairs then spoke directly with Cavanagh. They decided all parties should meet at Losheimergraben on October 11, 1988. They also decided not to invite German police or forest rangers. Tocchetti's objective was to validate the discovery and to survey the location. He met Cavanagh, Seel, and Speder in the parking lot of the Hotel Schröder, one of two commercial establishments at tiny Losheimergraben. Cavanagh also invited Maurice Sperandieu, a Belgian who served as a noncommissioned officer with Patton's Third Army during the Bulge. The gathering also included a sergeant who belonged to Tocchetti's staff. Together, the six men filed into the forest with the two diggers leading the way. To establish the validity of the discovery, Tocchetti first examined the bones to determine if they were human or animal. The answer was immediately obvious—human. He also examined the collection of personal effects, including the two dog tags and necklace. Everything was authentic. Until that time, the Belgians had not tampered with the leather wallet. As Seel explained, "For me, the billfold was a private thing. That's why I never opened it. When I gave all the material to Tocchetti, I asked him to check the billfold. He did so and immediately pulled out one dog tag, then another." There were now a total of four brass tags embossed with Sito's name and serial number. The pair in his wallet had a next-of-kin name and address: ANNA SITO, 2324 FLEET ST., BALTIMORE, MD.

Satisfied the discovery was genuine, Tocchetti made arrangements to conduct a recovery operation the following week. He and four other members of Memorial Affairs would carry it out. When they arrived at Losheimergraben on October 20, the day was foul and wet. Rain bounced off the pavement on the road outside the forest, but inside the woods the downpour diminished. Tightly woven tree limbs created a natural umbrella, albeit a leaky one. Beneath the drizzling branches, the recovery team turned the ground with shovels and spades. All team members wore civvies, which eventually became soaked. Cavanagh and the Belgians looked on as the crew first enlarged the slit trench and then sifted all loose dirt through wire screens. Tocchetti hoped to find those parts of the skeleton still missing, in particular, fourteen vertebrae and forty-nine small bones of the hands. None surfaced. Animals may have taken them, but another possibility loomed. The soil in the forest was naturally acidic due to all the spruce needles. That by itself made little difference, but when combined with rainwater or snowmelt, the results could be highly corrosive. Many of the recovered bones showed exfoliation due to destructive agents in the soil.

After all the digging and sifting, the army team boxed up the personal effects and skeletal remains of the young soldier who had presumably died on that ground forty-four years earlier. The recovery operation was over, and, thankfully, nobody from the German forestry service had chanced upon the scene. Perhaps the rain had kept them indoors.

Back at the Frankfurt mortuary, Tocchetti oversaw the completion of maps, reports, and other paperwork. Then a commercial airliner flew the bones and artifacts to Honolulu, home of the U.S. Army Central Identification Laboratory, Hawaii—commonly referred to by its acronym CILHI (pronounced "Sil-Hi"). Staff members at the laboratory would officially determine the dead man's identity through scientific examination. In the interim, his remains received the designation X-9463.

The identification process impressed Seel and Speder. It represented a remarkable contrast to the simple routine followed by German authorities when they recovered one of their missing servicemen. The Germans often used dog tags as the sole basis for identification. That seemed almost lackadaisical compared to the U.S. approach. The Americans considered dog tags and other artifacts as circumstantial evidence that required corroboration with biological evidence. Forensic anthropologists and odontologists in Hawaii looked for matches regarding age, race, gender, height, and dental anatomy. Any discrepancies had to be reconcilable.

FROM A SCIENTIFIC STANDPOINT, the experts in Hawaii could determine if X-9463 was truly Alphonse Sito. But what were the circumstances of his death, and what events led to it? Cavanagh undertook a quest for answers. He knew that Company B, 394th Infantry Regiment (part of the 99th Division) fought in the forest section where the grave had been found. He also knew there were living persons with firsthand information about what had happened in that forest, at that exact spot. The 99th had a well-established veterans association with more than 2,900 members. One of those was Otto "Bill" Meyer, a newspaper publisher and elder resident of Marion, Kansas. He printed the town's only newspaper as well as the *Checkerboard*, the official publication of the 99th Infantry Division Association. The same day Cavanagh learned about the grave site, he telephoned Meyer. It became one of multiple calls the two exchanged that day. Meyer knew several veterans of Company B, and he immediately phoned them, hoping to gain insight. All of them remembered Sito, an amiable kid with a ready grin, dark eyes, and coal black hair.

One of the men was Robert Muyres of Minneapolis, Minnesota, the same person whose dog tag Seel had found. The sixty-three-year-old veteran distinctly recalled the opening hours of the Bulge and Sito's death (but Muyres had no recollection of losing the dog tag). Another veteran, George M. Ballinger, a widower and retiree from South Bend, Indiana, also possessed firsthand knowledge. His rubber stamp, B 5011, had been found at the grave site. During the Bulge, he was a staff sergeant and leader of the Company B machine-gun section, a twelve-man outfit to which Sito belonged. Nearly a year after Bill Meyer first spoke with Ballinger, Speder wrote to the Indiana resident. Although the young Belgian's self-taught English was a bit broken, Ballinger had no difficulty understanding his words. The former section leader responded with an eleven-page handwritten letter. Speder later remembered, "The first time I read George Ballinger's story, chills went down my back."

Ballinger wrote that his section occupied a position nicknamed Creepy Corner, which lay on the extreme left flank of the Company B area. The position faced a shallow ravine that cut across the wooded landscape. An undefended gap separated the men at Creepy Corner from Company C, their left-hand neighbor. The Germans soon discovered the gap and often exploited it. That was easy to do during the autumn and winter when fog wrapped the forest in a white shroud. Enemy patrols used it as cover to infiltrate the American front line, which was more a series of isolated strongpoints than a contiguous line. Hunched in their foxholes, Ballinger's men snapped to alertness at every sudden noise and peered into the gloom. The world around them was a place of shadows. At any instant, the Grim Reaper might reach through the murk and tap them with his bony finger. That was Creepy Corner.

On the eve of December 16, 1944, Private First Class (PFC) Alphonse Sito kept watch from inside his foxhole. An ammunition bearer, he helped operate one of two light machine guns in Ballinger's section, but Sito's weapon had been damaged several days earlier, and nobody had procured a replacement gun. Under cover of night, he and his foxhole mate huddled together to ward off the biting cold. The nearness of enemy observation posts ruled out making campfires for warmth. An icy mantle of snow covered the forest floor, and a freezing mist hung in the air. It was also the premiere of the new moon, leaving absolute darkness for the soldiers positioned below.

At 5:30 A.M., along the eastern borders of Belgium and Luxembourg, German rockets and artillery shells plunged from the predawn sky. The savagery quickly swelled beyond the deepest dread of any GI facing the enemy that winter. An unthinkable reality flashed in the darkness. Adolf Hitler's armies in the West, supposedly on the brink of collapse, were now on the march. The greatest trial of blood and fire in U.S. Army history was at hand.

All around the Company B area, enemy artillery and rockets punched through the treetops. The scene beggared description. Several yards from Sito's foxhole, Ballinger hunkered in a log-covered shelter as shells burst all around. "When one exploded very close," he recalled, "it seemed as if my body was being compressed, and my vision was distorted, as if my very eyes were being squeezed out."

The roaring fury raged without lull until daylight when the tumult finally abated. Somehow, nobody in Ballinger's section died, although their platoon leader sustained mortal wounds when his shelter took a direct hit. Several other men received injuries. In the appalling silence that followed the German barrage, the men of Company B waited—waited for what? They heard the faint clink of equipment as gray forms moved like phantoms in the shifting fog. Ballinger described what happened next:

"The Germans, who had moved up quite close, began yelling loudly and in unison, probably to make us think there were more of them than there really were. When they stopped yelling, it became very quiet, and we wondered what they were going to do.

"Shortly, to our left front, a German scout appeared from behind a tree. He stood beside it and looked in our direction for a full minute. We kept quiet and did not move. The scout went back behind the tree, and we now thought they would attack for sure."

The soldiers of Company B expected a massive frontal assault, but the Germans remained cautious. A half-dozen enemy infantrymen came into view from behind the tree where the scout had appeared. They edged forward, straight into the firing zone of Ballinger's one machine gun. The triggerman was PFC George Boggs from West Virginia.

"He wanted to begin firing right away," Ballinger remembered, "but I could see there were others coming from behind, so I told Boggs to wait until I told him to fire. Those in the rear caught up with the first six, and they stood in a close group talking to each other. There were twelve or thirteen of them, and they seemed to be unaware of our presence. Finally, one of them placed a tripod on the ground, and another put a machine gun on it. They were about sixty yards or less away. One of them dropped to his knees behind the gun, and I told Boggs to fire."

The eager gunner opened up with a long burst, and all the Germans crumpled as the stream of bullets sliced into them. That seemed to be the signal for everyone in the area to begin shooting. Within seconds, the forest reverberated with a chorus of machine-gun and rifle fire. A torrent of copper-cased slugs emanated from the ravine where a sizable German assault force had taken up position.

The earsplitting din reached a crescendo as Alphonse Sito strained to shout above it. Ballinger recalled, "Sito, who was to the right of our dugout, was telling us where most of the fire was coming from, which was from our right. The one gun we had was not positioned to fire that far right. There was a BAR (Browning Automatic Rifle) team filling in for our missing gun, and they were covering that area. After a while, Sito told us that the Germans had broken through and were getting behind us. Then he told us that the BAR team had been wiped out."

Those were his last words to Ballinger.

An enemy bullet slammed into Sito's forehead. He never had a chance to scream for help. The young soldier slumped backwards as his last breath escaped into the frigid air, like smoke from a snuffed-out candle. He was just one month past his twentieth birthday. Robert Muyres witnessed the fatal shot. "I wasn't more than three or four meters away. When you see a lot of people killed, it's hard to remember details, but his death I remember, maybe because it was so quick—it was instant."

Muyres, who occupied a foxhole with Staff Sergeant Robert W. Davis, came close to death himself. "Our foxhole was hit by a machine-gun burst," he recalled. "I was hit slightly in the arm and severely in the upper leg, breaking it. Shortly after that, I was knocked unconscious by an explosion, probably a shell burst."

Ballinger had three men with him in his shelter and another three next-door at Boggs's machine-gun emplacement. All were still in fighting fettle, though hopelessly pinned down by the enemy. "It seemed as if all their firepower was now being concentrated on our position. Our shelter and machine-gun pit had been dug down and then covered with logs and dirt. The logs were disintegrating under steady machine-gun and rifle fire, which was now coming so low we could not get our heads off the floor.

"Throughout all this time, a German medic was out in front of us attending the wounded, paying no attention to us or to all the bullets so close to him. He was attending a German who had fallen about fifteen feet from our dugout. He looked at us and shook his fist. None of us ever took a shot at him."

The first enemy advance had been timid and blind, but once the shooting started, the Germans smashed forward with the weight of an entire infantry battalion and swamped the Company B defenders. Only fifty-eight escaped the forest, although some took nearly two weeks to rejoin their unit and some departed through medical channels. The remainder had no chance to withdraw. Outgunned, outflanked, and almost out of ammunition, only two options remained—capitulation or death. The latter seemed a foolish gesture to Ballinger and those at his position. "We decided it would be best for us to surrender." In the bottom of their dugout, the men buried all their letters and money, which totaled more than two hundred dollars in French francs. According to Ballinger,

"We fastened a white undershirt to a machine gun cleaning rod and stuck it out the shelter opening. All the firing stopped instantly, and the Germans began yelling. It became quiet again, and they shouted for us to come out.

"Sgt. George Grimm, who was in the dugout with me, stepped out, and a German shot at him but missed. Grimm dived back into the dugout, and we now thought the Germans were not going to be satisfied with a surrender. They shouted to us again and told us the shot had been a mistake, and it would not happen again. Grimm crawled out again, and nothing happened, so we all went out.... As far as I know, we were the last of Company B's resistance. All the others had been killed, captured, or wounded with the exception of those lucky enough to have gotten out."

Before the Germans led their captives away, Ballinger and two of his compatriots made a move, which met with immediate disapproval. "Sgt. Grimm, Sgt. Mathena, and I started to go to the hole where Sito was, with the idea of getting him out and covering him with a blanket, but the Germans would not let us get close to the hole. They said it would be taken care of." In retrospect, Ballinger added, "Evidently it wasn't."

The battle ended for Ballinger and ninety-four other members of his company who became prisoners of war. The majority ended up within the confines of Stalag XIIID, near Nürnberg. Later the group endured a forced march to Stalag VIIA at Moosburg. Robert Muyres, nowhere among them, was a prisoner, though he never made it to a Stalag. As dusk settled on December 16, he remained at Creepy Corner, where he had been wounded and left for dead.

"When I regained consciousness, it was getting dark, and I was bleeding slightly from the eyes, nose, and ears. My left arm was bleeding a lot more and my leg hardly at all." Muyres also discovered that he was lying beside a wounded German infantryman, who had been hit in the chest and stomach.

The next morning, Muyres, still in the hole, noticed four enemy soldiers wending their way through the forest. Although two of them had been slightly hurt, they improvised a litter and picked up the German with the chest and stomach injuries. They also assured Muyres they would return for him. Fat chance, he thought. But, true to their word, the four men came back and fetched the disabled GI. "They carried me a long way through the woods," he later explained. "The snow was deep, and the 'ride' was very painful. I fell off the litter several times. We arrived at a German aid station where there were many wounded, mostly Germans but also three or four Americans."

Muyres spent the remainder of the war in German hospitals.

OVER FOUR DECADES AFTER THE BLOODSHED AT CREEPY CORNER, a sense of shock hit Alphonse Sito's family. In late 1989, his oldest brother, Stanley, received a call from the U.S. Total Army Personnel Command in Alexandria, Virginia. He listened in disbelief as a stranger's voice told him that skeletal remains had been found in a German forest and positively identified at a special lab in Hawaii. Stanley thought the story might be a hoax, so he contacted his local congressman for assistance. Several days later, he got a definitive response. The story was true.

Prior to the call from Alexandria, the last communication from the army had been in 1951 when Alphonse's parents received a letter stating that all efforts to locate his body had failed. Now, after all the years of silence and uncertainty, the missing soldier's remains had been accounted for and would be returned to his family.

Stanley Sito initially suggested that his brother's final interment be at a military cemetery. That idea seemed quite appropriate. He and his wife had both served as army officers during World War II. Their only son, Richard, was an army officer on active duty, as was his spouse. Both of Stanley's surviving brothers were veterans. (Unfortunately, military service left one brother with post-traumatic stress disorder and the other with alcoholism.) The burial spot Stanley had in mind was the Ardennes American Cemetery in Belgium, which he had visited in 1985. But his younger sisters opposed anything associated with the military. Richard later summed up the situation: "They disliked the military because of what happened to Alphonse, and they took no pride in his service. They also held the military responsible for the maladies suffered by two other brothers."

In accordance with government policy, the ultimate decision rested with Stanley, the oldest living family member. He acquiesced to the wishes of his sisters and requested that a casket be shipped from Hawaii to Baltimore, Alphonse's hometown.

On Monday, December 18, 1989, a small group of family members congregated at St. Stanislaus Kostka Church in the Fells Point district of Baltimore. (At that church Alphonse had received the sacraments of baptism and confirmation.) The parish priest conducted a funeral mass for the fallen soldier. Afterward, a cortege of several vehicles including a hearse motored through the neighborhood where Alphonse grew up. It was a gray morning with low clouds and temperatures below freezing. The destination, St. Stanislaus Cemetery, lay in a crumbling community known as O'Donnell Heights. In recent years, the Archdiocese of Baltimore had used guard dogs to protect the cemetery at night from vandals, drunks, and junkies. Chain-link fencing and barbed wire also protected the grounds. The community itself was a sorry sight, tarnished with graffiti and boarded-up buildings. Amid that scene of urban decay, the cortege entered the cemetery through its main gate and twisted through a maze of headstones and markers before stopping beside the Sito family plot. The graveside service was brief and primarily a religious ceremony with no army rifle team or casket bearers. The only military tribute was a tape-recorded version of "Taps." Alongside the casket, the funeral party stood silent, hands thrust into pockets. After the priest read a concluding prayer, the cluster of mourners slowly vacated the grave like a tide withdrawing from shore. Cemetery workers then delivered Alphonse Martin Sito back to the earth—the reddish soil of his native Baltimore.

In Belgium, Seel, Speder, and Cavanagh had no knowledge of Sito's burial or the whereabouts of his family. The three men were still in the dark when Robert Muyres arranged a visit with Seel and Speder in July 1990 while vacationing in Europe. They found him to be an instantly likable person, who had a round face, pudgy nose, and a roll of flesh above his belt line. He also bore the physical scars of combat. His left leg was two inches shorter than the right one, and he suffered from chronic stiffness in his left knee, all the result of a shattered femur. Though less than limber, he had no difficulty following his two guides into the forest, where he soon located his old foxhole. As he stood there in the mild summer air, visions of a frozen December morning floated up before his eyes. The Belgians listened intently as the Creepy Corner survivor described every detail of the German attack. They gained insights unobtainable from any artifact or history book. Before he departed Europe, Muyres had the opportunity to hold the dog tag bearing his name. Seel offered him the relic, but Muyres left it in the possession of the young man who found it.

That same month, anxious for information about Sito, Cavanagh wrote to his friend Rex Whitehead, a 99th Division veteran living in Utah. Maybe he could locate the dead soldier's family. Whitehead queried several government agencies, but was rebuffed each time. As a last resort, he mailed a letter to the "current occupant" of 2324 Fleet Street, Baltimore—the address on two of the dog tags found at the grave site. Unbeknownst to Rex, his letter went to Alphonse's brother Frank, who still lived in the family home. Frank forwarded the letter to his brother Stanley, who sent it to his son, Richard, stationed in Germany. The army officer responded to Rex, and that initial contact culminated in a pilgrimage one year later.

Stanley and his wife traveled to Europe in the fall of 1991 to visit their son and his family, which included a newborn baby. Toward the end of that visit, on October 13, Richard chauffeured his parents to Losheimergraben for an afternoon rendezvous with Seel and Cavanagh. (Speder had a prior engagement with a tour group of 99th Division veterans.) It was a typical autumn day—cool and misty. Seel and Cavanagh guided the Sito family around the former battleground and finally to the foxhole where Alphonse died. The forest around them stood tranquil and serene. It was hard to imagine the horrors of 1944. Yet the sight of that foxhole stirred a cauldron of emotions in Stanley. Tears welled up in his eyes at the thought of his brother lying there like rubbish for so many years. Stanley turned away and wept, his wife too. He had been unprepared for the feelings that overcame him. After gathering himself, he questioned Seel and Cavanagh about events during the first day of the Bulge. Stanley also raised his 35-mm camera for a few photos. The heart-wrenching pilgrimage left him with a sense of understanding, something that had always eluded him.

Seel and Speder's fortuitous discovery at Creepy Corner had resolved the mystery surrounding the fate of Alphonse Sito. But the find raised new and larger questions. How many other 99th Division soldiers were still missing, and what could be done to find their lost graves? The ensuing adventure would unfold in ways the two Belgians never anticipated, and it would reshape their attitude toward battlefield-relic hunting.

Chapter 2
DIGGING INTO HISTORY

Jean-Philippe Speder had a penchant for practical jokes. He contrived one in early 1980, hoping to outwit his friend Jean-Louis Seel. The teenagers had met the previous autumn while attending the Institut Provincial d'Enseignement Technique in downtown Verviers, a former industrial city near their homes. Speder had already begun relic hunting and had a collection of battlefield artifacts. He described the collection to Seel, who reacted with skepticism. It seemed impossible that someone could find rifles, bayonets, and helmets in the forest. Speder invited his doubting friend to view the items for himself and try his hand at relic hunting. The offer met with eager acceptance, and that gave Speder an idea for a bit of trickery. He planned to ensure that his friend scored a resounding success. The scheme involved planting several artifacts for Seel to find.

Speder lived in a stone farmhouse in a narrow, forested valley below Verviers and several kilometers from the nearest town. The Wayai River flowed along the bottom of the valley and ran directly behind the house. It was there that young Speder invited his friend Seel. Before the rendezvous, Speder removed about ten objects from his collection, dashed across a busy road in front of the house, and toted the objects up a wooded slope on the other side. He used a shovel to secrete them in the ground. Before returning to the house, he tamped down the freshly turned earth and camouflaged each location with leaves and twigs.

After Seel arrived, Speder launched into a tall tale about a ferocious confrontation that occurred in the Wayai Valley in 1944, when American forces engaged several German battalions. He described a clash of monstrous fury. Flaming tanks, mangled corpses, equipment strewn everywhere. Seel believed every word. His friend also hauled out an impressive-looking metal detector, a C-Scope TR 400 manufactured in England. He explained all of its features and demonstrated the proper way to tune it, and then he handed the device to Seel. Time to put it to use. The two teenagers crossed the road and climbed partway up the slope where Speder had buried the artifacts. He motioned around and said that part of the 1944 battle occurred here. The novice relic hunter began scanning the forest floor, the steady hum of the detector audible throughout the expanse of hardwood trees. Speder looked on with anticipation, like a parent watching a child on an Easter egg hunt.

The sound coming from the detector suddenly spiked. Seel dropped to his knees and began digging at the "hot spot." He plucked out two clips of ammunition for an M1 rifle. Picking up the detector, he resumed searching. His eyes focused on the ground as if trying to see through the soil. The detector emitted another positive signal. He knelt and pulled up a bayonet. The next signal was so loud that Seel knew he had something big. He pawed through the earth until he uncovered the remnants of an M1 rifle. His eyes bulged, and he held up the weapon in triumph. Speder had a giant smile on his face, and he struggled to keep from laughing. His friend went back to work, retrieving more items that included a mess kit and an American grenade. He finally raked in all the planted items, but he had no inkling of the ruse, so he kept on searching.

Then it happened. The detector sent out another loud signal. That alarmed Speder because he had buried nothing else. He watched as Seel shoveled through the dirt and shouted, "Yeeees, another rifle!" He lifted out a German K98 bolt-action rifle. Speder's smile disappeared. He charged over to the spot and examined the hole and noticed a rust halo around the place where the rifle had lain. The artifact had been there for decades. The joke suddenly was on him.

Speder confessed all that he had done. Seel felt naive for having believed the story about a huge battle, but he had the final laugh.

Speder would never forget the episode. "That was my first experience with the outrageous luck of Jean-Louis."

How did the K98 end up at that place? Speder surmised the answer. On September 9, 1944, soldiers of the U.S. 3rd Armored Division liberated the nearby town of Theux. That day, or shortly thereafter, a column of GI vehicles advanced into the valley. Speder's mother was an eyewitness. She and her two older brothers, along with their mom, stood beside the road, curious to see the approaching Yanks. The lead jeep stopped, and one of its occupants traversed a machine gun toward the forest and opened fire. Apparently someone had spotted three Germans in the trees. Afterward, two of the enemy soldiers tossed aside their weapons and hastened down the wooded hill with their arms raised. The third soldier lay dead.

After the war, local kids found three German weapons in the forest—two K98s and an MG 34 machine gun. The children built a fortified camp in the woods and played war, using the firearms as toys. Time passed and other entertainment became more important. The kids abandoned the camp and discarded the guns. Everything remained lost until Seel's lucky discovery.

THE EXPERIENCE OF FINDING a German rifle captivated Seel, and he wanted to find more artifacts and on real battlefields. Speder obliged by taking him to a forest near the rural town of Waimes, Belgium. They traveled there on motorbikes, too young to drive automobiles. In the woods, Seel observed scores of foxholes, all the handiwork of bygone U.S. infantrymen. He was a city kid, having grown up in a suburb of Verviers, and he never dreamed that such vestiges of the war still existed. The place had a magic feel to it.

Speder switched on his C-Scope and held its sensing loop several centimeters above the ground. He tuned the detector by adjusting its transmitter-receiver until a faint but steady hum became audible. The loop emitted an electromagnetic signal, and the hum increased when the loop passed over something metal. An abrupt change hinted at something close to the surface; a subtle change suggested something deeper. The tonal quality provided a clue about the composition of the metal, ferrous or nonferrous. A brass cartridge casing sounded different than a rusted chunk of shrapnel, providing the two lay at the same depth.

Seel took a turn with the detector and located several American items: rifle ammunition and MKIIA1 fragmentation grenades. He later watched as his buddy demonstrated how to defuse the grenades. When Speder unscrewed the fuse assembly of one device, a hissing sound caused Seel to recoil backward. He thought the little bomb was about to blow. Speder chuckled, and said the sound was just air pressure being released. Seel gave a sheepish grin. He learned that MKIIA1 grenades came in two varieties: one filled with granular TNT and another filled with EC blank powder. The latter appeared reddish orange in color as opposed to TNT, which had a dark yellow color. (When detonated, EC powder was smokeless. TNT produced a black cloud.)

The experience at Waimes left Seel with new knowledge and even more enthusiasm. During subsequent weeks, he followed Speder to a forest north of Rocherath, Belgium, a much better sector for finding relics. Other people also searched there, and the place became somewhat of a training ground for relic hunters. Battlefield debris existed in abundance. The two friends traveled there a couple times a month, usually gathering items for Speder's collection. But sometimes Seel went alone in search of artifacts for himself.

Because he had no metal detector of his own, Seel borrowed his friend's C-Scope when venturing out on solo missions. One occasion was June 29, 1980. That day Seel drove through Rocherath and parked a couple kilometers north of the village. He walked into a crop of young spruce trees and began searching along a firebreak. He worked in a systematic manner, keeping track of the ground he covered, so he would avoid going over it again. The detector suddenly gave off a resounding *whump*. That signaled a good target below. He picked through the rocky soil and uncovered a cache of coins. Many dated way back, including a silver Louis-Philippe coin minted in France and dated 1833.

Nestled among the coins, Seel found a bead-link chain holding three brass dog tags. They bore the name Max Wisnieski, the serial number 36210978, and the address of Wisnieski's mother in Waukesha, Wisconsin. The chain also held an abundance of perforated coins, the type made with a central hole for carrying on a string. It appeared the little treasure trove had belonged to Wisnieski, who must have been an avid collector.

Days later, Seel returned to the site and found more coins that he had overlooked. He also discovered a big Mercedes parked inside the forest, and he spied a young couple inside. Their tangled movements suggested one thing. He distanced himself from the car, but eventually the driver-side door opened. Seel described what occurred next. "The guy came out and walked over to me. He studied my detector and asked, 'Are you looking for mushrooms?'"

Seel eventually sold all the coins, but he retained the dog tags and chain. They intrigued him. Who was Max Wisnieski? Was he still alive? Seel had no idea how to find answers, but he knew enough to store the tags someplace safe. He tucked them in a nightstand drawer beside his bed.

At the time Seel began searching for artifacts, he and Speder knew little about the Battle of the Bulge and its history. They had no idea what German and American units had clashed in the areas where relic hunting now flourished. The two Belgians had never heard of the 99th Infantry Division.

SEEL AND SPEDER HAD THEIR ROOTS IN WALLONIA, the French-speaking part of Belgium. Seel belonged to a family of five that included two sisters and a stay-at-home mother. His father worked for the Union Mutualiste Verviétoise, a nonprofit organization that furnished various forms of social-welfare coverage, including health and disability insurance. The Seel family lived in a housing development on the edge of Verviers in a town called Stembert. Built after the war, homes in the development were multiunit dwellings with plain lines and nothing that appeared uniquely Belgian or even European. Functionality superseded all else. The development was known as an HLM, which stood for Habitation de Loyer Modéré (Affordable Housing). Similar developments existed on the fringe of urban areas across Belgium and in neighboring countries. Residents typically paid monthly rent based on their annual income.

The austere, modern appearance of the HLM contrasted with the Old World look of the farmhouse that Speder called home. He was an only child and lived with his parents and maternal grandparents. His father managed an autobody shop at a Ford dealership in Verviers, and his mother worked at home as a housewife. She had lived there since her birth in 1939, and her parents resided in half of the house. They had been the last ones to operate the property as a farm and had maintained a herd of dairy cows in earlier times.

Throughout their childhood, Seel and Speder heard stories about World War II and the liberation of Belgium. Seel's parents told him that as kids they ran alongside American troop convoys and shouted, "*Chocolat* for Mama? Cigarettes for Papa?" The soldiers in the vehicles tossed down candy bars, chewing gum, and even boxed rations. The city of Verviers became a rest area for American troops. Soldiers on twenty-four- and forty-eight-hour passes rotated in and out of town. Many times the men stayed in civilian homes and brought food for their hosts. The GIs kept many families fed. The Americans gave away much of what they brought, but they also liked to trade. Seel's grandmother recalled one night when a GI knocked at her door brandishing a pistol and knife. He wanted to swap them for alcohol. "Unfortunately she turned down the deal," Seel said. "I'd have a better collection today if she had accepted."

The stories had an impact on him even as a child. When he played army with neighborhood kids, he always insisted on being a U.S. soldier, never wanting to be a German. Speder felt the same way when he played army. When the two friends began searching for battlefield artifacts, they had an affinity for American items.

Three days before finding Max Wisnieski's dog tags, Seel turned eighteen, and his parents gave him money to purchase a metal detector. He quickly placed an order and anxiously waited. When the new device finally arrived, it allowed him to search more often for relics on his own. He also continued searching with Speder, and together they befriended other relic hunters like Philippe Haulotte and Raymond Rahier. The foursome worked as a team on many occasions, searching areas near Rocherath. Each digger built a larger collection with almost every outing.

Seel kept the majority of his relics in the basement of his parents' home, and one day his mother chanced upon the full extent of his gatherings. She got an eyeful, discovering an American antitank mine and a German 7.5-cm shell, both full of explosives. She summoned her husband to the basement to see the troubling items. Their son immediately faced a barrage of angry questions and criticism. "I'd sooner have you break a leg than continue searching for that stuff," his mother said. She ordered him to remove the two pieces of ordnance. He hauled them away and buried them in a nearby forest. He hoped to retrieve both pieces later, so he could render them inert.

Relic hunters routinely defused ordnance to make it safe for inclusion in collections. Inert ordnance was legal to own and had monetary value. The trick was making it inert. Relic hunters shared defusing techniques, but sometimes tackled a particular weapon without knowing precisely how it functioned or what type of explosive it contained. Any wrong move had the potential to cause instant death, and Belgian newspapers occasionally carried stories about people killed while tampering with unexploded munitions. Despite the stories, relic hunters routinely defused ordnance. Success bred confidence.

Eventually, Seel and Speder learned to defuse artillery projectiles. The first step entailed placing each shell in a vice and using a wrench to unscrew its fuse and booster charge. That step usually brought the greatest danger. A fuse that malfunctioned in 1944 might suddenly fulfill its intended purpose. Unfired projectiles were the safest to handle but never risk free. Removing the fuse and booster exposed the interior of the projectile and its main charge—TNT in many cases. The charge existed in solid form and could not be poured out like the granular material found inside hand grenades. Relic hunters sometimes used a stick to break up solid TNT so they could empty it out. Other times they ignited it and allowed the projectile to blaze away like a Roman candle. The flames eventually extinguished when nothing combustible remained inside. Many relic hunters felt comfortable handling TNT because it had a reputation for being stable over long periods of time. It also had no sensitivity to jarring and required a booster charge or similar device to initiate an explosion. Some relic hunters discovered that TNT dissolved in benzene, and that occasionally worked for removal purposes but had the disadvantage of leaving behind a toxic mess.

White phosphorus presented a different challenge. The U.S. military used it in grenades and projectiles designed to produce white smoke. The substance readily combined with oxygen, which resulted in spontaneous combustion and thick, white clouds. It burned at 5,000 degrees Fahrenheit. The smoke also happened to be caustic and proved effective in clearing enemy trenches and bunkers. The Americans color-coded WP grenades and projectiles by painting them gray. On numerous occasions, Seel and Speder encountered M15 hand grenades, which each contained fifteen ounces of white phosphorus. The defusing procedure first required clearing a wide area of all combustible material like dry grass and dead leaves. The next step was to unthread and remove the fuse assembly from the grenade canister. The final step involved puncturing the bottom of the canister to release its contents, which slowly seeped out and burned with a greenish glow and twists of white smoke. The contents often took hours to burn out. Some relic hunters expedited the process by putting a flame to the escaping white phosphorus. That produced a fiery jet and clouds of noxious, foul-smelling smoke. Sometimes residue from the fire sealed the hole and caused hot gas to build up inside the canister. That usually resulted in an explosion. Persons who burned WP grenades learned to stand well away and upwind.

Aside from the perils of defusing ordnance, Seel and Speder often braved adverse weather to pursue their hobby. The teenagers rode little motorbikes and commuted several hours to and from battlefields. That put the boys at nature's mercy. Rain frequently slicked road surfaces, and fog often played havoc, enveloping the countryside. The roads themselves were narrow, meandering, and had plenty of slippery hairpin curves. When on relic-hunting missions, the two diggers each brought a duffle bag containing a shovel, mattock, metal detector, and a change of clothing. The bag also held food and water. On return trips, all newly discovered relics had to fit in the bag, sometimes adding considerable weight.

One weekend, Seel had mechanical difficulties with his motorbike, so he and Speder doubled up on one bike, duffle bags included. The pair took off for Rocherath amid sheets of rain. The precipitation lasted all day, and the diggers found nothing but a 75-mm shell, which Speder stowed in his bag. Filthy, and soaked to the bone, the pair resembled desperados from a Mad Max movie. They climbed on the bike and headed home. Less than halfway there, Speder made a wrong turn and immediately tried to reverse his mistake. He lost control of the vehicle. Water sprayed from the pavement. The bike slid out from under the two riders, and they spun through the air, landing smack on their bellies. "Then, like in slow motion," Speder recalled, "my duffel bag opened and out came the shell, gently rolling into the middle of the road." The bruised riders looked at each other for a moment and then laughed with the exhilaration of having survived.

Expeditions to Rocherath and other points became easier when Seel obtained a driver's license in February 1981. His new privilege also meant that he no longer had to rely on a bus for transportation to and from work. He had recently accepted an entry-level job with the Belgian railway. He obtained the position with the help of his youngest sister's fiancé who worked for the railway. Seel started his career working on the tracks, replacing wooden ties.

Speder was a year younger, and by the time he obtained a license in April 1982, Seel had temporarily quit relic hunting and the railroad. He now wore an army uniform.

Belgian law mandated that at least one son from every family serve on active duty for twelve months. Seel was the only male child in his family, so he had no choice. Since he had an appetite for adventure, he volunteered for a commando unit, which added three months to his military service. Seel departed for training, leaving behind his job with the railway, although the position would be his again when he finished his stint on active duty.

The Belgian Army's commando school was at Marche-les-Dames, near the city of Namur. The school served as the primary training center for the Régiment Para-Commando, an elite unit that constituted the upper crust of the entire army. When Seel arrived at Marche-les-Dames, he underwent three months of basic training and then embarked on commando training, a workout that crushed many recruits. The physical and psychological rigors far surpassed those imposed upon any other soldiers in the army. Half of all volunteers washed out, but Seel weathered the test and moved on to jump school. To earn his wings, he completed eight practice jumps: four from a balloon and four from a C-130 aircraft. One jump was at night and one with full equipment.

He became a member of the 3ème Bataillon de Parachutistes stationed near Tielen, Belgium. The battalion had two companies of Flemish-speaking soldiers and one company of French speakers. Seel joined the latter but stayed only a short while at Tielen before his company transferred to the 2ème Bataillon de Commandos at Flawinne, Belgium. The company exchanged places with the only Flemish-speaking company at Flawinne, thus making the 2ème all French and the 3ème all Flemish. Seel added to his combat skills by attending sniper school, where he earned his sniper brevet, a small crest emblazoned with a crown, wreath, and crossed rifles. That was the last qualification he gained before his active-duty commitment ended in June 1983. He returned to the Belgian railway, where his military time counted toward a government pension.

By the time Seel became a civilian again, his friend Speder had entered the army. He too was the only son in his family, indeed the only child, and that meant mandatory service. He reduced his active-duty term from twelve to ten months by volunteering for the Forces Belges en Allemagne (Belgian Forces in Germany). After training, he joined the 2ème Bataillon de Carabiniers Cyclistes, an armored infantry unit stationed at Siegen, Germany. When his tour of duty ended, he opted to join the reserves and became a noncommissioned officer with an infantry unit located near his home in Belgium. He also took a job selling cars at the Ford dealership where his father worked.

THEIR ACTIVE-DUTY SERVICE COMPLETE, Seel and Speder resumed relic hunting together, and in early 1984, they met Will Cavanagh, who had recently moved to Belgium with his family. Cavanagh first met the two diggers through a mutual friend, and several weeks later he bumped into them on a forest trail while guiding a busload of American veterans. The new resident had grown up and attended college in England, but his mother was Belgian and had worked for the U.S. Army during World War II. That led to his interest in the war and the Bulge in particular. German and American veterans were his chief curiosity. He had already spent twenty years gathering their stories and photographs. Seel and Speder had never met anyone like Cavanagh. They learned about the 99th Infantry Division and other American units that fought at places now popular with relic hunters.

Seel mentioned Max Wisnieski's dog tags, and Cavanagh said he could probably trace the soldier and determine his whereabouts. The tags indicated that Wisnieski came from Waukesha, Wisconsin, and declared Catholicism as his religious preference. Seel had difficulty reading and writing English, so Cavanagh wrote a letter on his behalf. The letter went to St. Joseph's Catholic Church in Waukesha. Perhaps someone there had relevant information.

While waiting for a response, the search for battlefield artifacts took an unexpected turn on September 12, 1984. That evening, Seel received a phone call from his friend Philippe Haulotte, who described his latest relic-hunting expedition. He had found several U.S. ration cans while searching a one-man foxhole in a Belgian forest near Losheimergraben. Beneath that trash, he uncovered a German dog tag made of zinc. Then he noticed bones—human ribs. He continued digging and found a complete skeleton lying facedown at the bottom of the foxhole. The dead German still wore an overcoat and had a pipe and watch in his pockets. Haulotte reburied everything. He wished to report the grave but feared getting in hot water because he had no permission to dig there.

The discovery interested Seel. He knew that other relic hunters had found the remains of German soldiers, but the relic hunters merely plumbed the dead men for artifacts, leaving their bones in the wilderness. Haulotte had taken nothing from the grave site. Seel proposed that he and Speder exhume the remains and transfer them to Belgian authorities for eventual reburial at a German military cemetery. His conscience told him that was the only proper course. He had certainly taken greater risks defusing unexploded ordnance. He promised to withhold the name of the person who actually found the burial place. Haulotte said okay.

The exhumation began on September 13, when Haulotte guided Seel to the site. Speder later joined them. The foxhole lay sandwiched between two bomb craters. One had enough depth to swallow a car. Other craters lay elsewhere in the woods. Seel and Speder tried to picture the earthquake that must haven taken place, but that was too much to imagine. They focused on removing the hapless German soldier from his resting place. Many of his bones had sustained fractures at the moment of death. Piece by piece, the young Belgians reassembled the skeleton on a bed of spruce needles beside the foxhole. It became apparent that Haulotte had overlooked the long bones of the arms and small bones of the hands. The diggers found them by enlarging the hole, and in the process, they discovered a gold wedding band. The Belgians wondered about the man who wore it. Where did he grow up? Did he have children? What was his name? The dog tag offered only an enigma:

2020A

2./Jnf.Ers.Btl. 465

The soldier received the number 2020 when he joined the 2.Kompanie of Infanterie-Ersatz-Bataillon 465, his basic-training unit. For security reasons, German dog tags seldom revealed the name of the wearer. Company-sized units regularly created personnel rosters, which recorded dog-tag numbers and corresponding names, and those rosters became the only way to trace a name. The letter A on the dog tag represented the soldier's blood group.

Following the exhumation, Haulotte departed for home. Seel and Speder drove to the house of Werner Colonerus, a forest ranger they had met three months earlier. Colonerus listened to their story about a relic hunter having uncovered the grave of a German soldier. The forest ranger accompanied Seel and Speder to the forest. The group switched on flashlights, their bright beams tunneling through the blackness. The trio zigzagged between trees until a shaft of light caught the shape of a skull. Colonerus surveyed the ghostly scene. Seel pointed out all the artifacts, and the forest ranger squinted to read the markings on the dog tag.

The next day, Colonerus reported the grave to municipal-government officials in the nearby town of Büllingen. They removed the skeleton to the city hall and contacted the Deutsche Dienststelle in Berlin. That agency maintained millions of wartime documents, including casualty reports and personnel rosters. Sealed in an envelope, the dog tag went to Berlin, where an archivist deciphered the inscription. It belonged to Franz Kuwilsky, a thirty-three-year-old Gefreiter (corporal) from Dederstedt, Germany. He died on December 24, 1944, while assigned to the 3.Batterie of Volks-Artillerie-Korps 402. His unit reported him missing in the forest where Philippe Haulotte chanced upon the grave. Subsequent research revealed that RAF Mosquito bombers raided that forest on December 24, unleashing 500-pound bombs in a rain of ruin. Kuwilsky ended up facedown in a foxhole between two of the many craters.

The story ended when the Deutsche Dienststelle sent instructions for the government officials in Büllingen to transfer Kuwilsky's remains to a German military cemetery in northern Belgium. The long-missing soldier at last received a dignified burial. Unfortunately, nobody from his family received word of the interment, because his hometown lay behind the Iron Curtain in East Germany. (The Deutsche Dienststelle mailed the dog tag to Seel in 1993 after he sent a letter requesting it.)

TWO WEEKS FOLLOWING THE RECOVERY OF KUWILSKY, Seel attended the wedding of Speder and his fiancée, Sonia Goffin. Three summers earlier, destiny intervened after Seel and Speder had concluded a solid week of digging. According to Speder, "We stopped in Verviers to chat with a friend who said, 'Such-and-such guys are on the Normandy beaches for vacation, and they're with four girls. Why not go there and stir things up?' That sounded like fun. The four girls were Sonia, her sister, and two of their friends. I met Sonia on Dog Green beach, famous to anyone knowledgeable about D-Day. I learned that she grew up about twenty kilometers from my home. Ironically we had to travel all the way to France to meet for the first time."

Speder soon discovered that Sonia's father had an interest in the Bulge, and he collected military relics. He worked as a letter carrier for the Belgian Postal Service and had gathered memorabilia from persons he met while delivering mail. Over the years, his mail routes included former battle areas like the towns of LaGleize and Stavelot. In those areas, he collected uniforms and equipment left behind by soldiers of the 1.SS-Panzer-Division. Those relics were the most valuable ones in his collection. Sonia had spent all her life around such items and had developed an interest in history as well as antiques. "I certainly picked the right woman to marry," Speder said. "She understood my interest in World War II and encouraged me to pursue it."

While the newlyweds were enjoying their first days of wedded bliss, Seel received a call from Cavanagh. His letter to Waukesha, Wisconsin, had brought a typewritten response from Mrs. Mary Wisnieski. "The dog tags found in a forest near Rocherath belonged to my husband, Max Wisnieski, who is now deceased." Max served with Company A, 38th Infantry Regiment, which was part of the 2nd Infantry Division, a unit that fought alongside the 99th Division during the Bulge. Mary went on to explain that she and her husband owned a small restaurant in Waukesha, and they had no children. He died in 1970 at age fifty-four. She closed by saying, "If you have further questions, do not hesitate to contact me, and please feel free to keep the dog tags if you have any use for them."

The letter from Wisconsin had a profound impact on Seel. One artifact in his collection had regained its history, no longer just a piece of metal from the forest. Between 1980 and 1984 the young Belgian had found eight American dog tags and one sterling silver ID bracelet. Speder too had found dog tags and bracelets. Both diggers became engrossed in research, trying to ascertain everything they could about the GIs who once owned the artifacts.

Seel learned more about a dog tag he recovered in September 1980. It had belonged to a soldier named Neely W. Wyatt. Cavanagh sifted through his archives and found a book with a KIA roster that listed Wyatt as a sergeant who died on December 18, 1944, while serving with the 23rd Infantry Regiment of the 2nd Division. Subsequent research revealed that he was a squad leader with Company I, and his family had him interred in Texas after the war. The dog tag came from the forest area where he had lost his life fighting enemy soldiers of the 12.SS-Panzer-Division.

Cavanagh also helped Seel learn about an ID bracelet that he had acquired from a relic hunter named Freddy Lemarcotte. The object belonged to an officer named Matthew L. Legler. Cavanagh recognized the name as being that of Major Legler, a 1939 West Point graduate and commander of the 1st Battalion, 393rd Infantry Regiment of the 99th Division. The major had hoped to make the army his career but retired on disability in 1946, having suffered a mangled leg in a land mine blast. Lemarcotte found the bracelet near a sawmill south of Rocherath, and that location meant something to Cavanagh. He possessed a "combat interview" from January 1945, and the document indicated that Legler and portions of his battalion retreated past that sawmill on December 18, 1944. Such information excited Seel and Speder as much as any artifact.

The diggers always recorded when and where they found each dog tag, bracelet, or any other item identified by a particular name or army serial number. Few other relic hunters bothered with such documentation. Seel and Speder saw value in preserving history as well as gathering artifacts. The two relic hunters came to believe that a collection had to serve a purpose greater than merely being an assemblage of material. They understood that archeological data could help reconstruct the past. Plucking up artifacts without recording location information meant destroying part of the historical record.

SEEL LIVED IN THE HILLTOP HAMLET of Becco, Belgium. After his discharge from the army, he moved there and rented half of an old farmhouse on the edge of town. Above one doorway, a stone lintel bore the date 1774. The structure had two stables, which now served as garages. One belonged to Seel, and above it he had a storage room for his artifact collection. The room had been the village dance hall in days gone by.

The new resident soon made the acquaintance of Pierre Chaufheid, who lived in the other half of the building. Chaufheid had an interest in firearms and enjoyed shooting skeet with his shotgun. Seel occasionally joined him. The surrounding countryside was endless pastureland and hedgerows, a perfect place for shooting. One day, the two neighbors exhausted Chaufheid's supply of clay pigeons, but Seel thought of another target. He had several German rifle grenades that he had yet to render inert. They contained a waxy, pink explosive called Penthrite. Seel and Chaufheid wedged one of the grenades under a tree stump and walked away to a safe spot. They opened fire with a .22-caliber rifle, aiming for the detonator at the tip of the grenade. They traded the gun back and forth after each shot. Chaufheid hit the detonator on his sixth try. *Ka-whoom!* The stump disappeared. Dirt and hunks of wood rained down. The explosion rattled windows and terrified neighborhood cats. Seel decided against any further grenade shooting. He defused the other grenades and disposed of their Penthrite wax in less tumultuous fashion.

Unexploded ordnance, like the rifle grenades, littered every corner of the Bulge area. After five years of digging, the two Belgians had located an example of almost every type of explosive device used during the battle. The diggers even encountered Soviet munitions, which the Germans captured on the Eastern Front and used on the Western Front. The Soviet material consisted of a hand grenade and a giant 120-mm mortar shell. The pair also found hand grenades made by Czech, French, Belgian, British, and Italian manufacturers.

During the summer of 1985, Seel and fellow relic hunter Raymond Rahier found a German weapon that neither had unearthed before. It was a solid-fuel rocket fired from a Nebelwerfer. The projectile had a crushed nose cone, superficial damage that undoubtedly occurred on impact. Seel wanted to save the item, but Rahier refused to transport it. "No, no, not in my car!" he said. "You can have the rocket, but you must come later with your own car. That damn thing's too dangerous!" Rahier had plenty of defusing experience, but he knew nothing about the internal workings of a Nebelwerfer projectile. Neither did Seel, but he had no fear and returned to fetch it.

At home in Becco, he tinkered with it, trying to open the base of the projectile. That appeared safer than messing with its head, which he guessed held a fuse and booster charge as well as TNT. Seel tried to open the base with various wrenches and even thumped on it with a hammer. He did all that without a wrinkle of worry but finally gave up after thirty minutes. He switched to the head, first removing the damaged nose cone and then opening the forward compartment of the projectile. Nothing inside. It had contained sticks of propellant and was empty because the Germans had launched the rocket. Something immediately dawned on Seel. The fuse, booster, and TNT were at the base of the projectile, the very end he had hammered. That realization caused him to gulp hard.

The Germans had used a special tool to open and close the base of the projectile. Seel gave up on the rocket and called a friend who collected World War II ordnance, and he promised to help. Seel drove to his home, and the Nebelwerfer round changed hands. The following day, Seel received a call from his friend, who said, "Come over and see what I found inside." He had removed two kilograms of TNT and discovered a wartime newspaper that looked brand-new. The Germans had wrapped the paper around the TNT charge so that it fit snugly inside the shell casing. Seel felt lucky to be alive when he saw the charge and the fuse and the booster. His friend asked if he could keep the projectile and the newspaper. Seel traded them for a German dog tag and several other small relics. The tag had received a direct hit from a piece of shrapnel, and Seel eventually traced it to a teenage member of Grenadier-Regiment 989 who died in combat on December 20, 1944. The ordnance collector framed the newspaper and restored the projectile. He even fabricated a new nose cone for it.

When Speder heard about the Nebelwerfer episode, he marveled at the charmed life of his friend. Seel had been lucky since the day he first picked up a metal detector. Speder was the more conservative of the two and always felt skittish about defusing certain types of ordnance, especially German ones. During World War II, the German munitions industry resorted to ersatz materials and slave labor. That resulted in unreliable ordnance. More than one German soldier died when a Panzerfaust antitank weapon exploded in his hands as he attempted to launch it. Speder had defused several of those weapons, but he eventually lost all stomach for it. He had no intention of selling his life for a Panzerfaust or any other weapon, and besides, he had a wife to consider.

Speder also had another interest besides relic hunting. Before his marriage, he purchased a dilapidated Ford GPW, more commonly known as a jeep. He had acquired the wreck from a farmer. The serial number on its frame and the registration number painted on its hood both indicated a date of manufacture sometime in January or February 1944. (The vehicle lacked all but one of its data plates, which made determining the exact date impossible.) Speder's father, who managed a body shop, helped with the restoration project. The task spanned four years and produced a vehicle that looked factory new.

Speder still found time for using his metal detector, and he continued searching for dog tags and personalized artifacts. One Sunday morning, he decided to search near Kalterherberg, a German village on the Belgian border. He went along with Francis Van Damme, a fellow jeep owner. While hiking, they encountered Philippe Haulotte and Raymond Rahier.

Rahier showed off his latest discovery, an American 105-mm howitzer shell. It had all its original paint, a rarity after so many years in the ground. Yellow markings identified the type of round: 105H, H.E.A.T., SHELL M67. That nomenclature denoted an antitank projectile filled with high explosives. He coveted such a well-preserved shell and considered it safer than any Nebelwerfer rocket or Panzerfaust. He had found an identical shell the previous week and easily defused it.

That afternoon, Seel learned about the latest discovery. He worked until 2:00 P.M. at a rail yard near Montzen, Belgium, and on the way home, he stopped to visit Haulotte and heard the story. Haulotte said, "We saw Jean-Philippe today, and Raymond found a beautiful shell with all its paint." Seel agreed that finding a shell in that condition was rare. He asked if any dog tags had turned up. Nothing. He soon made his way home.

His girlfriend, Cathy, lived with him, and she greeted him at the door and said that Haulotte's mother had called moments earlier. She sounded frantic, something about a terrible accident involving Rahier.

Seel grabbed the phone and returned the call. Mrs. Haulotte said her son had just rushed out, heading for Rahier's house in Stembert.

"Why? What happened?" Seel asked.

"Raymond had an accident. He's dead!"

"What?"

"Yes, yes, an explosion!"

Seel dropped the phone and scrambled to his car. His girlfriend jumped in the passenger seat, and they raced fifteen kilometers to Stembert and parked in the center of town. The entire population seemed to be outside and milling around. The two charged uphill into a swarm of local residents. Brick rowhouses crowded both curbs along rue Grand Vinave. Fire engines and police cars clogged the street. Shattered windows abounded. Chunks of brick littered the road, and a huge hole yawned in the facade of Rahier's home. The explosion had torn out an interior wall that separated the garage and living room. The destruction left Seel bereft of speech. He glanced down and spotted a lump of human scalp stuck to the pavement. Blood and flesh speckled the face of a building across from the damaged house.

The crowd gossiped about the tragedy. Rahier was the only casualty, and the detonation apparently occurred in his garage. Someone heard that he caused the blast while working on his car, perhaps a fuel-tank explosion. Seel knew better. He spotted Belgian Army explosive-ordnance experts probing the rubble. They too understood what had occurred. He also noticed plainclothes policemen from the BSR (Brigades de Surveillance et de Recherche). They specialized in explosives and firearms.

Investigators concluded that Rahier died while trying to defuse the antitank shell he had found earlier in the day. That type of projectile had a base-detonating fuse. Police officials speculated that Rahier became frustrated when he had difficulty unscrewing it, and he employed a desperate tactic. He used a torch to heat the metal for several seconds in hopes of loosening the stuck fuse. That hypothesis seemed plausible, yet many relic hunters found it ironic. Rahier had a reputation for caution when dealing with unexploded ordnance. He refused to fiddle with many items, but he felt comfortable with certain American shells, perhaps too comfortable, like a lion tamer who had lost fear of his animals. Or perhaps Rahier was just not as lucky as Seel.

The dead relic hunter had no immediate family other than a sister living in France. She buried her brother in the Stembert cemetery, and a large gathering of his co-workers attended the funeral. He had worked for the Belgian railway along with Seel.

Raymond Rahier died at age twenty-eight. His black granite headstone had spruce trees engraved on it as he had spent his happiest hours in the forest.

THE BELGIAN POLICE HAD NO TOLERANCE for relic hunters who collected munitions. Such persons jeopardized lives beyond their own, and that was true of Rahier. Flying debris from the blast that killed him could have harmed others. The police also had other worries at the time. Several terrorist groups operated in Western Europe, and all of them sought to acquire the type of explosives that relic hunters routinely discovered.

The terrorists labeled themselves as Marxist guerrillas, and they carried out numerous bombings and assassinations during the 1980s. One infamous German group detonated a car bomb at an American airbase several days after Rahier died. The German group had underground ties to a Belgian organization called the Cellules Communistes Combattantes. Belgian police officials feared that CCC members would obtain explosives from an unwitting relic hunter anxious to earn a few francs. Anyone caught searching a battlefield without permission became subject to a fine and metal-detector confiscation. Anyone caught with weapons or live ordnance could face imprisonment.

Philippe Haulotte, Rahier's best friend, quit relic hunting and disposed of his collection, giving away some items and selling others. Seel and Speder soldiered on, but refrained from gathering ordnance. They focused on their favorite artifacts, those identified with individual soldiers. The two diggers also leveraged their friendships with farmers and forest rangers and obtained verbal permission to search in certain areas.

Only the bravest souls still harvested unexploded ordnance from the forest. Freddy Lemarcotte was among them. He belonged to the first generation of relic hunters, the ones who began prospecting the Ardennes during the mid-1970s. In those halcyon days it was possible to search for several hours and come away with enough material to fill an entire car trunk. Over the years, Lemarcotte developed a real nose for finding great artifacts. He also dealt in firearms, and the police had collared him for illegal sales and possession. His arrest during one episode became a news item. "He was on the front page of a local newspaper," Seel recalled. Lemarcotte did jail time and ended up on probation but continued relic hunting. In August 1986, one year after the Rahier tragedy, he accompanied Seel northwest of Rocherath into a forest adjacent to Camp Elsenborn, a military-training ground and an artillery range. Seel and Lemarcotte had no permission to dig there. If caught, Lemarcotte faced harsh consequences. The slightest mishap had the potential to land him behind bars. Lemarcotte put that out of mind as he and Seel poked around the fringe of Camp Elsenborn. His nose for relics eventually led him to five metal containers filled with German 8-cm mortar shells, all in mint condition. Someone had buried the containers on top of each other. Underneath the pile, Lemarcotte located a German P-38 pistol wrapped in an American blanket, but severe corrosion had left the weapon inoperable. Seel discovered nothing worthwhile. He had found two dog tags the previous month but nothing today.

Hoping to improve his luck, Seel joined Lemarcotte about a week later on another foray into the same area. This time Lemarcotte brought a rookie relic hunter, a sixteen-year-old kid on his first search expedition. The outing passed without cause for anxiety until a vehicle roared up from behind. The three diggers whipped around and spotted a police car barreling along a forest trail. The vehicle was almost on top of them. The trio instinctively took off like spooked deer. The car braked to a halt. Its two occupants sprang out, weapons drawn. The diggers surrendered, caught with no place to run. The vehicle occupants turned out to be a police officer and a forest ranger, both armed with automatic pistols. They ordered their captives to kneel. Seel soon had the muzzle of a pistol pressing against the back of his neck. He gave up his ID card, and his companions did the same. Within minutes the police officer returned the cards. "What's next?" Seel asked. "That's it," the officer said. "You can all go home, but we're confiscating your detectors, and you'll receive citations." The diggers signed the paperwork, glad to be free. They lingered for a while and told the officer about unexploded ordnance they had noticed. He thanked them for the information and radioed it back to his station in the town of Elsenborn.

As the relic hunters prepared to leave, another police car arrived. The driver jumped out and privately conversed with his colleague and the forest ranger. The newly arrived officer approached the diggers, and said, "Hand me your identification cards." He then asked them to have a seat in the rear of his car. Seel had a bad feeling when the officer subsequently drove them to the Elsenborn station. The diggers waited inside the building and watched as the officer jabbered on a telephone. He put down the receiver and swaggered over to them with a giant smile on his face. "I'm terribly sorry. You're all under arrest." He turned to a co-worker, "Please put them in handcuffs."

Earlier that day the officer had overheard all the radio traffic about relic hunters, and he recognized the name Freddy Lemarcotte. That name stirred the officer to action and triggered the arrest of all three diggers.

The prisoners departed Elsenborn under guard, bound for jail cells where they spent the night. In the morning, the threesome faced a judge in Verviers. They shuffled into a courtroom, each digger with rumpled hair, grimy hands, and dirt-stiffened jeans. They looked and smelled like forest creatures. The judge had Lemarcotte's police record, which looked "thick as a dictionary" according to Seel. The repeat offender received a "six-month sentence, effective immediately." Seel and the teenage kid received no punishment beyond their night in lockup. They had no prior record, so the judge released them.

Seel thumbed a ride home, anxious to clean up. Soon after reaching his house, policemen knocked at the front door. They had a warrant to search his premises for explosives. The searchers felt cocksure they would find a munitions trove. They intended to rearrest Seel but gradually became frustrated when they found nothing dangerous. They conspired to save face. In the attic they discovered American MKIIA1 grenades, each one empty and with no fuse assembly. The police put on a big show, pretending the inert items were hazardous. The searchers gingerly carried each one as if it were a Fabergé egg. They also removed a mortar shell and a Panzerfaust, both empty and harmless. "The police would have arrested me on the spot if any of that had been illegal," Seel commented. "I'm sure all the confiscated material ended up in somebody else's collection."

Seel eventually received his metal detector back. The police at Elsenborn had no authority to dispose of it due to a legal technicality. Seel resided in the French-speaking part of Belgium, and Elsenborn lay in the German-speaking area. With the exception of illegal items, such as narcotics and unexploded ordnance, the police had to return most property seized from persons who lived outside the German-speaking area.

AFTER HIS BRIEF INCARCERATION, Seel shied away from the Camp Elsenborn vicinity. He and Speder also enlarged their search area to include battlefields well beyond the bounds of the Elsenborn police. The forest north of Schoppen, Belgium, was such a place, and Seel decided to explore there in June 1987. He knew that few relic hunters had ventured there, because nobody considered it a prime location.

His search began on June 8, when he meandered across a marshy glade and climbed uphill into a copse of young spruce trees. Low branches forced him to work on his hands and knees. Daytime resembled night under the dense canopy of spruce boughs. Seel crept uphill until he reached the far edge of the wooded area. Outside he could see the grassy fringe of a cow pasture. He remained under the trees and kept searching. His metal detector led him to the remains of an optical sight from a German heavy machine gun. Nearby he noticed a large dimple in the forest floor. Its size suggested a shell crater, and close to its center his detector indicated a deep target. His best judgment said forget it, just a corroded ammunition can from the machine gun, but his gut said dig.

Seel followed his gut and burrowed into the damp earth. He struck rusty metal. In the dim light he could see that its surface curved outward like a helmet. He reached down, cleared away more dirt, and worked one hand underneath. Several unseen objects tickled his fingertips, and awareness suddenly hit him. Human teeth! Seel jerked away from the hole. He had shoved his fingers in the open mouth of a skull.

The stunned digger paused and looked around at the already excavated soil. Ribs and vertebrae lay among the dirt and rocks. The shell crater served as a makeshift grave. He picked out all the bones and then resumed digging in the hole. The rusty artifact was indeed a helmet, but no ordinary one. Seel recognized it as the type worn by German paratroopers. The interior of the steel shell contained a liner made of leather and foam rubber, and it held a complete skull. Dirt packed both eye sockets, and the open mouth had a frozen expression of terror. The teeth impressed Seel, all present and textbook straight with no dental work or staining. The dead man must have had a perfect smile.

Back in the hole, Seel discovered a second skull beside the first one. No helmet this time. The new skull lacked all its facial bones and mandible, and that painted a gruesome picture of violent death. Seel presumed that a shell fragment caused the damage, and he imagined the face of the unfortunate soldier disappearing in a red spray of blood and bone.

Seel resumed digging until he heard movement from behind. Beneath the tightly laced branches he spied a pair of boots sidestepping along the edge of the pasture. Was somebody sneaking up on him? He had no time to ponder the question. The body of a gray-haired man plunged headfirst into the trees. "We came face-to-face," Seel recalled. "Both of us screamed, and I toppled backwards."

The man who lurched into the trees had no idea anyone was inside. He recovered from the shock and asked an obvious question.

"What are you doing here?"

"I'm searching the battlefield," Seel said. "Right now I'm disinterring the grave of two German soldiers."

"German soldiers? I was in the German Army. Let me see."

The man introduced himself as Emile Jacquemin, a retired farmer from the nearby village of Faymonville. He spoke French and German, and Seel asked him why he jumped into the trees. Jacquemin replied that he had been hiking when he noticed a helium balloon caught in the trees. He jumped to grab a card dangling from it. Schoolchildren often launched such balloons. The attached cards offered a small prize to whomever returned one from farthest away, but the offer only lasted for a certain number of weeks. Seel had encountered similar balloons himself.

Jacquemin retrieved the card and then helped exhume the two German soldiers. The heads of both men rested deep at the center of the crater, and their boots lay at its rim under a thin layer of soil and spruce needles. The boots must have poked through the surface decades earlier. The scene looked familiar to Jacquemin. He said that in combat he and his comrades buried dead soldiers that way, their boots sticking up from the ground. The purpose of burial was to cover a body just enough to hold down the odor of rotting flesh. The footwear helped mark each grave for later disinterment. After the Bulge, civilians living in the area also used that burial method according to Jacquemin.

Unfortunately, the grave yielded only one dog tag, and it belonged to the soldier with the paratrooper helmet and perfect teeth. The German Army veteran asked Seel what he planned to do next. Seel said he intended to have the skeletons interred at a German military cemetery. He mentioned the recovery of Franz Kuwilsky three years earlier. Seel scribbled his address and phone number on a piece of paper and promised to follow up.

Seel immediately sought help from Speder, who used his German-language ability to write a letter to the Deutsche Dienststelle in Berlin. The letter provided details of the recovery and included all the markings on the dog tag. Seel asked another friend and fellow relic hunter to store the bones. Seel was leery about keeping human remains at his house because he had no idea if the police would make another surprise visit. Several weeks later, Speder's letter generated an official response from Berlin with instructions to deliver the remains to a German cemetery near Recogne, Belgium. The letter also identified the owner of the dog tag: Herbert Meister, a seventeen-year-old paratrooper from Landau, Germany. He perished on January 16, 1945, as a member of Fallschirmjäger-Regiment 5.

On the day of delivery, Seel picked up the two sets of remains, and his friend came along. Speder also joined the group, and they drove south to Recogne. The cemetery had a red sandstone chapel at one corner and a sandstone wall enclosing part of the burial ground. In the parking lot, Seel decided to check the bones one last time. He made a disturbing discovery. There was an unfamiliar skull in the plastic bag containing Meister's remains. At that very moment, the cemetery superintendent approached. He was a Belgian from the German-speaking region of the country, and he immediately began complaining.

"You've caused me a great headache. Did you know that one of the soldiers you found already has a grave here? Herbert Meister rests in block 4, grave 235. Now I have an order from Berlin to disinter those remains and replace them with the skeleton you found. Well, I won't do it. The bones of both your soldiers are going into a mass grave. No individual burials, not even as unknowns."

The superintendent grabbed both sets of remains and stomped off.

Seel threw up his hands in disgust, but he also had another reason for displeasure. He confronted his friend who had stored the bones. "What did you do with Herbert Meister's skull?" The friend denied any chicanery, and a heated debate ensued, but it resolved nothing. The original skull was gone. "The guy probably sold it," Seel later commented. "The one he replaced it with was complete but in poor condition and missing most of its teeth. Meister's skull was perfect, and some collector undoubtedly put it on display in a showcase. I trusted the wrong man."

News of the fiasco soon reached Will Cavanagh, and he just shook his head. He told Seel and Speder to please inform him if they ever found an American grave. He could help prevent another travesty like this one.

The two Belgians continued relic hunting, and, thanks to their friendship with Cavanagh, they had frequent contact with American veterans. The old soldiers often visited Belgium to see where they fought during the Bulge, and Cavanagh acted as their guide. Seel and Speder joined the tours. Neither Belgian spoke much English, although Seel had studied it for five years in school. As he put it, "School was mainly a place to have fun with my friends, not to study foreign languages or anything else." Speder had been a more serious student but never took English. Both Belgians learned the language from Cavanagh and the veterans. French-English dictionaries also helped, as did books on conversational English.

Speder took a keen interest in Bulge history, analyzing wartime documents and reading postwar books about the battle. He had learned to speak German in school, and that aided his quest for knowledge, but a majority of the books and documents were American. That made learning English imperative, but he soon had other subjects to learn about, too.

He became an expert diaper changer after his wife delivered a baby boy during the autumn of 1987. Besides embarking on parenthood, he changed careers and took a job as a technician at a water-treatment plant in the city of St. Vith. He had much to learn about his new duties, which included survey and repair work. Yet despite the changes in his life, he still found time to study Bulge history and to make trips to the forest with his pal Seel.

In September 1988, the two friends asked Cavanagh for suggestions in hopes of finding a new hunting ground, and it had to be well away from Camp Elsenborn. He tapped on a map and advised them to search in Germany southeast of Losheimergraben. Infantrymen of the 99th

Division saw heavy combat in that wooded area. Neither digger had ever searched there, and Seel was anxious to give the place a try. He had a new metal detector and had found twenty-one American dog tags that year—sixteen in one day—more than in all previous years combined. He was on a roll.

That lucky streak and Cavanagh's suggestion led to the discovery of Alphonse Sito's grave.

Chapter 3

"CAN YOU HELP FIND THEM?"

I had never heard of the 99th Infantry Division when I joined the U.S. Air Force in 1984, but my interest in World War II and European history compelled me to volunteer for overseas duty while a trainee at the U.S.A.F. Security Police Academy in Texas. I hoped to spend two years in Europe but instead received orders to Okinawa, an island on the opposite side of the globe. Anxious to avert that assignment, I scrambled to find anybody who had orders to Europe and who would trade with me. One person came forward. His destination was Spangdahlem Air Base, Germany, and he agreed to swap after speaking with a sergeant who belittled Spangdahlem as a boondocks and lauded Okinawa as a "party island."

My overseas adventure began in May 1984, when I arrived at Spangdahlem and joined the 52nd Security Police Squadron. The base was indeed a boondocks, hunched on a bald plateau in the wooded Eifel hills. After two months of getting acclimated to my job at "Spang," I purchased a '76 Ford Escort (built in Cologne) and set out to find World War II battlegrounds. The base library had an ample supply of military-history books, and I referred to their maps for travel destinations. One of the volumes had a wartime illustration depicting a Battle of the Bulge scene near Büllingen, Belgium. Part of the caption read: "500 German dead were found in the woods to the left of the drawing." What evidence of that carnage remained after four decades? I decided to investigate.

Büllingen was about an hour away, and I drove there one Thursday in October. I walked into the forest and immediately found foxholes and abandoned equipment—canteens, gas masks, mess kits. Everything lay in plain view on the forest floor, and that kept me wandering all day. Surprised by my discoveries, I decided to spend the night in Büllingen and continue exploring the next day. I wanted to find more foxholes and relics, but I had a larger purpose. Early in life, I had developed a talent for oil painting, perhaps inherited from a grandmother who painted landscapes. In recent weeks, I had envisioned creating a series of Bulge paintings, but nothing specific had crystallized in my mind. Maybe an idea or two would come to me if I sketched some of what I had seen in the forest. I planned to make that my goal the next day.

The main street in Büllingen offered an obvious choice for lodging. The facade of the Hotel Dahmen displayed six oversized replicas of U.S. Army shoulder patches. I recognized the Big Red One of the 1st Infantry Division and the Indianhead of the 2nd Infantry Division. Both units fought in the area during the Bulge. The other patches looked unfamiliar, including a checkerboard insignia, which I later discovered was the emblem of the 99th Division.

I checked into the hotel and retired to a second-floor room. In the morning, I drifted downstairs and into the dining room, where Janine Greeven had breakfast waiting. She and her husband, Paul, owned the hotel and lived there as well. We conversed in a mix of English and German, and Janine said that an American author and Bulge veteran had spent the night at the hotel. Perhaps I had heard of him—Charles MacDonald. That name definitely rang a bell. The Spangdahlem library had a couple of his books, and I had recently begun reading them. During the Bulge, MacDonald wore the Indianhead patch and commanded a rifle company. He later ascended to the rank of colonel and retired in 1979 as deputy chief historian for the U.S. Army. Janine said he had come to the hotel with his "baby," a new book on the Bulge. She asked if I wished to meet him, and I answered yes before she finished the question. According to Janine, the venerable author was late for breakfast, and that worried her. She explained that a group of 99th Division veterans stayed at the hotel the previous month, and one of them died in his sleep. Oversleeping veterans were now a cause for concern.

Eventually the dining room door opened, and there stood MacDonald, pencil slim with curly gray hair. Janine chatted with him, and the two laughed. He then walked over to my table and introduced himself. I invited him to have a seat, and he ate breakfast while we talked about his experiences during the Bulge. I opened my briefcase and pulled out a sightseeing brochure, which had a map printed on one page. MacDonald used a pen to mark the position occupied by his battalion on the morning of December 17, 1944. He told me about the company he commanded and how his men defended the battalion's left flank and blasted back six or seven frontal attacks. The final assault forced his surviving men to fall back in retreat, their ammunition exhausted. During the melee, the company commander witnessed two soldiers earn the Medal of Honor, one losing his life in the process. MacDonald's compelling story gave me several ideas for paintings. He said the events of that day filled a chapter in his first book, *Company Commander*, a million seller originally published in 1947 and still in print when I met him that day in 1984. He then showed me an advance reader's proof of his latest work, a book titled *A Time for Trumpets: The Untold Story of the Battle of the Bulge*.

After discussing the new book and my artistic ambitions, MacDonald asked if I had any pressing business that day. If not, he offered to introduce me to a young Englishman who had served as his chief collaborator during the preparation of *A Time for Trumpets*. I had no plans more important than spending time with this Bulge veteran and whomever he wanted me to meet.

I followed MacDonald as he drove to the tiny community of Hédomont, where Will Cavanagh and his family lived in a white-stucco house. MacDonald introduced me to his colleague, who simply addressed him as "Mac." The author then produced two bottles of Glenfiddich Scotch, and said to Cavanagh, "One for you, and one for me." After pouring three glasses of the malt whiskey, Cavanagh invited me to inspect his collection of Bulge-related material. He grabbed several thick albums from his desktop and plunked them on a table where the three of us sat. The albums contained letters, signed photographs, and other memorabilia he had received from veterans. The former soldiers ranged from ordinary infantrymen to illustrious generals with names like Gavin, Bradley, and Eisenhower. While I leafed through the albums, Cavanagh and MacDonald talked shop. They reviewed a book-length manuscript Cavanagh had written about the 2nd and 99th Divisions and their part in the Bulge. MacDonald critiqued the manuscript, and I bent an ear, trying to absorb every word.

MacDonald was a fount of historical knowledge, and I became enthralled with his work and that of his British friend. They promised to help me conduct research for my paintings. Before we parted company, Cavanagh welcomed me to visit his home again, and I accepted. My unexpected meeting with the two historians turned out to be a watershed event, and it also happened to be my twentieth birthday.

WILL CAVANAGH, HIS WIFE, DENISE, and their two children moved to Belgium in May 1983, along with his bachelor brother, Jean-Pierre, or J.P., as everyone called him. The family had previously lived in County Durham, England, but a mediocre school system convinced Cavanagh and his wife to relocate. Belgian public schools were far better, and the Cavanagh children were young enough to learn French quickly. Their dad had an undergraduate degree in education, and he planned to make a living as an English tutor. He embarked on the plan with his brother, who also tutored. Their business cards read: "We speak fluent English. Can you?"

Cavanagh had family ties in Belgium. During the war, his mother, a French-speaking Belgian, lived near Verviers under Hitler's hobnailed boot. She also spoke English, and when American troops liberated the city, she found employment as an interpreter with the Civil Affairs Detachment of the First U.S. Army. She later transferred to a similar position with the Third U.S. Army. Two years after the war ended, the young Belgian woman traveled to England on holiday and met the family of her former English teacher, which included Cavanagh's father. During the war, he had worked at an armored car factory and also had a job as an air-raid warden. The two married in April 1949, and Will Cavanagh came into the world nine months later at a maternity home in County Durham.

While growing up in England, Cavanagh and his schoolmates read World War II books and swapped militaria, like swastika flags and Japanese swords. He also made frequent visits to maternal relatives in Belgium, and that sparked his interest in the Bulge. His mother lived in Verviers at the time of its liberation, but her family originally came from Waimes, a farming community that sat astride the front line during much of the Bulge. Cavanagh became well acquainted with Waimes and the surrounding countryside. He saw wooden grave markers with rusty German helmets roosting atop them. There were also less grim reminders of the war. "My uncle had a truck, and he used to go around to farms, picking up milk churns and delivering them to a dairy in nearby Malmédy. I used to ride in the truck. The farmers all had Zeltbahns covering the milk churns to protect them from the summer sun, and many farms had American helmets serving as flowerpots." (During the war, the typical German soldier carried a Zeltbahn, which was a tent section that could be worn as a waterproof poncho or camouflage garment.)

In the mid-1960s, a teenage Cavanagh wrote to the U.S. Army Center of Military History and received a reply from one of its leading historians, Charles B. MacDonald. He remembered Waimes and had spent a frigid night there in January 1945. The two continued corresponding, and in 1969, MacDonald asked his pen pal to help guide a group of veterans returning to Belgium for the twenty-fifth anniversary of the Bulge. Cavanagh's fluent French and familiarity with the countryside impressed the army historian. He came to rely on the young Briton to help guide veterans back to the fields and forests where they fought and froze during the last winter of the war. Cavanagh also undertook World War II research as an avocation, gathering documents and chasing down details of Bulge events.

Soon after I first met Cavanagh in 1984, his passion for the past led him to accept a job managing a museum and militaria shop in downtown Malmédy. Behind a storefront window, Cavanagh worked alone, operating a cash register and selling war relics and military surplus. The museum occupied two side rooms, and visitors paid a fee to enter through a curtained doorway. World War II veterans entered free of charge. Glass showcases lined the walls and held mannequins outfitted in uniforms and equipment worn by German and American troops during the Bulge. Artifacts and photographs enhanced the display, and big-band music played in the background. Cavanagh's job at the store and museum supplemented his tutoring income, and the museum became one of my frequent haunts. He and I spent countless hours there hashing over Bulge history and discussing ideas for my paintings.

Another frequent haunt was the Hotel Dahmen, where I originally met MacDonald. Cozy and unpretentious, it had no touristy glitz. Deer antlers and rustic furniture accented the dining room. Beer mugs and tankards hung by the dozen above the bar. French doors opened on a leafy courtyard, and a creaky, wooden staircase led upstairs to the guest rooms. Paul and Janine had two children about my age and one much younger. They also had a fat house cat named Napoleon, who frequently sat on the bar and lapped milk from a saucer. Paul happened to be an accomplished artist, and his paintings adorned several walls in the hotel. He worked in the manner of the French Impressionists, and his creative process was an incredible frenzy of brushstrokes that captured his personality as much as it did the landscapes he painted. His technique fascinated me. I had a different creative process and worked in the meticulous, patient way of Dutch still-life painters. Paul also possessed considerable talent in the kitchen and kept his guests well fed. His hotel was usually my first destination when I had time off from my military duties.

At Spangdahlem, my fellow security policemen and I guarded three squadrons of fighter aircraft (F4 Phantoms) and nuclear weapons. We typically worked eight-hour shifts for six consecutive days and then enjoyed a three-day break. I spent most of my break time in Belgium, and the Dahmen became my headquarters. I occupied my days hiking over battlegrounds, sketching scenery, and shooting photographs with my Nikon, or I visited Cavanagh at the museum.

More than a year after my arrival in Europe, I met my first 99th Division veteran—Howard I. Bowers from Oak Ridge, Tennessee. He and his wife stayed at the Dahmen, and I guided them to a grassy ridgeline where PFC Bowers had resided in a frozen foxhole for almost two fortnights after retreating cross-country from the German border. He told me about enemy attacks against the ridgeline, and he eloquently described several incidents during the retreat, one of which inspired an idea for a painting:

"We could hear rifles and the rapid fire of German burp guns and the slower firing of American machine guns. We soon left the forest, and a flare suddenly lit the night like day as we crossed into the middle of an open field. My squad leader yelled, 'Freeze!' I can still see a tableau of soldiers frozen in different positions like statues. I held my breath waiting for the burp guns to open fire and wanting to hit the ground. But no one moved, and no one fired on us. After an eternity, the flare burned out. . . . Even now I can close my eyes and see the flare and wait for the burp guns and feel the fear."

After Bowers and his wife returned home, I received an unexpected letter from Walter E. Schroeder, secretary-treasurer of the 99th Infantry Division Association:

"The Association has a number of Associate Members, and Howard Bowers proposed an Associate Membership for you. However, to keep the Association solvent, we have yearly dues of $5.00. This includes about six issues of our newspaper, the *Checkerboard*, and also information on upcoming reunions, etc. We would be very happy to have you as an Associate Member."

I mailed a check, and soon the *Checkerboard* began arriving in my mailbox at Spangdahlem. The newspaper editor annually published the names and addresses of over 2,900 members of the 99th Association. I kept busy with the list, typing letters at the base library in hopes of corresponding with veterans who could help me. I intended to create historically accurate paintings, and I needed details, everything from weather conditions to clothing and equipment. Some veterans sent written descriptions, and others sent wartime snapshots. I also obtained photographs from Belgians who lived in the area where the 99th Division fought. They had pictures of their homes and villages before and after the Bulge. They also shared stories about the battle, and, in the course of our conversations, I learned about the culture and geography of the Ardennes, the region where the Bulge took place.

THE FOREST MASS KNOWN AS THE ARDENNES featured rocky soil, deep valleys, and meandering streams. Stone-built villages dotted the rolling landscape, as did castles constructed at strategic locations. The entire expanse of forest sprawled across maps, extending from Belgium into France, Germany, and Luxembourg.

After World War I, a section of the forest became a contentious borderland. That area was the German-speaking part of Belgium known as the Eastern Cantons or Ostkantone. The Belgians established the cantons after receiving frontier territory stripped from Germany under the Treaty of Versailles. The territory had been part of Germany since Napoleon's defeat at Waterloo, when the Prussians acquired the land as reward for having helped defeat the French emperor. The German districts of Eupen and Malmedy became the Belgian cantons of Eupen, Malmédy, and St. Vith. The German population became an ethnic minority within the country. Many people adapted to the change, preferring the more relaxed Belgian manner to the strait-laced Prussian system. Other people rejected the change and formed opposition groups, one of which aligned itself with the Nazi movement in Germany.

When Hitler invaded in 1940, he quickly pulled the cantons back into the Fatherland. Thousands of male residents served in German uniform, which also had been true during World War I and earlier days, but this time the ranks included more reluctant conscripts than zealous volunteers. Ostkantone citizens also joined resistance movements opposed to Hitler. When Anglo-American forces liberated Belgium in 1944, the cantons came under U.S. military governance. German forces later reoccupied much of the territory during the Bulge. The 2nd and 99th Divisions were among the American units that won back the lost ground. After the war ended, the Belgian government regained control of the Eastern Cantons, and the German-speaking population once again became an ethnic minority.

DURING MY TWO YEARS IN EUROPE, I occasionally used a metal detector that I acquired in high school and brought overseas. I never found a dog tag or anything identifying an individual soldier; however, I often chanced upon unexploded ordnance but never felt the urge to defuse any of it. The idea seemed especially unwise after Cavanagh told me what happened to Raymond Rahier.

Most artifacts that I found required no metal detector to locate. I merely bent over and picked them up off the forest floor. Acting on a suggestion from Cavanagh, I sometimes patrolled garbage dumps looking for relics that local farmers had discarded from their barns. My best luck came at a small landfill near the twin villages of Krinkelt and Rocherath. My finds included GI overcoats, ration boxes, and German leather gear.

On one occasion, Cavanagh and I teamed up on a relic-hunting expedition. We had one objective, to find remnants of several German assault guns (Sturmgeshütze) knocked out in a snow-covered ravine while being used to attack 99th Division soldiers. Cavanagh had wartime documents that identified the general location, but I needed greater precision to paint the scene. He told me that after the war, salvage workers dismantled destroyed tanks and usually buried miscellaneous debris that had no monetary value. The farmer who owned the ravine gave me written permission to dig there, and Cavanagh and I went to work with metal detectors. We pinpointed several debris pits, all containing assault-gun wreckage.

None of the artifacts I found that day or any other day rcompared to the rare and spectacular ones found by Jean-Louis Seel and Jean-Phillipe Speder. Cavanagh introduced me to the Belgians at the Hotel Dahmen in 1986, several weeks before I departed Europe for reassignment stateside. Cavanagh seldom cooperated with relic hunters, because most of them cared only about gathering goodies for themselves or for sale. Seel and Speder impressed him as different. Bulge history fascinated them, as did the soldiers who fought the battle. I shared a few beers with Seel and Speder, and we discussed a topic of practical use to them—American English. They quizzed me about slang words and colloquial expressions. The Belgians hoped to improve their ability to communicate with U.S. veterans. After our conversation, we shook hands and parted company. I expected never to see them again.

I left Europe in May 1986 with a one-way ticket to Tinker Air Force Base, Oklahoma. My baggage included hundreds of Kodachrome slides and pencil sketches. I also had file folders stuffed with letters, black-and-white photos, and copies of wartime documents, many obtained from Cavanagh. My home at Tinker was a barracks, and that thwarted my desire to start painting. My roommates had no tolerance for the stink of turpentine and linseed oil. Unable to paint, I continued sketching and studying Bulge events. The pace of my research increased because I was able to interview veterans over the phone, something too costly at Spangdahlem, where calls to the U.S. ran five dollars per minute. I also took the time to visit 2nd and 99th Division veterans in Texas, Kansas, and Oklahoma. In a town near Tulsa, I called on the sister of a 99th lieutenant who died in combat soon after the Bulge. More than a month before dying, he had battled the German assault guns that interested Cavanagh and me.

My stateside assignment ended in January 1988, when my term of enlistment expired. I declined an offer to reenlist, choosing an honorable discharge instead. One reason I joined the air force was to obtain money for college, and each month I had diverted part of my paycheck into the Veterans Education Assistance Program. I had designs on attending my father's alma mater, The Ohio State University. With Oklahoma in my rearview mirror, I drove for Ohio and the halls of academia.

I had to wait until spring quarter 1988 before starting freshman courses, and during the delay I received a new edition of the *Checkerboard* and immediately spotted an intriguing headline: "Belgian Makes Big Discovery." Jean-Louis Seel wrote the article that followed, and he described having recently found sixteen American dog tags stacked one on top of the other. Perhaps they belonged to 99th Division soldiers? Seel had no idea, but he had found the tags in an area once occupied by the 393rd Infantry Regiment. The article contained all sixteen names and serial numbers, and it also included ten other names from tags and bracelets he had recovered over the years. The Belgian hoped that *Checkerboard* readers could shed light on the men, and he provided his mailing address. I checked the membership roster of the 99th Association and found three of the sixteen names. The trio were veterans of Company K, 393rd. Perhaps one of them would respond to Seel's article.

After beginning college classes, I continued to read the *Checkerboard*, expecting to see a follow-up article about the sixteen dog tags. Nothing appeared. I later learned that Seel received several direct responses to his article, including a telephone call from a history buff in Belgium. He received the *Checkerboard* and informed Seel that all the tags belonged to Company K men.

Cavanagh and I maintained periodic contact, and he informed me of the unfortunate demise of the museum in Malmédy. Its owner had defaulted on financial obligations, including wages owed to Cavanagh. The British ex-pat searched for employment, his tutoring work having faded away. He formed a business partnership with an American tour operator living in Germany. The two men guided busloads of U.S. Army officers on "staff rides," which amounted to battlefield lectures held at various locations in the Bulge area.

Several days after Christmas 1988, I received a letter from Cavanagh. He and his wife planned to attend an upcoming 99th Division reunion scheduled for June in Dallas, Texas. He hoped to see me there. Before closing the letter, he included a paragraph about Seel and Speder's discovery of a 99th soldier in a foxhole near Losheimergraben. The letter described artifacts found with the dead man. Cavanagh went on to explain that both relic hunters came to him for help, and he recounted all that followed. I wondered whose name appeared on the dog tags. The letter made no mention.

The next edition of the *Checkerboard* featured a piece on Seel and Speder, but the editor omitted the name of the dead soldier. Cavanagh had promised the army he would keep the name out of print, pending closure of the identification process and next-of-kin notification. The editor, Bill Meyer, wrote:

"It may be six months before the name will be released. After forty-four years, the family will have to wait another few months. In the meantime, some relative may die without the peace of mind knowing that his/her loved one's remains have finally been discovered. No longer is he 'missing in action and presumed dead.' . . . Your editor contacted Senator Bob Dole, a veteran who has helped the 99th often in the past, and told him the story. Dole is trying to speed things up with the army. But the process is slow."

I called Meyer about three months later, but not to inquire about the discovery made by Seel and Speder. The reunion slated for Dallas was fast approaching, and I asked Meyer if Cavanagh still planned to attend. I knew the two kept in regular touch. Meyer said that our mutual friend would be there, and afterward he hoped to visit a 99th Division veteran named Dick Byers, who lived near Cleveland, Ohio. That news pleased me. I had no time or money for Dallas but could manage an excursion to Cleveland, only two hours from my apartment in Columbus. I eventually phoned Cavanagh to confirm his schedule, and we had our first conversation since my departure from Europe. He welcomed the opportunity for a get-together and suggested I call Byers and make arrangements. I had never met Byers, although, in a recent *Checkerboard*, I read a poignant narrative he wrote titled, "Artilleryman's Recollections of Bulge." Cavanagh gave me a telephone number, and I dialed the 99th Division veteran later that day.

STAFF SERGEANT RICHARD H. BYERS NARROWLY ESCAPED becoming a prisoner of war. His brush with enemy captivity occurred near a Belgian railroad station during the predawn hours of December 17, 1944. He belonged to a forward-observation party from Battery C, 371st Field Artillery Battalion, which had gun positions several miles away. The sergeant and two other artillerymen sacked out in the cellar of a stone farmhouse across from the station. Around them lay slumbering riflemen from an infantry company.

Outdoors, in a black soup of fog and night, the mechanized muscle of a German battle group edged closer and closer to the station and farmhouse. The approaching enemy soldiers were paratroopers and Waffen-SS men, and they formed the spearhead of Kampfgruppe Peiper. American sentries at the farmhouse sensed the danger and alerted the sleepers. The infantrymen ran up from the cellar and darted toward foxholes in nearby woods. Byers later wrote: "On the way out, one of them shook me and urgently whispered, 'Get up! There's tanks outside!' I mumbled something, rolled over, and went back to sleep."

One of the three artillerymen did awaken and rushed to exit the cellar. That was the lieutenant in charge of the forward-observation party. Byers and the other artilleryman remained asleep. They rested beside a shell-shocked infantryman who had narrowly survived a near miss the previous day. The dazed soldier sensed the exodus, and yelled, "Wha's goin' on? Wha's goin' on?" The lieutenant heard the voice and shone his flashlight in that direction. There he saw the soldier and two sleeping beauties. He charged over and kicked them awake. According to Byers, "He *really* woke us up! We grabbed our coats and helmets, buckled on our pistol belts, and headed for the stairs."

Outside the house, the three artillerymen stumbled toward a stone barn where they had parked a jeep. It had an SCR-610 radio, and the men planned to use it to call down artillery fire on the enemy. They opened the back door of the barn and discovered German paratroopers entering from the opposite side. The GIs reversed direction and ran through a wooden gate between the house and barn. Byers followed the lieutenant. The third member of the party knelt down to buckle his overshoes because they were jingling. In an instant, the paratroopers cornered him, and he raised both hands.

Byers and the lieutenant escaped into the woods without seeing their friend fall into enemy hands. The lucky pair trudged overland until they finally reached the gun positions of their battery. The two men climbed aboard trucks and pulled out with the unit, staying just ahead of the German onslaught and eventually reaching new positions near Elsenborn, Belgium. Byers and his comrades went into action there, showering the enemy with high explosives for over a month.

By February 5, 1945, the Germans had lost all their territorial gains in Belgium, and Byers had received a battlefield commission, becoming a second lieutenant. His war abruptly ended that day while bouncing along a forest trail in a jeep. The rear of the little truck fishtailed and struck a Tellermine. The blast launched the rear of the vehicle skyward, and two backseat passengers rocketed out. One died of shock due to blood loss, and the other broke his back against a tree trunk. The driver flew straight forward and died within minutes from internal injuries. Byers and a fifth passenger landed directly in front of the jeep. Stunned and barely aware of what had happened, Byers caught sight of the vehicle as it stood upright, teetering on its front bumper. One absurd thought flashed through his mind as the jeep started to fall. "Christ, I hope it doesn't tear my trench coat!" The truck came down on top of Byers, pinning his derriere under the passenger seat and entangling his legs with the steering wheel and the gearshift lever and the legs of the fifth passenger, who had somehow survived, too. Byers pulled and wiggled his way out from underneath the mass of metal.

He had a fractured pelvis and spent the remainder of the war convalescing in hospitals from Paris to England. He returned to the United States with a rear-echelon logistics unit, the 15th Major Port Battalion. Wearing a Purple Heart ribbon on his Ike jacket, Byers arrived home to East Cleveland and rejoined his wife, Jean, and their three-year-old daughter. He received an honorable discharge just before Christmas 1945.

The postwar years brought two additions to the Byers family, a son and another daughter. The father of three had only a high school diploma and found employment with the Iron Fireman furnace company, first as an installer, then as a salesman, and finally as a sales manager. In the 1960s, he accepted a marketing position with Mussun Sales, a commercial heating and air-conditioning firm. He rose to become its vice president of sales. Byers and his wife eventually moved from East Cleveland to Mentor-on-the-Lake, where they lived in a ranch home overlooking Lake Erie. It was there that I met him in June 1989.

CAVANAGH AND HIS WIFE FLEW TO CLEVELAND after the Dallas reunion and took over a guest bedroom at the Byers residence. I had seen pictures of Byers in the *Checkerboard*, but none of them had accurately portrayed his physical presence. He filled the front door of his home when he greeted me. We shook hands, and I glanced down and noticed sneakers big enough to belong to an NBA player. He guided me through the house to an enclosed patio in the back where his wife and guests had made themselves comfortable in lounge chairs. Besides Will and Denise Cavanagh, I recognized Pierre Dullier, a Belgian police officer whom I remembered from my days in Europe. He had restored a jeep and painted it in the markings of one that Byers drove during the war.

The group of old and new friends discussed everything from the nautical history of Lake Erie to the recent massacre at Tiananmen Square in China. I brought along an oil painting I had started, and everyone gathered around for a look. It depicted the ruins of Krinkelt, Belgium. Cavanagh voiced his approval, saying he liked the winter sky, the only part I had completed. Byers and Dullier agreed and asked several questions about my technique. Our conversation then turned to Cavanagh's new career as a tour guide. He talked about the "staff rides" he had recently conducted for the U.S. Army, and he mentioned his involvement with the army after Seel and Speder found the remains of a 99th Division soldier. Byers and Cavanagh reviewed details of that episode, and I learned that Alphonse Sito was the person identified on the dog tags. The name sounded unfamiliar to me, but I nevertheless made a mental note of it. The Sito recovery especially interested Byers because he belonged to the Archives Committee of the 99th Association. The committee had five members, and they worked to document and preserve 99th history.

Sometime before sundown, everyone vacated the porch and strolled down to the rocky beach behind the house. We gazed across the water, and Byers said that his curiosity once compelled him to find out what was on the other side in Canada. He consulted topographic maps and determined the line of longitude that ran through the center of his property. He traced that line across the water to a point in Canada. Unsatisfied with a mere map exercise, he drove six hours around the lake to see the place for himself. He just had to set foot on the other side. Byers had curiosity all the way to the marrow of his bones, and he always enjoyed an intellectual challenge. He also possessed a creative streak. Cavanagh made a comment that prompted Byers to relate a "home-repair story" from his army days.

In early December 1944, Byers and his comrades occupied a front-line house once owned by a German Army officer and his wife. The building had indoor plumbing and a downstairs toilet. "Unfortunately it was unusable," Byers recalled. "The previous GI occupants had used it but never flushed it, there being no running water in the village." Wearing a gas mask, Byers cleaned the vile mess with sticks, brushes, liquid soap, and gasoline. He then went about making the porcelain fixture operable. He climbed upstairs and tinkered with a bathtub directly above the toilet. He disconnected the tub and elevated the cast-iron vessel atop ammunition crates, raising it above the plumbing. Using whatever tubing he could scrounge, including vacuum cleaner hose, the inventive staff sergeant connected the tub drain to a coldwater pipe that had poured into the tub and also ran downstairs and fed the toilet tank. Hanging out a bathroom window, he wrenched loose a downspout and pulled it inside so that it drained into the tub. Gravity forced rainwater and snowmelt into the bathtub, then into the coldwater pipe, and on down into the toilet tank. That provided what Byers described as a "gen-u-wine, white-china, self-flushing, sit-down toilet as good as any throne in the world."

I had read the story in the *Checkerboard* but nonetheless enjoyed hearing Byers tell it himself. He also related other stories and told me about his 1969 trip to Belgium for ceremonies marking the twenty-fifth anniversary of the Battle of the Bulge. He had visited Belgium several times since. I drove away from Lake Erie that night happy to have seen my European friends and pleased about meeting a member of the 99th Archives Committee. He had enthusiasm for my artwork and offered to help me in any way possible.

As I reflected on my visit to Byers's home, one thought nagged at the edge of my mind. How many 99th Division soldiers like Alphonse Sito were missing? I wondered if his name appeared on an honor roll I once had seen in an old edition of the *Checkerboard*. I eventually dug through my pile of back issues and found the honor roll. It included only 99th soldiers interred overseas, and the name of each soldier appeared along with the location of his grave. Some names had no grave location, only the abbreviation, W. of Missing, which stood for

Wall of the Missing. I counted thirty names with that abbreviation, including Alphonse M. Sito.

An idea struck me as I pondered the names. Seel and Speder had located Sito without intention. What if they began using a more deliberate approach? They could probably find other missing soldiers. I felt certain there were 99th veterans with firsthand information that could guide the two diggers, and the *Checkerboard* seemed an obvious way to reach those veterans. I suddenly envisioned a coordinated team effort, and I prepared a list of all thirty names. It deserved publication in the newspaper, but I had no illusions about what could result—a project consuming reams of paper and hundreds of hours. At the time, summer classes at Ohio State and full-time employment had me swamped, so I tucked the list into a file folder. It remained out of sight but never out of mind.

The list languished until fall quarter when my workload eased, and I finally pitched my idea to Byers. The proposal appealed to him, and he said that he anticipated no problem getting the list published in the *Checkerboard*. I suggested he become the point of contact for all correspondence. Veterans of the 99th would be more likely to respond to a fellow 99er, especially a member of the Archives Committee. He agreed, and I promised to send him a copy of my list. After he received it, I called and suggested he obtain a date of death for each missing soldier by writing to the American Battle Monuments Commission (ABMC). That organization maintained all U.S. military cemeteries overseas and could provide the necessary information. Byers sent a letter that day.

In January 1990, he received a package from the European office of the ABMC. The package held a seventeen-page computer printout. It included information on all 99th soldiers buried in Europe and commemorated on Walls of the Missing (or Tablets of the Missing at some cemeteries). The document gave each man's name, rank, unit, serial number, home state, date of death, burial location, plus awards and decorations. Byers examined the data and found thirty-seven soldiers listed as missing. My tally had been incomplete. When he called me to discuss the matter, he suggested that just thirty-three names be published, because only those men died during the Bulge. The other four perished afterward. I had no objection, so Byers sent an updated list to Bill Meyer.

The March 1990 issue of the newspaper featured a bulletin with the headline: "MIA, Still Missing After 45 Years, Can You Help Find Them?" The updated list followed along with a request:

"If you have any knowledge of what happened to these men during the Battle of the Bulge, please get in touch with Dick Byers. With a few facts about where and how they disappeared, a search could be started. Do not think that what you remember is not important. A little bit from you, matched to a small piece from someone else, might complete the puzzle."

I had just received my copy of the newspaper when Byers called to say that letters had already begun arriving in response to the bulletin.

Chapter 4

THE TRIUMPH OF TEAMWORK

Columns of infantrymen slogged along both sides of a muddy forest trail. The boots and tires of previous traffic had churned the route to a gooey morass. The men ignored the muck underfoot and thanked Providence for a rare day without rain or snow. Several jeeps crawled through the mud, passing the troops, who traded rumors about a newly arrived captain in charge of their outfit. These were the foot soldiers of Company K, 393rd Infantry Regiment, and they had orders to dig in one mile behind the front line at a battalion-reserve position.

Second Lieutenant Lonnie O. Holloway Jr. (who preferred to be called L.O. or Larry) belonged to the company, and he marched with his thirty-five-man Weapons Platoon. In addition to rifles and pistols, his troops carried two Browning light machine guns and three 60-mm mortars—the Company K "artillery." The lieutenant carried a compass and a topographic map, but he had little use for them at that moment because the wooded terrain around him was familiar. The date was December 1, 1944, and Company K had spent most of the previous month in that same area.

The company had arrived in Belgium in early November and reached the front on the tenth day of the month. Fresh to combat, the men relieved veteran infantrymen of a unit that had fought from North

Africa to Belgium. Company K took over from the battle-tested warriors and maintained defensive positions in the forest but also patrolled into enemy territory. The company had the code name Bedbug, and its officers also had code names. Holloway was Bedbug Four. During November, the outfit suffered forty-eight "nonbattle casualties," primarily trench-foot cases resulting from a dearth of waterproof overshoes among the men. The outfit also had five men killed in action and six wounded. The first man KIA was a machine gunner in Holloway's platoon. Fragments from a mortar shell mortally wounded him in the groin. Two other members of his gun crew sustained injuries but survived. The company took on replacements and spent the last five days of November at a regimental rest area. The entire unit lived in crudely made log huts with canvas roofs and bunk beds. The men rotated on twenty-four-hour passes to nearby Krinkelt, Belgium, where they took showers, obtained clean clothing, visited a Red Cross canteen, and cheered on USO girls who performed a song-and-dance routine at an improvised theater that had been a dance hall. The men also watched a movie starring Ann Sheridan, but an enemy buzz bomb struck the town during the show, and the film stopped. Nobody got to see its ending.

The company retraced its bootsteps on December 1, and reentered the forest, marching to the battalion-reserve position. The sound of picks and shovels echoed among the trees as the men burrowed into the wet, rocky ground. That same day, the unit gained a new company commander, Captain Stephen K. Plume Jr., a West Pointer (class of 1941). He had graduated in the bottom quarter of his class after five years at the academy, and his senior yearbook, the *Howitzer*, described his academic record as one of "almost constant deficiency." When he joined Company K, he replaced another officer who had spent only twelve days with the company before the regimental commander relieved him for alleged "incompetence." Holloway had never met Plume before, but a fellow platoon leader already had become acquainted with the captain.

Second Lieutenant Joseph F. Dougherty, leader of the First Platoon, met the West Point graduate while crossing the Atlantic on a steamship that carried the 393rd Infantry and other elements of the 99th Division. The captain was a "severe alcoholic" according to Dougherty, and their meeting came at the behest of the assistant division commander.

"General Mayberry had me capture Plume on the troopship after he was found dead drunk several days out. I didn't know him very well then, although I had heard a lot about him. He had all booze and no equipment in his duffle bag." According to Dougherty, the captain's misadventures continued after being apprehended. "He was locked up on the S.S. *Argentina*. Went AWOL in England. Caught. Crossed the Channel and later went AWOL in Belgium."

The lieutenant colonel commanding the 393rd transferred Plume from a cushy, rear-echelon job to a weapons platoon, a combat unit normally led by a second louie like Holloway. The purpose of that lowly assignment was to "dry out" the captain. The 393rd commander was a fellow West Pointer, and he vowed to shape Plume into a leader.

When Plume took charge of Company K, his second in command was First Lieutenant John W. Fisher, but he remained scarce according to Dougherty. "Fisher, the company executive officer, spent little time with the combat elements. He was mostly in the rear, I presume with the cooks, supply vehicles, maintenance, etc. I rarely saw him."

Fisher was nowhere near the company command post on December 5, when the battalion operations officer summoned Plume. Company K had orders to relieve a front-line company, but Plume had been on another bender, according to Dougherty. He found the captain passed out in his sleeping bag, and that created a predicament. Who would lead the move and set up the new command post? The company had three other platoon leaders, but one lay hospitalized with influenza, and another had been with the unit for less than two weeks and lacked experience. Holloway had experience and seniority, but he had to stay with his men because his platoon sergeant was out sick. The task fell to Dougherty.

"I went to battalion, received the order, conducted the move of Company K to the new area, set up the CP, went back with a jeep and trailer, put Plume, sleeping bag and all, in the trailer, and reinstalled him in his tent in the new area."

Bitter weather blew in that day, and snow flew from the low sky. The company moved out amid the whirling white, and the men hunched their shoulders against cold, stinging gusts of wind. The steel of their helmets and rifle barrels held the numbing chill. Bundled in jackets and overcoats, the soldiers trudged forward, their gloved fists clenching rifle slings and ammo cans. Holloway carried his topographic map in one hand and dogtrotted alongside his platoon, bucking up the troops with words of encouragement.

The trail everyone followed had no proper name. The soldiers referred to it as the main supply route or MSR. Toward the end of its length, the trail twisted and turned and exited the forest. Just before that point, the road descended into a wooded hollow, and at its bottom lay Olef Creek. Holloway had a goose egg drawn on his map near that ribbon of frozen water. His mortar crews set up their guns in a small clearing there, and he established his platoon headquarters there, too. The machine gunners had to hike farther, to positions at the forest edge.

The forest did have a proper name according to Holloway's map. The Dreiherrenwald encompassed four hundred acres of spruce trees. The name, which meant "Three Lords' Forest," referred to a trio of medieval blue bloods: the lord of Bütgenbach, the lord of Schleiden, and the lord of Schönburg. Rather than war over possession of the forest, the lords conceded to control it jointly. Such peaceful compromise was remarkable for an age characterized by barbarity and innumerable wars. Five centuries later, in a more civilized age, those who controlled the forest held no hope for peace. Survival was their only desire, and the men of Company K wondered and worried about their fate under the West Point captain.

THE DAYS REPEATED THEMSELVES with dreary sameness, the weather alternating between snow and rain. Holloway occupied an earth-and-timber dugout that served as his platoon headquarters and provided overhead protection from the weather and enemy shells. Several paces away from the dugout, Holloway's mortar men had log-covered holes for sleeping and rectangular pits for their guns. The pits had no overhead protection. Half a mile away, at the forest's edge, Holloway's machine gunners also had covered holes for sleeping and open entrenchments for their weapons.

Staff Sergeant Dwight C. Bishop led the Machine Gun Section, and Holloway hiked up there almost daily to visit the sergeant and his men, usually bringing rations, new socks, and other quartermaster wares. The two men enjoyed shooting the breeze, and a day seldom passed without some nostalgic remark about home. Bishop found the lieutenant to be an effective leader and also easygoing. "He once told me to call him L.O., rather than lieutenant," Bishop remembered, "but I kept things military and addressed him as lieutenant. He didn't mind, and we became good buddies. I never encountered a finer officer during my twenty-six-year career in the army. He had a real feel for enlisted men and showed genuine concern for his platoon."

Holloway understood enlisted men because he had been one himself. He joined the army in 1942 after having grown up in Texas and Oklahoma as the son of an auto dealer. The future lieutenant served as a corporal with a heavy weapons company of the 89th Infantry Division at Camp Carson, Colorado. His enlisted service ended after he gained acceptance to officer candidate school and obtained a commission in 1943. The new officer received orders to an infantry training battalion posted in a California desert. During the summer of 1944, he transferred to Company K, stationed at Camp Maxey, Texas. Bishop and Holloway first became acquainted there. Bishop had grown up in Mississippi and joined Company K in 1942, when the unit originally formed. The two men had known each other for six months by the time they took up residence in the Dreiherrenwald.

The eastern edge of the forest pressed against the Belgian-German border. Bishop had two machine guns, one positioned just inside Belgium and the other gun positioned a few yards inside Germany, where a narrow finger of the forest poked across the border. The finger almost touched a highway that ran parallel to the border. Felled trees blocked the highway, and it marked the beginning of no-man's-land. The landscape beyond the road had the white patina of winter and the dark designs of war. Trip wires and minefields lay under patches of snow. Frost clung to rows of concertina wire. Antitank obstacles serrated the frozen nap of pastureland, which rolled away to the stark little village of Ramscheid. The enemy town lay behind a curtain of barbed wire and concrete bunkers, and Holloway occasionally spied on the place with his binoculars. Dougherty did, too. No civilians had lived there for months, only German troops inhabited the area, and they loped around outside their bunkers and trenches ignoring the American observers. The German defenses represented the forefront of the Westwall (or the Siegfried Line as Anglo-American soldiers called it).

Both sides moved around at will, with no small-arms firing unless a patrol penetrated too deeply. If the wind blew right, the Americans occasionally heard the enemy troops singing "Lili Marlene." Sometimes men of Company K crooned the English-language version. Day and night, the Germans frequently used colored signal flares as a means of communication in lieu of field telephones, for which wire was in short supply. Each morning, in ritual fashion, American artillerymen registered their guns on Ramscheid, striking the village with a few shells. The enemy sporadically fired back, lobbing shells into the American-held forest. Rarely did the blasts cause harm.

There were also other explosions, ones that Captain Plume created. "He liked to walk alone," Dougherty remembered, "throwing frag grenades into puddles. That was behind the front line. We would form a three-man patrol to check out these noises. There, 100 or 200 yards behind us, would be Plume contemplating a small crater."

Dougherty never hated Plume, unlike some members of Company K, but the lieutenant understood that in combat there were only two types of soldiers: those who got the job done and those who failed. Dougherty wore the weight of responsibility on his shoulders, determined never to shift it upon others. Holloway felt the same. The welfare of his men always came first.

On December 15, Holloway penned a letter by candlelight to his folks in Corpus Christi. He reassured them he was "getting along swell," and he mentioned his men. "My biggest worry and trouble over here is the 35 men in my platoon. Believe me, I have the best damned platoon in the world, but still, men have to be fed, clothed, and sheltered, and that is my problem.... We (the officers) received a liquor ration the other day. I sort of hated to, but I gave all mine to my men. Well, they deserve it more than I."

The lieutenant mentioned nothing about recent enemy activity that had drawn the attention of almost everyone in his company. For two days, the men had listened to the constant thrum of vehicles moving behind the German lines. The enemy camp bustled with preparations. The men sent reports up the chain of command, but the messages alarmed nobody at higher headquarters. The sounds probably indicated that a new enemy unit had arrived and was relieving front-line troops. Strictly routine. Nothing to fret about.

NOBODY ON THE AMERICAN SIDE saw them creeping through the mist and predawn darkness. Quiet as mice and clad in white camouflage,

German Army engineers cleared pathways through the minefields and concertina wire in front of the Company K position. After completing that thorny chore, the enemy sappers melted away. The countryside lay in silence, cemetery silence. That was about to change.

The shriek of incoming artillery shells broke the stillness. They exploded all over the Company K position. The sleet of steel began at 5:30 A.M. on December 16, 1944, and engulfed an eighty-nine-mile stretch of front line. The Germans aimed to make short shrift of American front-line defenses. Shells and rockets ran riot through the night. Awakened by the drumbeat of death, Holloway and everybody else inside his platoon headquarters pressed themselves to the dirt floor of their dugout. It felt like being aboard a submarine during a depth-charge attack. There was no place to flee. The men could only grit their teeth and pray.

The firing eventually shifted to targets behind the Bedbug position. Like curious prairie dogs, the men of Company K poked their heads above ground. Bulging eyeballs surveyed the damage and searched for any indication of enemy movement. Bishop could hardly believe that he had survived, as had everyone at his position. The Germans had drubbed them but failed to score a direct hit. Holloway's dugout also escaped a direct hit, as had all the other holes at the mortar position.

Before exiting the dugout, the lieutenant spoke to Nello Bartolozzi, a sergeant from Pennsylvania. Bartolozzi never forgot what happened next. Holloway turned to him and said, "Bart, here's a pair of binoculars. I'm giving them to you. Someday you may want to see an opera or a baseball game." The young officer took the binoculars from around his neck and handed them over.

"He must have sensed something," Bartolozzi recalled. "I figured he thought he was going to get killed. He also gave me several morphine syrettes, and showed me how to administer them. He said, 'If one of your men gets wounded, give him a shot of this.' That's the last time I spoke with Holloway."

Staff Sergeant Arthur E. Hicks, another Pennsylvanian, was also in the dugout. He led the Mortar Section, and Bartolozzi was one of his three squad leaders. Sergeants Oscar F. Hillring and James R. Beck, both natives of Indiana, had the other squads. The mortar crews rushed to their gun pits and prepared for action. Holloway and the mortar men had no telephone communications with anyone outside their area. The artillery bombardment had torn apart all the phone lines.

Bishop had a bigger problem. Minutes after the barrage lifted, he spotted shoals of enemy troops moving to his right and making an all-out frontal assault. They wore snow-colored jackets and trousers and had whitewashed helmets. As the onslaught rolled forward, German searchlight beams bounced off low-hanging clouds, creating artificial moonlight to aid the attackers, but it also permitted the Americans to see what was descending on them. The enemy soldiers wielded assault rifles and squirted quick bursts while charging ahead. Bishop had one machine gun at his position, and its crew threw back return fire. Dougherty's platoon also cut loose. One of the men, PFC Curtis L. Amuedo, drew a bead on an enemy trooper who rushed within several strides of the forest. Amuedo squeezed the trigger of his M1 rifle, and a bullet caught the German squarely in the forehead. American fire decimated the attackers, downing them fast, but more Germans followed on their heels and pushed ahead. Mortar shells began bursting amid the stampede.

The mortar barrage came from Holloway's position. His mortar gunners had no visual contact with the enemy but could hear the frenzied crackle of rifles and the steady *tum-tum-tum* of machine-gun fire. The mortar crews sprang to work. They had range cards with predesignated targets that interdicted avenues of approach to the Company K position. The cards provided all necessary data: range, elevation, deflection, and propellant increments. Hicks and Holloway unfolded a map and selected targets based on the battle sounds. Hicks shouted fire commands, and the mortars opened up. For more than a month, the mortar men had stockpiled ammunition, accumulating over one thousand rounds. The Americans had enough shells to bloody an attacking force of any size.

Salvo after salvo fell on two areas just in front of Company K. Those were the points where the German infantry struck. Grenadier-Regiment 991 hit the right flank of Dougherty's platoon, which also happened to be the right flank of the company. Bishop battled that assault. Grenadier-Regiment 989 hit near the center of Company K and straight up the main supply route, which twisted and turned all the way back to Krinkelt. The Germans wanted that route and made its capture a key objective of their attack. They massed two regiments against the 172 men of Company K, creating a lopsided fight.

Dougherty's platoon cracked first. His riflemen ran out of ammunition, and so did Bishop and the machine gunners. Onrushing enemy soldiers stormed over the bodies of dead comrades and entered the forest. Curtis Amuedo crawled under low spruce boughs and slipped unseen into a gully behind his position. Dougherty and other members of his platoon did the same thing. Bishop had no way to escape. He fell into enemy hands as did the other GIs in the finger of the forest. The victors lined up their captives. "I knew what they meant to do," Bishop recalled. "It was obvious they planned to mow us down, but then a German officer appeared and stopped everything. He needed us to help carry wounded Germans, and that's what we did for the rest of the day."

Alone and in small groups, the survivors of Dougherty's platoon retreated to the company command post. Sergeant Otha L. Langford and his squad were among the first to arrive, and they encountered Captain Plume. His attire surprised PFC Donald W. Rader, who later wrote about Plume. "He apparently had been in his sleeping bag during the artillery barrage and ensuing infantry attack and had just slipped on his combat boots and leather jacket over his silk pajamas." The captain addressed Langford.

"Sergeant, we're surrounded. You'd just as well surrender."

"Captain Plume, you can go straight to hell," Langford said. "We're getting out of here."

Langford stormed away and led his men in the direction of Holloway. They found Bedbug Four and his mortar men furiously pumping out shells. The lieutenant gave no thought to surrender and ordered Langford to position his squad beside the mortars as part of a perimeter defense. Other members of Company K trickled in and joined the defense. That included two radio operators from company headquarters, PFCs Thomas D. Price and Louis F. Gainey. They had abandoned their commanding officer. Price later explained:

"Lou Gainey came to me shortly after the barrage lifted and told me the captain said he was going to surrender as soon as the rifle platoons checked in. Up until that time we had not even seen the enemy, although we had heard a lot of small-arms fire and machine guns all along the front of our position and presumed we were under some type of attack. Neither Lou nor I had a desire to surrender, so we took off in a northerly direction along a road to the west of our company HQ. In about fifteen minutes, more or less, we encountered Lieutenant Holloway."

Price and Gainey told the lieutenant that Plume intended to surrender, and Holloway said, "Okay, well, come on in here and join us. We're going to hold this position as long as we can."

Alone and freezing cold, Amuedo also reached Holloway. The twenty-year-old rifleman from New Orleans had somehow escaped the onslaught that overran the right flank of Company K. He knew of no other survivors from his squad. After joining Holloway's band of holdouts, Amuedo discovered that German troops also had pierced the center of Company K and were pushing forward along the main supply route. The Germans had most of the company caught in the pincers of a two-pronged assault.

Amuedo, and everyone at the mortar position, saw enemy soldiers advancing along both sides of the supply route. Some wore greatcoats and others had snowsuits. They headed straight for Holloway's little bastion but failed to spot the Americans, because their position had splendid camouflage provided by treetops brought down during the artillery bombardment. The mortar men quietly readjusted their gun tubes for close range and dropped in shells with minimal propellant. The projectiles sailed high before plunging through conifer limbs and bursting above the Germans. Amuedo and the other riflemen ripped at the enemy with bullets, while the mortar shells sprayed down steel death.

The Germans faltered but regrouped and pushed forward again. Hicks and Holloway coordinated the response, but a problem developed. The mortar men could only elevate their tubes to 84°, making it impossible to drop a shell closer than one hundred yards. Enemy soldiers were now within that range, having crossed Olef Creek. Each mortar had bipod legs that restricted its elevation. The gunners detached the legs and held the tubes at 89° by hand. That solved the dilemma. Mortar shells flew again and burst directly in front of the American position. The gunners used blankets, cardboard, and bits of wood to insulate their hands from the blistering heat of the tubes.

Nello Bartolozzi helped his squad feed shells in their mortar, and he sniped at the enemy with his rifle. He emptied an eight-round clip and reloaded. "The M1 rifle sings out when it's empty," he recalled. "I can still hear the metallic ping of a clip being ejected."

The Germans fell back, having failed to claim a single American casualty. Holloway congratulated his men on their expert shooting. He and Hicks expected the enemy to request artillery support and to attempt a flanking maneuver. Instead another frontal assault materialized. The mortar men went to work again, and so did everyone holding a rifle. About then, Bartolozzi suffered an injury. "Something hit my left eye. It was tree bark. That's how close the Germans came to my head. I couldn't see out my left eye for three days. Despite my injury, I saw two Germans run up a little hill. They planted a machine gun so fast, I didn't have time to get them before they shot."

The enemy gun crew lay prone with a light machine gun mounted on a bipod. Their first blast stitched Holloway. Bartolozzi squeezed off several shots and hit both crew members. "I wounded one and killed the other," he recalled, but he went on to explain that his accurate marksmanship brought no feeling of success. "I wasn't fast enough, and they got the lieutenant."

Hicks saw the enemy machine-gun crew but never saw Holloway fall. As the Germans withdrew yet again, Hicks shouted a question for the lieutenant and received no reply. That bothered Hicks and caused him to investigate. He found Holloway seated in the entryway of his dugout, head sagging forward. Hicks knelt down and found three purplish holes at the base of Holloway's neck. One of the slugs had apparently broken a collarbone and deflected downward, piercing his heart. The stalwart officer died at age twenty-three.

Hicks informed everyone of the sad loss, but it was only a momentary distraction. The enemy struck again, and the Company K soldiers hurled them back as before. According to Hicks, "The Germans attacked us a total of five or six times, but, to my knowledge, they never physically penetrated our area."

The troops of Grenadier-Regiment 989 finally bypassed the persistent GIs. German medics cleared away scores of dead and bleeding. Only one American perished during the struggle: Lieutenant Holloway.

MORE THAN AN HOUR PASSED without a single German soldier coming within sight of the mortar position, and the Americans decided to take advantage of the lull. Amuedo and seven others volunteered to attempt a breakout in hopes of getting reinforcements. After moving several hundred yards, the eight men unknowingly walked smack into the crossfire of two German machine guns. Amuedo avoided being hit, but as far he could determine, nobody else survived the crossfire. Alone and with a knot of fear in his stomach, he found a hiding spot and waited for an opportune moment to make a break for the mortar position.

While Amuedo kept out of sight, his ears picked up the sound of vehicles in the distance. His comrades at the mortar position also heard the noise, and Hicks sent one of his mortar gunners on a scouting mission. He returned and reported the situation: "The whole damn German Army's up there!" The soldier described a pasture crawling with fresh troops, who were assembling for an attack into the forest.

Hicks said, "Okay, we'll go up and pay them a visit. They've paid us several visits." He intended to set an ambush in the forest. The sergeant grabbed an M3 "grease gun" and recruited two assistants, including the scout. Before departing, he spoke to everyone at the mortar position. "When we get back, be ready to move."

The ambushers vanished into the trees and crept up to the main supply route, where they selected an advantageous position. Plenty of Germans soon came within range, but Hicks restrained his assistants. Then he noticed what appeared to be enemy officers, and he gave the order to fire. The Americans unleashed a volley of bullets, but none came from Hicks. A maddening malfunction silenced his grease gun, and he tossed a couple grenades instead. After seeing several enemy soldiers spin to the ground, the little group of marauders fled toward the mortar position. (The Germans belonged to SS-Panzer-Grenadier-Regiment 25, which sent a reinforced battalion into the Dreiherrenwald shortly after noontime on the first day of the Bulge.)

The ambush party reached the mortar position, where everyone already had their gear packed. The entire group abandoned the position and retreated toward the rear. After less than a mile, the group entered a broad clearing and came under fire—friendly fire. An unseen GI assailed them with a .50-caliber machine gun. Hicks crawled under the bullets until he got close enough to shout, "Hold that fire!" The fusillade ended, and Hicks stood up and identified himself. He and his buddies had escaped the German noose, at least temporarily. It was about 4:30 P.M., and night had begun dropping its dark veil over the battlefield.

Feeling safe in the gathering gloom, Amuedo crawled out of his hiding place and stalked through the forest until he located the mortar position. Its defenders had pulled out, leaving Holloway's body in the entryway of his dugout. Amuedo found three live soldiers who had arrived following the pull out—a Company K medic and two gravely wounded men. The medic had both casualties inside a log-covered hole about fifty feet from Holloway's dugout, and Amuedo helped care for them. "We only had morphine and used the last of it during the night," he recalled.

Before daybreak on December 17, 1944, the Germans established a command post in Holloway's dugout, unaware that live Americans lay in their midst. Strong winds earlier that night had caused several shell-damaged trees to fall, and one of them toppled over the hole occupied by the GIs. That concealed their presence until daybreak, when the morphine ran out, and the wounded men began groaning in pain. The medic and Amuedo agreed that surrender was their best bet and the only chance the casualties had for survival. Amuedo buried his rifle and trench knife inside the hole and then climbed out, hands raised. German litter bearers soon hauled off the injured GIs. The medic accompanied them, and Amuedo followed later, his feet so frozen he could barely walk. He eventually encountered the medic, who said that both wounded soldiers succumbed to their injuries.

Amuedo became one of eighty-seven Company K soldiers listed as "missing in action." That number translated to twenty dead and sixty-seven prisoners of war. The captives included Captain Plume and Lieutenant Dougherty, who spent time at three POW camps: Stalag XIIID, Oflag XIIIB, and finally Stalag VIIA. Amuedo dwelled in the sullen confines of Stalag IVB before being transferred to an Arbeitskommando (work detail) at Falkenstein, Germany. He and other forced laborers escaped in April 1945 by killing a guard.

WILL CAVANAGH GAVE ME Joe Dougherty's address. The two men had corresponded in 1982, and I hoped the ex-POW could answer several questions about the 393rd Infantry. I needed details regarding a particular aid station and battalion command post that I intended to depict in separate paintings. During the closing days of 1985, I sat at the Spangdahlem library and typed a letter to Dougherty, and included a photocopy of a wartime map that Cavanagh allowed me to borrow.

I received an eight-page, handwritten response dated January 7, 1986. Dougherty answered my questions and expounded on the events that resulted in his capture. His letter included a typewritten "statement" that he wrote shortly after the war. The letter and statement explained that he and survivors of his platoon withdrew to the company command post after the Germans overran their right flank. They set up a defensive position near the command post and exchanged fire with the enemy. Captain Plume took no part in the shooting and offered "no leadership," and "he made the decision to surrender." Dougherty complied with the decision and waved a white flag and arranged a ceasefire.

"I regret having surrendered part of Company K," he told me. "We would have been defeated anyway because of the size of the German offensive, but we could have done better without Plume." Dougherty spoke highly of the enlisted men in his platoon. "I saw no one run, quit, defect, or otherwise abandon our unit. We lost the battle by defeat in ground combat. Rifle platoons don't get a second chance."

In his January 7 letter, Dougherty told me that he rendered his statement under oath to a "Board of Investigation on Company K." The board convened at Fourth Service Command headquarters in Atlanta, Georgia, and Dougherty surmised its purpose. "I assumed it was to eliminate Captain Plume from the service." (Although repeatedly passed over for promotion, Plume remained in the army. His career ended in 1953 after a court-martial convicted him of "dereliction of duties" and "drunk and disorderly conduct." The court sentenced him "to be dismissed from the service and to forfeit all pay and allowances.")

Dougherty served as a company commander during the Korean War and received the Silver Star Medal for "gallantry in action." Defeat and captivity during World War II drove him to success in Korea.

"I was a journeyman in the trade, no War College, no Harvard short course. When the outfit was in trouble, I got the job to bring it back. That was based on my experience in Company K, 393rd. I promised myself I would never lose again. . . . I learned not to answer the radio in combat, just to do the job, make the decisions, and bolster *my* people. I answered the questions of my superiors after I had everything in control. I passed on solutions with problems. That way, I got my own way."

The former Company K platoon leader retired from the army in 1975 as a full colonel. His last duty assignment brought him to Hawaii, and he decided to remain there, spending much of his time on a forty-foot sailboat named *Patriot*. He often wrote to me on days when stormy weather kept him off the open water. His Company K recollections were detailed and informative, and I decided to add Dougherty and his platoon to my list of artwork subjects.

One February day in 1986, I drove from Spangdahlem to the area where his platoon made its last stand. I carried a sketchbook, my trusty Nikon, and a copy of his statement, which included a map of the Company K area. The accuracy of the map amazed me, and I immediately located the remains of the dugout that served as Dougherty's platoon headquarters. The square hole had an entryway on its north side and was about chest deep. Relic hunters had picked over the area, leaving behind only K-ration cans, communications wire, and rusted metalwork from pup-tent poles. I photographed the hole and sketched my impression of what it may have looked like in 1944.

I also inspected Plume's command post and all the other points on the map, except one spot—the Weapons Platoon mortar position. Young spruce trees covered that area of the Dreiherrenwald, and their interwoven limbs precluded easy access, which made photography and sketching impossible. I remained on a forest trail and wondered if mortar pits lay somewhere beneath the trees.

Holloway never came up during my correspondence with Dougherty because he had forgotten the lieutenant's name. However in one letter, he mentioned the death of the Weapons Platoon leader, but Dougherty had not witnessed the killing, so he had no information beyond hearsay. When I compiled my original list of missing 99th Division soldiers, I learned that Holloway belonged to the 393rd Infantry, but I had no idea what company he served with. Dougherty had been the only Company K veteran with whom I corresponded, so I had no other information source.

Although Dougherty had forgotten the name Holloway, another Company K vet had no such difficulty. Curtis Amuedo reacted with alarm upon seeing Holloway's name on the list of missing soldiers published in the March 1990 *Checkerboard*. He wrote to Dick Byers and explained that Holloway could not be missing because he, Amuedo, had seen the lieutenant's body. Byers ironed out the misunderstanding with a phone call. Holloway was indeed dead, but the army had never recovered his body.

Byers forwarded me a copy of Amuedo's typewritten letter along with all other letters and notes he had received regarding missing 99th Division soldiers. As I sifted through the stack, the Amuedo letter stood out from all the others. I knew the places he mentioned, but I had never known that Holloway led the Weapons Platoon and died at the mortar position. Amuedo wrote, "Lt. Holloway was dead, laying facedown in the snow. The lower part of his body was half in and half out of his bunker." When I read those words, one thought came to mind: Eureka! I remembered Dougherty's 1945 map, which located the mortar position. I also remembered the day when I walked through that area, and I now wondered if I had passed within yards of Holloway's grave. It all seemed so easy. I had anticipated spending months or years conducting research. The notion never occurred to me that I had already gathered relevant material. My next move was to call Byers and tell him what I knew about the location where Amuedo last saw the lieutenant. Byers asked if I could pinpoint the spot, and I said that I could come close.

Dougherty had not drawn his map to scale, so his work required interpretation on my part. I circled my best guess on a modern topographic map and mailed it to Byers along with copies of Dougherty's map and statement. Byers sent my findings to Amuedo, and he agreed with the location of the mortar position, but he wanted to investigate further. "Certainly someone else must have seen Holloway's body besides me," he wrote in a letter.

Upward of ninety veterans from his company belonged to the 99th Infantry Division Association, and Amuedo contacted two of them. One published a Company K newsletter called *Kapers*, and the other one had served as company clerk during the war and knew unit personnel better than anyone. Neither man had knowledge of events at the mortar position but provided Amuedo with a list of Weapons Platoon members who belonged to the association. None had responded to the *Checkerboard* bulletin, so Amuedo decided to make a direct appeal for information. He sent each one a letter. That tactic paid off. Art Hicks and Nello Bartolozzi came forward with information about Holloway's death. During a telephone conversation, Hicks said he could draw a sketch of the mortar position, and he provided the name of another man who had seen the lieutenant's body.

Two months after the *Checkerboard* bulletin, Byers received a letter from Tom Price, a new member of the 99th Association. He had learned about the organization from Jean-Louis Seel, who traced him after finding a dog tag with his name and home address (one of the sixteen Company K tags that Seel found in 1988). Price also had seen the lieutenant's body. The letter that Byers received had a narrative account of December 16, 1944, events and a sketch of the mortar position. The letter commented on Holloway's battlefield leadership. "He had the courage to organize what few forces he could muster and gave us the determination to hold off a numerically superior enemy force for a couple hours," wrote Price. "I doubt that we may ever recover the body of Lt. Holloway, but for the knowledge and comfort it may provide his family, he was a fine officer, highly respected by his platoon and other men in the company."

I had more optimism about the chances of locating Holloway, and felt certain we would find the missing lieutenant if he still rested at the mortar position. Byers and Amuedo shared that belief, but all of us understood that Holloway might be in an "unknown" grave at an American military cemetery in Europe. I had visited several of those cemeteries and had seen the marble crosses engraved: HERE RESTS IN HONORED GLORY A COMRADE IN ARMS KNOWN BUT TO GOD. There were thousands of such crosses, and one could easily have been a marker for Holloway's grave.

Three months after the search for Holloway began, the 99th Division Association held its annual reunion, this time at a hotel in downtown Louisville, Kentucky. I drove from Ohio to attend. That was my first reunion and my first meeting with Amuedo, who flew in from Colorado along with his son. Byers attended, too, and wore his trademark bolo tie with an enameled 99th Division insignia. As he had done at two previous reunions, the former artilleryman orchestrated the so-called War Room, a display of World War II memorabilia— uniforms, equipment, and weapons. Byers collected most of the items from 99th veterans, but Seel and Speder also had made several donations. The collection filled a small banquet room and became the place where Amuedo and I discussed the Holloway case.

We spread out maps and other documents on an empty table, and I soon discovered that Amuedo had an expert eye for maps. He had no difficulty interpreting the contour lines on a topographic map and visualizing the three-dimensional forms the lines represented. His cartographic fluency came by way of his professional training as a geologist. He was part owner of Amuedo and Ivey, Inc., a geological consulting firm in Denver that specialized in mineral and petroleum exploration. Maps and aerial photographs were part of his livelihood, and he easily followed along as I referred to this or that map during our conversation. We quickly agreed on the location of the mortar position. Amuedo said that none of his research contradicted my original approximation based on Dougherty's map.

We adjourned from the War Room, and Amuedo introduced me to numerous Company K veterans, including one of Holloway's section leaders, Dwight Bishop. I heard about his wartime experiences for the first time, and he asked that I keep him updated on the search for Holloway. I also met Joe Dougherty, and he expressed surprise when he saw me. "I didn't know you came to these things," he said. I explained that I was attending for the first time, and he welcomed me aboard. We engaged in a discussion about Holloway, and Dougherty expressed embarrassment for having forgotten the name. There had just been too many names during his thirty-one years in the army. I told the retired colonel about the value derived from his map, and he asked that I keep him abreast of developments regarding Holloway. I heard that request again and again as I spoke with Company K veterans. The men of that ill-fated company were a tightly knit brethren and always had a large turnout at 99th reunions. Many were former POWs, and the events of December 16, 1944, had bonded them for life, though they heartily welcomed veterans who joined the company as replacements during and after the Bulge. Only one man was persona non grata—Stephen Plume. The very mention of his name brought raised eyebrows, as though someone had rudely passed gas. Nobody had a kind word.

The main event of every reunion was a Saturday-night banquet, and Company K had fifty-one men present at Louisville, the most of any 99th Division company or battery. That earned the men recognition from the convention chairman, who awarded their group a bottle of Kentucky bourbon. Dougherty received recognition for being the veteran who traveled the greatest distance to attend the reunion. As a resident of Hawaii, he usually had that distinction when he attended reunions.

The reunion ended the morning after the banquet, and I spoke with Amuedo one last time. I said that I intended to prepare a map and report, instructing Seel and Speder where to search for Holloway.

Amuedo mentioned that, if that search resulted in success, a Company K veteran living in Texas knew the whereabouts of Holloway's family so that they could be informed.

CLASSES AT OHIO STATE kept me preoccupied until the end of summer, when I had a short recess before fall quarter. The break gave me time to create a map and supporting documentation. I kept in regular contact with Dick Byers, and he asked me to send him everything. I obliged and passed the ball to him. He had corresponded with Seel and Speder and arranged for a face-to-face meeting to explain every detail of the Holloway case and to discuss other missing soldiers of the 99th Division. Byers planned to visit Belgium for the dedication of a monument commemorating the 99th.

He was among over two hundred veterans and family members who witnessed the monument unveiling on October 6, 1990. Hundreds of Belgians also attended, and that included Seel and Speder as well as Speder's pregnant wife and toddler son. After the event, Byers met with the diggers, as planned, and presented my material. He dubbed them the On-site Search Team and accompanied them to the Dreiherrenwald. Together they hunted for the mortar position where Holloway died. Their mutual friend Pierre Dullier came along and observed the reconnaissance operation. Young spruce trees covered the area, but the searchers squeezed their way in and eventually found a cluster of eighteen holes. These included three holes resembling mortar pits and the remains of a dugout with an entryway, just like the one described by eyewitnesses who saw Holloway's body. The location was a stone's throw from the spot I had marked on the map. Seel and Speder decided to return at a later date with metal detectors and digging implements. Byers returned to the United States and updated me.

Speder delayed the start of digging because on October 9 his wife delivered their second son. Bottles, diapers, and sleepless nights followed. Besides a new baby, the young couple also had a new home. Speder and his wife had recently moved to an Ostkantone village called Thirimont, where they purchased a 250-year-old farmhouse that had stone floors, eighteen-inch-thick stone walls, and exposed-beam ceilings. Like most rural architecture in the region, the building was a Quereinhaus, a combination house and barn. A previous owner had transformed the barn into a garage, and Speder stored his jeep there and built a workshop. He turned a second-floor bedroom into a museum where he displayed his artifact collection. The room also became On-site Search Team headquarters.

During the first week of November, the team finally went to work. The baby was sleeping through the night, and Speder had time to start excavating the suspected mortar position. For the first time, he and Seel entered the forest without the intention of finding artifacts. They had come to solve a problem, to find a missing soldier. The two friends crossed a threshold that would separate all that came before from all that came after.

Seel and Speder began by working in the holes that resembled mortar pits, and the diggers soon found 60-mm shells and empty containers for them. One hole also yielded a cleaning kit for a 60-mm mortar. Little doubt remained. The site was indeed the Company K mortar position. Additional evidence came when Speder located the bottom half of an American mess kit, and it had the name Hillring crudely engraved. Seel dug up a canteen cup that had the mark H-9264. Both items belonged to Oscar Hillring, one of Holloway's men. Less noteworthy discoveries included toothbrushes, shaving cream tubes, and rotted clothing. After two days of digging, the two Belgians had cleaned 70 percent of the holes but found no trace of human remains. That included the dugout with the entryway.

Before making a third visit to the mortar position, Seel asked relic hunter Jean-Michel Roth to lend assistance. He had helped excavate Sito's grave, and Seel was present in February 1989 when Roth discovered the remains of a Wehrmacht soldier. The Deutsche Dienststelle later identified the soldier as nineteen-year-old Alois Adelmann from Eggenberg, Austria. The teenager eventually found a final resting place at a German military cemetery in northern Belgium. Roth had a sixth sense for finding artifacts, and by November 1990 had found no fewer than forty-three dog tags and eleven identification bracelets. He had a reputation for success and was also an entrepreneur, selling or trading many of his discoveries. He accepted Seel's invitation and joined the search in the Dreiherrenwald on November 9, 1990.

The day dawned clear and cold, but the rising sun gradually burned off a heavy frost that had fallen during the night. The soft perfume of spruce balsam drifted through the forest while the three diggers turned the earth with shovels and picks. They worked in different holes and found artifacts similar to those already discovered.

Darkness had begun falling when Seel and Speder decided to knock off for the day, but Roth wanted to remain a little longer. He was busy in a small slit trench. Someone else had previously grubbed around there and pulled out pieces of mortar-shell containers and discarded them as junk. Roth dug deeper and found a Bakelite case for German binoculars. The little entrenchment lay directly behind the dugout with the entryway, and Roth expected to find more artifacts underneath the case. He kept digging and unearthed fabric. Speder identified the cloth as herringbone twill, the type used for GI fatigue clothing.

Roth requested a hand. "He asked me to dig because he was tired," Seel recalled. The two men exchanged positions, and Seel promptly struck a bone, a human tibia. The Belgians worked to enlarge the hole, and in the process, they removed a pair of rubber boots, all the long bones of two legs, and a set of pelvic bones. The grave contained several artifacts: a broken compass, two MKIIA1 hand grenades, a magazine for a .45-caliber automatic pistol, and a sterling silver ID bracelet with no name engraved on it. The most important artifact was a leather wallet containing a laminated identification card with Holloway's name and signature. The wallet also held photos, but they had all turned to soggy pulp.

Nighttime finally forced the diggers to quit. They concealed the grave site, and made plans to return the following day. On the way home, they visited Will Cavanagh and informed him of the discovery.

November 10 was damp and misty. The trio arrived in the afternoon and resumed work. They began by sifting all the previously excavated dirt. It contained no additional bones or artifacts. For the next four hours, the Belgians carefully removed the bones of Holloway's upper body. His right collarbone had a fracture, probably resulting from one of the bullets that killed him. One rib was also broken. More artifacts emerged. The diggers uncovered a pair of stainless-steel dog tags on a bead-link chain around Holloway's neck. The chain had a break probably caused by one of the bullets. The lieutenant's skull displayed remnants of a wool knit cap and tufts of brown hair. His outerwear consisted of a wool greatcoat and overalls made of herringbone-twill fabric. The collar of his overalls had rank insignia for a second lieutenant and crossed rifles for an infantry officer.

One of his pockets contained remnants of red and blue colored pencils, which he probably used for map work. (Red was the color for enemy forces, and blue represented friendly forces.) His pockets also held two Belgian coins.

The location of Holloway's grave suggested the Germans had moved his body. He had died in the entryway of his dugout, and that was the spot where American eyewitnesses last saw his body. Amuedo later observed German soldiers using the dugout, and the dead lieutenant was no doubt in their way, so they probably stuffed him in the slit trench behind the dugout. The diggers found no pistol or wristwatch. Holloway's remains lay facedown, and his wallet rested on top of his greatcoat and in the middle of his back. It was easy to imagine an enemy soldier rifling through the wallet and tossing it in the grave.

Speder checked the time. It was 4:30 P.M., and all bones and artifacts were out of the ground. The diggers had relieved the fallen officer from his post after nearly forty-six years.

BYERS RECEIVED AN EXCITED CALL from Seel, who said he and Speder had recovered Holloway's remains. He also said that Roth was the person who found the grave and that Will Cavanagh would contact the U.S. Army and arrange a transfer. Byers immediately called me. I had been optimistic about the search effort but never expected the excavation phase would conclude on the third outing. The operation was a signal triumph, proof that what I envisioned could be accomplished.

Byers also telephoned Curtis Amuedo to inform him of the discovery and to make a request. We needed a name and address for Holloway's next of kin. The family had lived in Jacksboro, Texas, during the 1930s but moved to Shawnee, Oklahoma, before the war and later moved to Corpus Christi, Texas. Although the family never returned to Jacksboro, a maternal uncle named John C. Winters still lived there in 1990 and so did a Company K veteran named Robert L. Peterson. The former Company K man received a call from Amuedo, who explained the situation. Peterson subsequently visited eighty-three-year-old Winters and relayed news that a search team had found Holloway's grave. Winters said, "Well, well, after all these years." He also said that Holloway had a younger sister living in Corpus Christi.

Sarah Holland was the only surviving immediate family member. After receiving her address and phone number, Peterson passed that information to Amuedo, who gave it to Byers and me.

In Europe, Cavanagh telephoned Mike Tocchetti, director of the U.S. Army Memorial Affairs Activity–Europe. Tocchetti had received Alphonse Sito's remains in 1988, and he well remembered Seel, Speder, and Cavanagh. The director of Memorial Affairs arranged to receive Holloway's remains on November 26, 1990, and to check the grave site for any bones or artifacts inadvertently overlooked. As in 1988, he would transfer everything to the Central Identification Laboratory in Hawaii.

Byers passed Holland's address and phone number to Cavanagh, who promised to give them to Tocchetti when he came to collect the remains. The information would hopefully save time because it might take the army weeks or months to locate Holloway's next of kin. Amuedo telephoned Cavanagh and told him that Holland knew about the discovery. Her uncle had broken the news. Amuedo also asked a question about financial compensation. He wondered if Seel and Speder had incurred any expenses by undertaking the search. Cavanagh had an immediate answer. "They would be offended if anybody did anything in the way of monetary remuneration." He said the team conducted the search for the "sake of doing it, and that's all."

Amuedo and I spoke several times during November 1990, and he felt that someone from Company K should contact Holland and provide her with more information about her brother. He also felt that Art Hicks would be the best person, because Hicks had served as a section leader under Holloway and had a close relationship with him and had firsthand knowledge of his death. I had one bit of advice. Whoever contacted her should make certain she understood that army scientists would conduct a forensic analysis, and there was no guarantee of a positive result. She also needed to understand that the identification process might take a year or more.

Hicks called Sarah Holland first, and Amuedo called two days later. The flood of news about her brother left the sixty-five-year-old Holland in an emotional quandary. "I had mixed feelings," she later recalled. "I was relieved to know that at last he would be put to rest, but saddened that my parents weren't around to know." She said her mother left behind a collection of plaintive letters from the army that documented a lengthy and fruitless effort to locate a grave site. Amuedo explained what the Belgian search team found in the Dreiherrenwald and what prompted the search. He also said that scientists at an army laboratory in Hawaii would analyze the recovered bones and artifacts and attempt to establish positive identification. Prospects looked good, but nothing was definite. Amuedo went on to inform her of how long the process might take. Holland said she would be patient and hope for the best. She asked Amuedo about the circumstances of her brother's death. Her family had only sketchy information prior to the recent call from Hicks. Amuedo shared his remembrances of December 16, 1944, and how he became a prisoner of war. For the first time, Holland understood precisely what happened to her brother. "All of this is so incredible," she told Amuedo. "I can't tell you how much I appreciate what you and all the other men have done. This all helps so much, just to know."

Tocchetti learned about Sarah Holland when he traveled to Belgium with a search-and-recovery team from his mortuary at Frankfurt, Germany. Seel and Speder handed over the remains, and Tocchetti scrutinized them. He turned the skull in his hands, and said, "Male, Caucasian." He studied the hipbones, and said, "Twenty-three to twenty-seven years old." Cavanagh looked on, as did two Belgian forest rangers, Adolphe Collard and Erich Hönen. The American team screened the grave area and found no additional remains or artifacts. Back at the Frankfurt mortuary, Tocchetti designated the remains as X-9472 and transferred them to Hawaii. He included artifacts, next-of-kin information, a summary of the recovery operation, a sketch of the recovery site, and letters written during the spring of 1990 by Company K veterans who assisted the search effort.

Besides Holloway's remains and associated artifacts, the mortar position had yielded many more items. Seel and Speder decided to send almost everything (except the 60-mm mortar shells) to Dick Byers, letting him keep what he wanted for the War Room and giving the rest to Company K veterans. Speder packed everything in a cardboard box and shipped it across the Atlantic. The lot included two special pieces of GI equipment—Oscar Hillring's canteen cup and the bottom half of his mess kit. Speder instructed Byers to mail them to Hillring, along with a request for a signed photograph. Byers followed through and reunited the equipment with its original owner, who responded with an autographed picture. Byers kept a selection of artifacts but sent the bulk to Amuedo. Speder also sent me a small package with several artifacts.

Besides distributing artifacts, the diggers traveled to the United States in June 1991 to attend their first 99th Division reunion. Cavanagh also attended, along with Byers and me. Everyone gathered at the San Francisco Airport Marriott where the five-day shindig took place. Once again, the veterans of Company K won an award for having the most men present from any 99th company or battery. Joe Dougherty made a brief appearance and informed Amuedo and me that he had recently visited the Central Identification Laboratory, which was near his home in Hawaii. He introduced himself to the laboratory commander and inquired about Holloway. The scientific staff had completed all analysis work, and the resulting positive identification awaited final approval from a review board. There had been no hitches. I passed the good news to Art Hicks, who showed up despite an ongoing battle with brain cancer. He had received the Silver Star Medal for his actions in the Dreiherrenwald, and I interviewed him on tape about his experiences. San Francisco was our first meeting. He flew there from his home in Florida because he wanted to meet everyone involved with the search for Holloway, and he wished to meet the lieutenant's sister.

Sarah Holland had been a widow for three years and flew alone from Corpus Christi, where she ran an insurance agency. Sarah was a hard one to overlook. Even at age sixty-five, she had a gracile figure and could turn heads in an evening dress. She made a lasting impression, and events in San Francisco made a similar impression on her. "The convention was absolutely fantastic," she wrote afterward. "I have been to a lot during my lifetime but none that had the camaraderie this one had." The Company K veterans accepted her into their family. She told me that being with them made her feel as though a part of her brother were still alive. She became an associate member of the 99th Division Association and hoped to attend all future reunions.

Three months later, six of those veterans attended her brother's funeral at Fort Sam Houston National Cemetery in San Antonio, Texas. One of the veterans eulogized the fallen officer during a chapel service and later offered a closing prayer at the interment. The ceremony ended with a rifle salute, the playing of "Taps," and the presentation of a folded flag. Amuedo stood at the rear of the funeral party and watched in silence. Earlier in the day he had spoken to journalists. "The service and burial received wide radio, newspaper, and television coverage in

San Antonio and all of south Texas," Amuedo recalled. "TV cameras were there from all three San Antonio affiliated TV stations of ABC, CBS, and NBC. It was also on the Spanish-language TV station and radio."

After the ceremony, Holland held a reception in her hotel suite. One of the Company K men remembered, "She, her daughters, and friends prepared an elaborate buffet of delicious snacks and drinks. Sarah's uncle, John Winters, brought one of his famous home-baked cakes all the way from Palo Pinto County. It was an appropriate ending to a final farewell honoring a comrade listed as missing for forty-seven years and now laid to rest."

Holland stayed in regular contact with the veterans who served with her brother, and she attended every reunion. She also joined a group of 99th Division veterans who toured Belgium in 1994, two months before the fiftieth anniversary of the Battle of the Bulge. A film crew from ABC News followed the group and documented their journey. Cavanagh and the diggers escorted Holland to the Company K mortar position, and a TV cameraman recorded the scene. Later, the entire group visited the mortar position and observed a minute of silence in remembrance of all who perished in the Dreiherrenwald.

In 1995, the 99th Division reunion took place during July at a hotel in downtown Pittsburgh. Holland had a direct flight from Houston to Pittsburgh, but stormy weather and turbulence forced her aircraft to land in Cleveland. All her life she had been fearful of storms, and that day was no exception. She sounded nervous when she called home. Her middle daughter begged her to get a hotel room and wait for the storm to pass. Holland refused. Determined to make it to the reunion without delay, she rented a car and set out on the two-and-a-half-hour trip to Pittsburgh. Sadly, she never arrived. While driving through a torrent of rain, her car spun out of control on the Ohio Turnpike. She survived the wreck but lay comatose on a ventilator in an intensive-care unit. Her daughters flew to Ohio, and several weeks later they transferred her via air ambulance to a Houston hospital. She emerged from the coma but had unfortunately suffered brain damage. Her alertness improved enough for her to speak a few words, but she remained bedridden and frequently required the ventilator. She had been off the breathing apparatus for ten days and in good spirits when she died of a pulmonary embolism on October 6, 1995.

Chapter 5

UNKNOWN SOLDIERS

Four years before Sarah Holland's tragic accident, a newspaper reporter interviewed me about the search-and-recovery operation, and he asked how my colleagues and I bankrolled our work. He knew that Department of Defense personnel spent millions of dollars each year searching for missing servicemen. I laughed and said that my colleagues and I had no budget. Money was a minor ingredient in our success. Know-how and persistence were the linchpins. Seel and Speder lived in the search area, and that made our work feasible from a financial perspective. If we pursued cases in France or Italy, for example, costs would rise exponentially and quickly become prohibitive. By confining our work to the Bulge area, we eliminated money as a significant factor.

While speaking with the reporter, I referred to the search for missing 99th Division soldiers as the MIA Project. The reporter asked me about the name. I said that Dick Byers and I came up with it after the recovery of Holloway. We decided the search needed a proper name, and I designed a logo that combined the name with a dog tag and a 99th shoulder patch. The logo had begun appearing in the *Checkerboard* along with updates on the search. I then admitted the name was something of a misnomer because no GIs remained "missing in action" from World War II. That surprised the reporter. I said the term MIA only applied to missing servicemen for whom no death report existed, and that no longer held true for any of the missing from World War II. The military had long since declared them dead. Eyewitness testimony verified many of the deaths, but the armed forces only considered officers as reliable eyewitnesses. Without an officer eyewitness, the military made a "finding of death" under the provisions of the Missing Persons Act (Public Law 490, Seventy-Seventh U.S. Congress). That allowed next of kin to collect death benefits and to settle other legal or financial matters. Missing soldiers like Sito and Holloway had a special status: "body not recovered," or BNR. That abbreviation was unfamiliar to the reporter, and he understood why Byers and I chose the name MIA Project. The lexicon of American popular culture included the abbreviation MIA, which had come to refer to any missing serviceman. The term had developed a meaning beyond its legal definition.

The reporter then asked me how many U.S. servicemen were still missing from World War II and listed as BNR. I had no reliable number to offer. After the war, the American Battle Monuments Commission (ABMC) commemorated 78,956 missing servicemen at its cemeteries and memorials around the world. The names appeared on Walls of the Missing and Tablets of the Missing, but thousands of the names belonged to men whose bodies the military had recovered and positively identified. Many were sailors buried at sea, and the navy never considered them missing. Those men simply had no graves on land, so government officials decided to include them among the missing commemorated by the ABMC. The reporter asked how many sea burials took place. I had seen widely conflicting numbers, so it was impossible for me to say, but there were more than sea burials to consider. The military had recovered and identified the remains of many servicemen after the ABMC established its 78,956 figure. No accurate count of those recoveries existed. As the reporter and I continued talking, we discussed servicemen lost at sea in sunken ships and downed aircraft and even amphibious tanks. We also discussed servicemen interred as "unknowns" at ABMC cemeteries, and I told the reporter that some of those burials consisted of unidentifiable body parts from GIs who occupied known graves.

The issue of missing servicemen had layers of complexity beyond what the reporter had imagined. Byers and I routinely grappled with some of those complexities, and to help manage them we began grouping BNR cases into three categories:

1) further pursuit
2) no further pursuit
3) investigation deferred due to lack of leads or exhausted leads

The no-further-pursuit cases included a 99th soldier killed by a massive blast triggered when he opened a booby-trapped door. The explosion left nothing large enough to recover. Another no-further-pursuit case involved a soldier who drowned in a river. Byers and I considered him "lost at sea." We also decided against pursuing three other cases, because they involved soldiers who became prisoners of war during the Bulge and later died at POW camps deep in Germany. Seel and Speder had no way to search those areas. We eliminated the case of PFC Richard G. Gastelum upon learning that Belgian foresters had recovered his remains in September 1959, after the ABMC had inscribed his name of the Wall of the Missing at the Henri-Chapelle American Cemetery.

Holloway had been a further-pursuit case, thanks to Amuedo's research. More than a dozen other soldiers fell in that category, and that included PFCs Jack C. Beckwith and Saul Kokotovich, missing soldiers of the 395th Infantry Regiment. Two of their wartime buddies, Vernon E. Swanson and Byron A. Whitmarsh, began gathering information just as Amuedo had done for Holloway. They worked with Byers and me, and together we funneled data to Seel and Speder.

The two diggers had established a relationship with Erich Hönen, one of the forest rangers present for the handover of Holloway's remains to American authorities. The Holloway recovery impressed Hönen because it was no accidental discovery. He had an interest in history and admired the Yanks who liberated Belgium, and he agreed to support future search operations. The ranger became an ally for Seel and Speder, and they often visited him and secured approval to dig at locations deemed as possible burial sites. Several times he granted permission to search in a remote wooded area called the Hasselpat. Vern Swanson had an uncorroborated report that American medics buried Saul Kokotovich near a battalion aid station or battalion headquarters in that area. Seel and Speder knew both locations and searched them in hopes of finding the missing soldier. They also searched for him on a forested hill in Germany, where more reliable reports indicated medics buried him along with Jack Beckwith. Soon, though, a different mystery intervened, taking Seel and Speder's quest along another path.

HÖNEN HAD A STONE-AND-BRICK HOME in the village of Rocherath. A pair of deer antlers decorated the building just below the peak of its gabled roof. The ranger happened to be there on June 25, 1992, when Seel knocked on the front door. He found Hönen attired in a natty green uniform, standard apparel for members of the forestry service. Seel intended to ask permission to continue searching for Kokotovich in the Hasselpat area, but Hönen had surprising news.

He and another forester and several lumberjacks had discovered a grave in a five-hundred-acre forest known as the Elsenbüchel. The group of woodsmen found a freshly dug hole with bones lying around it. Several minutes later, and thirty meters away, they noticed an arrangement of four bones beneath a downed spruce tree. The collection consisted of two hipbones and two arm bones. Whoever arranged them had set the arm bones into the hipbone sockets. Someone partially encircled the bones with a rusted ammunition belt for a German machine gun. Before leaving the forest, Hönen collected the bones from beneath the downed tree and the other bones at the freshly dug hole.

After returning home, Hönen telephoned the police to ask what should be done with the bones. "We don't know," was the reply. "Contact the Rocherath Bürgermeister." Hönen telephoned the Bürgermeister, who recommended the bones go into a pauper's grave at the Rocherath cemetery. No further action took place until Seel entered the picture. Hönen had been preoccupied with other matters. Seel immediately suggested that he and Speder go to the hole with their metal detectors to search for dog tags or other identification. Hönen liked that idea, and they set a date.

On July 3, Hönen led the way into the forest. He first showed Seel and Speder the freshly dug hole, and they immediately recognized it as the work of an unscrupulous relic hunter. The culprit (or culprits) had looted the grave without compunction, flinging dirt and bones all around. Not more than six months had passed since the ransacking.

Hönen then pointed out where the arrangement of four bones had lain beneath a downed tree. Someone had recently unearthed and discarded German small-arms ammunition beside the tree. No bones remained there, so Seel and Speder returned to the hole.

The two diggers culled the dirt in and around the hole, and they accumulated a sizable collection of bones. Beneath spruce needles outside the hole, the diggers found bones that had lain undisturbed for years, perhaps pulled to the surface by scavenging animals. Besides human remains, Seel and Speder found rotted shreds of GI winter clothing as well as snaps, buckles, and other hardware from American combat gear. The Belgians also found one empty BAR magazine, several unfired .30-caliber cartridges, two charger clips for an M1 rifle, and an ammunition belt for an American machine gun. No German clothing turned up at the site. Unfortunately, the diggers recovered no dog tags or other identification media. If such artifacts once existed, whoever robbed the grave snatched them along with anything else of monetary value. Among the junk left behind, Seel and Speder made a significant find: deteriorated chevrons for a U.S. Army sergeant. Although rotted and broken into pieces, there was no mistaking them.

By day's end, a skeleton, albeit incomplete, had taken shape. The skeleton lacked shoulder blades, several long bones, most of its skull and teeth, and numerous small bones from its hands and feet. But the situation was more complicated. There were duplicate bones, including extra arm bones, an extra clavicle, and an extra leg bone. The remains belonged to at least two persons. The commingling of their bones caused concern as to which bones belonged to which individual. Segregating the bones was beyond the capability of Seel and Speder, but they knew the army had forensic anthropologists in Hawaii who could handle that job. The diggers transported all their discoveries to Hönen's home for safekeeping.

The Belgians now focused on the most obvious question. Who were the unknown soldiers? The only clues immediately apparent were the shreds of GI clothing and the chevrons. That evidence pointed toward one possible conclusion: some of the remains belonged to an American sergeant. Seel and Speder knew of only one missing sergeant associated with the Elsenbüchel forest. Sergeant John T. Puckett disappeared on January 15, 1945, while on a patrol in that area. The two Belgians had learned about the patrol after Seel wrote to the U.S. Total Army

Personnel Command in 1991 and requested information regarding several missing 99th Division soldiers, including Puckett. The army maintained an individual deceased personnel file (IDPF) for every soldier who perished during World War II. Those records, also known as 293-files, contained documents relating to cause of death, recovery or nonrecovery of remains, disposition of personal effects, and funeral records if there was a burial. Seel received a smattering of documents from the Puckett IDPF, and they included a memorandum mentioning the patrol but providing few specifics. No officer witnessed the death, so the army declared Puckett dead in 1946 under the provisions of the Missing Persons Act.

Seel telephoned Dick Byers to inform him about the Elsenbüchel discovery, and Byers immediately called me. He asked if I could obtain more information about Puckett's death and identify other missing soldiers associated with the grave. I offered to undertake that research and prepare a report, but I said it would require several months and a visit to the National Archives. Byers said okay, and I started work by writing a letter to the army requesting a complete copy of the Puckett IDPF. Byers called Belgium, and all parties agreed the time had come to notify Mike Tocchetti of Memorial Affairs Europe. The diggers called him and arranged a rendezvous. Byers also called Tocchetti and promised him a copy of my report as soon as I completed it.

In the meantime, Seel and Speder returned to the site on July 10, and they brought Cavanagh. With his help, they spent the day digging and sifting dirt. For all their efforts, they recovered only several skull fragments. Tocchetti and a four-man team arrived on July 20 and inspected the entire assemblage of bones and artifacts at Hönen's home. The bones possibly represented three individuals according to Tocchetti. He also noticed several of the bones had greenish traces of moss or lichens, indicating they had been aboveground for a long period. The next morning, the team entered the Elsenbüchel along with Seel, Speder, and Cavanagh. The group dug and sifted for more human remains but found only one tooth and a handful of small bones. Tocchetti closed the site and transported all bones and artifacts to his mortuary at Frankfurt, Germany. He designated the remains as X-9476, and shipped everything to Hawaii.

My task was now to produce the report I offered to create. During the summer of 1992, I had only two classes at Ohio State, which gave me plenty of free time. I had originally planned to work on an oil painting and help Cavanagh conduct research for his next book, a history of the 99th Infantry Division. The X-9476 case altered my focus, and I made that my priority.

CAVANAGH TRAVELED TO THE STATES in August 1992 to conduct research for his book. Byers and several other 99th veterans met him at the National Archives, and I did, too. We stayed at a hotel in Suitland, Maryland, for most of one week, and our group spent eight hours a day at the archives. I helped Cavanagh but occupied half my time with X-9476 research. My first chore was to determine every American unit that had entered the Elsenbüchel forest. I had started that task on the day Byers called me, and I finished it at the National Archives. The result was a detailed chronology.

The Elsenbüchel forest fell to the U.S. Army on September 15, 1944, fourteen weeks after the Normandy invasion. Troopers from the 4th Cavalry Group captured the forest. The cavalrymen encountered resistance in nearby villages, but the Germans conceded the forest with little or no resistance. Their battered forces were too busy retreating to the relative safety of Westwall fortifications along the Belgian-German border. After a fortnight, the 4th Cavalry Group relinquished the forest to the 28th Infantry Division, which occupied it for a brief period during October until relieved by the 102nd Cavalry Group. Soldiers of the 99th Division arrived in early November and relieved the 102nd. The forest was a quiet sector and behind the front line. The quiet lasted until the Bulge began. The Germans seized the forest on December 20, 1944, by which time the 99th had withdrawn to defensive positions along a barren expanse of high ground just west of the forest. That ground became known as Elsenborn Ridge.

For the remainder of December and all of January, the Germans entrenched themselves in the Elsenbüchel, vis-à-vis Elsenborn Ridge. The forest inhabitants survived mortar and artillery bombardments and frequent visits by patrols from the 99th Division. The 99ers finally launched a major effort on January 30, 1945, aimed at removing the Germans from the forest, but the attack had inadequate artillery support. After two days of murderous fighting, the poorly supported assault finally broke the German hold on the forest, and it soon became a rear area, well behind the front line.

My research on the forest identified all the American units associated with that piece of terrain and the X-9476 recovery site. My research also identified the dates those units were there. That information served as my guide as I perused lists of missing servicemen on computer printouts, which Dick Byers obtained from ABMC cemeteries in Holland, Belgium, and Luxembourg. I found only four missing soldiers associated with the forest and the recovery site: Private Earnest E. Brown, Private Harold E. Dechon, PFC William D. Cooper, and Sergeant John T. Puckett. All four belonged to the 394th Infantry Regiment, and all died in January 1945 while on patrols that penetrated or attempted to penetrate the forest. I researched those patrols during my time at the National Archives. The records of the 99th Division contained dozens of relevant documents: patrol reports, field orders, map overlays, unit journals, casualty lists, after-action reports, S-2 periodic reports, S-3 periodic reports, and prisoner-of-war interrogation reports. I photocopied the documents, and they helped me gain a better understanding of events, but the archival research provided no information specifically pertaining to the missing soldiers. Eyewitness testimony helped fill that gap.

After visiting the National Archives, Dick Byers and I telephoned and corresponded with 394th Infantry veterans who served with the four missing soldiers. The membership roster of the 99th Division Association was our starting point, and I made an audiotape of each telephone interview I conducted. Byers placed a bulletin in the September 1992 edition of the *Checkerboard*, and he received several letters in response. Byers also helped me by providing an aerial photograph made of the Elsenbüchel forest as it appeared on Christmas Day 1944. He obtained the black-and-white image from an artilleryman, who had used it as a map while in combat.

After gathering documents and eyewitness accounts, analysis consumed my time. I had originally correlated four missing soldiers with the X-9476 recovery site. I now had research that tended to disassociate William Cooper and Harold Dechon with the site. They died within one kilometer of it but on patrols that never penetrated the forest, although information on Dechon was too meager to establish anything with certainty. The same research strongly linked Earnest

Brown and John Puckett with the site. Both men belonged to Company B, 394th Infantry, and they died on an ill-fated patrol that penetrated the forest. The patrol route passed directly over the recovery site. Several questions still remained about Brown and Puckett, but I found it unnecessary to have all the puzzle pieces in order to see the picture.

ON THE FIFTH DAY OF THE 1945 CALENDAR, Sergeant Jack Puckett (he preferred Jack instead of John) became a member of Company B along with eighteen other replacements. The Wichita, Kansas, native had no prior battle experience. Combat and freezing weather had taken a huge toll on the company prior to his arrival. He found scruffy-looking survivors with soiled and sagging clothes that looked as foul as they smelled. Every soldier had matted, greasy hair and cheeks crusted with soot and whiskers. Not a glimmer of youth remained in their eyes. The sergeant and his fellow replacements looked like creatures from another world, with their bright eyes and clean uniforms.

When the Bulge began, Puckett lived in a Nissen hut at Danebury Down, England, where he served as a squad leader with the 272nd Infantry Regiment (69th Infantry Division). His regiment received an order on Christmas Day to supply seven hundred men as replacements for Bulge casualties. Some of the selectees, including Puckett, later embarked on a motor convoy through snow and cold to a Naval yard. They boarded an LST (landing ship, tank) and crossed the English Channel amid heavy seas. On the other side, the replacements climbed into "forty-and-eight" boxcars and moved by train from Le Havre, France, to Welkenraedt, Belgium. The mass of men stayed overnight at a brick factory and then rode by truck to within hiking distance of front-line units. Puckett was among a contingent assigned to Company B, which occupied foxholes on Elsenborn Ridge.

Foot soldiers of the 2nd, 9th and 99th Divisions held sway over the ridge and frequently sent patrols into German territory. The patrols scouted enemy defenses and picked up prisoners but sometimes fulfilled a larger purpose. Higher headquarters announced plans for a major attack beginning on January 15, 1945, and instructed the 99th to launch five raiding patrols that day as diversionary cover for the push. Staff officers picked Company B to furnish one of the patrols, and First Lieutenant Roger C. Lenihan became the patrol leader. He was the company executive officer and one of two experienced officers in the unit. His patrol plan called for thirty enlisted men, and that included replacements like Puckett as well as Sergeants Emanuel Rind and Clifford B. Selwood. They had also joined the company on January 5 and had served with the 272nd Infantry. The three sergeants first met after being drafted as replacements. They became assistant squad leaders due to their lack of combat experience, although Rind received a temporary assignment as a platoon guide. The patrol would be their first piece of the war.

Lenihan and several senior officers convened a briefing on January 14. It took place among front-line foxholes so everyone could survey the intended patrol route that led to the Elsenbüchel forest. While walking to the meeting spot, Rind and several other battlefield neophytes bunched together as they traipsed through the snow. One of the officers shouted at them to spread out, but the binoculars of an enemy observer had already caught the careless action. The Germans sent three calling cards. *Pom! Pom! Pom!* Mortar shells flew out of the forest. The first explosion severely wounded an infantryman sitting on the edge of his foxhole, and a miniscule sliver from the shell penetrated Rind's groin. The other two shells fell farther to the rear and hurt nobody. The air was too frigid for Rind to drop his britches and inspect the tiny puncture wound. He pressed on, telling nobody about his injury. Medics hauled the severely wounded man away on a sled. He survived, but Rind only learned that fact decades later. "I thought he had been killed, and I felt guilty about it, since we had drawn the Kraut fire by bunching up."

Still shaken by the close call, Rind listened to Lenihan and Technical Sergeant George E. Speace as they explained details of the raiding patrol, code-named Topper. The patrol included the entire First Platoon, which had only two rifle squads remaining despite the influx of replacements. The squad leaders, Sergeants Thomas J. Cornett and Robert E. Doebler, had both worn PFC stripes when the Bulge began. Besides being a squad leader, Cornett doubled as bazooka man for the patrol because he had the most experience with the rocket launcher. The patrol planners augmented the platoon with a radioman, medical technician, and a light machine gun crew. The planners scheduled the operation to commence at 6:10 A.M. when 4.2-inch mortars would begin dropping smoke shells and high explosives in front of the forest and inside it. Five minutes later, at H-hour, the patrol was to move out toward the forest. After passing the line of departure, known as phase line 1, the patrol members had over nine hundred yards of open snow to cross. Phase line 2 was at the forest edge, and shortly before that point, the radioman had instructions to call a halt to the shelling. Part of Cornett's squad was to remain outside the forest as a support echelon while everyone else entered. Enemy soldiers of Grenadier-Regiment 991 occupied the area. The patrol had two more phase lines and nearly three-quarters of a mile to cross before reaching its objective, a bridge spanning a narrow creek. That marked the point of withdrawal for the patrol.

Lenihan and Speace both had combat experience and were the senior-most soldiers on the patrol. The two squad leaders also had experience, but other patrol members had veteran status, including PFC Carl W. Combs. He had just returned from a hospital in Liège, Belgium, and had earned a Purple Heart and Combat Infantryman Badge. His experience made him an immediate candidate for the mission. As he later recounted, "This patrol was made up of a few old hands and the rest rookies, even some transferred from the air force." Combs had four men under his charge. "I was assigned a BAR man, Private Earnest Brown, and three riflemen. Our mission was left-flank protection for the patrol."

Brown had been in the States when December 1944 began, and he journeyed overseas as a replacement. On the morning of January 3, he had joined Company B on Elsenborn Ridge, as did fifty-one other replacements. The twenty-nine-year-old Virginian had a wife and three children and had been in the army for less than a year. He lacked combat experience but knew how to operate his weapon with proficiency, which set him apart from the air force replacements who barely knew how to fire a rifle. He and the other patrol participants assembled near the line of departure during the first hours of January 15. They watched as unseen enemy soldiers occasionally popped amber and white flares into the night sky.

Deadpan faces among the would-be attackers betrayed their anxiety. They prayed the 4.2-inch mortars would smother the forest with smoke and explosives and screen the patrol from German eyes. The men imagined the consequences if the mortars failed to deliver, and the picture made everyone queasy. Enemy bullets and shells might pick off the GIs like birds on a fence.

Sergeant Rind girded himself for combat, loading up with hand grenades and ammunition bandoliers. He unfastened his sergeant's stripes, which he kept fixed to his jacket sleeves with safety pins. Disclosing his rank to the enemy was a quick way to become a preferred target. He tucked the stripes in a pocket. Rind also partook in a momentary diversion from thoughts of battle. "A sergeant came up and produced two bottles of Calvados. He said he had just come back from town, and we could all have a swig for breakfast. As I remember, some of the guys passed on the drink, but it sure felt good warming my belly on that cold morning."

H-hour arrived, and the patrol moved out in two parallel columns through the darkness. Scouts led the way. Deep snow fettered the long march across no-man's-land. As platoon guide, Rind brought up the rear and had the job of reining in backsliders, but only one man fell behind. "When I told him to move faster, and he said he was moving as fast as he could, I told him my rifle butt or bayonet up his ass would make him move a little faster." The straggler sped up but not fast enough for Rind. Halfway to the forest, Rind said, "So long, I'll be seeing you." The sergeant lit out to catch up with his column, and the laggard came hustling after him, not wishing to be left alone in the middle of no-man's-land.

Someone at the front of the formation called for the radioman, and other patrol members echoed the call. The clank and clunk of equipment heightened the ruckus. Sound carried well in freezing cold weather, but the Germans were unable to spot the approaching patrol, despite its lack of noise discipline. Mortar shells had clouded the Germans in white-phosphorous smoke. Before reaching the trees, Lenihan requested a halt to the mortar shells. His radioman sent the request and also reported that the patrol was "receiving no enemy fire as yet." Despite Lenihan's request, shells continued to fall and some burst dangerously close to his men as they neared the forest. The contents of a smoke shell blinded one American, but he was the only one hurt. Lenihan later noted the casualty in his patrol report but also praised the fire support. "The effectiveness of the 4.2 mortars was excellent," he wrote.

Lenihan fanned out the majority of his troops, and when he blew his whistle, they marched forward into the forest, hip-firing their weapons to keep enemy heads down. The lieutenant had positioned the support echelon outside the woods. Rind was in charge of the men outside, and they scrunched down along a row of tall conifers extending perpendicular from the forest.

Inside the Elsenbüchel, the Americans found no enemy soldiers entrenched at the forest edge, but as the patrol continued forward, its men suddenly faced concertina wire and enemy bullets. The clatter of German machine guns filled the air. "We encountered eight automatic weapons in one spot and two in another," Lenihan reported. "The enemy had lanes cut from which they could fire down our flanks and fire on us at close range. They had wonderful fields of fire." German mortar gunners soon joined the fight and began lobbing in shells. The forest became a pantheon of dangers. The Americans risked death from five directions: mortars from above, antipersonnel mines from below, grenades and bullets from the front and sides.

Amid those dangers, Sergeant Selwood—one of Doebler's men—took cover at the base of a spruce tree. He fired his rifle at enemy muzzle flashes and the darting silhouettes of German soldiers. Several yards to his right, PFC James R. Latham lay beside a tree and fired his rifle. The wild roar of battle surrounded the men. The sergeant glanced over and noticed that enemy bullets had chewed off the tree bark above Latham's helmet. Selwood shouted, "Keep your damn head down! Roll over and look at the tree above your head. There isn't any bark up there." Latham did so and hollered back, "You better keep your damn head down, too. Look at your tree."

Elsewhere in the woods, Sergeant Puckett had assumed a prone position alongside his buddy Private Eugene A. Lett from Wisconsin. The two men had served together in the same company with the 272nd Infantry and had shared a foxhole on Elsenborn Ridge as members of Cornett's squad. During the firefight, Lett heard someone shout, "We gotta rush 'em. When I give the signal, everybody jump up and charge." Lett sprang to his feet at the signal. He was the only one. Nobody else moved. "It seemed like I stood there for a year," he recalled. "I felt about ten feet tall, but nothing happened." He dropped back into the snow, embarrassed but alive.

The din and fury of combat continued, and Lett observed a BAR man pounding on the receiver of his automatic rifle. Snow had gotten inside it, causing the weapon to malfunction. The man suddenly stuck his head up, disregarding the hail of death around him. He called out to the Germans: "Mine won't work!" His nonchalance made the battle seem like a game of cowboys and Indians, but this game was for keeps. While busy shooting, Lett caught a sidelong glimpse of Puckett's helmet lying in the snow. "Jack, put your hat back on," Lett said. He turned for a better look. Puckett lay facedown with a gunshot wound to his forehead. Lett grimaced and shouted for the medic. Technician Fourth Grade Guerrina J. Prola approached, but enemy fire drove the aidman back. He instead concentrated on casualties he could reach, and there was a growing number as the situation worsened. The patrol had lost all forward momentum.

Communications broke down between the GIs inside the woods and those outside. Rind had no radio, so he waited for Lenihan to dispatch a messenger. None arrived. Unwilling to sit still while disaster threatened, Rind decided to enter the forest in hopes of locating the lieutenant to determine if he wanted the support echelon committed to the fight. Rind instructed the men under his charge to stay put until he returned. He could hear the sounds of battle spreading, which indicated the Germans had begun a flanking maneuver.

Carl Combs, Earnest Brown, and three riflemen anchored the left flank of the force in the woods. The enemy slashed at them with a scythe of machine-gun bullets. One of the Americans went down, his right ankle smashed by a bullet. The medic rushed to his aid. Combs returned fire with his M1 rifle, and he caught a glimpse of Brown as he rose with his BAR to blast one of the enemy guns. A German bullet drilled Brown just as he squeezed the trigger. The force of the impact jerked him upward, and he dropped into the snow facedown. The medic sprinted to his side. Combs charged the enemy gunners and silenced them and then returned to check on Brown. The medic had rolled him over and retrieved his dog tags. "He's done for," the medic said. The unfortunate soldier had a bullet buried in his brain. Combs latched onto Brown's BAR and collected his remaining magazines.

The nearest rifleman inherited the weapon and magazines, and he took over for Brown as BAR man. Meanwhile a pair of enemy soldiers grabbed one of the silenced machine guns and attempted to reposition it farther to the left. Combs raised his rifle, took quick aim, and knocked down both Germans. More enemy soldiers surged forward from deeper in the woods and increased pressure on the left flank. The BAR man laid down a base of fire, which permitted Combs and a rifleman to maneuver left and spoil the flank attack, at least temporarily. The rifleman stayed in position alone as Combs hastened back to the BAR man, who had one twenty-round magazine remaining. Combs helped him by reloading an empty magazine with bullets he hastily shucked from M1 rifle clips. No more ammunition remained.

Dodging enemy bullets, Combs weaved his way to Lenihan and told him the left flank verged on collapse. The men there had little ammunition, and one of them had sustained a fatal head shot, and another lay wounded with a shattered ankle. The lieutenant said the entire patrol had almost exhausted its ammunition, and he had just received permission to withdraw. The pullout was to begin in a moment, and the left flank had to hang on a little longer. "He asked if we could hold for five more minutes," Combs recalled. "He gave me a full BAR magazine and some extra M1 clips and one rifleman to help get our wounded man." Combs and the rifleman dashed to the left flank, ducking behind trees on the way. The BAR man had just run out of ammunition when they arrived, and the new magazine brought his weapon back to life. Lenihan had given the left-flank defenders permission to withdraw after they expended their ammunition.

Unable to reach Lenihan because of enemy fire, Sergeant Rind sprinted out of the forest and discovered the support echelon had vanished, contrary to his instructions. The men had either made a beeline for friendly lines or plunged into the melee. Rind caught his breath and sprinted back into the trees. He never found the men. The sergeant joined a couple of other friendly faces and started blasting away at the enemy. He rapidly expended all the rifle clips in his cartridge belt and reached for one of his bandoliers, but he encountered a problem. "I found all the clips frozen to their cardboard pouches and the pouches frozen to the cloth of the bandolier." As Rind cursed his frozen ammunition, he noticed the action seemed to be easing up. The patrol had started to disengage from the firefight.

On the left flank, the BAR man ran out of ammunition and pulled out of the forest. Combs stayed and took a few more shots. "I used one clip of ammo to shut down a machine gun and then turned to leave, and there was the young man with the injured ankle." Two riflemen had started to tote him away, but a bullet wounded one of them. The unscathed rifleman hauled away the hurt one. Combs grabbed the man with the injured ankle and pulled him over one shoulder. They emerged from the forest, and a spray of bullets came their way. After diving for cover, Combs looked up to see a German charging at them, his machine pistol blazing. Combs used his last clip of ammunition to drop the attacker, and then he resumed retreating toward friendly lines, still carrying the injured man.

Rind and members of Cornett's squad covered the withdrawal from just inside the forest. They watched Doebler's squad and Lenihan hightail it home in a single column. Rind and Cornett ordered the men around them to vacate the area. At the same time, Rind discerned the sound of German mortars firing in the distance. As the men got up to leave, he heard a mortar shell breaking branches above his head. He started to look up when the shell detonated. The blast flattened Rind. It tore off his helmet and ripped away his rifle. Shell fragments peppered his face, chest, hands, and legs. One fragment cut a groove in his skull and another almost severed his left ring finger. He felt blood running over his face, and he tasted something coppery in his mouth. He could hear one of the men in his group calling for a medic. "Can we help you?" a voice said. "Scram, get your asses the hell out of here!" he said. Everyone around him disappeared.

He raised himself and staggered out of the forest. "I may have moved thirty to fifty feet when I came upon a dead GI in my path. The corpse was on its back with its arms spread-eagle, still clutching a box of machine-gun ammo in each hand. Its eyes were wide open, and the whites were purplish. The irises were black-purple, and the skin was a dark purplish color." Perhaps the soldier died on a previous patrol. Rind could do nothing but leave him, but after he moved around the cadaver, the Germans began sprinkling the area with mortar shells. The severely wounded sergeant flopped on his back to avoid being hit. The shelling stopped, but Rind was unable to pull himself upright.

Helpless and defeated, Rind spotted a solitary GI emerge from the woods. It seemed impossible that any live Americans remained in the area. The man had a leg wound but hobbled along at a good clip. He ventured over to Rind and offered help. The sergeant refused, telling the man to clear out and save himself. The limping soldier took off, promising to dispatch a medic and litter team, but there was little chance of them making a successful rescue in daylight.

The sun rose behind the Elsenbüchel forest, and Rind wondered when the enemy would come out and finish him off. Somehow he managed to open his canteen, but the water was solid ice. He decided he would probably freeze to death before the Germans got to him. Numbness and fatigue washed over him. He watched as two enemy soldiers stepped from the forest. They propped their rifles against a spruce tree and donned Red Cross identification vests. One of them carried a litter. Several German infantrymen had gone down outside the forest, including the one Combs dropped. The two medics began checking them. "*Todt,*" the medics said as they inspected each body. They spoke loudly enough for Rind to hear, and he knew *todt* meant "dead." His mother was an Austrian Jew who spoke German and Yiddish, and he had learned both languages as a child growing up in Brooklyn, New York.

The medics slowly headed in his direction as they examined corpses. He had four hand grenades in the pockets of his field jacket, and he decided to use one. "I'm dying anyway, why not take a couple of 'em with me?" he thought. The medics carried rifles, and that made them combatants and fair game. The sergeant reached for a grenade. One of the medics noticed Rind move, and said in German, "There's one that's still kicking." They walked toward the American, and he fumbled with the grenade. It slipped out of his hand and fell back into the pocket. He tried two more times and the same thing happened. His fingers were too frozen and mangled to extricate the grenade, and he gave up on the idea. He instead reached for his canteen, one thing he could still grasp. He tried in vain to suck water from it. One of the medics lifted it from his hands. The two Germans loaded him on the litter and carried him into the forest to a foxhole, which was apparently their base of operations and a casualty collecting point.

"They searched me and found my stripes and whistle in my pockets." Rind recalled. "As they came to each hand grenade, they gave me a dirty look and cursed me. About half a dozen Krauts milled around the hole, the highest-ranking one being their equivalent of a tech sergeant." The medics had several men stretched out beside the foxhole. At least two of them wore GI clothing. Rind had a clear view of an American with locks of blond hair poking out from under a head bandage. Blood drizzled from beneath the cotton dressing. "His breathing was difficult and sounded raspy," according to Rind. "He seemed to be in bad shape, and I didn't think he would live." The blond-haired man lay on the boundary between life and death, and the Germans wasted no time on him.

When the medics finished with Rind, two litter bearers picked him up and began a one-mile journey to a Verbandplatz (aid station). They each wore a shoulder harness to support the litter. Another pair of litter bearers walked alongside to provide relief for the first two when they became tired. The wounded sergeant lay on his back, gazing skyward at a universe of snow-laden spruce trees. Their branches looked exquisite, tinseled with ice and glittering in the sunlight. The only sounds were the crunch of German boots and the hard breathing of the litter bearers. Rind drifted into unconsciousness.

The sergeant awoke at the Verbandplatz, an isolated house with a picket fence. In happier days it had been a hunting lodge called Sam Suphy and the primary residence of the Hönen family. Before the Allied liberation of Belgium, Friedrich Florian, a Nazi Gauleiter, controlled a huge tract of adjacent woodland and stayed at the lodge while hunting deer and wild boar. He sometimes brought distinguished guests, including Adolf Galland, one of Germany's preeminent fighter pilots and recipient of the Knights Cross, further decorated with oak leaves, swords, and diamonds. Sergeant Rind had no knowledge of that history. All he saw was a ramshackle building with antlers hanging on one of its interior walls.

One of the Germans at the Verbandplatz was a short, redheaded lieutenant, who spoke fluent English and conducted prisoner interrogations. The 99th Division had launched five patrols that day, and the Germans had other prisoners besides Rind. One of them promised to reveal everything he knew in exchange for morphine. The interrogator eventually approached Rind and talked about American football and compared the engagement in the Elsenbüchel forest to a football game. He asked for help scoring the game and encouraged Rind to disclose his unit and the names of all its officers and noncoms. The sergeant refused to cooperate. "Every time he asked me a question, I just moaned," Rind later recalled. The interrogator gave up, but only after revealing detailed knowledge about the 99th and its order of battle. He knew more than Rind.

Medics loaded the American sergeant and other patients on a truck and drove them eighteen miles to Steinfeld, Germany. The village had a fortresslike monastery, which medical personnel of Sanitäts-Kompanie 277 converted to their Hauptverbandplatz (main aid station). German Army doctors performed surgeries, and Catholic Sisters tended to the patients. The doctors repaired Rind, and the nuns nursed him back to health.

Back in Belgium, the 99th Division posted Rind as missing in action along with two other patrol members, Private Brown and Sergeant Puckett. Patrol survivors claimed to have seen Brown and Puckett killed, but no officer (namely Lieutenant Lenihan) had witnessed the deaths. The War Department eventually used the Missing Persons Act to declare both men dead.

I COMPLETED A 103-PAGE REPORT on the X-9476 case after three months of research, analysis, and writing. The report identified all missing soldiers associated with the case and provided a narrative account of the circumstances surrounding each man's death. The report also included maps, overlays, photographs, and numerous wartime documents gathered from the National Archives. I added dental records and other IDPF material obtained from the army.

The final pages of the report presented a summary analysis. Brown and Puckett were the missing soldiers most associated with X-9476. The recovery site lay along their patrol route, and the site jibed with the location where Emanuel Rind described having seen two American casualties, including the dying soldier with blond hair and a bandaged head. Brown sustained a head wound, but he had brown hair according to his IDPF. Puckett also sustained a head wound, and he had blond hair. One piece of material evidence pointed toward Puckett. The set of sergeant's stripes that Seel and Speder recovered at the grave site corresponded with Puckett's rank, but I now wondered if the stripes might have belonged to Rind. German medics had removed his stripes before evacuating him to Sam Suphy.

I finished my report on October 8, 1992, made eight copies, and disseminated them to persons involved with the X-9476 case. Dick Byers mailed one to Mike Tocchetti in Germany, and he forwarded it to the Central Identification Laboratory in Hawaii. He also asked that we send a copy to Douglas L. Howard, a mortuary affairs specialist who worked at the U.S. Total Army Personnel Command in Alexandria, Virginia. I followed through on Tocchetti's request. The army now had two copies of the report.

The lack of dog tags or other identification made X-9476 a challenging case. The ghouls who plundered the grave probably absconded with material evidence. My treatise provided historical evidence and data analysis that partially compensated for whatever the grave robbers might have taken, but the army also needed conclusive biological evidence in order to establish positive identification. Because X-9476 represented the incomplete remains of two or three persons, the situation became more complicated, raising another issue. I could only associate two missing GIs with the grave, so if the remains belonged to three persons, the third individual was perhaps a German. That possibility demanded consideration even though no German clothing turned up at the site. The scanty amount of dental anatomy further compounded the difficulty. All factors considered, X-9476 represented an almost impossible challenge but for one ray of hope. The new technology of DNA analysis offered a potential solution to the mystery. Maybe the army could extract DNA from the bones and compare it to DNA from family members of the soldiers named in my report. Army scientists had begun doing that type of analysis with remains recovered from southeast Asia.

Each of the unknown soldiers collectively labeled X-9476 had a name when he died, and each deserved to have it back. DNA analysis could take years, so Byers, Seel, Speder, Cavanagh, and I prepared for a long wait. Tocchetti promised to inform us of developments. While waiting, we continued the search for other missing 99th Division soldiers.

Seel and Speder picked up where they had left off when they first learned about the Elsenbüchel grave. They had been searching for the resting place of Saul Kokotovich. That case, and the related cases of Jack Beckwith and David Read, kept all of us busy. I also found time to finish an oil painting that depicted a bedraggled infantryman. I gave the painting to Cavanagh, and he later reproduced it on the cover of a 1994 book about the 99th. After completing that artwork, I abandoned my ambition of creating a series of oil paintings. The search for missing servicemen like Beckwith, Kokotovich, and Read seemed a more worthwhile use of my time.

Chapter 6

IN SHALLOW GRAVES

January 4, 1945. Frank Read heard the telephone ring and a sense of foreboding struck him. He knew what it meant. "My brother's been killed in Europe," he blurted out.

"What are you talking about?" asked one of his roommates.

Moments later, somebody called Frank to the phone in the hallway of his dormitory at the U.S. Navy training facility near Del Monte, California. The call was from his parents in Hudson, Ohio. They had just received a telegram from the War Department. Frank's brother, PFC David A. Read, was dead—killed in action on December 15, 1944. Even more bad news came later: his brother's body was lost.

Seven years after David's death, the army mailed a sad letter to his father:

"It is with deep regret that your Government finds it necessary to inform you that further search and investigation have failed to reveal the whereabouts of your son's remains. Since all efforts to recover and/or identify his remains have failed, it has been necessary to declare that his remains are not recoverable." That seemed the final word, a heartbreaking epilogue to a promising life that began on February 8, 1925, in Brownsville, Texas.

The fourth of six children born to Verne and Ethel Read, David's birth came while the family wintered at their Texas property. When not in Texas, the Reads lived in Akron, Ohio. The family dry-cleaning business, the Read-Benzol Company, was in the city, and David's father served as its vice president and treasurer, and eventually its president.

In 1935, the Reads took up residence in Hudson, Ohio. They initially lived in a rented house, but later David's parents purchased a home at 35 Church Street. A real Victorian-era showpiece, the house included a pyramidal-roofed tower at one corner, a full facade porch with a spindlework balustrade, and a profusion of other gingerbread details. Many Hudson residents considered it the finest home in town. (In 1973, the property gained a spot on the National Register of Historic Places.) The picturesque community, reminiscent of a New England village, included the Western Reserve Academy, a prestigious prep school for boys. Verne and Ethel moved to Hudson so their five sons could attend the academy as day students rather than as boarding students.

David entered the academy in September 1939, the same month World War II erupted in Europe. The school grounds featured sweeping lawns and Greek revival architecture. Mighty elms flanked the main roadway, their intertwined branches forming a shadowy tunnel across the street. These stately surroundings had an aura of learning and high purpose. Over the course of David's four years there, he earned a reputation as a "conscientious, hard worker" whose warm personality won him friends everywhere. He played varsity football and became first man on the tennis team. He also competed as a varsity swimmer and springboard diver. Outside of school, he was a big-band aficionado and a record collector.

During the summer months, David and his siblings worked at the family business, the largest dry-cleaning company in Akron. One of their sundry tasks involved inspecting all garment pockets for foreign objects, especially kitchen matches or other items that might ignite solvent fumes during the tumble-drying phase of the cleaning process. "We earned a dime an hour searching pockets," Frank Read recalled. "Plus we got to keep whatever coins we found providing they totaled ten cents or less. Anything greater had to be returned to the customer." The kids also made money cleaning rugs and upholstered furniture. When David was old enough to operate a motor vehicle, he drove a delivery truck around the Akron area, picking up and returning rugs, clothes, draperies, and furniture.

Also during the summer there was leisure time. David and some of his classmates often relaxed and reveled at nearby Silver Lake. David's youngest brother, Doug, fondly remembered:

"David was a great big brother to me. Whenever he went swimming at Silver Lake with his high school friends, he would take me along. He and his friends made me feel like one of the gang, even though I was six years younger.

"One time, there were twelve of us crammed into Dad's nine-passenger Lincoln, and David stopped to pick up a sailor in uniform hitchhiking to Akron. The sailor was thrilled and—as I like to tell it—sat on the lap of one of David's beautiful girlfriends."

David's trips to Silver Lake ended in June 1943 after he graduated from the academy. He had a scholarship to attend Amherst College in Massachusetts, but a draft notice interrupted his plans. After entering the service, David took basic infantry training at North Camp Hood, Texas, a desolate, chigger-infested spot that abounded with sand, sagebrush, and cacti. He remained there for about three months before being transferred to the Army Specialized Training Program (ASTP). His high intelligence earned him a place in that unique organization created to meet the army's future demand for college-educated specialists.

Enlisted men who joined the program received orders to attend colleges and universities around the country. David went to John Tarleton Agricultural College in Stephenville, Texas. There he studied pre-engineering like a majority of his fellow "student-soldiers." His coursework included history, English, geography, physics, chemistry, and mathematics. In addition, military drill and physical conditioning kept him grounded in the rigors of army life. After four months of study at Tarleton, classes abruptly ended in March 1944. The army radically reduced the ASTP to help offset a severe manpower shortage among combat units.

David joined several thousand other ASTP men recently assigned to the 99th Infantry Division at Camp Maxey, Texas. Among the throng of new arrivals was Saul Kokotovich. Though he and David never met—then or afterward—the two soldiers were similar in several respects. Both grew up in the Midwest, both came from families of six children, and both were draftees. They were also nearly the same age, less than three months apart.

SAUL WAS BORN ON NOVEMBER 20, 1924, in Gary, Indiana, as the third child of Serbian immigrants George and Stella Kokotovich. Their birthplace was the rural village of Kosinj, in the Lika province of the Austro-Hungarian Empire. George, whose Serb name was Gjuro, emigrated to the United States the year before World War I began. His bride-to-be, Stoja Paripovich, reached America in 1921 and married George sixteen days after her arrival.

The following year, the newlyweds moved into a single-story house at 1697 West 11th Avenue in Gary, Indiana. That became the birthplace for all six of their children. Situated on the south shore of Lake Michigan, Gary swarmed with immigrants from eastern, southern, and central Europe. For all of its ethnic diversity, the city had but one industry—steel. George worked at the Gary Works, a gargantuan network of mills and finishing plants built and operated by the U.S. Steel Corporation. The most striking characteristic of the town was its smoky skyline. Day and night, rows of soaring chimneys pumped plumes of pollution into the heavens. Mountains of coal, slag, and iron ore punctuated the scene. This industrial landscape became the backdrop for the childhood years of the Kokotovich offspring.

Saul's given name was actually Savo, but few people outside of the family used that Serbian name. His oldest sister, Mary, remembered, "When we went to school, nobody used our real names. I was Maria, but they called me Mary. Savo was Saul, and my sister Millie was Mildred. My brother Vasily was Bill or William. The two youngest kids, George and Helen, had no Serbian names. By the time they were born, my parents were pretty much Americanized."

Like most inhabitants of Gary, the Kokotovich family lived comfortably in boom times when demand for steel ran high, and the mills operated at peak capacity. But during economic downturns or labor strikes, the huge blast furnaces, coke ovens, and rolling mills ceased production or slowed to a sluggish pace. City residents quickly felt the pinch as layoffs and unpaid bills beset their lives. Clear skies over Gary meant rough times.

The hardest period came during the 1930s with the catastrophe of the Great Depression. Saul's youngest brother, George, recounted its impact on their father and the family. "Pop, if he worked, it was only one or two days a week in the mills. The situation got to the point that our water and electricity were turned off. We couldn't afford them. Pop eventually sank a well in the basement, and we used a hand pump to get water. For light, we had kerosene lamps." The Gary Relief Council doled out flour and other food staples, which the family supplemented by raising chickens and ducks. A large vegetable garden helped, too. As soon as Saul was old enough, he took a job as a paperboy for the *Gary Post-Tribune*.

Amid the struggle to carry on through the Depression, tragedy visited the Kokotovich household. In early 1935, city officials quarantined the family in their home after Mildred, age eleven, contracted scarlet fever. The only doctor available was one provided by the Gary Relief Council, but in the era before antibiotics, no effective remedy existed. The young girl died in her bed. The wake took place at home, but, due to the quarantine, friends and family could not enter the house to view her body. They stood outside and peered through a window at the dead child. Mercifully, none of the other Kokotovich children developed scarlet fever, and they eventually returned to school.

In 1938, Saul entered Tolleston High School, within walking distance of his home. He earned Cs in English and mathematics, and collected Ds in Latin. Two of his favorite subjects were ROTC and shop class. He never scored less than a B in either. But Saul's greatest interest was music. At an early age, he learned to play the *brach*, an instrument similar to a mandolin and popular in Serbian culture. His first music teacher, George Kachar, lived in the nearby town of Hammond, Indiana. In later years, Saul attended a local studio of the Wurlitzer School of Music and became an accomplished accordionist.

As a child, while taking music lessons at George Kachar's home, Saul met his future wife, Martha Serbian, a brown-eyed brunette from Des Moines, Iowa. She often traveled to Indiana to visit George and his wife, who were her aunt and uncle. The relationship between Saul and Martha began in grade school, blossomed in high school, and continued after Saul received his diploma in June 1942. Besides dating Martha when she was in town, he got a job sorting metal fasteners at the Gary Screw and Bolt Company, one of the few firms in town independent of U.S. Steel. The burgeoning war effort meant long hours, but for Saul that abruptly ended when he received a draft notice.

At 7:00 A.M. on February 23, 1943, he reported to the Greyhound terminal in Gary and was bussed to the armed forces induction station at Fort Benjamin Harrison, Indiana. There he underwent a physical examination to determine his fitness for military service. The medical staff judged him to be class 1A, eligible for active duty. He was sworn into the army and then, as was standard practice, granted a short furlough to return home and set his personal affairs in order. Afterward, he reported to the Army Reception Center at Benjamin Harrison. At the center, he received uniforms, shoes, a pair of dog tags, and had his head shaved. He also received a battery of inoculations and took the Army General Classification Test, an "intellectual capacity" assessment that consisted of 150 multiple-choice questions. After several days at the center, he and a cavalcade of other former civilians boarded a troop train bound for Camp Swift, Texas, and the 97th Infantry Division.

Saul underwent basic infantry training at Camp Swift, but his tenure with the 97th lasted only five months. Due to his high score on the classification test, he received orders to attend the Army Specialized Training Program at John McNeese Junior College at Lake Charles, Louisiana. There he began a pre-engineering curriculum that lasted until the army curtailed the ASTP in March 1944 and many of its participants went to the 99th Infantry Division at Camp Maxey, Texas. Before leaving school, he proposed marriage to Martha. She accepted, and the two announced their engagement, though they set no wedding date.

ONCE IN TEXAS, SAUL BECAME ACQUAINTED with Jack Beckwith, a fellow ASTP man. The two soldiers belonged to the same rifle company. Born in LaMoure, North Dakota, on March 12, 1924, Jack was the second child of Norman and Verlie Beckwith. The couple divorced before he turned five, leaving his mother to raise him and his older sister, Norma Jean. The two children and Verlie lived with her mother, father, grandfather, and unmarried sister. That extended family of seven lived in a two-story farmhouse on the edge of the city. Their rustic dwelling had a three-hole outhouse and no running water, although it had electricity for incandescent lights. In cold weather, a cast-iron stove in the middle of the living room provided warmth and a rosy glow.

In 1930, there was a total of 889 souls in the little city of LaMoure. Among prairie communities, it exhibited a measure of prosperity. As one of Jack's childhood friends Jerry Gleesing put it, "If a town had a water tower and two or three grain elevators, then you knew it was a good place." LaMoure met that standard, although the water and sewer systems stopped a block short of the city limits.

Jack was seven years old when his mother married Severt Ohnstad, who, along with an older brother, owned the LaMoure Hardware Company. After the wedding, Jack took the surname Ohnstad, and his family moved a block away into a small, square-shaped house with a stucco exterior. Two years following the marriage, Verlie gave birth to Jack's half brother, Samuel J. Ohnstad. The baby arrived during one of the toughest years of the Great Depression. To understand its harshness, it is necessary to remember the calamitous situation in North Dakota and other states, where a drought of unprecedented length and severity left America's breadbasket an arid dustbowl. Again and again, a hostile wind eroded the rich farmland and the lives of all who depended on it.

Picture the giant dust storms that blackened the sky with flying topsoil. Picture the residents of LaMoure cloistered in their shaking homes as the wind shrieked and flogged them with the earth itself. No escape existed from the choking dust. "It was impossible to keep it out," Jerry Gleesing recalled. "Everybody jammed wet rags around their windowsills, but you couldn't stop the stuff.... The wind blew strong and hot, very hot. Sand and little pebbles destroyed crops, just cut them down. In areas where the soil was lighter than ours, it actually stripped paint off houses."

On occasions when the crops survived to harvest, depressed commodity prices made profit impossible. Thousands of farmers defaulted on their mortgages, which led to bank foreclosures and disaster for merchants like Severt and his brother. They had supported farmers by granting them lines of credit that now went unpaid, which propelled the LaMoure Hardware Company into bankruptcy. Salvation came in the form of a plump, middle-aged Canadian named Oscar "Stubby" Wankel, who rescued the failed business by purchasing it. He gave Severt a job working for the company he once co-owned.

At the age of twelve, Jack got a job with Oscar, too. He held it for six years, working evenings and Saturdays. On the Sabbath, he sang with the choir at the local Presbyterian church, one of five places of worship in LaMoure. He also rang the church bells, stoked the furnace, and cleaned the building after Sunday services. Jack spoke many times about his wish to study theology and become a minister.

Besides work and churchly matters, there were triumphal times on the basketball court, baseball diamond, and gridiron. Jack played football for his high school team, the LaMoure Lobos. His quick mind and physical strength earned him a starting position every year. "Jack played guard," Jerry Gleesing remembered, "and he was the one who announced the next play in the huddle. It was an unusual thing to have a guard who called all the signals." Jack, the brightest guy on the team, led the Lobos to conference championships, and football coaches across North Dakota voted him to all-conference and all-state teams.

In June 1942, Jack graduated in the upper percentile of his class. The following autumn, he matriculated to Jamestown College, a North Dakota school affiliated with the Presbyterian Church. He immediately won a starting position on the football team, but his gridiron days lasted only one season. The U.S Congress lowered the draft age from twenty-one to eighteen, and that led to Jack's induction into the army on February 17, 1943, at Fort Snelling, Minnesota. There he swore an oath of allegiance, took the Army General Classification Test, and reverted to the surname on his birth certificate—Beckwith. Afterward, he traveled by train to Fort Lewis, Washington, for basic training with the newly activated 44th Infantry Division. Like many who took the AGCT, he heard assurances that a sufficiently high score would qualify him to join the Army Specialized Training Program and avoid combat overseas. There was a widespread witticism that ASTP stood for "all safe till peace." While training with the 44th, he received notice that he had been selected for the program. His first collegiate assignment after Fort Lewis was the University of Idaho, but he spent only two weeks there before being transferred to the University of California at Los Angeles. The program at UCLA lasted nearly nine months for Jack. Several weeks before it folded, he applied for cadet training with the U.S. Army Air Force, but his hope of becoming an aviator was short-lived. He and thousands of other ASTP men boarded trains, buses, and trucks bound for Camp Maxey, Texas, and the 99th Infantry Division.

OLD-TIMERS IN THE 99TH GREETED the new arrivals with disdain, and mocked them with epithets like "campus commandos" and "college boys" (or "college fucks" in less polite parlance). Harsh training in the sun-parched back country of east Texas would callous them, transform the "quiz kids" into dog-faced infantrymen and prepare them to meet the Germans or Japanese. When speaking of his troops, the commanding general of the 99th reportedly remarked, "I intend to make it so goddamn tough on these men that they will be glad to go overseas and lead an easy life." An editorial writer for the division newspaper commented, "Many former ASTP men no doubt find that their transfer from college to the infantry closely resembles a cold bucket of water down the neck. . . . We extend our sincere welcome to you and our deepest sympathies to your feet."

Since most ASTPers had previously undergone infantry basic training, the initial regimen at Maxey seemed familiar, although more grueling—dawn to dusk, seven days a week. The men underwent that workout separately from the rest of the division because of uncertainty about the effectiveness of their previous training. The segregation soon proved unnecessary, and the newly anointed infantrymen joined the balance of the division. Together, the troops underwent specialized courses in close combat, infiltration, and village fighting. There were also countless training films, road marches, and classes on topics like first aid and map reading. Weapons training took place routinely at several firing ranges. Field exercises and mock battles helped the soldiers turn their skills into the reflex responses necessary for survival in combat.

David Read, Saul Kokotovich, and Jack Beckwith were members of the 395th Infantry Regiment—part of the 99th. David became a rifleman with Company F, but a reshuffle landed him in Cannon Company, where he trained as a cannoneer and later as a radio operator. Saul and Jack became members of Company C and quartered in adjacent barracks. Initially, neither man knew what his occupational specialty would be within the company. Saul held little hope for a position corresponding with his abilities. "Do you know what they have me classified as on my service record?" he wrote his mother. "A mechanic!... I sure hope that's the kind of job they give me, but you know the army, it's all screwed up. An expert mechanic turns out to be a company clerk or mail orderly, and they make a machine gunner out of a businessman. Their motto, 'Every man in his right place.' Ha! What a laugh."

Saul and Jack both ended up carrying a rifle but not an ordinary one. Their instrument of war was the Browning Automatic Rifle. To aid them in firing this twenty-pound brute, each man had an assistant gunner and an ammunition bearer. Jack joined a rifle squad with the Third Platoon. Saul joined the Second Platoon and a rifle squad under the leadership of Staff Sergeant Michael Gracenin, a Pennsylvanian born to Serbian parents. Immediately curious about his new subordinate's background, the sergeant asked if he was Jewish. The answer was no.

"But your name is Saul," Gracenin said.

"My real name is Savo. I'm Serbian."

"What's a Serbian?"

Gracenin played dumb as Saul rendered a lengthy explanation. Finally, Gracenin interrupted in fluent Serb, "*Ide Cragu!*" (loosely translated: "Go to the devil!") The two men laughed and thereafter became friends.

Once Saul established himself in Texas, his fiancée joined him. On Saturday, July 8, 1944, the couple exchanged wedding vows at Camp Maxey in a little white church with clapboard siding. The next day they sent a Western Union telegram home. "Dear Mom, we were married last night at the camp chapel. Having a wonderful time. Wire $30 immediately.... Love, Saul and Martha."

Like other married soldiers, Saul found accommodations for his bride in the nearby town of Paris, Texas. He often finagled overnight passes so he could be with her, but each time he had to be back at the barracks for reveille. Every morning, a bus returned the married enlisted men to camp. As the men of Company C stood at attention for roll call, they often heard footsteps racing from the street. Moments later, Saul elbowed his way into the formation, just in time.

Unmarried soldiers like David Read and Jack Beckwith seldom loafed around their barracks during free time. That was a fast way to get snagged for a work detail. Instead, the men frequented the Post Exchange and lounged outside in their summer khakis, downing soft drinks or knocking back bottles of 3.2 beer. Other times, they congregated at the regimental recreation hall to shoot pool, bowl, or play basketball. There were also two service clubs and five movie theaters at Maxey. Each service club had a library, where soldiers could write letters, read books, or listen to phonograph records.

On weekends, it was periodically possible to obtain a twenty-four- or forty-eight-hour pass. David and his buddy, PFC Warren F. Thomas (a fellow Ohioan and friend since ASTP), did that on several occasions. One time, the pair visited Dallas at the invitation of a lieutenant colonel in the Medical Corps. "He had a daughter," Warren remembered, "and he asked if I could bring somebody with me because she had a friend. I got Dave to come along." The colonel's home had a large swimming pool. "That did me in," Warren declared. "As soon as Dave got in the pool and started to do his dives, I might as well as have gone back to Camp Maxey. Both girls ignored me completely. Normally, if I went anywhere with Dave, that's how it worked out." Warren's compatriot often made a big splash with his athletic ability, genial personality, and movie-star good looks.

Moments of leisure were inevitably fleeting and the gravity of war inescapable for infantrymen. The 99th Division completed its training in Texas and, in mid-September 1944, departed by train for an undisclosed port of embarkation and combat overseas. When the railcars began rolling toward the East Coast, it was apparent to all aboard: they would fight the Germans. The train trip ended at Camp Myles Standish near Taunton, Massachusetts, one of several embarkation points for troops heading to Europe. Its facilities operated around the clock, processing the continuous stream of army units headed across the Atlantic. To support this ceaseless operation, Jack Beckwith and several members of his company found themselves on midnight KP in a cavernous mess hall that served meals at all hours. PFC Vernon Swanson worked with Jack, and remembered, "Each morning, we emerged from the darkness of the mess hall kitchen, blinking our eyes at the daylight. We called ourselves the Mole Club." Jack and Vern became pals, and when not on KP duty, they had abundant free time because no training schedule existed at the camp. Passes flowed freely, and the two amigos went on junkets to Providence, Rhode Island, and Boston.

While at Myles Standish, David Read telephoned his brother Verne, an army lieutenant posted at the U.S. Weather Bureau in Washington, D.C. He and David both arranged short furloughs and agreed to meet in New York City. After a memorable evening at the St. James Theater, where they watched the Rodgers & Hammerstein musical *Oklahoma!*, the two brothers hung out for a day in the city before bidding each other farewell. David departed from Grand Central Terminal, and Verne left from Penn Station.

AFTER A FORTNIGHT OF FINAL PREPARATIONS, the officers and enlisted men of the 99th hiked up the gangplanks of oceangoing vessels like the S.S. *Explorer*. On September 29, that troopship, crammed with more than 2,400 soldiers, carried the 395th Infantry (minus one battalion) onto the vast nether spaces of the North Atlantic. Destination—Gourouck, Scotland, and then, by rail, Dorchester, England.

Several weeks before the lumbering steamer put out to sea, newlywed Martha Kokotovich moved from Texas to Indiana and took up residence with her husband's family. She shared a room with his sister Mary, whose husband was in the Pacific serving with a Marine Raider unit. The two women could do little more than wait, wonder, and pray. They, and millions of others, kept up with events abroad by monitoring the radio, reading articles, and watching for the mailman. There was generally a two-week delay in receiving letters from servicemen overseas, although Jack Beckwith reduced the lag time by spending six cents for airmail whenever possible.

During the voyage to Scotland, Jack wrote his mother. "Whatever you do, don't worry about me. You've told me often that you haven't, but I still like to tell you again. I'm like you in that I feel I'm in pretty good hands, and I don't mean the army. That's for certain."

He closed by saying, "I'm more thankful than ever that I have the kind of family I do have and that I was taught to appreciate a few of the finer things of life, which, sadly enough to say, is something a lot of fellows haven't learned, believe me. . . . Good night for now, Mom. God bless you as well as the others. I thank Him for the privilege of having a mother like you often. Keep the chin up, and don't worry."

After a brief sojourn in the United Kingdom (where Jack mailed his letter), the 99th Division reached the port town of Le Havre, France, by the first week of November 1944. From that bomb-ruined city, the division began a 285-mile "motor march" across the conquered and reconquered lands of northern France and Belgium. The route passed through a kaleidoscope of cities, countryside, and a countless number of forgettable villages. It ended near Aubel, Belgium, where the 99th spent four rain-drenched days while reconnaissance parties surveyed the front-line sector soon to be occupied by the division. Some 99ers billeted in homes and barns, and escaped the beating downpour. The less fortunate, including most of the 395th Infantry, bivouacked in leaky pup tents. Vern Swanson remembered, "My tent buddy was Milford Keeney. He was the

BAR man and I the assistant. Sometime during the four days at Aubel, Keeney slipped on wet ground, fell, and broke his arm. Jack Beckwith became his replacement. Why I didn't become the BAR man, I don't know." Whatever the reason for the decision, Swanson and Beckwith became almost inseparable as members of the same BAR team.

Swanson grew up as an only child and resided in Duluth, Minnesota, until age five when his father, a civil engineer, died of tuberculosis. Penniless, he and his mother moved to Chicago and lived with a maternal uncle who had never married. Swanson graduated from high school and completed four quarters at Iowa State University before being drafted in January 1943. After basic training at Camp Hulen, Texas, he joined the ASTP at Texas A&M and that eventually led to Camp Maxey, where he first met Beckwith. Seven months after that meeting, the two friends bivouacked near Aubel, and Beckwith wrote home and described his comrade as a "big Swede from Chicago, formerly of Duluth." Beckwith characterized the Belgian climate as "damp and cool," a definite understatement.

The autumn rains turned to snow on November 9, 1944, as the first elements of the 99th began leaving Aubel in convoy. The trucks sloshed their way to the Belgian-German frontier, where the troops dismounted. That was the front line, the ramparts of Nazidom. Evergreen forests and cow pastures dominated the sector occupied by the 99th. The placid area had seen little enemy activity since the region fell into American hands during the final week of summer.

Beneath high conifers planted row on row, David Read and his comrades in Cannon Company, 395th, built log huts for shelter, each large enough for two men. The diminutive structures had straw-lined floors and paraffin candles for light. After nightfall on Thanksgiving, David relaxed in his hut and conjured visions of home as he took time to write his brother Verne:

"Today I imagine the Davies were up for dinner, and I can see everyone now. Dad either working in the yard or taking a nap and Uncle Stan listening to the games. I can enjoy thinking about it even if I'm not there. Today we did have a fine Thanksgiving dinner, but I didn't get enough turkey or cranberries until I went back for seconds. . . . Well, it's about time I blow out our candles, Verne, and get some sleep."

November saw no fatal casualties in David's company. The situation was different in Company C, where Saul Kokotovich and Jack

Beckwith lost two comrades, one on Thanksgiving Day. The soldiers died after detonating antipersonnel mines while on reconnaissance patrols in the dense forests along the Belgian-German border. Both men were BAR gunners.

Jack made no mention of the deaths when he wrote home on December 3:

"Just ending my last day of a 48-hr. pass at a rest camp in a Belgian city. We sleep on canvas cots in part of a hotel. Meals are free and home-cooked. A USO show and movies in a modern Belgian theater. Showers, clean clothes, and a PX are also available. Seems like a dream almost, although I haven't been away from these things so terribly long. Oh yes, the Red Cross has a 'donut dugout,' where you can get coffee and donuts for about 4 francs (= 9¢). A barbershop and money exchange are also at our disposal. After hearing some good GI swing music, I feel much better. Americans in the States are fortunate, believe me."

Jack concluded the letter by writing, "Well, I wish that I was going to be able to spend Christmas with you, but seeing that I can't, we'll hope that by next Christmas all of us will be together. Good night for now. Keep well, and, Dad, don't work so darn hard. All my love, Jack."

Like all denizens of the front line, censorship rules precluded Jack from disclosing information of potential military value to the enemy. That "sensitive" material included place names, unit designations, casualty figures, and operational activities. The rules also forbade mentioning anything of propaganda value such as unseemly incidents, judgment errors, animosity or low morale among the troops, and heroism on the part of enemy soldiers. Criticism of Allied leaders was also taboo.

When Saul wrote home on December 6, he too followed the rules. The dateline of his v-mail letter began with the words "Same ol' place," and the body of the letter described nonmilitary happenings:

"Just finished the morning fire, and everyone is still sleeping, so I'm dropping you a line as I wait for daybreak. It's snowing but melts as soon as it hits the ground. Today we're going to begin construction on a log cabin, so we won't have to sleep on the ground—pioneers, that's what we are. Wish you could see me now, 190 lbs. and all brawn from swinging a big ax at 50-foot trees. I may come home a lumberjack if we stay here much longer.

"Listen, Mom, please send me the *Gary Post* and also the *Srbobran* regularly—Mike and I are dying for something to read. Send me a package for our Christmas, Mom, with food that won't spoil, like fruitcake, nuts, chocolates, also can some *jeladija* [jellied pigs feet] for me. I'll probably think of more by the time I write again. I'll write a long letter next. Hope all is well at home. Write often Mom—no mail lately. Your son, Savo."

David also kept up with his correspondence and penned a letter home on December 8. These were his final sentences:

"You all have been fine about writing, and there is hardly anything I could want more—a word from any of you. When I don't get letters, though, I still know you are sending your love, and that's really what counts. Letters are more or less just a visible means of receiving one's love and thoughts, isn't that right?

"It's time I must close and get some sleep. Goodnight. I love you more than tongue can tell."

The following week, David heard scuttlebutt that part of the 99th Division would soon launch an attack into Germany and that his Cannon Company would lend fire support for this push. The company consisted of 118 soldiers, twenty vehicles, and six 105-mm howitzers. David served as a radioman with the Third Cannon Platoon. Under the leadership of First Lieutenant Harold S. Smith of Arkansas, the platoon wielded two of the six howitzers assigned to the company. During combat operations, Smith led a forward observation party that included himself, David, and Corporal Robert J. Beilman of Pennsylvania. The nature of their work meant they operated near enough to the enemy to adjust artillery fire by direct vision. As such, they had "one of the toughest and most hazardous assignments in combat," according to PFC George H. Kennedy, a cannoneer with David's platoon. (The two men were close friends who first became acquainted while in the ASTP. After the war, Kennedy found fame and success in Hollywood as a film and television star. His performance in *Cool Hand Luke* won him the 1968 Oscar for best supporting actor.)

ON DECEMBER 14, 1944, David and his two compatriots, Smith and Beilman, found themselves at the forefront of a full-scale attack or at least one prong of it. The trio trudged over the German border along with other foot soldiers of the 395th. Snow and ice hampered their march. The route crossed rugged terrain covered by spruce trees of the Schleiden

Forest. In many instances, the men pulled themselves uphill, tree trunk by tree trunk, or they grabbed roots and branches. It was a precarious balancing act for David who had a forty-pound radio strapped to his back. The tiresome trek finally halted atop a wooded hill, where the GIs assaulted and captured a concrete bunker and nearby dugouts, then scratched out foxholes in the rocky soil. Army maps labeled the place Hill 627 (named for its height in meters). Enemy artillery and mortars soon walloped the area. Among the blizzard of incoming shells were 88-mm artillery projectiles. For the troops who occupied the hill, the 88s turned their surroundings into the epicenter of hell on earth.

Thanks in part to Smith and Read, the Germans, too, endured the satanic fury of shellfire. Smith barked out gun commands. David, bent over his SCR-300, radioed them to platoon headquarters. His words heralded the swishing sound of shells on their way overhead.

Besides directing cannon fire, Smith and Read had other chores. During the daytime hours of December 15, Smith received word that a supply of boxed rations had arrived. He sent David to fetch some. When David failed to return, Smith dispatched Beilman to ascertain the reason for the holdup. He came back with tragic news.

David was dead. An enemy mortar shell had ended his life.

The calamity left Smith's gut in a knot. "It hit me hard," he remembered. "I was married at the time and had a baby girl. I often remarked that if I ever had a son, I hoped he'd be like David. He was that type of young man."

David Read was the first member of Cannon Company to die in combat.

At the time of David's death, Saul Kokotovich was also on Hill 627, enduring the German mortars and artillery along with the rest of his company. He was one of 180 men in Company C on December 15, a day that saw the capture of several more bunkers and dugouts. Toward evening, Saul and his assistant gunner crouched in their foxhole as night pulled its blackness over the hill. Despite the dark, the implacable anger of the enemy guns continued.

Explosions danced in the treetops and on the forest floor. The hill was a wilderness of ruin, its slopes and summit fouled with shell craters, fractured tree limbs, and the cloying aroma of high explosives.

Near Kokotovich's foxhole, his squad leader, Mike Gracenin, sat curled in his own hole. By the final hour of December 15, Gracenin drifted to sleep despite the violent tumult outside his shelter.

Suddenly, someone shook him awake. It was Kokotovich's assistant gunner, PFC Joseph A. Leschetsko. He was desperate.

"Mike, Koke wants you. I think he's dying."

After telling Leschetsko to stay put, Gracenin scrambled to the hole of his Serbian buddy.

"I crawled in," Gracenin remembered, "then covered the hole with my poncho and gathered Savo in my arms. I lit my cigarette lighter and saw nothing could be done." Concussion from a shell burst had shattered his organs. He was bleeding to death internally.

Gracenin gave his comrade last rites. "I said the *Oce Nas* [Lord's Prayer] for him, as he asked me to do should anything ever happen to him. I crossed his arms, made a cross sign over him three times, and sadly returned to my hole."

Dim and misty, daylight eventually returned to the hill, but not before word of Kokotovich's death spread along the line. When Vern Swanson got the news, he was alone in the slit trench he shared with Jack Beckwith. The BAR gunner from North Dakota had departed that morning for the battalion aid station in hopes of getting medical attention for himself.

Along with many others, Jack had trench foot. A debilitating condition, it resulted from having wet feet and being unable to dry them for days on end. Freezing weather exacerbated the problem. In most cases, a victim's feet would initially swell and appear white. Burning pain often accompanied these symptoms. This usually preceded a color change to blue, gray, or dark purple and then complete numbness. In severe cases, the nerves died, and the feet became black.

As Beckwith made his way toward the aid station, he chanced upon another member of his company with trench foot. Sergeant Harold B. Wright's feet had been totally numb for two days. A medic on Hill 627 had examined him and discovered a black spot on his right big toe. Wright explained to Beckwith, "The medic told me I have to go back to the aid station."

Beckwith replied, "My feet are just killing me. I'm going with you."

The pair of invalids set out together for the aid station, two hills in the distance. It was a bearable journey for Wright, who had lost all feeling in his feet. The opposite was true for Beckwith. Each step radiated pain through his swollen feet.

At the bottom of Hill 627, the duo crossed paths with a bleary-eyed GI in a curious dreamlike state. A shell fragment had smashed the butt of his rifle. Perhaps that close call had loosened his grip on reality. Beckwith and Wright both questioned him. "What company are you with? What's your name? Are you okay?" No response. Before resuming their trek, the two trench-foot victims pointed the forlorn soldier in the direction of the American positions on the crest of Hill 627.

After struggling over the next hill, then up another, Beckwith and Wright reached the aid station. One at a time, a medic ushered them into a tent, where they met the battalion surgeon, First Lieutenant Marcus P. Graeber. He quickly surveyed Wright's condition and made a diagnosis. "You've got dead flesh on your foot—that black spot." Graeber then explained the necessity of hospitalization.

An ambulance waited outside the tent to transport him and several other casualties to the rear. Before climbing in the vehicle, Wright saw Beckwith emerge from the tent. "Hey, Jack, what happened?"

He replied in a despondent tone, "The doc looked at my feet and said he couldn't see enough wrong. I'll have to go back up." Since no replacement troops were available, the surgeon relieved from duty only the most severe cases.

Back on Hill 627, Swanson thought Beckwith was on his way to a hospital bed. But soon he spotted his friend traipsing back through the ankle-deep snow. Swanson climbed out of their foxhole and greeted his returning comrade. "How'd ya make out?"

Beckwith explained that only guys with blackened skin on their feet merited evacuation. The rest had to go back because there was nobody to replace them.

As Swanson listened, there was a burst of flame, too quick for definition. Concussion rocked the air.

The blast toppled both men and blew Beckwith fifteen to twenty feet.

Unhurt, Swanson rose. His eyes were wild, searching, frantic. They quickly rooted on the sight of his friend's broken body.

White-hot mortar fragments had ripped Beckwith apart. They severed his left foot and smashed his left leg. Blood oozed from smoking holes in his abdomen and head.

Swanson screamed and screamed. "I shouted for the medics," he recalled. "I saw warm air rising from Jack's mouth. He appeared to be breathing. Finally, somebody grabbed me and said, 'He's dead.' I can't remember what I did after that point."

Someone eventually covered Beckwith's body with a shelter half. He lay there for the rest of the day before litter bearers carted off his mortal remains.

History records the date of Beckwith's death as the day Hitler unleashed his legions against American forces in the Ardennes region of Belgium. The young North Dakotan died during the first hours of the Battle of the Bulge.

"The Germans poured into Belgium on our right flank," Swanson remembered. "We were in danger of being cut off. Thus, we received an urgent order to abandon Hill 627 and retreat to a particular ridge in Belgium."

As the retreat began, the weary troops, fatigue pulling at their bones, trudged past an improvised cemetery on the reverse slope of the hill. Several fresh mounds of earth blemished the forest floor. Here were the shallow graves of David Read, Saul Kokotovich, and Jack Beckwith. Swanson observed that Beckwith's grave marker was "a dog tag lashed to a short stick." Other passersby recall seeing one or more M1 rifles used as markers.

HALFWAY AROUND THE WORLD, on a snowy day in January 1945, word of David's death reached his parents in Hudson, Ohio, via Western Union telegram. Sadly, that was not the first time Verne and Ethel Read endured the loss of a child. Their only daughter, Aileen, had died at age eighteen in December 1936, when the car she was driving collided with a passenger train in Cuyahoga Falls, Ohio.

David's youngest brother, Doug, recalled his parent's courage despite immeasurable anguish:

"Their grief and sorrow must have been tremendous, having lost two children. Yet I never heard a word of regret or self-pity. In fact, I remember my mother worrying about, and spending time consoling, another Hudson mother who was having a hard time coping with the death of her only son. That was just a week or two after we heard about David."

The same dreadful day the Read family learned of David's death, an army officer knocked at the front door of the Kokotovich home in

Gary, Indiana. He held a telegram from the War Department. At his side was a next-door neighbor whom the officer had asked to help him deliver the news. "We were just dumbfounded," Saul's sister Mary remembered. "All he wanted to do was get out of the war and build a house for his wife, Martha." Several days after the telegram arrived, the postman delivered a letter from Saul. According to Mary, "That caused everyone to wonder if he was really gone. Maybe a mistake had been made." The Kokotovich family yearned for more information, details, but all they received from the army were condolences and a vague assurance that Saul had been laid to rest at a military cemetery in Belgium. Returned mail also began arriving. Each envelope had a stamp with the words "Deceased" and "Return to Sender."

Concurrent with the arrival of tragic tidings in Indiana, a telegram reached the rural community of LaMoure, North Dakota:

32 Govt   WUX   Washington D C   239 PM   Jan 4 -1945

Mrs Verlie B. Ohnstad,
LaMoure, N.Dak.

The Secretary of War desires me to express his deep regret that your son Private First Class Jack C. Beckwith was killed in action on sixteen December in Germany, confirming letter follows.

> *Dunlop,*
> *Acting, The Adjutant General.*

Jack's loss struck his family on the heels of his younger brother's near death. Sam, age eleven, almost succumbed to appendicitis in early December 1944. The youth lay in bed with stomach pain and nausea for three days before his appendix ruptured, and his condition became a crisis. The fifty-mile trip to the hospital came close to killing him. "They examined me in the hallway and rushed me straight into the operating room," he recalled.

Chapter 7
CHASING THE PAST

By the summer of 1945, the war in Europe had ended. After a short assignment in the Philippines, Vern Swanson returned home to Chicago with a Combat Infantryman's Badge, a Bronze Star Medal, three Purple Hearts, and four Battle Stars. He then hustled off to Iowa State University and resumed his studies interrupted by the war.

In March 1946, Swanson penned a note to the army asking for the location of Beckwith's grave. The reply was disconcerting. His remains had not been recovered or positively identified. Search efforts were under way, but as yet nothing was known.

The same was true of David Read and Saul Kokotovich. Their loved ones wrote letters hoping to gain answers. But the army could offer only "deep regret" and folded American flags. Kokotovich's widow received one other thing, a small parcel containing her husband's personal effects: letters, photographs, an army paybook, an Expert Infantryman Badge, a tattered wallet, and a broken pair of wire-rimmed spectacles. Beckwith's mother inherited a package with similar contents. Read's parents received nothing.

In 1951, the army deemed the remains of Read, Kokotovich, and Beckwith to be "nonrecoverable." Their case files were closed.

The war years became a distant episode as Swanson returned to the mainstream of civilian life. His postwar world revolved around family and work. He graduated from Iowa State with a civil engineering degree and married his college sweetheart. The newlywed couple moved to an apartment on the South Side of Chicago and lived there when their first child arrived. They raised four sons while traveling the globe as Vern pursued his career. The Swansons lived in Spain for two years while Vern helped design military bases for the U.S. Navy and Air Force. His family then spent five years in Pakistan, where he worked on the development of water, land, and power resources in the Indus River Basin. He also had short assignments in Egypt, El Salvador, Kuwait, Lebanon, and Saudi Arabia. Vern eventually earned an M.B.A. from the University of Chicago and became vice president of a consulting firm that specialized in real-estate research. He and his wife settled in the north Chicago suburb of Deerfield.

During the crowded years that followed his military service, Vern lost contact with all but a handful of his army buddies. He attended a couple 395th Infantry reunions shortly after the war, then withdrew from such activities. Nearly thirty years passed before he went to another reunion. In 1980, he attended a gathering of the 99th Infantry Division Association held in Chicago. "I went there half expecting to see nineteen-year-olds," Swanson recalled. "Instead I found a bunch of old people, and I didn't know a single one of them." Nobody from his company attended the reunion. Swanson quickly lost interest in such events, although he remained a dues-paying member of the association.

Vern's passive feelings lasted until March 1990, when he noticed the bulletin that Dick Byers and I placed in the association's newspaper. Its bold headline read: "MIA, Still Missing After 45 Years, Can You Help Find Them?" As Vern skimmed over the accompanying list of missing soldiers, he recognized several names. One struck him like a lightning bolt—Jack Beckwith.

Across the chasm of a prosperous lifetime, Vern suddenly realized he had unfinished business. The remains of his buddy had to be found. Vern telephoned one of his wartime cohorts, Byron Whitmarsh of Richardson, Texas. Both men had seen Beckwith's grave on Hill 627 as well as the graves of other GIs buried next to him.

Like Vern, Byron also had noticed the newspaper bulletin and also felt the same sense of unfinished business. Byron, an Oklahoma Panhandle native, had retired in 1983 after a thirty-four-year career that began with a stint with the Army Corps of Engineers and ended as co-owner of a construction company. He and his wife had two daughters and a son born in Oklahoma and raised in Texas. During the war, Byron served as a squad leader with Company C until his combat tour ended in March 1945, when a German rifle bullet shattered his lower right arm. That injury permanently disabled his right hand and earned him a medical discharge from the army. He returned to the "sooner state" with two Battle Stars, a Purple Heart, a Bronze Star Medal, a Silver Star Medal, and a Combat Infantryman's Badge.

IN 1990, HOPING TO FIND BECKWITH'S GRAVE, Swanson and Whitmarsh joined forces with Byers, Seel, Speder, and me. Our search quickly expanded to include Kokotovich, whose name Swanson and Whitmarsh also recognized on the list of missing soldiers. Both men knew him, and they were aware that he died on Hill 627. It seemed logical that he, too, rested in a grave on the hill.

That autumn, Swanson and Whitmarsh joined a contingent of 99th Division veterans and their families—more than two hundred strong—who traveled to Belgium for the unveiling of a granite monument dedicated to the division. The ceremony and preceding events lasted five days. On the first afternoon, the entire contingent visited the Henri-Chapelle American Cemetery. Unlike most large groups that came to the cemetery, this one did not remain bunched together and attentive to the words of a tour guide. These visitors needed no history lesson. They spread out across the cemetery in ones, twos, and threes. Here and there, a man knelt down or bowed his head upon finding the burial spot of a fallen friend. For Swanson and Whitmarsh, this was their first visit to the cemetery since the war. Together, they sought out the graves of five soldiers from their company. As the two veterans gazed at the white marble crosses, the same thought gnawed at each man. There should be two more crosses at this hallowed place, one for Beckwith and another for Kokotovich.

The trip to Henri-Chapelle ended with a wreath-laying ceremony and a bugler playing "Taps." Four days later, the entire tour group congregated at a small park across the street from the church in Krinkelt, Belgium. The crowd listened to speeches and a brass band before everyone witnessed the unveiling of the 99th Division monument. Afterward, many group members, including Swanson and Whitmarsh, gathered for lunch at the Hotel Dahmen.

Following the meal, Seel rendezvoused with Swanson and Whitmarsh at the hotel. The three drove to Krinkelt and the home of the forest ranger Erich Hönen. The four men set out to find the hill where Beckwith and Kokotovich died. Swanson and Whitmarsh had only a fuzzy recollection of its location and no memory of its height in meters. Hönen guided them into Germany and atop a wooded summit called the Wiesenhardt. During the war, the GIs referred to it as Purple Heart Hill or Hill 621. "The territory was familiar," Swanson recalled, "but we had a gut feeling this was the wrong place. The terrain and the approach to the hill didn't seem quite familiar. Whitmarsh felt 'our' hill probably was the next one to the right."

Several months later, research confirmed that Whitmarsh was unerring. The correct location was slightly to the southeast—Hill 627. Besides the initial confusion regarding geography, Swanson and Whitmarsh had no inkling that David Read also had died on the hill. Because he was not a member of their company, they had little knowledge of his life or death.

Two people well acquainted with David were his older brothers, Tommy and Verne, who first came in contact with the 99th Infantry Division Association in 1986, and flew to Belgium in 1990 for the monument dedication. Tommy, now retired and suffering from rheumatoid arthritis, traveled from Akron, where he lived with his wife. Verne's home and family were in Milwaukee, and he had a law practice there as well. Before going to Europe, neither man knew precisely where their brother had died. In hopes of learning more, they joined the tour group of 99th veterans. A large motor coach took them to places where troops of the 395th Infantry lived and fought—but not Hill 627. On several occasions, the passengers strolled a short distance into the forest and were able to see old foxholes, dugouts, and shell craters. That experience brought Tommy and Verne closer to David.

"We wanted to see where he was and get a feeling of what he was going through," Tommy told an interviewer. "The battle situation here in 1944 is now much clearer to us. A lot of questions have been answered, such as how battles were fought in these woods. It was much different in the Army Air Force where Verne and I served." Tommy spent the war years stationed at Westover Field, Massachusetts, where he taught instrument flying to aviation cadets. Verne served with weather-forecasting units in the eastern United States and the Azores.

Although Verne and Tommy found answers to some of their questions, other uncertainties about David remained. "We also hoped to find someone on this trip who knew him and could tell us more about what happened," Tommy said, "but we didn't."

The families of Beckwith and Kokotovich also harbored questions. After returning home, Swanson established contact with them and delivered news of the ongoing search operation and its progress. The Belgian "diggers" were now surveying Hill 627 and mapping its numerous man-made features such as bunkers and foxholes. I busied myself creating a map based on wartime documents obtained by Swanson, Whitmarsh, and me. I mailed a finished copy to Whitmarsh, who then penciled in the area where he remembered seeing graves. This squared with Swanson's memory, and it seemed to narrow the search area though it did not pinpoint a precise location.

Besides preparing a map, I wrote to Kokotovich's oldest sister, Mary. My letter was dated April 29, 1991:

"Vern Swanson advised me last night that he contacted you in reference to the ongoing search for your brother's grave.... Hill 627 is a rugged and densely wooded hill in Germany several hundred yards east of the Belgian border. Fortunately, our two-man search team is more than up to the task. There is undoubtedly no one more capable and experienced than they." I offered no guarantee of success but held out hope for the future. "Who knows, the discovery could come tomorrow or ten years from now."

The day after mailing the letter to Mary, I wrote a similar letter to Beckwith's mother, who was eighty-seven years old. Both women expressed gratitude for our efforts, and they furnished photographs of Jack and Saul.

Two months after writing the letters, I flew to San Francisco for the forty-second annual reunion of the 99th Infantry Division Association. There I met Swanson and Whitmarsh, our first face-to-face meeting. Seel and Speder also made the trip to California. The five of us attempted to get our minds around the facts as we pored over maps and documents. The most spectacular item was an aerial photograph recently acquired from the National Archives. It showed Hill 627 as it had appeared to an American reconnaissance aircraft on Christmas Day 1944.

The reunion stretched over five days, during which time Swanson spoke with me in detail about Beckwith's death. I had never heard the full story before.

"The shell that killed him could have ended your life instead," I commented in amazement.

Vern nodded, "You could easily be here today talking with Jack about my death and long-lost grave. I was just lucky. No other explanation. And lucky several times after that."

He went on to explain that he had been injured in combat three times: December 20, March 1, and March 2. The first occasion, he told me, was the most severe, a shrapnel wound to his neck.

"I was hit in the throat and couldn't make a sound because blood was pouring down my windpipe. I was put on a litter and carried by jeep to an aid station, where a chaplain was in attendance. As he walked up to my stretcher, I could dimly make out his collar ornament, a Star of David. He, in turn, misread my dog tag, thought I was a Catholic, and gave me last rites. I remember thinking that I really had all bases covered."

When Vern and I last spoke in San Francisco, he expressed renewed hope that graves would soon be discovered on Hill 627. All members of the search team shared his optimism. Less than a month later, a burial site came to light, but not on the hill. The Elsenbüchel forest yielded the skeletal remains of two, possibly three, individuals. That was X-9476. I became preoccupied with the case for the next three months. During that time, the search for Beckwith and Kokotovich faltered. Seel and Speder found no evidence of graves in the area that Whitmarsh indicated on my map. Furthermore, doubt arose concerning the location of Kokotovich's grave. The source of that controversy was Mike Gracenin, who had been Kokotovich's squad leader.

While speaking with Swanson on the telephone, Mike added a new wrinkle to the mystery. He and another squad leader, Staff Sergeant Roger L. Davis, had helped evacuate Saul's body from the hill. "Davis and I put him on a stretcher," Gracenin recalled, "and four stretcher bearers prepared to take him back. The medic who accompanied them saw the tears in our eyes and pulled out a bottle of whiskey. He told us both to take a good slug because we looked as though we needed it.

"The next morning, we were given orders to withdraw. We threw away much of our heavy equipment and retreated. As we reached our deserted battalion headquarters, Davis came over to me and said that he ran into one of the stretcher bearers and was told it took the four of them eight hours to get [Saul] back to where he was buried."

In an attempt to corroborate Gracenin's story, Swanson tracked down Dr. Mark Graeber, who had been the battalion surgeon. He was presumably in a position to know if anyone buried bodies in the vicinity of his aid station or the battalion headquarters. "He's alive and well, seventy-five years old and practicing in a VA hospital," Swanson reported to me, "and he does not recall that his people buried any dead."

Undaunted by the Kokotovich confusion and the general lack of progress, digging in the forest continued until early November 1991, when a hiatus became necessary. "We have to forget Saul and Jack for a couple months," Speder wrote to me. "It's now hunting season and it could be dangerous to walk in front of a hunter's scope."

In the States, the families of the missing soldiers provided assistance. Beckwith's mother sent a letter to the army requesting a copy of her son's IDPF. Kokotovich's sister did the same for her brother. In response, the army furnished all requested files in less than two months. I subsequently borrowed the stack of documents and photocopied them for my records.

While perusing Beckwith's file, a single sheet of paper grabbed my attention. It was a crude map drawn in 1948 by Donald O. Woolf Jr., who, like Swanson, had been a member of Beckwith's BAR team and had seen his grave. Woolf drew the map to aid the army's search effort after the war. He noted the graves near a triangular outcropping of trees at the edge of a huge clearing. Unfortunately, he got the compass direction wrong, as well as the grid coordinates. The army investigators who studied the map drew no meaning from it. I understood its significance. Woolf's errors were easy for me to see because I knew what hill his map depicted. But finding the clearing and the outcropping of trees proved problematic. They had long since disappeared. Evergreens now covered the entire hill.

The key was the aerial photograph from the National Archives. I compared it to Woolf's map and instantly recognized the clearing and outcropping, then transferred their locations to a modern topographic map.

Armed with my findings, Seel and Speder hiked to Hill 627 in February 1992. They immediately found an M1 rifle, three U.S. Army combat shoes, and an American hand grenade at the precise spot where I had pinpointed the graves. "It was a great moment," Seel recalled. Surely they had the right place. The rifle must have been one of the grave markers. The two Belgians dug countless holes and trenches but found nothing. The area yielded only frustration.

Elsewhere on the hill, the diggers unearthed a trove of American artifacts. That section of forest had lain untouched since the war. In a letter to me, Seel listed the contents of one particularly bountiful foxhole:

60 M1 rifle charger clips, each with eight .30-caliber rounds
8 pairs of arctic overshoes, size 10
6 M15 white-phosphorus grenades
6 M1 rifle-grenade adapters for MKII hand grenades
3 .30-caliber ammunition boxes (each containing 250 rounds of belted ammunition)
3 first-aid packets
3 toilet kits, each with razors, comb, shaving cream, toothpaste, toothbrush, shaving brush, plastic soap box
3 mess kits (one engraved Billy Worley Jr and another engraved L.F.)
2 M1 bayonets with M3A1 scabbards (one scabbard marked G-9955)
2 ten-pocket cartridge belts, M1923
2 pup tents rolled in blankets
2 mattock picks
2 canteens
2 overcoats
1 pair of service shoes, size 11½
1 signal lamp with red lens

In another hole, Speder dug out the rotted remains of a cartridge belt filled with charger clips for a Springfield rifle. Each clip still held five .30-caliber rounds. There was also a white-phosphorous grenade and an M3 trench knife in its scabbard. On another occasion, he excavated the interior of a collapsed dugout. "I found two M1 rifles," he recalled, "and the broken butt of a BAR. I never dug so fast, but the rest of the BAR wasn't there." Nearby, Seel found an M1 rifle, a pile of clips for it, several overcoats, and broken Polaroid lenses for goggles.

While on the hill and at his home, Speder drew scale maps of the area where excavation work had taken place. He noted the dimensions of foxholes, slit trenches, and bunkers. He also indicated where artifacts had been discovered. Besides recording site data, there was the task of identifying the owners of artifacts that bore personal markings. The Belgian team liked to return these things to the appropriate veteran or his surviving family.

It seemed an easy job to trace the original owner of the corroded aluminum mess kit marked Billy Worley Jr. On a current list of 99th Infantry Division Association members, Seel found one man with that name: William K. Worley Jr., a retired colonel living in Johnson City, Tennessee, who, during the Bulge, served as a lieutenant with the 99th Reconnaissance Troop. That puzzled Seel because nobody from that unit fought on Hill 627. So how did Worley's mess kit get there? Seel eventually packaged the object and mailed it to him. Worley gratefully accepted it but admitted, "I don't remember losing it." He then added, "You couldn't remember a thing like that, not with all the confusion."

Years later, Seel learned the truth. He had sent the mess kit to the wrong man. It actually belonged to PFC Billy Worley Jr. of Company D, 395th Infantry, a heavy weapons unit that definitely fought on Hill 627. He resided in Levelland, Texas, until his death in 1989. What were the odds that two men with that particular name would be members of the 99th Division?

Among the other artifacts found on the hill, one item held particular interest for Swanson. He had previously told the Belgians that he inadvertently left an M3 trench knife in his foxhole. He also lost an ID bracelet there. Both items apparently became buried in the muck at the bottom of the hole. The knife found by Speder may well have belonged to Swanson, although no bracelet was found near it. Nonetheless, Speder decided to send it to him. "It's on my desk now," Swanson said "and the thing that surprises people is that the leather on the handle and the lanyard are in great shape, as is the scabbard. It's still capable of killing or wounding someone." Swanson then admitted that during the war he never used his knife in combat. The weapon was used only "to open number-ten cans."

The discovery of more artifacts continued, as did efforts to determine the number of soldiers buried on the hill and the location of their graves. Swanson eventually zeroed in on David Read as one of the casualties. The circumstances of his death emerged during a telephone conversation between Swanson and Harold Smith. He had been David's lieutenant and knew how he died, but Smith had no other information. He recalled nothing about David's burial. The possibility that his body lay interred on the hill led us to seek help from his oldest brother, Tommy. On our behalf, he wrote to the army and requested a copy of his brother's IDPF. Unfortunately, nothing in the file specified a burial location.

Anxious to bring the search to a successful conclusion, Swanson and Whitmarsh journeyed to Europe in October 1992. Perhaps they could locate the burial site if they visited the hill in person. They traveled with another former member of their company, Rudolph Zehnder. It marked the first time any of the three veterans had been atop the hill since 1944. At that time, it was the last place on earth they ever wanted to see again. Now, as old men, they were anxious to return.

Upon reaching the hilltop, they wandered out among the towering spruce trees. It was an easy task to find the string of foxholes and bunkers once occupied by their company. Seel and Speder listened as Whitmarsh explained, "That dugout over there was our company command post. It was originally a German bunker covered with logs and earth." His two contemporaries nodded in agreement.

Swanson then wheeled around, "And the graves were in that direction." He pointed west, but could not be more specific. Too many years had passed, and the forest had changed too much. The trio of veterans spent nearly a week tramping about Hill 627 and other locations in the forest. In the end, no breakthrough resulted.

One hypothesis emerged as the most likely reason the graves could not be located. Someone had discovered the dead infantrymen during the war or soon afterward, but army examiners could not positively identify the bodies and buried them as "unknowns" at an American military cemetery. That was a disheartening notion but a real possibility. Nonetheless, the search continued.

Before his October visit to Europe, Swanson requested and received a batch of "morning reports" from the National Personnel Records Center in St. Louis. Every company in the army from 1912 through 1974 created such reports. Their purpose was to record any change in status of a company member. These changes included being killed, wounded, missing, hospitalized, reassigned, promoted, demoted, court-martialed, on leave, AWOL, or the recipient of an award.

The reports Swanson received were for Company A, 395th Infantry. That was the other rifle company that fought on Hill 627 alongside Swanson's outfit. According to the reports, only one soldier from Company A died on the hill. The unfortunate GI was PFC John G. Sims of Chattanooga, Tennessee. At some point, the army recovered his body and made positive identification. That fact prompted Swanson to immediately request a copy of Sims's IDPF. How and where had the army found his remains?

The answer surprised Swanson and me. In 1946, German civilians discovered Sims's grave in the woods near Hellenthal, Germany, a town close to Hill 627. The civilians pulled skeletal remains from the forest, placed them in a wooden casket, and interred everything at the village cemetery. The soldier's name eluded the Germans because no dog tags or other identification could be found, but the decedent appeared to be American. Remnants of a GI overcoat and wool drawers clung to the skeleton. Shortly after the reburial at Hellenthal, a U.S. Army Graves Registration team passed through the area and stopped at the Bürgermeister's office. The team learned about the American buried there and exhumed his remains. Everything found in the casket went to the U.S. military cemetery at Neuville-en-Condroz, Belgium. The unidentified soldier became X-2676. A cursory examination revealed numerous missing or fractured bones. That pointed toward artillery fire as a possible cause of death.

Almost three years elapsed before the army made a connection between Sims and X-2676. The place of recovery was the first clue. A battle-casualty report indicated that Sims died "near Hellenthal, Germany." The report also explained the circumstances:

"On the day of his death, there were several sharp, vicious barrages with a high percentage of tree bursts, resulting in several wounds to members of his company. Sims, having delivered a message to his platoon leader, started back to the company command post, when the first round of the next shelling struck the ground within fifteen feet behind him. He was killed instantly by the concussion and was also riddled by shell fragments."

Another clue was the estimated height of the "unknown." That measurement agreed with Sims's height. More definitive evidence also existed. The "unknown" had extensive dental work. All but one of the remaining teeth displayed amalgam or silicate fillings. Unfortunately, army tooth charts for Sims provided insufficient data for comparison. They showed only minor work done while he was in uniform. Civilian records offered the only hope. The army contacted Sims's parents in 1949 and asked them to provide whatever records they could obtain. They responded with dental charts from two civilian dentists. These documents allowed the army to establish positive identification. In June 1950, the family of John Sims consigned his remains to a final resting place at Chattanooga National Cemetery.

While leafing through the pile of documents pertaining to the Sims case, Swanson discovered a typewritten letter from the personnel officer of the 395th Infantry. He wrote it eight days after the soldier's death and offered condolences to his mother. The officer concluded by saying, "Burial services were conducted by our Protestant chaplain, and after the final rites, John was laid to rest in a military cemetery in southeastern Belgium."

Swanson found a similar note from the battalion chaplain. "I personally saw him and know he was properly buried, and you will be comforted to know he was not mutilated but looked as if asleep."

After reading the words of the personnel officer and chaplain, Swanson felt disgusted but not surprised. The families of Beckwith, Kokotovich, and Read also had received mailings from the personnel officer. Swanson characterized them as "typical army bullshit . . . form letters with false information that led to misunderstanding and pain." The resulting grief emerged in correspondence written by John Sims's mother, brother, and sister. They begged the army for an explanation. Why was John still missing if he had been interred at a military cemetery? In response, the army questioned the personnel officer. He replied, "I have no personnel file concerning casualties during the war, and out of the numerous cases handled doubtless would not recall any particular one."

The army also queried the chaplain. "It was impossible for me personally to get up to the section of the front line where this boy was killed," he confessed in a letter. The chaplain went on to explain that "medics buried five boys" in that forward area. He also explained what happened when he later encountered the medics. "They gave me the personal effects of these men, and I returned them through channels to the relatives."

The same day the chaplain divulged the truth to the army, he wrote to John's mother and told her the opposite:

"I did see him after he was killed and was able to take his personal effects, but seeing he was dead, I covered him and attended to the seriously wounded and then with a litter case went back to the aid station. It was impossible for me to return to the place of your son, and therefore two of the medics that were still there placed five of the dead in foxholes and buried them right on the field of battle."

Though the chaplain made contradictory statements, he was consistent about one thing. Medics buried five bodies in the field. Swanson and I attempted to corroborate that assertion, but we could only confirm that four men died on Hill 627. Who was the fifth soldier? By some accounts, that man was PFC Dean W. Sword, who belonged to David Read's company. After David died, several men reportedly drew straws to determine who would replace him. Dean picked the short straw, or so the story went. The only verifiable facts were that Dean died on December 16, 1944, and the army found his remains in March 1945. According to the official burial report, his body came from an "isolated grave" in Belgium. The precise spot was a forest area more than a mile from Hill 627.

No matter how many graves were on the hill, the Sims case raised a larger question. Why was his grave the only one found if there were other men buried nearby? Swanson ruminated on that mystery. Maybe the German civilians noticed only Sims's resting place because an M1 rifle marked it. Swanson knew that a short stick and dog tag had marked Beckwith's grave. He and Kokotovich were BAR gunners, and their weapons were too valuable to be used for anything but their intended purpose. (Swanson inherited Beckwith's BAR, and someone else got the one that belonged to Kokotovich.) As for David Read, his firearm was an M1 carbine. Sims was the only one of the four men who carried an M1 rifle. If that became his grave marker, the civilians may have easily spotted it. Sticks with dog tags would have been much less obvious, especially if they had fallen over and debris had covered them. And the detritus of war indeed littered the forest floor. The devastating artillery fire left shattered tree limbs and branches strewn everywhere.

The task of unraveling events on Hill 627 carried on through 1994. That year, the search team expanded in size when Seel and Speder invited two friends to join them. Their new colleagues were Marc Marique and Jean-Luc Menestrey, who had both known Seel and Speder for nearly fifteen years. Marc lived in Visé, Belgium, and was a civilian employee of the Belgian Army. He had been searching battlefields throughout the region since 1976 and formerly held membership in the Centre d'Archéologie Militaire (CAM). Jean-Luc lived in Stembert, Belgium, a suburb of Verviers. An electrician by trade, he worked as a handyman at a plastic-bottle factory and had been searching battlefields since 1980. Like Marc, he had been affiliated with CAM until both men left that organization to join Seel and Speder and the search for missing U.S. servicemen.

The addition of Marique and Menestrey added valuable experience to the team, but it brought no end to the stymied search on Hill 627. In December 1994, Swanson and Whitmarsh traveled to Europe and met with the Bürgermeister of Hellenthal. They discussed the possibility of finding whoever had exhumed John Sims' body from the forest shortly after the war. By determining the precise location of his forest grave, perhaps that would lead to Beckwith, Kokotovich, and Read. The meeting, held in the Bürgermeister's office, included Seel, Speder, and Karl Lüttgens, a scholar who specialized in local history. After listening to a presentation made by Swanson, Lüttgens agreed to spearhead an effort to track down anyone in the area who had pertinent knowledge.

Besides the conference in Hellenthal, Swanson and Whitmarsh had come to Europe to inspect Hill 627 once again and to mark the fiftieth anniversary of the Bulge. They were among thirteen 99th Division veterans who made the pilgrimage despite frigid weather. Television cameras from CBS, CNN, Belgian TV, Dutch TV, and Luxembourg TV were on hand to cover their visit and to record a solemn ceremony held at 5:30 A.M. on December 16, 1994. At that exact moment, five decades earlier, the battle had begun. In addition to filming the commemoration ceremony, a CNN correspondent and camera crew followed Swanson, Whitmarsh, and Rudy Zehnder to Hill 627. The resulting story aired around the world. "To this day, the foxholes these men fought in are still there," the correspondent told viewers. "But it's not just a trip down memory lane for them. They're looking for the bodies of fallen comrades, U.S. soldiers still missing after fifty years."

The camera captured a tight shot of Swanson, decked out in a brown parka and a Chicago Bulls cap. He explained the battle situation on Hill 627 and he told of the shell burst that killed Beckwith. "I was blown down on the ground, and he was riddled with shrapnel." Swanson then summed up his feelings about the ongoing search for graves on the hill. "None of us like to leave bodies behind even though it's been fifty years."

After returning home to Illinois, Swanson began corresponding with Karl Lüttgens and also pursued a new angle. He learned about ground-penetrating radar (GPR) upon reading a brochure he received from a Colorado organization called NecroSearch International. The pamphlet explained that NecroSearch operated on a nonprofit basis and consisted of "law-enforcement investigators and scientists frustrated by conventional grave location methods such as large-scale ground searches and trial-and-error excavation." GPR was their solution. Swanson and Whitmarsh had no qualms about the cost of renting or purchasing that equipment. Their chief concern was the practical application of such technology on Hill 627. After consulting with a GPR specialist, Swanson decided the device would provide no advantage to the search. The soil on the hill was rife with shell fragments that would distort the radar signal and resulting readings. Distortion would also result from the abundant tree roots on the hill. There was also a safety concern regarding whatever unexploded shells lay beneath the forest floor. They might be detonated by the electromagnetic signal emitted by the device.

At about the same time that Swanson abandoned the GPR idea, he received a disappointing letter from Lüttgens. He had been unsuccessful in his effort to help. The only eyewitness he found was a man who, as a kid, watched the disinterment of American and German soldiers buried at the Hellenthal cemetery. He knew nothing about an American grave in the forest. Lüttgens also placed an ad in a community newspaper, enquired at the local Catholic and Protestant churches, and interviewed forestry officials. All that came to nothing. Sadly, the quest for Beckwith, Kokotovich, and Read ended, again. It was tough news to deliver to their families.

Despite the lack of success, one of Read's brothers wanted to see Hill 627 for himself. Verne Read and a friend traveled to Europe in October 1995 and met with Swanson, his wife, and Speder. The group drove to the hill in two restored World War II–era jeeps, both painted in 99th Division markings. Speder was at the wheel of one vehicle and Swanson drove the other. They reached the hill after a brisk and bumpy ride. Speder showed Verne the location where I had pinpointed the burial site based on Woolf's map and the aerial photograph from the

National Archives. Verne learned about the M1 rifle and combat shoes discovered at that spot. The next day, the group visited the Ardennes American Cemetery near Liège. It was the first time Verne had seen the cemetery and the name David A. Read inscribed on the granite Tablets of the Missing. During the visits to Hill 627 and the cemetery, Seel had been busy at work, but he managed to join Verne and his friend before they left Europe. The friend had served as an officer with the 28th Infantry Division during the Bulge, and Seel helped him locate a bridge near Bastogne where German troops had nearly captured him.

After Verne and his friend returned home, Seel and Speder had little reason to visit Hill 627. The search effort faded into memory as other events overshadowed it. In August 1997, a German-language newspaper in eastern Belgium carried the headline, "*Grabungen sollen Gewißheit bringen über das Schicksal von Air-Force-Lt. Wilton G. Erickson*" (Excavation Should Bring Certainty over the Fate of Air Force Lieutenant Wilton G. Erickson). The article told the story of a German team of aviation archeologists who discovered the crash site of a Lockheed P-38 near the village of Lanzerath, Belgium—about twelve kilometers south of Hill 627.

The team members, Manfred Klein, Peter Drespa, and Josef Schaefer, were all in their twenties and lived in the Eifel region of Germany, vis-à-vis the Belgian-German border. They had civilian occupations and were also members of the German Army Reserves. In their spare time, mostly on weekends, they researched the fate of Allied and German aircraft lost over the wooded hills of the Eifel. Their first news-making discovery came in June 1993, when Klein located the crumpled wreck of an American fighter plane that crashed in a cow pasture owned by a distant relative. This proved to be the resting place of First Lieutenant Roger T. Lane of Portland, Maine, who died on Christmas Eve 1944 when his Republic P-47 was shot down near Prüm, Germany. The U.S. Army Memorial Affairs Activity–Europe excavated the site in August 1994 and forwarded Lane's remains to the Central Identification Laboratory at Hickam Air Force Base, Hawaii, where staff members established positive identification in late 1996.

About the time the army closed the Lane case, Klein identified another crash site, this one near the Belgian hamlet of Lanzerath. The location, along a small stream, turned out to be the muddy tomb of Second Lieutenant Wilton G. Erickson of Cleveland, Ohio. He had failed to return from his first combat mission in December 1943. Klein reported his findings to David B. Roath, the new director of Memorial Affairs–Europe. He gladly agreed to dispatch a recovery team to assist Klein, Drespa, and Schaefer with the excavation. The recovery operation began on August 18, 1997, and lasted nine days. Afterward, a military escort accompanied the shattered remains of the pilot to Hawaii. Scientists made positive identification six months later. At the request of Erickson's family, the army cremated his remains and returned the ashes to Ohio for burial.

While Erickson's remains were still in Hawaii, another recovery occurred in Europe. The location was the village of Kommerscheidt, Germany—about twenty-five kilometers north of Hill 627. In January 1998, a father and son found the skeletal remains of an American infantryman in the garden behind their home. The soldier still wore his combat uniform, helmet, and dog tags. That was Sergeant Lemuel H. Herbert of Scranton, Pennsylvania. A member of the 28th Infantry Division, he died of a head wound in November 1944 during the Battle of the Hürtgen Forest. Memorial Affairs–Europe eventually received his remains and flew them to Hawaii for identification. Herbert's family laid him to rest at Arlington National Cemetery in March 1999.

The following year, another accidental discovery took place in the Hürtgen Forest. The find occurred when an ordnance-disposal team swept the area with metal detectors to rid it of all remaining bombs, mines, shells, and other explosive devices that still lingered from the war. Near the remnants of a concrete bunker, the team found the skeletons of two German soldiers and one American. The dead GI was PFC Robert T. Cahow, a BAR gunner from Clear Lake, Wisconsin. He had served with the 78th Infantry Division and died one freezing night in December 1944 after detonating a German mine. More than five decades later, the U.S. Army took custody of his remains, positively identified them in Hawaii, and returned a casket to his family for burial in Wisconsin.

News about Cahow, Herbert, and the work of Klein's team brought a sense of enthusiasm to all those involved with the Hill 627 search. My Belgian colleagues befriended Klein and his partners, began sharing information, and helped establish a museum under the auspices of the Belgian Army at Camp Elsenborn. On the downside, the three recoveries reminded us that our best efforts had failed to locate

Beckwith, Kokotovich, and Read. We were also cognizant of that shortcoming when Beckwith's mother died in 1997 at age ninety-three. The sharpest reminder came on March 6, 2001, when Dick Byers passed away at a nursing home in Ohio. The seventy-nine-year-old veteran of the 99th Division had been a driving force behind our hunt for missing soldiers. Without his support, my idea of a coordinated, multilateral search might never have become reality.

As I sat among the mourners at Dick's funeral, I listened to a clergyman speak about the search efforts over the past decade. He then read several eulogies, one written by Jean-Philippe Speder. Since Dick had chosen cremation, there was no graveside service. Inside the funeral home, his family and friends glanced out a window to watch a rifle team fire a salute on the front lawn. A bugler played "Taps" and an army lieutenant presented a folded flag to Dick's widow. There was a sad finality to it all. Perhaps our search for missing servicemen had culminated.

But the ghosts of Hill 627 lingered.

EIGHTEEN DAYS AFTER DICK'S DEATH, Seel received a phone call from Marc Marique. He had alarming news. Another digger had just brandished a set of dog tags belonging to Jack Beckwith. The tags seemed freshly dug from the earth, both made of brass, and one of them pierced by shrapnel. The digger also recovered a half billfold with the tags. Anxiety gripped Seel. Had that relic hunter looted Beckwith's grave?

Seel immediately drove to Hill 627 with Erich Hönen, the forest ranger who had been a loyal supporter for ten years. They found no sign of fresh digging. The dog tags and billfold apparently came from someplace else. But where?

On April 11, 2001, Seel decided to double-check the hill. He scanned the suspected graves area with his metal detector, crossed a forest trail, and continued exploring. He quickly uncovered an American hand grenade. Its safety handle protruded outward at an irregular angle, a deformity probably caused by shrapnel. Three steps from the grenade, he heard a familiar sound through his earphones. It was the telltale echo of a nickel-alloy dog tag. Seel flipped it from the soil with his shoe.

"I read the name," he recalled, "and it took a few seconds to realize this dog tag belonged to one of the missing—David Read. Then, it is difficult to describe my feelings, but I became nervous, almost crazy."

Was this the burial site? Less than two feet from the dog tag, Seel found a collar disk, the type made of brass and worn by enlisted men in the infantry. Before the day ended, he also uncovered remnants of a GI cartridge belt.

Seel made plans to return with Marique. Early on Tuesday, April 17, the pair ascended Hill 627. Two hours later, Speder joined them, as did forest ranger Hönen.

In late afternoon, Speder fired off a short e-mail to Swanson, Whitmarsh, and me: "Jack Beckwith, Saul Kokotovich, and David Read no longer on the MIA list. Bodies found today. Complete report tonite."

After more than five decades, Hill 627 had finally relinquished the last of its dead. The three soldiers occupied graves a mere thirty yards from the 1992 search area.

Seel later explained that the discovery came about when his metal detector emitted a sharp "positive signal." He dug down about twelve inches and struck a hipbone. Beside it lay a brass belt buckle. That was Beckwith's grave. One of his brass dog tags later set off Seel's detector as he scanned the forest floor nearby. Several paces away, Seel culled yet another brass dog tag from the topsoil. That one belonged to Kokotovich. His grave lay alongside. It now seemed obvious that Read's interment place must be near the spot where his dog tag turned up the previous week. That proved correct.

Beckwith and Kokotovich rested side by side, and Read lay about two meters downhill from Beckwith's feet. The graves formed a pattern that suggested there had been a fourth grave—John Sims's original burial spot.

It took two days to complete the exhumation process. Each soldier had a dog tag marking his grave and another tag around his neck on a bead-link chain or on a shoelace in Read's case. The diggers found rotted clothing along with the remnants of canvas leggings, boots, and overshoes. Beckwith and Kokotovich each wore an M43 field jacket, while Read had a winter combat jacket. One PFC stripe survived on Read's left sleeve, but no trace of clothing remained on his right arm. Close examination of his boots—actually service shoes—revealed a faded ink stamp: R-2803. That mark agreed with Read's name and the last four digits of his serial number.

Medics had apparently removed each man's personal effects before burial in 1944, but there were several exceptions. Read had a leather wallet and a teaspoon in his right shirt pocket. (Many front-line GIs lived out of their pockets and considered a spoon the only necessary eating utensil.) Unfortunately, the paper contents of the wallet had turned to mush. The most spectacular item emerged as the diggers delicately peeled away the decayed vestiges of Kokotovich's wool gloves. Among the small bones of his fingers, a platinum ring glinted in the dirt. The dead soldier's hands were folded on his torso, making it impossible to determine on which hand or finger he had worn the ring. The Belgians doubted it was a wedding ring because the object was not band shaped. It was a signet ring with no engraving. What was the significance of that piece of jewelry?

Read's remains were the hardest to reach because the roots of an evergreen tree had enveloped his grave. It required an entire day to dig around the tentacles of that conifer. The painstaking task went on despite a sudden snowfall, an occasional springtime occurrence in the Ardennes region.

After excavating the three burial spots, the diggers photographed each skeleton as it lay in its grave, and then they extracted the bones. Read was the most difficult to remove. Seel grasped the young soldier's skull and gave it a gentle tug. Nothing budged. The skull was still connected to cervical vertebrae. Seel tugged harder and separated the bones. He felt a queasy sensation in his stomach as he pulled the soldier apart. Near the graves, Speder carefully reassembled each skeleton, arranging the bones in the order they had occupied in life. He noted that several teeth and small bones were missing. These little objects, if they still existed, would be left for an army recovery team to sift from the earth.

Once excavation work in the forest ended, Erich Hönen transported the remains to a storage cabinet in his home. Seel then e-mailed David Roath of Memorial Affairs Europe. They arranged a meeting for the end of April at a hotel in the nearby town of Monschau, Germany. At the agreed-upon place and time, Roath and an assistant rendezvoused with Seel, Marique, and Menestrey. The group exchanged greetings and handshakes, and then departed the hotel and drove to Hönen's house to view the skeletons and artifacts. A journey to the graves area followed, and afterward, the group scheduled another visit. Roath would bring a recovery team and take custody of the remains.

The team arrived on May 14, 2001. Roath brought four specialists from his unit as well as two other members of the organization. In addition, a DNA expert from the University of Salzburg tagged along as an observer. Roath and his colleagues took possession of the remains, set up a field lab on Hill 627, and began the official identification process. The lab consisted of two white tents, a wooden table, and a pair of canvas litters for laying out the remains. At the graves area, team members removed the uppermost layer of soil and stretched a grid pattern over the area with string and wooden stakes. That aided the mapping process. Roath selected Manfred Klein as the chief surveyor and mapmaker. The young German, a civil engineer by profession, came equipped with the instruments of his trade.

While Klein collected data, Roath's crew reexcavated the graves in hopes of finding additional remains and artifacts. Workers used quarter-inch mesh screening to sift through all the excavated soil. Under the tents, Roath washed the remains and rigorously examined them. As he cleaned Beckwith's skull, several tiny objects dropped from the cranial cavity. They were mortar-shell fragments. Of the three soldiers, only Beckwith's remains showed evidence of traumatic injury. The damage closely matched the frightful wounds Swanson remembered. Roath and several helpers diligently recorded every bone and artifact. Part of that job included sealing the items in Ziploc bags, labeling the bags with a felt-tipped marker, and establishing a chain of custody.

To aid the identification process, Speder prepared a detailed report that included wartime documents ranging from after-action reports to dental records. He also provided eyewitness accounts from 99th veterans as well as an analysis of the GI clothing and footwear found with the remains. Speder included next-of-kin addresses and telephone numbers. Photographs of the decedents were part of the report, too. The picture of Kokotovich showed a distinctive gap between his front teeth. On his remains, Roath noticed an identical gap. He also observed similarities between Kokotovich's dental charts and his remains.

After three days, Roath's team placed each soldier in an aluminum casket known as a transfer case, and restored the entire area to its natural order. No trace of human hands remained other than a simple wooden cross erected by a German forester. Its inscription read, "*Im stillen Gedenken an 3 amerikanische Soldaten Dezember 1944 hier ihr Leben gaben*" (In Silent Remembrance of Three American Soldiers Who Gave Their Lives Here in December 1944).

Roath now focused on satisfying all legal requirements regarding the recovery of remains on foreign soil. Some of his predecessors had overlooked such formalities and had gotten away with it, but Roath was a stickler for detail. He adhered to every letter of the Geneva Conventions and Protocols as well as the NATO Status of Forces Agreement and its related supplements. Germany had a unique arrangement with the U.S. military because American forces "occupied" the country after World War II. Roath possessed authority to take custody of American remains without notifying the host government, except in criminal cases like murder. Other NATO countries required official notification and documentation showing the transfer of remains to U.S. control. Since Roath had a free hand in Germany, he notified the host government as a matter of courtesy and to promote good public relations. He and representatives of the Volksbund Deutsche Kriegsgräberfürsorge (German War Graves Commission) arranged for a memorial service known as a fallen-soldier detail. The event took place on May 18, 2001, at a German military cemetery near the town of Hürtgen. An honor guard of nearly four dozen Americans arrived by bus from their barracks at Kitzingen, Germany. The soldiers all wore blue ascots and belonged to the 4th Battalion, 3rd Air Defense Artillery (1st Infantry Division). They received three flag-draped cases and marched out of the cemetery, moving between rows of crosses roughly carved from gray limestone. No gleaming white marble like American military cemeteries. Everything about the place spoke of catastrophic loss and wasted German lives. In the parking lot, the troops slid their honored cargo aboard a line of parked vehicles, one hearse and two vans. Roath's organization possessed only one hearse, so the vans were stand-ins that day.

American journalists and cameramen recorded the event for armed forces television as well as *Stars and Stripes* newspaper. One member of the honor guard shared his thoughts with a reporter. "During the ceremony, I just kept thinking about how those guys probably died, the scenario they went through," Specialist Ramon Benitez said. "I know their families will be happy to finally have their loved ones returned home."

Jean-Philippe Speder stood in front of a TV camera and answered questions. When asked why he and his Belgian colleagues felt so passionate about recovering missing American servicemen, he answered, "It's a way to thank them for what they did. . . . They liberated us."

Chapter 8
ON THE DEVIL'S ANVIL

Marc Marique had the distinction of being the oldest of the four diggers who unearthed Read, Beckwith, and Kokotovich, and he also had the most experience searching for battlefield relics. He began hunting for them in 1976 when he was fifteen years old. At first his only tool was a shovel, which he used to explore old foxholes and caved-in bunkers. His technique improved two years later when he acquired a British-made metal detector. On his first outing with the new gadget, he unearthed an M1 rifle, two 60-mm mortar rounds, and two American fragmentation grenades.

His success continued until 1980 when he joined the Belgian Army and had to give up his hobby temporarily. Marique spent ten months with the 17ème Brigade Blindée, an armored brigade stationed at Siegen, Germany. He served as a mechanic, repairing tanks, trucks, self-propelled guns, and armored personnel carriers. After his discharge from active duty, he found civilian employment with the army as a mechanic. His workplace was the Arsenal de Rocourt, a large military depot near Liège, Belgium.

Besides starting a civilian career, Marique resumed relic hunting in his spare time. In doing so he teamed up with a childhood friend, Jean-Luc Menestrey, who had begun searching for battlefield artifacts in the spring of 1980. He was two years younger and had grown up in

Ensival, a suburb of Verviers. That was also Marique's hometown. Together, the pair looked comically different, resembling Mutt and Jeff, those affable cartoon characters who are remembered for their disparity in physical height. Marique was slight in stature, round headed, and almost bald. Menestrey was tall, long faced, and had more hair than his friend. The disparate-looking duo pursued their avocation by joining a confederation of about twenty relic hunters known as the Centre d'Archéologie Militaire. The group operated as a collective. All artifacts recovered by its members belonged to the group and were put on public display and never sold. One of their specialties was the excavation of aircraft crash sites. The group also recovered the skeletal remains of two German infantrymen, but had never managed to find a GI. Seel and Speder were the ones with that distinction. And that was one reason Marique and Menestrey teamed up with them in 1994. Seel and Speder were as much interested in the history and personalities behind the artifacts they found as the objects themselves. The two men spent countless hours corresponding with German and American veterans and escorting them around the former battlegrounds of the Ardennes. All of that appealed to Marique and Menestrey, who shared the same fascination with history and the people who made it. Many CAM members had no desire to delve into the historical background associated with the relics they culled from the earth.

For Marique and Menestrey, the discovery on Hill 627 confirmed the wisdom of their decision to leave CAM. The discovery left all four diggers stoked with enthusiasm and hungry for another success.

Shortly after the Hürtgen ceremony, Marique visited Seel's home at Ensival. He lived in a modern trilevel brick row house. Its one-car garage was on the lower level, as was a small basement, which he had transformed into a museum for his dog tag collection. He often referred to the room as his "bunker." The two diggers met upstairs in the dining room and indulged in several cups of coffee while they hashed over future plans. One suspicion loomed in their minds: Maybe they had missed other graves by a few yards, just like the ones on Hill 627.

Together, Marique and Seel pored over case files for missing 99th Division soldiers. One of them pertained to Sergeant Frederick F. Zimmerman, and it included a map sketched by a former 99th medic. His rendering showed a "forward aid station" where he last saw Zimmerman's body. Another veteran asserted that he helped carry PFC

Stanley E. Larson's body to the aid station. He too was among the missing. A third eyewitness reported seeing PFC Ewing E. Fidler's body in the same vicinity. He was also missing. The documents in the Zimmerman file had been collected a decade earlier by Rex Whitehead and me.

IN MARCH 1990, ALVIN REX WHITEHEAD, a 99th veteran from Logan, Utah, saw the names of thirty-two missing soldiers listed in the *Checkerboard*. He had known three of them, including Larson and Zimmerman. They served together in the same unit—Company H, 394th Infantry Regiment.

Rex was born in the farming community of Grace, Idaho, during the spring of 1925, and was the only son of Alvin and Mae Whitehead. The family was Mormon, though not devout. They lived on Main Street in a two-story, flat-roofed home with art deco lines—rather stylish for a rural town. Alvin managed the only bank in town, and he also owned a Swiss cheese factory as well as an insurance company. His prominence in the community left Rex feeling a bit self-conscious. "I always disliked the fact that I was a 'banker's son.' Even though my family was not wealthy, we had more than most." Rex labored at the cheese factory during the summer months and was always anxious for the start of school in the autumn. He answered the call of his local draft board three months after he graduated from high school in 1943. Then it was off to Fort Benning, Georgia, for basic training. After thirteen weeks at Benning, he joined the ASTP unit at Arkansas State University in Jonesboro. When the ASTP underwent its severe personnel reduction in 1944, Private Whitehead and most of his fellow classmates found themselves assigned to the 99th Division at Camp Maxey, Texas. He became a mortar gunner with the 81-mm mortar platoon of Company H. There he first encountered Larson and Zimmerman, who belonged to different platoons.

FRED ZIMMERMAN WAS A NONCOMMISSIONED OFFICER and member of the company since its formation. He entered the service from Ohio where he had lived since his birth on January 16, 1922. His family originally resided on a farm in rural Hardin County. Before he entered grade school, his parents, Lloyd and Ethel, quit farming and moved their family eighty miles away to the vicinity of Groveport, Ohio.

Lloyd worked at an electric power plant, but his employment there ended during the Depression when he received a layoff notice. Lloyd then landed a position with the Works Progress Administration, where he labored on construction crews that built parks, bridges, roadways, and other public works. He found the work agreeable but felt many of his co-workers were unambitious or "shovel leaners" as he called them. That grated on his work ethic, and he returned to his first vocation, agriculture. His family relocated to an eighty-acre farm south of Groveport, where they grew hay, corn, and wheat for several years before moving a short distance to another farm of similar size. Lloyd rented both properties.

Fred Zimmerman was one of five children in the family. He had three sisters, one of whom died as an infant, and he had a younger brother named Bill, who was born in 1930 and was the baby of the family. Bill recalled that Fred took after the maternal side of the family. "My mother's relatives were all Irish, and they joked around and enjoyed life. My dad's family was German, nice people but rather stoic. I think Fred had more of the Irish in him. He was fun loving and had a good sense of humor. He also liked sports and was good at it." As an adolescent, Fred stood a head taller than his parents and had a body stacked with muscle. He also had a quick mind but no academic ambitions. "Fred never finished high school," Bill remembered. "He was an intelligent guy but not interested in school."

Fred left the classroom and began driving a truck for the Pickerington Creamery. He motored around the countryside to dairy farms and cream stations, collecting cans of the oily, yellowish liquid. He also immersed himself in religious activities. His family belonged to the Church of Christ in Christian Union, which advocated a Puritan lifestyle unblemished by "sacrileges" such as dancing, drinking, and even motion pictures. "The true believers were real salt-of-the earth people and very honest," Bill recalled. "You could trust them with anything, but I felt they were a little too controlling. Under that influence, Fred seriously considered going to a Bible college in Cincinnati. Eventually that ambition faded when he got out into the world and saw how the other half lived."

An automobile provided one means of getting out. Fred bought a car with money he earned as a driver for the creamery. That purchase led to near tragedy one evening on a country road near Groveport. Fred was behind the wheel with a buddy at his side. As they crested a hill, another vehicle burst into view—in their lane. With no time to react, the two cars struck head-on. Everyone survived the collision, though all suffered ill effects. Fred had cuts, bruises, and a dislocated shoulder. He recuperated at home where his family doctor treated the injuries and returned periodically to change bandages. The episode left Fred with a knot in his right shoulder and chronic pain.

About the time World War II set Europe ablaze, Fred's father gave up farming. It had never amounted to more than a break-even existence. He took a job with one of the nation's first grocery store chains, which owned a meatpacking operation where he cared for livestock before the animals went to slaughter. The Zimmerman family moved to a rented house on Elm Street in Groveport. They later moved down the street to another residence, which Fred's father purchased. Across the street stood the home of William Meuser, who also worked in the meatpacking industry. He had a dark-haired daughter, Martha Jane, who was two years younger than Fred. Her soft face caught his eye, as did her warm and genuine smile. According to Fred's brother, "Martha Jane was about the only girl I ever saw him have much interest in." The two dated and could often be seen around town in his glossy new '41 Chevrolet coupe.

After the United States entered the war, Fred decided to volunteer for the Army Air Corps. When he informed his mother, she derided the idea as foolhardy, and she pointed out a pragmatic reason against it. "You've got that bad shoulder. You won't pass the physical." Rather than agitate his mother, he took a job with the Seagrave Corporation in the nearby city of Columbus. By that time, his father had quit the grocery store chain and also worked for Seagrave. Their employment came by way of Brother William Goble, evangelical pastor at the Church of Christ. The reverend worked as a foreman for the company, which manufactured fire engines. Fred was a wrench turner on the assembly line and toted a toolbox to work every day. His father operated a spray gun and gave the engines their cherry red finish. (A close connection existed between the Goble and Zimmerman families. Goble's son married Fred's oldest sister, Esta.)

Fred's work at Seagrave ended with a draft notice. On November 30, 1942, he reported to Medical Examination and Induction Board

No. 5 in downtown Columbus. He received a short furlough after being sworn in to the military, and then he left Ohio on a troop train bound for the Army Reception Center at Fort Thomas, Kentucky. After several days of in-processing, he boarded another train, and this one steamed south to Camp Van Dorn, Mississippi.

Fred underwent basic and advanced training at Van Dorn as a member of the newly formed 99th Infantry Division. The camp opened in November and had a raw, makeshift look. All the barracks were dull black, their walls made of tarpaper nailed to stick frames. Many of these shanties stood on cinder blocks, which elevated the buildings above the red, viscous mud that pervaded the place. Wooden walkways connected the structures and bridged drainage ditches. It was a kind of army purgatory, a place where Fred Zimmerman shed his civilian self and learned the business of killing. Company H, 394th Infantry became his surrogate home and family, but many of Fred's newfound brothers departed the company after less than a year. They shipped out as replacements for units already in combat.

THE RANKS OF COMPANY H eventually refilled with fresh draftees. One of the rookie infantrymen was Stanley Larson, who had been in high school when the company first came into existence.

Larson entered the army from Rochelle, Illinois, where his family moved when he was a toddler. He was born on February 11, 1925, in Benton Harbor, Michigan, and was the youngest of three children born to Elmer and Ella Larson. After moving to Rochelle, Stanley underwent an informal name change. One day while playing outdoors, he stopped to watch a group of carpenters as they hammered together a new house next door. None of the workers knew the boy's name, so one of them decided to call him Mike. The moniker stuck. By the time he entered school, many people in Rochelle had no idea his real name was Stanley. Only his mother used it.

There was also another change in the youngster's life. His parents separated and then divorced. In later years, he rarely spoke of it, but his friends detected an undercurrent of resentment toward his father. Mike blamed him for the breakup.

Mike's dad defined himself as a businessman rather than a husband or father. After separating from Ella, he left Rochelle and moved to nearby DeKalb where he owned a trucking company, which evolved into a construction business and gravel quarry. When in public, he maintained an air of formality, always outfitted in suit and tie and with a demeanor even primmer than his wardrobe. One of Mike's friends described Elmer Larson as being "colder than a well-digger's butt." His aloofness contrasted with his former wife, who beamed with charm and cheer. Mike gravitated toward her despite her frequent absence from their home. As a single mother, she worked long hours at a local drugstore to support her children and herself. Mike worked, too. During his last two years of grade school, he and his buddy Lyle Kunde cut asparagus for the Rochelle Asparagus Company.

"It was the toughest job in my life," Lyle remembered. "Various private growers sold to Rochelle Asparagus, and we worked for one that was just a couple blocks from our homes. We got up before daylight and cut until it was time to go to school. We walked in mud and rain, baskets hanging at our sides, and we had to cut every day asparagus was in season. It was rough work, earning only a few pennies per pound. Not every kid could do it."

When Mike and Lyle entered high school, they landed jobs working for the Del Monte Corporation, which had a vegetable-packing operation in Rochelle. "Mike worked in the canning end of it, testing vegetables to ensure they had been properly cooked before a machine funneled them into cans. I worked as a gofer for two scientists, who bred and propagated pumpkins, tomatoes, and so forth. Mike and I began at 17½ cents an hour and worked our way up to 30 cents. We often spent six or seven days a week at Del Monte. The pea 'pack' started in early April and ran until we went back to school in September. Then there would be a break between peas and corn and between corn and pumpkin."

Despite his work schedule, Mike held an A average in school, won elections for class president (junior year) and student council president (senior year), and belonged to the National Honor Society. He also played cornet in the school band, and he performed onstage as a member of the drama club. But his tennis and basketball abilities eclipsed all else. He dominated in those sports and also played varsity football and ran track.

Mike's tennis doubles partner was Lyle Kunde, who described their game in nine words. "He had the mind, and I had the power." The pair smashed the adult competition and won the city championship in 1942. During their senior year in high school, they earned a trip to the state finals at Champaign, Illinois, and advanced to the championship match, but rain forced its cancellation. Tournament officials rescheduled the big event for a Saturday and moved it to Oak Park, Illinois, because the University of Illinois had dibs on the Champaign courts. "We went to Oak Park," Lyle remembered, "and played on a clay court for the first time in our lives. It was a different game, and we had a terrible day. The team that beat us was from Oak Park, and we played on their home court. If we had competed on asphalt, who knows. . . . "

Mike's athletic talent shone even brighter on the basketball court, where he captained the varsity squad and netted 260 points his senior year. Lyle played on the team too and described his friend as an all-round competitor. "Some players are great shooters, some are great rebounders, and some are great defenders. Mike did it all." He left an enduring mark on Rochelle High School, earning a spot on the "All Century Team" named during 1999–2000 basketball season. His on-court accomplishments were even more remarkable given his physical impairment. "Mike had terrible eyesight," Lyle remembered. "He had to ask me the score because he couldn't see the scoreboard. He played without glasses because safety lenses didn't exist in those days. His wire-frame glasses were okay for tennis, but on the basketball court and the football field he had to go without." (He also refrained from wearing glasses in many photographs.)

Lyle and Mike spent much of their free time together. When speaking of Mike, Lyle said, "He spent as much time at my house as his own. He became like a brother to me, and my parents treated him like a son." The two friends often double-dated, taking their girlfriends to a downtown Rockford eatery called Jack's or Better. They became such frequent customers, the house pianist greeted their arrival with a clamorous outcry: "The Rochelle boys are here!" When ordering supper, Mike always requested the same meal: steak and potatoes. And the pianist always tapped out Mike's favorite melody: "Tales from the Vienna Woods." That romantic Strauss waltz was also a favorite of his girlfriend, Maralyn Brennan, a slim-hipped brunette who wore ruby lipstick and wire-frame glasses. She delighted in big-band tunes and dancing, and hoped to become a music teacher. Her courtship with Mike began in high school and progressed toward marriage until he received a draft notice.

He joined the army on July 6, 1943, a month after graduating from Rochelle High. His relationship with Maralyn tapered to letter writing, and his college plans went on hold. He had academic and basketball scholarships to attend Purdue University, where he planned to study civil engineering. After basic training at Camp Fannin, Texas, Mike's intellect earned him an ASTP slot at Louisiana State University. He roomed in the football stadium along with all the other student-soldiers.

As MIKE LARSON SETTLED INTO the pre-engineering program at LSU, his future compatriot Rex Whitehead did the same at Arkansas State University. The military administrators at both schools divided the students into companies and assigned them to dorm rooms in alphabetical order. That arrangement kept Whitehead apart from fellow student and future 99er Ewing Fidler. At opposite ends of the alphabet, the two never met even though they belonged to the same ASTP unit.

Fidler's family resided in Ada, Oklahoma, where his parents raised three children—he as big brother, Thelma as younger sister, and Charles as little brother. Ewing came into the world at his grandparent's home on June 1, 1925. Charles recounted the circumstances:

"He was born at the Fidler farm. My folks went over for a weekend visit, and the South Canadian River came up during their stay because of heavy rainfall to the west. So they couldn't get back to Ada for several days. No bridges spanned the river in those days; everyone crossed on the riverbed. My parents stayed on the farm, and Mom gave birth to Ewing."

The baby boy shared the same first name as his father but had a different middle name. To avoid confusion, family members called the youngster "Sonny." His boyhood friends referred to him as Fid, a shortened version of his last name.

Before his parent's marriage, Sonny's mother had been a schoolteacher, leaving her career to raise children. His father owned a trucking company that employed about ten men. He and his workers transported household goods to all points in Oklahoma as well as Kansas, Texas, and Arkansas. Much of their business involved moving the chattel of oil-field workers.

Petroleum production boomed in central Oklahoma before and during the war. Derricks and pumping jacks studded the countryside around Ada, and pipelines carried black gold to refineries upstate. A steady flow of oil revenue kept the little municipality alive during the Depression, when many communities in western Oklahoma choked to death in dust storms that wasted crops and farmland. Most of the terrain around Ada was hilly and timbered with blackjack oak. At the height of the Depression, the downtown area included three retailing giants— JC Penney, Woolworths, and Montgomery Ward. There were also more than a dozen oil-field supply stores and service companies such as Haliburton and Schlumberger. The city had two other major employers, a cement plant and a glass factory that made bottles and jars.

Sonny grew up in a boxy, three-bedroom house at 225 West 21st Street. His parents bought the white bungalow just before the Depression. The street in front of their residence was a dusty gravel road. Only the downtown streets had paved surfaces, and it was there that Sonny's dad had his business office. Both Fidler boys worked for their father during the summer, loading and unloading trucks and accompanying him on occasional road trips. Sonny also peddled his red bicycle around the neighborhood, tossing the *Ada Evening News* onto porches and doorsteps. His brother inherited the route after Sonny took a job at Woolworths, where he worked evenings restocking shelves.

His earnings from the store financed his number-one hobby, model airplanes. The countryside around Ada afforded him plenty of space to fly his balsa-wood creations, powered by gasoline engines. In addition, he belonged to the local Boy Scout troop, where he garnered twenty-nine merit badges, more than enough to attain the rank of Eagle Scout. (That lofty distinction became official after he joined the service. At Camp Maxey, his company commander presented the Eagle Scout medal and a Bronze Palm award.) "He also liked to squirrel hunt," his brother recalled, "and he spent a lot of time doing that on my Grandpa's farm. Whenever we'd go over there, which was fairly often, he'd go squirrel hunting. I still have his .22 rifle, a Remington single shot." Sonny also owned a brass cornet and played first chair in the high school band. Occasionally, he blew "Taps" for a military funeral at the city's largest graveyard, Rosedale Cemetery.

Sonny had a soft, boyish face and used no profanity in his speech. Tobacco never tempted him, and he never sipped anything stronger than a Nehi Root Beer. His most outstanding trait was a scalpel-sharp mind, which served him well in school. One of his classmates, Mickie Bigham, remembered, "He was always the most brilliant student in his class. Even in grade school, if there was a scholastic award given, we all knew it would be he who received it." It came as no surprise that he graduated as valedictorian when he finished high school in June 1943.

Athletics were among his lesser talents, though he delighted in listening to baseball games on the family radio. His favorite team was the St. Louis Browns. After graduating from high school, he fulfilled a childhood dream when he traveled alone by train to St. Louis and attended a Browns game. That was his farthest excursion from home until he joined the army.

Ewing "Sonny" Fidler had never been inclined toward the military. He aspired to attend Oklahoma University, but an induction notice postponed those plans. On July 27, 1943, he reported for duty along with a group of other draftees from Ada and nearby communities. Their families saw them off that day. There was no patriotic hoopla, just hugs, handshakes, and good-byes. Charles Fidler recounted that event and what followed:

"We all went down to the courthouse. Every two or three days a busload of boys would depart for military service. We watched him leave from the Pontotoc County Courthouse. That's where the bus always parked. He went to Oklahoma City where he took physicals and so forth, and then he went on to Fort Sill. We didn't see him until he finished his basic training at Fort Benning, Georgia. They gave him a week or so leave. He knew then that he would be reporting to the ASTP at Jonesboro, Arkansas."

EWING FIDLER STUDIED PRE-ENGINEERING just like Stanley Larson and Rex Whitehead. All three eventually found themselves at Camp Maxey, Texas, after the army drastically downsized the ASTP during the spring of 1944. The new arrivals and thousands like them joined the 99th Infantry Division, which had departed Camp Van Dorn, Mississippi, slogged through a series of war games in Louisiana, and relocated to Maxey in November 1943. The contingent of student-soldiers replaced three thousand enlisted men, mainly privates, stripped from the division and transferred to units embarking overseas for combat in Italy. Most noncommissioned officers in the 99th survived the cannibalization, and many of them eyed the fresh faces with contempt. The reasons were manifold. One company commander had warned his noncoms, "We have some young college kids coming in to fill the ranks. They are smart, and if you guys do not shape up, they will soon have your stripes."

Fidler joined the 99th as a member of Company E, 394th Infantry. Larson and Whitehead joined Company G, 394th, but soon transferred within the regiment to Company H. The latter unit, a heavy weapons company, included Fred Zimmerman. The young buck sergeant led a machine-gun squad of seven men (one squad leader, one gunner, one assistant gunner, one jeep driver, and three ammunition bearers). His squad belonged to the Second Heavy Machine Gun Platoon, and his squad weapon was a Model 1917A1 water-cooled machine gun. Whitehead and Larson had little contact with him—or each other—because they belonged to different platoons, and they also had no contact with Fidler, who belonged to another company.

Unlike many of his fellow noncoms, Zimmerman felt no antipathy toward the ASTP castoffs. He welcomed two of them as ammunition bearers in his squad—Raymond P. Emmer and William Braxton Williams.

Emmer originally belonged to another company until a noncom thrashed him. Emmer had the dual disadvantage of being a "college puke" and Jewish. Anti-Semitism and every other form of racism stained the U.S. military during the 1940s. Many servicemen believed that "Wall Street Jews" caused the Great Depression, and that American involvement in World War II served no purpose beyond preserving the wealth of Jews like Emmer's father, president of a real-estate company in St. Louis. Anti-Semitism even affected Christians like Zimmerman whose surname led several bigots to conclude that he was Jewish, but no one dared poke a fist at him. His physical size and strength discouraged attacks. Emmer offered an easier target. Slender and unimposing, his appearance seemed to invite hazing. More than once, Zimmerman interceded to thwart assaults on his subordinate. The sergeant always seemed to be there at the right moment, like a good-guy sheriff in a Western movie.

Zimmerman's devotion to his men never wavered and neither did his devotion to the young lady in his life. He and Martha Jane Meuser planned to spend their lives together after the war. His brother remembered, "Fred came home on leave, and her uncle got them off to the side and said, 'I've got a piece of property that I can make available to you, and it would be a good place to build a house.' I recall them driving out to look at the place. It was right outside Groveport." (Zimmerman had a fourteen-day furlough, June 25 to July 8, 1944.)

Meuser traveled to Camp Maxey soon after Zimmerman's visit to Groveport. She and the sergeant married on July 16 at the 394th Infantry chapel and dashed off for an abbreviated honeymoon. One of his squad members, W. B. Williams, recounted what happened afterward. "I recall it took a telegram from Captain Mannheimer [the company commander] to convince Fred that he should return to camp. We wondered if he would go AWOL. I think he did for a day or two, but he was a good sergeant, so they let him off the hook. He was one unhappy trooper when he returned. Leaving his wife behind may have been the hardest thing he ever did."

The young bride returned to Ohio, where she took a job as a clerk for the Ohio Farm Bureau. The distance between home and Camp Maxey precluded visits with her husband.

For Ewing Fidler, the distance to home was two hours' driving time, assuming no flat tire along the way. He frequently spent weekends with his family in Oklahoma. "Occasionally he hitchhiked home," his brother said, "but most of the time we drove down and picked him up along with his best buddy, Billy Hoipkemeir, who was also in the 99th. They went through school and Scouts together and went to the same Baptist church, and they had the same hobbies. Sometimes Billy's folks would pick them up, and on Sunday afternoon one of the families would take them back. Now and again, Ewing thumbed a ride back to camp."

Rex Whitehead also saw his family while at Camp Maxey. His parents and sister journeyed down from Idaho during the first week of September 1944, and they spent all his free time together. He said good-bye to them on a Friday night, and the following week, the 99th Division began boarding trains, its soldiers bound for an undisclosed destination overseas. Whitehead and Larson shared a seat in the same Pullman car. The pair had bunked in different barracks at Camp Maxey but had known each other by name and occasionally chatted. "I liked Stan the moment I met him," Whitehead recounted. "He was personable, tall, good-looking, bright—the kind of guy you gravitated to." During the rail journey, which lasted four days, the two friends whiled away the hours, chatting about athletics and swapping high school experiences. Both had played varsity basketball and tennis. Rex was the champion tennis player at his school four years in a row.

The train trip ended at Camp Myles Standish, Massachusetts, where the troops organized a basketball league while they awaited orders for Europe. Larson and Whitehead became teammates. "In thirty seconds I could see that Stan knew what he was doing on the basketball court," Whitehead remembered. "I had never played with anyone as good." The two friends saw each other one final time in the locker room after their last game. On September 29, 1944, they and thousands of other 99ers boarded troop ships at the Boston port of embarkation. Larson, Fidler, Whitehead, and Zimmerman sailed for Scotland aboard the S.S. *Exchequer*.

After a week on the ocean, Fidler wrote home. It was the second such letter he penned while crossing to Europe:

"We're still underway on the high seas, that's about all I can tell you. We're not allowed to even date the rest of our letters. I've completely gotten over my seasickness and am beginning to kinda enjoy the voyage. The sea is much smoother, so that's a big help. Most of us divide our time during the day between staying out on deck and loafing, and reading in our bunks. Just lately, we've had a few classes of instruction and calisthenics. It seems funny taking exercises on the deck as it is heaving up and down."

After landing in Scotland, the British railway system conducted the 99th to southern England under rainy skies. Whitehead recalled "the green rolling hills, the red-roofed houses, and more than anything else, the feeling that we were there." His company stopped at the fishing port and seaside resort of Lyme Regis and billeted in an aging hotel, one squad per room with everyone on army cots and straw-filled mattresses.

Sergeant Zimmerman and his squad occupied a room with a stove, which provided warmth during chilly October nights. One evening, the squad members received a visit from a staff sergeant in their platoon. He was a Texan and an unabashed racist. His eyes fixed on Ray Emmer, the Jewish kid from St. Louis, who happened to be wearing a yarmulke atop his head. The staff sergeant became agitated, like a bull at the sight of a red cloth. He cut loose with a stream of pejoratives about the "goddamn Jew" and his "goddamn hat," which violated army regulation. Zimmerman sprang up. "That's enough! He's my man, and I'll take care of this. Get out!" The staff sergeant fumbled for words and retreated. He knew better than to challenge a man of Zimmerman's size. The remainder of the night passed without incident. Emmer kept his yarmulke.

IN EARLY NOVEMBER 1944, the 99th departed England, passed through the port city of Le Havre, France, and motored into Belgium. Larson wrote his mom on November 10 and passed word that he had reached continental Europe:

"Letters are going to be something rare coming from me now even more than before. Things are so indefinite that nothing can even be thought of being planned. We were somewhere in France but not too long. It snowed some yesterday, and things are pretty miserable, feet soaking wet and then sleeping is another thing. Last night we did get mail and that was certainly heaven sent. I received five letters, and that was really something. It's wonderful to receive them, but impossible to answer them all."

Four days later, the 394th Infantry Regiment arrived at the front line and relieved veteran campaigners of the 60th Infantry Regiment (9th Division). The newcomers took up residence in a spruce forest along the Belgian-German border. Fidler described his new digs in a letter home:

"Tonite finds me writing you from a foxhole up on the front in Germany. If you could only see me now, you could get an idea how it is with the ole infantry in the field in the dead of winter. Our foxholes are kinda elaborate for combat I guess. They're big enough for two men to sleep in them comfortably and keep warm. The outfit here before us had already dug them, so all we have to do is fix them up to suit ourselves. Even though there's about 18 inches of snow on the ground outside, you'd be surprised how warm we sleep in our sleeping bags. As yet, the only way the enemy has bothered us is by buzz bombs and sporadic firing which we don't pay much attention to."

Although Fidler belonged to a rifle company, he was neither a rifleman nor machine gunner. He served as a platoon messenger and had a foxhole a short distance behind the front line. Whitehead and his mortar platoon were even farther to the rear and in Belgium. Larson and Zimmerman were in Germany at forward positions along the forest edge, right under the enemy's nose. They could peer across an open meadow and see a belt of minefields, concrete bunkers, and antitank obstacles. The villages of Neuhof and Udenbreth lay amid those defenses.

Zimmerman's squad inherited four log-roofed emplacements from the 60th Infantry. One was a machine-gun position, and the others were two-man holes for sleeping. The Germans made little attempt to assail the newly arrived Americans. The war in that sector amounted to sporadic shellfire and reconnaissance patrols. Zimmerman and his men never participated in patrols because heavy machine guns were defensive weapons. Patrol work fell mainly upon riflemen. Despite the lack of serious combat, most soldiers did what soldiers do best—bitch about their circumstances. Zimmerman groused in a letter, "I just hope and pray that this thing will soon be over. I am so sick and tired of living like a backwoodsman. I never thought it was possible to live like this."

Several days after he wrote those words, one of his squad members received a dire letter from home. Ray Emmer learned his older brother was missing in action. He was a P-51 pilot and squadron commander, who had fourteen German aircraft to his credit, but enemy flak had downed him. The news crushed Emmer. No words of encouragement could rally his spirits. He knew his brother was dead. The following night, after he and W. B. Williams came off machine-gun duty, Emmer stood outside their sleeping hole and thoughtlessly lit a cigarette. It proved to be a tragic mistake. An enemy observer saw the flare of Emmer's lighter, and mortar shells fell within seconds. The first salvo took out the machine gun and hit Emmer along with two other members of his squad: PFCs Vincent C. Clark Jr. and Woodrow Smith. The latter two survived their wounds, although both required hospitalization. Emmer died where he fell. Another incoming shell bowled over Zimmerman and reinjured his bad shoulder. After the barrage ended, Williams slipped off Emmer's wristwatch and gave it to the battalion chaplain. Medics stuffed the dead soldier inside a mattress cover. Two days later, Graves Registration men unceremoniously dumped him in a muddy hole at a temporary cemetery near Henri-Chapelle, Belgium. (When Emmer died on November 18, his brother was still alive. Captain Wallace Emmer fell into Luftwaffe captivity after parachuting from his flaming aircraft. He sustained severe burns and succumbed to myocarditis on February 15, 1945. His German captors knew he was Jewish, but, out of respect for his elite status as a fighter ace, they gave him a hero's funeral complete with an honor guard.)

Zimmerman remained on duty for a couple of days until the pain in his shoulder became too intense. Medics suspected he had sustained a fracture, and they transported him to the 67th Evacuation Hospital. While there, he wrote to his mother but mentioned nothing about his shoulder. "Just a few lines to let you know that I am okay and wished I could say happy.... Please keep praying for me, and tell Dad and Bill that I said hello. Write whenever you can, and I hope to be with you real soon." As he lay in a convalescence ward, his squad marched off the line. Only three men remained: W. B. Williams, Ellery C. Morgan, and a jeep driver who stayed at the battalion motor pool and seldom spent time with his fellow squad members. Two replacements joined the outfit, and the group received a new machine gun. Woodrow Smith came back on November 28 with a bandage on his left thigh. Zimmerman returned to duty on December 1 with a sore shoulder. X-rays had revealed no fracture.

"He seemed cheerful," Williams recalled, "but he was more apprehensive than he had been before." Zimmerman had the muscle and stamina to endure the physical privations of combat, but the enemy shell that hospitalized him also shattered his sense of invulnerability. He had always believed his number would never come up. Now he knew otherwise. That realization left him anxious and acutely alert. He also bore a fearsome burden of guilt. Maybe he could have prevented Ray Emmer's death. The kid had been in shock over the loss of his brother and should have been closely watched. Perhaps that would have saved him. Before combat, every squad leader dreamed of bringing all his troops home alive. But after only four days, Zimmerman had lost one man. What chance did the rest have in the long run? He could do the math. Yet he still managed to put on a good face, which attested to his character as a leader.

When Zimmerman returned to duty, he found his squad manning a new machine-gun position at the forest edge, about two hundred yards from the previous position. Logs and earth covered both holes, but the new one was less than a foot belowground, which forced its occupants to remain in a prone position while on the gun. The men considered it a "piss poor" setup compared to what they had before. The previous hole was now among firing positions occupied by the First Heavy Machine Gun Platoon of Company H. That platoon included Stanley Larson, who served as an ammunition bearer with Sergeant Warren H. Wenner's squad.

Ewing Fidler also had a new home, which he described in an airmail letter dated December 3:

"Tonite, from candlelight, I'm writing you in our new log cabin. We've just completed it after three days of real hard labor, and man I mean manual labor! We hewed every log out by hand, and chinked the whole works with mud and chips. Talk about snug and cozy! Our bunks are built double-deck and banked with straw. After lying in that hole I had, this is almost heaven. This is one time the doughboy is pioneering the German frontier."

The cabin functioned as the headquarters of Second Lieutenant William D. Huttinger, leader of the Third Platoon, Company E. As platoon runner, Fidler had the task of carrying the lieutenant's verbal messages back to the company command post and to neighboring units and to the three rifle squads in the platoon. Because radio and telephonic communications were often fallible, runners or messengers remained a necessity on the battlefield. Fidler had to deliver messages accurately to the intended recipient and return with a reply for the lieutenant. That sometimes meant dodging enemy fire, and, more than once, the young Oklahoman barely missed being hit by shell fragments. His fringe benefit was a warm cabin and a bunk bed, as contrasted with the cold, soggy foxholes that most other platoon members lived in.

On the third anniversary of Pearl Harbor, he found time to jot down a few words and send them to his mother:

"The date on this letter has a much more important meaning to me now than it did that Sunday three years ago when I was a happy 16 year old in high school. Little did I realize that I would find an active part in this mess. But, as I've heard time and again, time changes all, and, everything turns out for the best for those whose faith is in the Lord. . . . Mom, I hope I can console you by begging you not to worry a lot, because I have a feeling that by the will of God, I'm coming thru okay. Not once since I've been in action have I been worried, and I've had some narrow escapes, too. My goodness, with Christian people like you-all at home praying for me, I've nothing to worry about at all."

On December 9, Fidler and the lieutenant relinquished the cabin when their company exchanged positions with Company G, 394th. The switch put the men in a new log hut, which lay a couple hundred yards behind Zimmerman's machine-gun emplacement. For the first time, Fidler, Larson, and Zimmerman were in the same forest area. Also for the first time, Rex Whitehead resided in Germany, where his mortar crew backed up Company G. He temporarily returned to Belgium on December 15 after he and a select group of soldiers boarded a truck bound for a rest center in the Belgian village of Honsfeld. None of the men had bathed or changed clothes since leaving England in early November. The center had a portable shower (which proved to be inoperable at the time) and an ample supply of clean uniforms. Best of all, film star Marlene Dietrich had a live performance scheduled at the center the following day. In advance of her arrival, foot troops of the 394th Infantry jammed the center, which forced Whitehead to spend the night sleeping on a bench.

As the Idaho native snoozed in Honsfeld, Zimmerman and W. B. Williams hunkered inside a machine-gun nest. Their fellow squad members slept in a single dugout aft of the gun position. The men took turns manning the weapon in four-hour shifts, two men per shift.

Williams and Zimmerman went on duty at 2:00 A.M. on December 16. Williams lay in a prone position to the right of the gun. Zimmerman lay on the left, but he soon asked to switch positions. His shoulder ached, and he wanted to try the other side of the gun for a while. As the night wore on, the two men peered through the firing slit of their gun position and scanned the misty darkness for any sign of hostile activity.

Two hours before daylight, the two machine gunners witnessed a peculiar and dazzling sight. Flashes of light twinkled on the horizon, well inside German territory. Within seconds the curious onlookers understood the meaning. The flashes were the angry pulse of enemy artillery and rocket launchers. A storm of shells stabbed through the darkness and burst all along the American front line. They poured in, too quick to count. Williams and Zimmerman pressed themselves to the dirt floor of their position. The crashing cadence of explosions beat against their eardrums, and the tang of TNT filled their nostrils. The

German artillerymen knew the whereabouts of every American machine gun, and each received attention, a special pounding on the devil's anvil.

One of the incoming shells detonated just to the right of the gun position inhabited by Williams and Zimmerman. Metal fragments blew in through the entryway, which was on the right side of the position. "I was hit in the right hand and arm," Williams recalled. "Fred was not so lucky—apparently the blast caught him full in the right side." Zimmerman flinched and swore and said he had to get to the nearest aid station. Fear sliced to his core. He bolted upright and Williams grabbed him and shouted for him to stay put. "I tried to hold him down, but he was a much bigger man than me." Zimmerman dashed outside into the maelstrom as helpless as a minnow in a tidal wave.

When the bombardment began, Ewing Fidler lay asleep in the cabin that served as the headquarters of his rifle platoon. He dozed beside Lieutenant Huttinger and Staff Sergeant Dominic Palermo. They were the only ones in the cabin. Among the first salvo of shells, a tree burst sent a piece of shrapnel through the log roof. The small fragment smashed into Fidler's back, but he never knew that. The nineteen-year-old died instantly.

Likewise, Stanley Larson never knew what struck him when a shell exploded atop his machine-gun position. His partner, PFC Andrew Woods, recalled the consequences:

"I was with Larson in the hole that morning and he caught most of the force of the shell, which saved my own life. One of my legs was shot up and broken and both hands damaged. Larson's gut was all torn up and his legs were almost gone."

Larson and Woods served in the same squad as PFC James S. Dickey. When the firing finally abated, he rushed over to the destroyed machine-gun position where other soldiers had already pulled out Larson. Woods was still in the hole and now unconscious. Dickey jumped in, applied a Carlisle bandage to the nasty leg injury, and then sprinted away to fetch a medic. He returned with an aidman, who went to work on Woods. Just then he heard someone yell, "Let's carry Larson to the first-aid station." Dickey helped transfer the mangled soldier to a litter and then hoisted one end of it. Sergeant Wenner grabbed the other end, and off they went. The aid station lay a half mile to the rear and a few short yards inside Belgium. The trek ended at a large dugout with slate shingles pilfered from nearby villages. The battalion surgeon, First Lieutenant James R. Swan of Pennsylvania, conducted business there. Outside his facility, bloody bandages lay in heaps, as did boots, web gear, and clothing scissored from patients. The place was a hive of activity. The doctor darted between casualties, clamping hemostats on torn arteries and blood vessels. Medical technicians pumped plasma into outstretched arms. The spectacle chimed with a symphony of groans, cries, and gurgles—animal expressions of agony and fright. Other men lay quiet, subdued by shock and morphine. Wenner wanted only to escape that theater of misery. "We just put the litter down and left," he said.

Back at Zimmerman's machine-gun position, Williams crawled outside when the enemy fire let up. He too had injuries that required medical attention. "The shelling stopped," he remembered, "and ten to fifteen minutes later medics began searching the area, and I heard one of them say these terrible words, 'Here's one—he's dead.'" The medic stood over the motionless body of Fred Zimmerman. Shrapnel had severed his right leg and femoral artery. No blood remained in his face, making it chalk white. Litter bearers subsequently hauled the dead man and his severed limb to the aid station.

The medic tended to Williams and pointed him in the direction of the aid station, which was the forward aid station of 2nd Battalion, 394th Infantry. Williams instead hiked along the log surface of a corduroy road, which was the battalion's main supply route and led to the battalion command post and rear aid station. He had been to that area before and knew the way. Once there, he boarded an ambulance and departed.

As Williams journeyed to the safety of a hospital, Rex Whitehead moved back to the front line from the Honsfeld rest center. (Marlene Dietrich's performance had been abruptly canceled.) After traveling by truck, he and several buddies walked up the corduroy road to a hut that served as the headquarters of their mortar platoon. Whitehead hollered in and announced their return. The reply: "Get the hell in here! Wanna get killed?" Just then an enemy shell slammed into the area, and everyone scrambled into the hut pronto. Whitehead soon learned about the artillery bombardment, which lasted ninety minutes that morning and claimed the lives of Larson and Zimmerman—men he knew. At first light, enemy foot troops had attacked in the wake of the bombardment and infiltrated into the forest to the left of the 2nd Battalion. German infantrymen also had assaulted the battalion head-on, but their efforts failed in the face of mortar, artillery, and automatic-weapons fire. The battalion held fast throughout the ensuing night.

The next morning, Whitehead surveyed some of the destruction inflicted the previous day. "I went out and looked around the area, and it was really torn up by shells—big jobs, which left a crater about five yards across." He finally returned to his mortar crew during the afternoon but stayed only a few minutes. The crew received orders to withdraw, as did the entire 2nd Battalion. The Germans had broken through to the left and right of the battalion and threatened it with encirclement. The vulnerable GIs abandoned their positions, including the forward aid station. Shellfire clawed at the withdrawing troops as they squirmed to escape the German vise. The retrograde movement ended more than a day later near Elsenborn, Belgium. Whitehead emerged as a survivor of the retreat. He then helped defend the bleak and barren ridgeline east of Elsenborn, which enemy forces assailed for over a month before an American counteroffensive chased them from Belgium permanently.

The misery and wreckage of those wintertime battles became a watershed for Whitehead, separating his life before from all that came after. He remarked in later years, "I was raised in Grace, Idaho, but grew up in Belgium during the Battle of the Bulge."

Chapter 9
THE LOST AID STATION

A messenger boy bicycled down West 21st Street in Ada, Oklahoma, and a cold drizzle fell as he peddled along the gravel road. He carried a leather satchel and wore a visored cap bearing the name of his employer, Western Union.

The kid had come from the company office in downtown Ada, and his satchel held a telegram received by wire at 3:20 P.M. (Central War Time) on January 4, 1945. Like most messengers, he had no opportunity to read the telegrams he delivered because each was confidential and sealed inside an envelope. But messengers could always tell when a telegram conveyed casualty information. Two blue stars stamped beside the recipient's address could be seen through a glassine window on the envelope.

The telegram received at 3:20 P.M. had two blue stars.

The boy parked his bicycle in front of the Fidler home, climbed the porch steps, and rapped on the front door. The noise brought Ewing Fidler's sister to the door. She and her younger brother, Chuck, were the only ones home. During the war years, the presence of a Western Union messenger at the door was always an anxious occurrence, like an unexpected telephone call in the middle of the night. Thelma Fidler signed for the telegram, tore open the envelope, and skimmed over the words pasted on the yellow sheet. Ewing was "missing" in Belgium.

The brief message concluded with an assurance: "If further details or other information are received, you will be promptly notified."

The following day, a similar telegram reached Rochelle, Illinois, hometown of Stanley Larson. The message went to his mother, who worked at Hayes Drugstore and lived alone in an apartment above the store. Stanley's boyhood friend Lyle Kunde happened to be in Rochelle that day on furlough from a navy flight school where he was training to become a marine corps aviator. Lyle answered a knock at the front door of his parent's home, and he found Stanley's mother standing there.

"She walked in the door," Lyle remembered. "We hugged, and she showed me the telegram, which read, 'The Secretary of War desires me to express his deep regret that your son, Private First Class Stanley E. Larson, has been reported missing.' I attempted to console her, but I think she probably consoled me as much as I did her."

No telegram had yet reached Groveport, Ohio, when Fred Zimmerman's wife, Martha Jane, and his younger brother crossed paths on a city sidewalk in January 1945.

"We were outside my parents' home," Bill Zimmerman remembered. "Martha Jane had just gotten the mail that day, and she said, 'Huh, this is kind of unusual. I got one of my own letters back, one that I sent Fred.' She took a second look at the envelope, and said, 'This thing's marked Missing in Action.' I'll never forget the astonished look on her face. We had received no prior notification."

Fred's wife finally received a telegram on January 22, and it verified what little she already knew. Uncertainty about his fate lingered until February 9 when a second telegram arrived. It conveyed the worst possible news about her husband: "Correct report now received states he was killed in action sixteen December in Belgium."

Bill Zimmerman recalled how he and his parents learned about the second telegram. "Martha Jane lived across the street from us, and she, or one of her parents, called my sister Esta in Columbus. Her husband subsequently phoned our home. I somehow ended up talking with him, and he said, 'I'm afraid Fred's not coming home.'"

After the call, Esta and her husband hurried to Groveport. She found a scene of despair at her parent's house. "My brother Bill took it the hardest, at least outwardly. He became so upset that my mother had to summon our family doctor who administered a sedative."

Stanley Larson's mother also received a second telegram that day. Three words hammered her heart: "killed in action."

In Oklahoma, the family of Ewing Fidler waited for word regarding his fate. They remained in suspense until March 4 when a belated death notice arrived via Western Union. The delay resulted because military authorities had difficulty locating an officer who had witnessed Ewing's death or had seen his body.

The officer who corroborated Ewing's death was his platoon leader, William Huttinger. The day Ewing died, a shell burst slammed the lieutenant to the ground and left him punch drunk and "white as a sheet" according to one witness. Medics evacuated him for "combat exhaustion." Paperwork regarding the dead soldier caught up with Huttinger in a Paris hospital, and he verified the date and place of death. He eventually wrote to Ewing's parents and furnished them with details beyond what little the army had provided, but he had no information about the location of their son's grave.

Ewing's mother attempted to gain clarification by writing to the army's Quartermaster General: "We have tried to locate his grave, to learn whether his body has been removed to an American military cemetery, but at this date, have not been able to do so. If you can help in any way, we will be so grateful."

She received a disappointing response: "It is with deep regret that you are advised that, up to the present time, information pertaining to the burial of the remains of your son has not been received in this office. Upon receipt of information you will be advised."

The families of Larson and Zimmerman also wrote letters and received similar responses. The army finally closed all three cases in 1951 and deemed each soldier's remains "nonrecoverable." The American Battle Monuments Commission later memorialized all three on the Tablets of the Missing at the Ardennes American Cemetery in Belgium. The names engraved on those granite slabs represented a last, sad roll call of missing servicemen.

Each family also erected a cenotaph—a monument honoring a person buried elsewhere. Fidler's parents purchased a headstone and placed it over an empty grave at Rosedale Cemetery in Ada, Oklahoma. The inscription read:

IN MEMORY OF
EWING E. FIDLER
JUNE 1, 1925
DECEMBER 16, 1944
KILLED IN ACTION
BATTLE OF THE BULGE

Larson's father installed a similar headstone above an empty grave at Lawnridge Cemetery in Rochelle, Illinois. Zimmerman's parents did the same in Ohio.

REX WHITEHEAD DEPARTED the 99th Infantry Division during the summer of 1945 and returned to the United States as a member of the 4th Infantry Division. Years later he described his arrival stateside. "The thing I remember best was that when we sailed up the Hudson River from New York harbor, all the tall buildings had signs reading, 'Welcome Home—Well Done.' Of course that did, and still does, remind me of the ones who really paid the price and did not return."

That 4th Division had orders to the Pacific, but first Whitehead obtained a thirty-day furlough and caught a train back to Idaho. During his visit home, two atomic bombs fell on Japan, and the war soon ended. The 4th remained in the States, and Whitehead stayed on with the division as a courts-martial clerk until January 1946, when he became a civilian again. "The happiest day of my life—nothing else is even a close second—was the day I got my discharge," he later recalled.

Whitehead's discharge certificate snapped a great shackle around his life. He returned to Idaho and resumed his long-interrupted civilian life. The erstwhile infantryman immediately enrolled in spring-quarter classes at Utah State University.

One day before school started, he traveled with his father to Utah on business. They stopped in Salt Lake City and visited a local bank where the elder Whitehead met with a colleague. Whitehead recalled what happened next:

"After the visit, we walked north across an intersection on Main Street and were halfway across the street when a driver hit his brakes, and there was a screech. I grabbed my dad, and I yelled as I dragged him to the pavement. I can't remember what I said, if anything, but I hope Dad knew what I was doing. I had not forgotten the sound of an 88 shell."

Whitehead found it difficult to release the past. At Utah State University, all his male friends were veterans too, and they often compared experiences and wrote about them for class assignments. Combat was a subject almost everyone understood, everyone except the female students. One of them, Paully Cardon, began dating Whitehead after meeting him at a fraternity party. The two often studied together at the library, and one evening they sat at a table with several other couples. Whitehead later recalled what transpired after a veteran at the table began reading aloud from a paper he had written about the war:

"One girl said she would scream if she heard or read another theme written by a veteran about his service experiences. All of the girls gave their endorsement, and a heated debate followed. I did some fast math and told them we knew little else, for in my case, I had just spent the most recent 15 percent of my life in the army. Besides that, all I could relate were childhood and high school experiences. The girls considered either of those preferable to war stories. The discussion continued later between Paully and myself, and I told her if she felt that way, and she did, I just wouldn't mention the army or the war again."

In April 1947, Whitehead and Paully Cardon married. Neither graduated from Utah State, instead choosing to settle in Idaho, where he went into business with his father. Whitehead worked at the bank for over twenty years, and thereafter spent most of his time managing the cheese and insurance businesses. Outside of work, he and his wife raised three daughters and relocated to nearby Logan, Utah. All the while he kept quiet about his army experiences.

He remained tightlipped about the war until age fifty-six, by which time his wife no longer viewed his military service as an unmentionable subject. Decades of silence had softened her attitude. In 1981 the couple traveled to England and Belgium, and they stayed in the Bulge area for a week. That visit sparked something in the aging veteran. He realized that his knowledge of the battle extended no further than his own experiences, and he wanted to learn more. After returning home he wrote to Charles B. MacDonald. The two men corresponded, and Whitehead mentioned that he planned to visit Belgium again. MacDonald recommended Will Cavanagh as a battlefield guide.

Whitehead contacted the young Briton, and they met in Belgium during 1984 and cemented a friendship. Whitehead returned to Belgium in 1986, 1988, and 1989. During the last of those visits, Cavanagh introduced him to Seel and Speder. Two more friendships formed.

Besides making new friends and learning more about Bulge history, Whitehead became a frequent contributor to the official newspaper of the 99th Division Association. He wrote articles about the subject he knew best, his own experiences. He also read each edition of the *Checkerboard*, front to back. While perusing the March 1990 issue, he spotted the bulletin about missing soldiers killed during the Bulge. Whitehead instantly recognized the names Stanley Larson and Fred Zimmerman. He also recognized the name Wilmer Smith, a combat medic from Ohio.

W. B. Williams, a retired college professor living in Nashville, also recognized the name Fred Zimmerman. The former professor wrote a letter to Dick Byers recounting the circumstances of Zimmerman's death. Byers also received a letter from Jerome G. Nelson of Wisconsin, describing the death of Ewing Fidler. "It is hard for me to understand why he would be missing," Nelson wrote. "Time, perhaps, did not allow for his evacuation and consequently, he will be forever MIA." Another 99th veteran responded to the bulletin by telephoning the *Checkerboard*'s editor, Bill Meyer. The caller, Gray B. Smeltzer of Tennessee, served as a medic with Company H, 394th Infantry. He reported that nobody removed Wilmer Smith's body from the spot where died. Smeltzer also reported that he last saw Zimmerman's body at a forward aid station.

Whitehead, Williams, and Smeltzer all remembered Fred Zimmerman, but the name also meant something to Seel and Speder. The Belgians knew of a relic hunter who years earlier had recovered six dog tags belonging to Zimmerman.

JEAN-PIERRE DESAUCY OFTEN USED his metal detector to find battlefield artifacts, including dog tags, which he collected for his father. Sometime in 1982 the young Belgian and a group of friends searched a wooded area near the crumbling foundation of a torn-down hunting lodge. The long-vanished building served as the command post for the 2nd Battalion, 394th Infantry until the second day of the Bulge, but Desaucy knew nothing of that history. Like most relic hunters, he concerned himself only with the objects he retrieved from the soil. About forty meters from the foundation, he unearthed six identification tags strung together on a long bead-link chain. The tags all belonged to one soldier, Frederick F. Zimmerman.

Desaucy showed his newfound treasure to the other people with him that day, and one of them immediately offered to purchase the artifacts. Albert Franssen tendered one thousand Belgian francs (about twenty dollars), and Desaucy accepted. One year later, photographs of three of the tags appeared in a French-language publication on American dog tags. The trio represented different dog-tag variations issued prior to the spring of 1944. One of them gave the name and address of Zimmerman's next of kin. News of the dog tags eventually reached Dick Byers and me in 1990, prior to the annual reunion of the 99th Division Association.

That year the 99th held its reunion in Louisville, Kentucky, and it was there that I met Rex and Paully Whitehead for the first time. They invited me to supper one evening at the restaurant on top of the downtown hotel where the reunion took place. Rex ordered a round of martinis, and we chatted about my background and how I became interested in World War II. By the time our meals arrived, the conversation had turned to Larson, Zimmerman, and Wilmer Smith, whom Rex referred to as Smitty the medic. I told Rex about the six dog tags, and that I could probably use the next-of-kin information to locate the Zimmerman family. He promised to research the deaths of the three soldiers and to begin that detective work as soon as he got home. (Dick Byers handled all research regarding Ewing Fidler.)

Whitehead telephoned and corresponded with dozens of veterans, including W. B. Williams and Gray Smeltzer. One former machine gunner, James "Sam" Dickey, recorded his story on an audiotape and mailed it to Whitehead. The Utah resident tried to corroborate each man's story with other eyewitness testimony and wartime documents. He struggled to reconcile contradictory information and to weed out inaccurate material. He learned firsthand that no battle ever appeared the same to any two people. History rarely takes a single course, a simple narrative of one event after another. Whitehead commented to me, "Sometimes I think I should go back to golf that I quit three years ago and forget the past, but then it sure as hell is interesting and a challenge." After two months of work, he managed to knit the facts into a tapestry that made sense. He produced a four-page report and mailed it to Dick Byers and me. The document included a statement from Dickey, who claimed to have helped carry Larson's body to the forward aid station of the 2nd Battalion, 394th. Smeltzer went on the record as having seen Zimmerman's body at the same place. The report also included a hand-drawn map by Smeltzer, and it showed the location of the forward aid station. (The rear aid station lay adjacent to the hunting lodge, which served as battalion headquarters.) I used computer software to enhance Smeltzer's map, and sent copies of the finished product to Byers, Whitehead, and our Belgian colleagues.

I also conducted genealogical research regarding Fred Zimmerman. My hunt for his family began at the library of the Ohio Historical Society, which was a short drive from where I lived in Columbus. Zimmerman's hometown, Groveport, lay several minutes south of the city. At the library, I pored over microfilm of the *Columbus Dispatch* for the months of January and February 1945, and I easily found an obituary for Zimmerman. It included a grainy photograph and details about his life and family. I gleaned more information from the 1945 city directory for Columbus, and from probate court records, where I found a marriage license application for his oldest sister, Esta.

My findings led me to Groveport in March 1991, where a woman from the local historical society directed me to an auto-parts store on Main Street. There I encountered Wesley Welch, a clean-shaven man in his early thirties who stood behind the cash register. I approached and asked if he knew the name Fred Zimmerman. "That was my uncle," he said. I explained my reason for asking, and the two of us conversed as he waited on customers. He grabbed a scrap of paper and wrote down my name, address, and telephone number. He promised to pass them along to his aunt Esta, who lived in retirement at Buckeye Lake, Ohio.

Esta eventually telephoned me, and we spoke at length about her brother. I explained the circumstances of his death, and she thanked me for the information I shared. The army had provided her family with no details. She then expressed amazement that anyone would dream of searching for his grave after so many years. I replied that my colleagues and I would make every effort. She told me about her surviving brother, Bill, and she thought he would like to speak with me. Bill lived near Kansas City, and Esta said she would give him my phone number. Before our conversation ended, I inquired if she had any wartime photographs of Fred. She said, "I have pictures, V-mail letters, and all the telegrams we received. You're welcome to borrow them if you like." I replied yes, and Esta agreed to dig out everything and send it to me.

Less than a month later, a package arrived in the mail. It contained all the mementoes Esta promised. She enclosed a handwritten note thanking me for my research efforts and those of my colleagues. "You will never know how much this has all meant to us."

About the time Esta's package arrived, I received a call from Bill Zimmerman. We talked for nearly an hour, and he told me about his service as an Ohio Air National Guard officer and that he spent a year on active duty in France during the Berlin Wall crisis. While overseas he and his family visited the Ardennes American Cemetery and saw Fred's name on the Tablets of the Missing. Bill mentioned that his job entailed extensive travel, and that he would look me up the next time his work brought him to Ohio.

Besides tracking down the Zimmerman family, I initiated a search for the family of Stanley Larson. I requested help from 99th Division veteran Roger Foehringer and his son Roger Jr. They lived in northern Illinois near Larson's hometown, and they had little difficulty finding the family. Older brother Leon Larson loaned us an eight-by-ten portrait of Stanley wearing cotton khakis and a garrison cap. Leon also let us borrow newspaper articles about his brother, and those yellowed clippings painted a picture of an extraordinary young man, a champion athlete who excelled in academics.

While I concerned myself with the families, Byers and Whitehead jetted to Belgium in March 1991, hoping to find the aid station on Smeltzer's map. Seel and Speder aided the search, as did Will Cavanagh. The night before each day of "operations," Byers planned an itinerary and sometimes a timetable. Whitehead and the others razzed Dick about his penchant for planning, but as Whitehead commented, "You need somebody like that if you're going to get anything done." The Belgian weather obliged with day after day of sunshine and mild temperatures. Speder chauffeured the two veterans in his 1944 Ford GPW, and they tooled around the terrain once occupied by Whitehead's battalion. The meadows and forests no longer resembled the grim landscape he remembered from the Bulge, but Whitehead nevertheless recognized two features depicted on Smeltzer's map: Corduroy Road and California Highway.

Near the junction of the two roads, Seel and Speder pointed out the location of a cabin that had been an aid station at some point. Nothing remained of the structure except mounds of earth that once reinforced its log walls. Relic hunters had recovered loads of American medical debris at that spot and had dubbed it the *hôpital*, or hospital. The discoveries included a plasma bottle that contained a human eye preserved in formaldehyde. Besides medical items, dog tags and other identification media had come from there, but none of the artifacts related to 99th Division soldiers. The aid station may have dated to February 1945 when troops of the 82nd Airborne Division occupied the area along with troops of the 69th Infantry Division. Equally significant, the aid station was north of Corduroy Road and thus different from the one on Smeltzer's map, which was south of the road. Seel and Speder went to work south of the road and swept over portions of the forest floor with their metal detectors. Whitehead followed them, as did Byers and Cavanagh. The map proved too vague to pinpoint Smeltzer's aid station, and no medical material emerged. Despite that shortcoming, Whitehead relished the search, as well as the oil smell and *put-put-put* sound of Speder's jeep.

He returned to Utah, bounced back from a cold he caught overseas, and wrote a thank-you letter to his Belgian hosts: "The highlight for this old dogface was driving up Corduroy Road in an honest-to-God army jeep with memories flowing back of when I did the same as a scared-shitless nineteen-year-old." Whitehead also commented, "After all the walking in the woods, I expected and hoped I had dropped a few pounds. I gained five! At least that indicates how much I ate and enjoyed your Belgian bread, plus the fine beer."

Whitehead continued his research, telephoning more veterans, including Stanley Larson's squad leader. "I talked to Warren Wenner," Whitehead told me in a letter. "He was in H Company and helped carry Larson back to the aid station." Wenner corroborated Sam Dickey's earlier assertion about the disposition of Larson's body.

According to eyewitness testimony, the bodies of Larson and Zimmerman made it to the aid station, but what about Ewing Fidler? Dick Byers received several letters regarding Fidler's death, but none of them mentioned the aid station. I eventually interviewed Angelo J.

Spinato, who served in Fidler's company, and he remembered viewing the dead soldier's body at the company command post. Spinato said, "I recall seeing his body myself, firsthand, at the company CP. I saw him on a stretcher. We probably left the body behind because we couldn't carry it due to the terrain. The only things I carried were my rifle to fight with, whatever mess gear I had, and my coat to keep warm. There was no way we could have carried a body."

By some accounts, the company command post stood adjacent to the aid station, but Spinato remembered no medical post nearby. Whitehead then found a battalion headquarters veteran who had a snapshot of the aid station. The photo showed a roofed dugout shrouded by snow and situated in a spruce forest. The caption on the back of the image gave no indication whether it depicted the rear aid station or the forward one, but the photo dated to the time period before the Bulge. The same veteran also had a snapshot of a dugout entrance, and he thought it might be the aid station, but the photo had no caption on its reverse side.

Whitehead and I needed more information.

During the spring of 1992, he requested the IDPFs for Fidler, Larson, and Zimmerman. The documents arrived two months later but made no mention of the aid station. Yet one of the files held a report that contained an intriguing statement: "Unknown X-287, United States Military Cemetery, Henri-Chapelle, has been associated with Sgt. Zimmerman, but positive identification could not be made."

Had the army found Zimmerman's remains decades earlier? The answer had to wait. The summer of 1992 brought the X-9476 case, and I suddenly became embroiled in research relating to it. Despite the resulting workload, I made time for a brief diversion when I received an unexpected phone call.

Bill Zimmerman called me in August and said he would be attending the Ohio State Fair on business. His employer, Encyclopaedia Britannica, had a booth at that seventeen-day extravaganza. I lived a short drive from the fairgrounds, and we agreed to meet. Bill stopped by my apartment one afternoon, and we met face-to-face for the first time. He was sixty-two years old, the same age as my father. I showed Bill my case file pertaining to his brother, and he studied it carefully. I pointed out the report concerning X-287, and I explained that Fred might already be at a military cemetery in Belgium. Bill also had news for me. He and his wife had recently traveled to Nashville and rendezvoused with W. B. Williams. Bill interviewed him and used a portable cassette recorder. I asked Bill to duplicate the tape for me, and he said he could do better. He would transcribe the interview and send me a copy. We continued our conversation and eventually adjourned to a nearby Chinese restaurant. After supper, we parted company, and Bill asked me to keep him informed when I learned more about X-287.

Once my workload declined, I obtained the IDPF for X-287, and I learned the remains consisted of eleven bone fragments: one section of left tibia, three rib-cage pieces, three small hand bones, and four arm-bone fragments. The burial report indicated the decedent died after being struck by an artillery shell. Zimmerman died from artillery fire but not a direct hit, although a postmortem hit was possible. The report also gave a grid coordinate for the location where a collection team recovered X-287 in January 1945. I opened my file cabinet and pulled out a wartime map. The coordinate lay about eleven kilometers from the spot where Zimmerman died, and the coordinate was outside the 99th Division area of operations. I recognized the recovery site as being in the zone where the 26th Infantry Regiment (1st Infantry Division) fought during the Bulge.

The burial report showed that Graves Registration troops at Henri-Chapelle interred X-287 beside X-286. The two nameless casualties came from the same area, but army technicians eventually identified the latter as Private Harold P. Lau of the 26th Infantry. He died on December 21, 1944, during a hellish clash with the 12.SS-Panzer-Division. I determined that two members of Lau's unit, who also died in that fight, were still among the missing: Staff Sergeant William W. Allen and Sergeant Mitchell T. Yowell. Those casualties had an undeniable link to X-287; however, the army never made that connection. Not that it would have made a difference. Given the fragmented and incomplete nature of the remains, such a connection would have meant little in the days before DNA analysis.

I concluded that X-287 had no correlation with Zimmerman. Perhaps his remains abided at or near the aid-station site, wherever that was. Rex Whitehead aimed to solve the mystery, and he returned to Belgium in October 1992. He motored around for two days in a rental car and drove along Bundesstraße 265, a two-lane road that traced the Belgian-German border. American soldiers knew it as California

Highway during the war. Whitehead stopped on the Belgian side of the asphalt at a border-crossing gate where Corduroy Road intersected California Highway. A padlock held the gate closed, so Whitehead ventured into the forest on foot and threaded his way between spruce trees. He soon encountered a rectangular depression big enough to have been a dugout, and it lay south of Corduroy Road. Had he found the lost aid station? And was a grave site nearby? Whitehead felt a surge of confidence. His discovery jibed with Smeltzer's map.

Whitehead also took time that October day to find the area where his friend Wilmer Smith died. According to Smeltzer's map, the approximate spot was on the German side of California Highway and near a section of dragon's teeth, those concrete antitank obstacles built by Hitler to impede attacking tanks and other vehicles. Whitehead inspected the teeth, now battered by fifty years of history and ensconced among trees. Many of the teeth displayed a thick coat of velvety moss. Whitehead snapped a few photographs and wondered if Smitty the medic rested nearby in an unmarked grave.

After two days of clear weather, rain moved in and Whitehead quit tramping around the forest alone. Meanwhile, the hotel where he stayed had become temporary headquarters for Vern Swanson, Byron Whitmarsh, and Rudy Zehnder. The three came to Belgium to hunt for graves on Hill 627. Dick Byers also joined the group, as did Seel, Speder, and Cavanagh. At the hotel, Whitehead told the two Belgians about the rectangular depression he found. They reacted with surprise. Neither of them recalled seeing it, and Speder promised to investigate. Whitehead hoped to return to the spot with them, but a cold and fever overcame him, and he spent two days bedridden. He eventually summoned enough strength to drive to Brussels. He grabbed a hotel room for the night, boarded a flight the next day, and came home a week earlier than planned. Weeks passed before he felt well enough to write me and describe his trip.

Whitehead pinned high hopes on the rectangular depression, but Seel and Speder squelched those hopes when they reported that no grave existed there, nor any debris associated with an aid station. Fidler, Larson, and Zimmerman remained lost in history's shadow, as did Smitty the medic.

Around that time, Whitehead began to wonder if he was spending too much time on World War II and not enough on family matters. He debated his continued involvement with the 99th Division Association. He belonged to its Archives Committee and had undertaken numerous research and writing projects, including the search for missing servicemen. But now Whitehead's desire to participate seemed near an end, like the sand running out of an hourglass.

Several months passed, and I received a typewritten letter from him. Much of it dealt with the 99th Association. "I feel overwhelmed with it, that it has taken a more important position in my present life than I want it to," he wrote. "I am anxious to get away for a year and then decide if I miss it or not. However, there will still be communication with friends, and between friends, but not as part of the association. I am a bad organization man—always have been—perhaps a trait I picked up in the army. I would rather work and think alone. You can be sure you will still hear from me, and I will always be interested in your fine work, for I have valued your friendship and will continue to do so."

Whitehead resigned from the Archives Committee, quit attending 99th Division reunions, and correspondence from him slowed to an occasional note. He did however host Speder and his wife when they visited Utah following a 99th reunion in Denver. Whitehead also kept track of happenings in Belgium, especially in the spring of 1994 when Stanley Larson's brother, sister, and their families visited the Bulge area. Speder and Cavanagh gave the group a tour of the sector where Stanley died. One family member recorded the event on videotape, and several others scrounged artifacts from the forest floor. The group also saw Stanley's name on the Tablets of the Missing at the Ardennes American Cemetery and had front-row seats for the annual Memorial Day commemoration at the cemetery.

More than a year later, Whitehead ended his hiatus and showed up at the Pittsburgh Hilton to attend the forty-sixth annual reunion. He kept a low profile and stayed for only part of the reunion, but he spoke with excitement about his intention to revisit Europe and resume search efforts, hopefully in 1996. His last morning at the reunion, Seel, Speder, Cavanagh, and I joined him for breakfast, and afterward we escorted him to an airport shuttle bus.

Our friend and colleague never returned to Europe. Within months his health crashed, and he learned that he had emphysema. I had never seen him with a cigar or cigarette and wondered how he contracted the

(Top) September 27, 1988: Seel and Speder with artifacts recovered from
Alphonse Sito's grave (J.P. Speder); (Middle) M1 Rifle from Hill 627; (Bottom)
June 24, 2002: Ruins of concrete bunker on Hill 627.

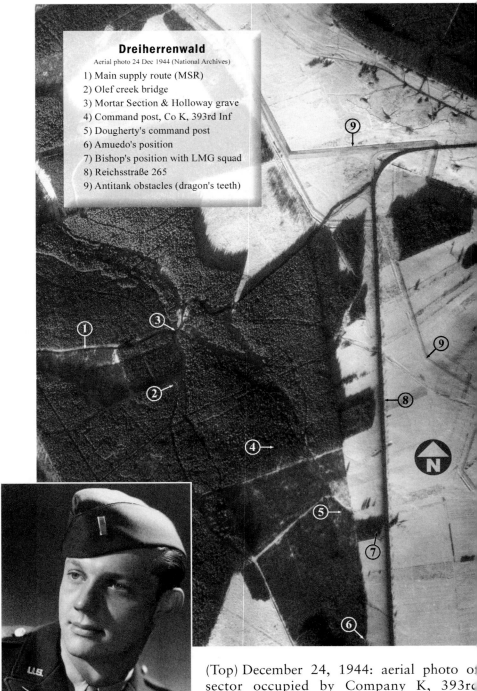

Dreiherrenwald

Aerial photo 24 Dec 1944 (National Archives)

1) Main supply route (MSR)
2) Olef creek bridge
3) Mortar Section & Holloway grave
4) Command post, Co K, 393rd Inf
5) Dougherty's command post
6) Amuedo's position
7) Bishop's position with LMG squad
8) Reichsstraße 265
9) Antitank obstacles (dragon's teeth)

(Top) December 24, 1944: aerial photo of sector occupied by Company K, 393rd Infantry (National Archives); (Left) Lonnie O Holloway Jr., Company K, 393rd Infantry (Sarah Holland).

Top) November 10, 1990: Holloway's dog tags emerge (JL Seel); (Middle)
Earnest E. Brown, Company B, 394th Infantry (Paul Brown); (Bottom)
July 1944: Maralyn Brennan and Stanley "Mike" Larson at his sister's farm
Mary Larson).

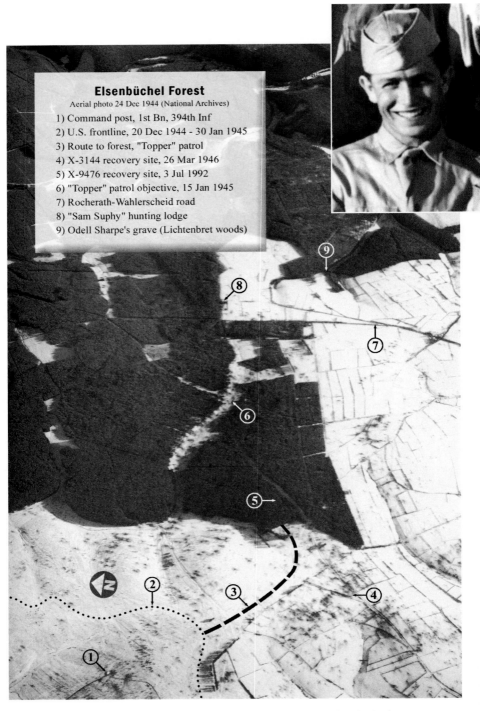

Elsenbüchel Forest
Aerial photo 24 Dec 1944 (National Archives)

1) Command post, 1st Bn, 394th Inf
2) U.S. frontline, 20 Dec 1944 - 30 Jan 1945
3) Route to forest, "Topper" patrol
4) X-3144 recovery site, 26 Mar 1946
5) X-9476 recovery site, 3 Jul 1992
6) "Topper" patrol objective, 15 Jan 1945
7) Rocherath-Wahlerscheid road
8) "Sam Suphy" hunting lodge
9) Odell Sharpe's grave (Lichtenbret woods)

(Top) December 24, 1944: aerial photo of Elsenbüchel forest (Nationa
Archives); (Right) Odell Sharpe, Company H, 393rd Infantry (Mary Miller)

(Top row, left to right) Beckwith, Kokotovich and Read; (bottom row, left to right) Fidler, Larson and Zimmerman; (Middle) Rex Whitehead's recovered pen; (Bottom left) John T. Puckett, Company B, 394th Infantry. Photo taken in summer 1944 while serving with Company F, 272nd Infantr. (Joann Bowman); (Bottom right) Alvin Rex Whitehead, Company H, 394th Infantry. Photo taken at Arkansas State University while serving with Army Specialized Training Program (Rex Whitehead).

Hill 627

Aerial photo 25 Dec 1944 (National Archives)

1) American attack route 14 Dec 1944
2) Gravesite per Woolf map
3) Triangular outcropping of trees
4) Gravesite discovered 17 Apr 2001
5) Command post, Co C, 395th Inf
6) Concrete bunker captured 14 Dec 1944
7) Spruce-tree nursery

(Top right) April 10, 1992: GI artifacts found in American foxhole on Hill 627.
The mess kit on the left had a name engraved: "Billy Worley Jr." (J.L. Seel)
(Left) December 25, 1944: aerial photo of Hill 627 (National Archives).

Top left) Vernon E. Swanson, Company C, 395th Infantry. Postwar photo
Vern Swanson); (Top right) June 24, 2002: Swanson on Hill 627; (Bottom)
March 1991: Dick Byers and Rex Whitehead at dragon's teeth (J.P. Speder).

(Top left) Mary Maisel with her brother's wedding ring; (Top right) June 18 2005: Joann Bowman places bronze rosette (inset) beside her brother's name or Tablets of the Missing; (Bottom) June 22, 2002: Zimmerman's casket on catafalque at Henri-Chapelle.

disease. He joked that he owed his difficulties to having inhaled sooty smoke from gasoline-filled bottles that he and his comrades used for heat and light in their foxholes. He thought that sounded more romantic than saying he had smoked Camels for twenty years.

Despite fatigue, chronic coughing, and shortness of breath, Whitehead continued typing occasional letters, and he eventually became e-mail savvy. One winter day in early 2001, he told me about a recent telephone conversation he had had with our friend and teammate Dick Byers, now fading away in a nursing home:

"Dick could only whisper and answer in one- or two-word expressions. It broke my heart. After mentioning a few names, yours included, I signed off with, 'I value our friendship, Dick' and he responded, 'It is mutual.'"

Whitehead then added, "Every time the phone rings, I expect it to be a call about his death." Whitehead closed his e-mail by wishing me well and harkening back to better times. "My life is slow, for my health is lousy, but find myself going back to fine memories of the MIA Project."

Byers passed away less than a month later, and I wondered how much more time remained for Whitehead.

TETHERED TO AN OXYGEN MACHINE, Whitehead sat at his computer on April 17, 2001, and opened an e-mail he received that day. The message came from Jean-Philippe Speder, and it delivered a bombshell. The diggers had found the graves of Beckwith, Kokotovich, and Read. Thrilled by the almost unbelievable news, Whitehead immediately telephoned Swanson, Whitmarsh, and me. After long conversations with each of us, Whitehead returned to his computer and composed a response to the e-mail:

"You have caused a lot of excitement in our little world today with your findings, and we salute you. I called Whit, and for a man who does not show a lot of emotion, he was in disbelief. He stated that he had given up on ever finding them, so a fitting end for him. . . . Really don't know how to explain how I feel about this happening but damned proud that I am associated in any way with men such as you. You just do not give up, and I hope your satisfaction justifies all of your efforts. Dick Byers would know just the right thing to say. Wish he were still with us."

During the days that followed, Whitehead became engrossed in the recovery operation and its aftermath. "Find myself waiting for another e-mail with more details, as if it were an all-important ball game or something." He wished he could return to Belgium and resume the quest he began more than a decade earlier. "I feel like taking off for California Highway and searching for the 2/394 guys."

He was not alone in thinking about the missing soldiers from his battalion.

Marc Marique took an interest in them. Spurred on by the Hill 627 success, he visited Seel on May 24, 2001 and decided to pick up where Whitehead left off. The two Belgians discussed Whitehead's research, and they also discussed the six Zimmerman dog tags found in 1982. Seel listened as Marique said that during the 1980s he attended a militaria show and saw a dog tag for sale that had the surname Larson on it. Marique no longer recalled the first name, but he thought it might have been Stanley. There was also another tag to consider. It bore the name Ewing Fidler and belonged to a collector named Johnny Esch, who lived in Malmédy, Belgium. Unfortunately nobody recorded the location of its discovery, which rendered the artifact useless as a clue to the location of the grave site. Only Smeltzer's map had value, and Whitehead was the person who originally obtained it. Marique departed Seel's home with the map as well as the entire Zimmerman file.

The following day, he drove to the area shown on the map and trekked into the woods with his metal detector. He selected a starting point and searched outward in ever-widening circles. After three hours, he worked his way into a stand of spruce trees near the highway that ran along the Belgian-German border. He found a deteriorating hole about twelve feet long and eight feet wide. It seemed to be the foundation of a dugout. Marique's detector went berserk near the hole. He rooted around and found rusty nails, pieces of tin containers, and eight morphine syrettes. Remnants of an aid station? He dropped his detector and shoveled away. More artifacts came to light, including a thermometer case. Amid one scoop of dirt, a corroded brass dog tag surfaced. It had a short bead-link chain looped through its eyelet.

Anxious to report the possible discovery of an aid station, Marique grabbed his cell phone and rang Seel, who was in his car driving home from work. As the two spoke, Seel asked whose name was on the dog tag. Marique had not yet picked up the artifact. Seel jokingly said,

"Check it. This one may belong to Fred Zimmerman."

Marique lifted the tag from the dirt.

"I won't repeat the word he shouted," Seel later recalled. Marique then read the name aloud—"Zimmerman, Frederick F."

That electrifying development triggered plans to scour the entire area.

Speder sent Whitehead and me an e-mail that contained an insightful observation about the tag. During World War II the U.S. Army altered its regulation governing the proper way to emboss identification tags. A total of four changes took place during the war, resulting in four types of tags, each one superceding its predecessor and specific to a particular time period. The final variant, authorized in March 1944, was the most current format in use when the 99th Division embarked for Europe. Speder observed that Sito, Holloway, Beckwith, Kokotovich, and Read all wore that final variant around their necks. The six Zimmerman tags unearthed in 1982 were earlier types. The one discovered by Marique was a final variant, but it was a single tag, and such items always came in pairs. Where was its twin? Around Zimmerman's neck?

Speder expressed cautious hope that an answer was near.

On Friday, June 1, 2001, one week after finding the dog tag, Marique returned to the exact location of its discovery and began excavating a sizable hole about fifteen feet away. Seel and Speder accompanied him and worked nearby in a two-man foxhole. By coincidence, that day happened to be Ewing Fidler's birth date. The teenager from Oklahoma would have been seventy-six years old.

The trio began digging at 12:50 P.M. Seel and Speder almost immediately began removing bedsprings and GI telephone wire from their hole. The two men soon decided to refill the hole after reaching its bottom and finding nothing significant. They started work in another foxhole of identical size.

Just then, Marique called out. "Hey, guys, come see. I have a snow boot." Without another word, Marique brushed away more soil. Bones!

He had found the grave of an American soldier, at least judging by the arctic overshoe and hunks of clothing that clung to the bones.

Speder hustled home to fetch his camera. Meanwhile, Marique and Seel continued digging. To their surprise, beside the snow boot a skull emerged. Its empty eye sockets stared outward, and its jaw hung open in a silent scream. Two soldiers rested in the grave. Speder learned of the second discovery when his cell phone rang as he motored home. He mashed the accelerator pedal of his Ford Fiesta and raced along village streets like a Grand Prix driver. At home he snatched his 35-mm camera along with a range of excavation tools including picks, trowels, brushes, plastic bags, and a sifting screen. He also called Jean-Luc Menestrey, who was at work and unable to get away for several more hours. While zooming back to the forest, Speder stopped briefly at the home of forest ranger Erich Hönen and left word of the discovery.

By the time Speder returned, Marique and Seel had come upon the remains of a third soldier. The diggers surmised that German troops had dumped the three bodies in the hole. Two of the dead men lay side by side. The third man rested on top of the others. The heap of bodies made excavating the grave a complicated undertaking. "In the center of the hole, we had a hodgepodge of bones," Speder recalled, "and we had to work with extreme care to avoid mixing them." However, some of the bones had already become commingled over the decades, but the Belgians knew the U.S. Army had forensic anthropologists who specialized in "segregating" the remains of more than one person.

The diggers first exhumed the remains of the soldier on top, the man whose overshoe heralded the discovery. The overshoe contained a size 10D service shoe along with a shell fragment about half the length of a railroad spike. It had pierced both pieces of footwear and its jagged tip protruded from the heel of the overshoe. All the diggers winced when they saw it. Inanimate objects sometimes spoke with incredible power. Shrapnel had obliterated a long section of the man's right leg, severing the foot and overshoe. The other leg remained intact, although minus footwear, which a needy German soldier probably swiped. The dead man wore a wool shirt, M43 field jacket, and a wool overcoat with plastic buttons. His jacket still displayed rank insignia—three chevrons on each sleeve. That meant the soldier probably was Sergeant Fred Zimmerman, even though no dog tag remained around his neck. His pockets held a toothbrush, a plastic comb, a stainless-steel knife and fork, unfired .30-caliber cartridges, and one .45-caliber cartridge. The diggers also found an M3 trench knife in its scabbard, but it was impossible to determine which one of the decedents had owned the weapon.

After removing Zimmerman from the grave, the Belgians began exhuming one of the soldiers beneath him. That particular man had no shoes and no dog tags or other identification. He wore only a wool shirt, wool trousers, and a knit sweater—all GI issue. His pockets contained two U.S. pennies, two Belgian coins, and seven British coins. One of the diggers found a belt buckle at his waist. Speder suspected the unidentified man was Ewing Fidler, although Wilmer Smith was a possibility, but eyewitness testimony indicated that no one moved his body to the aid station.

Jean-Luc Menestrey eventually joined his friends at the grave site, as did forest ranger Hönen, who surveyed the recovery operation. Work dragged on until dark, at which time the team decided to quit for the day. Only one soldier remained in the grave. Hönen took the recovered remains to his home for safekeeping.

That night, Speder e-mailed news of the discovery to Rex Whitehead, Vern Swanson, Byron Whitmarsh, and me. The message left us stunned, almost disbelieving. Whitehead and I spoke that night, and we marveled at the location of the grave. Relic hunters had searched that area for more than two decades, but the three soldiers had gone undetected.

The next day, under a steady rain, all four diggers converged on the scene at 10:00 A.M. Clad in camouflaged clothing, the diggers roofed the site by stretching a tarpaulin across a timber frame lashed to several tree trunks. Seel and Menestrey then climbed into the pit and began exhuming the third soldier. The other two diggers stayed topside and spread a green-plastic sheet on the forest floor. That became the stage for the task of skeletal reconstruction. The Belgians arranged each soldier's remains in anatomical order and determined which bones they had and which ones were missing and potentially recoverable. Artifacts also had to be photographed, identified, and inventoried.

One newly excavated artifact pointed toward the identity of the third soldier. The diggers found a damaged service shoe between his legs. Inside the shoe, Marique discovered no bones, but he did find a barely legible marking in white paint. It read L-6476, and that corresponded to the last four digits of Stanley Larson's serial number. The diggers continued working and carefully peeled away rotted shreds of the soldier's clothing. In the right shirt pocket, Seel uncovered a fountain pen. It still retained most of its red-striated color, but corrosion had frozen its filling mechanism, and oxidation had eaten into its metal clip.

"He handed it to me," Speder recalled. "It was a nice red plastic pen with a gold nib. I wiped away the dirt to look for a trademark." Engraved letters emerged, W, then H, then I. . . . It was the name Rex Whitehead.

Speder had to sit down. "My heart ceased to beat for a moment," he recalled.

The others seemed puzzled by his sudden silence. He handed them the pen. Everyone sat down. No one spoke.

In addition to the pen, Larson's pockets contained a GI spoon, a glass vial for water-purification tablets, a pillbox holding eight "wound tablets" (sulfadiazine), a plastic sleeve that probably had held photographs, and a handful of ammunition, .45 caliber and .50 caliber. The long bones of the lower legs attested to a violent death. Shrapnel had smashed the distal end of each tibia, nearly severing both feet. The bones also told another story. They displayed robust ridges where tendons and ligaments had attached and pulled. Ridges like that typified a person with well-developed muscles such as an athlete. Zimmerman's bones looked similar, whereas Fidler's bones were thin and suggested a person of slight build.

That evening, the team bagged the remains of all three soldiers and deposited them at the forest ranger's house for safekeeping. Upon returning home, Seel e-mailed two JPEG photos of the fountain pen. Both pictures showed Whitehead's name engraved in gold on the barrel of the pen. (The reverse side of the pen carried a manufacturer's marking: W.A. SHEAFFER PEN CO., FORT MADISON, IOWA, U.S.A.) When Whitehead downloaded the images, a bolt of astonishment struck him.

"What are you trying to do to an aging man who can't take such shocks every day?" he replied in an e-mail. "Wish I could, but I cannot explain my thoughts when the pictures came through, and I saw my name, after you had explained the 'surprise' was in Stan's pocket. Then the phone rang, and it was Bill Warnock asking if I had survived the shock. I think he felt it as much as I did."

Whitehead then admitted that he could not explain the pen. "I don't think I saw Stan after we left Boston on the ship, for machine gunners and mortar guys were seldom close when on the line. . . . I can only surmise that during the time before shipping out, I may have given the pen to him. It does not look familiar, but a pen is a pen. I can guess that my folks gave it to me as a gift, or even when they knew we were going overseas, they sent more than one. Those were the kind of parents I had, so generous. Anyway, I am wondering what tomorrow will bring, but nothing can be a bigger shock than your photos today."

Whitehead later told me that his businessman father often doled out pens, pencils, paperweights, and other trinkets to customers. He usually had the items embellished with a company logo, and he definitely had the wherewithal to have a pen engraved with a person's name.

It was time to contact the army. Seel called David Roath and apprised him of the latest discovery. He could scarcely believe what he heard. Seel said a full-scale recovery operation would be necessary because several small bones remained missing. Roath promised to once again deploy a team.

Before the team arrived, Marique returned alone to the grave area, tidied up the place, and continued to search the area with his metal detector. Over twenty feet from the burial spot, he dug out a stainless-steel dog tag belonging to Ewing Fidler. The tag was identical to the one in the collection of Johnny Esch. The newfound tag reinforced Speder's earlier supposition about the identity of the second soldier exhumed by the team. Speder also made a discovery about the soldier believed to be Zimmerman. One of his pockets held a plastic comb with most of its teeth broken off, but across its spine someone had etched the name Goble. Speder queried his database containing the names and serial numbers of several thousand 99th Division soldiers. No match. Later, while preparing documentation for David Roath, Speder came across a 1946 letter the War Department had sent to Zimmerman's sister, Esta—Mrs. Raymond Goble. Speder smiled; another mystery solved.

Roath and his team arrived on June 13, 2001, and began a three-day excavation of the entire aid station area, including the grave site. The goal was to recover additional skeletal remains and artifacts. As before, team members pounded wooden stakes into the forest floor and stretched a string grid over the area. The team also built a screening station where a trio of workers sifted soil and clay. There was even a white tent and plastic chairs, which team members used as a break area. As on Hill 627, Roath selected Manfred Klein as the chief surveyor and mapmaker. But unlike that earlier operation, which took place in a remote area, Roath decided against having a field laboratory because the aid station sat too near a major roadway. He wanted absolute privacy when processing human remains. The need for seclusion became apparent when several cars pulled off the road, and curious motorists trotted over to see what was happening. The sight of Roath's large team and their vehicles attracted the onlookers, including one relic hunter clutching a metal detector. The Belgians quickly dispersed the uninvited guests.

By the third day of work, Roath's team had managed to recover several of the missing bones and a few more artifacts. The team wrapped up by restoring the area to its original condition. Roath also took time that day for a meeting with local Belgian officials in the town of Büllingen, the seat of government for several villages in the area. Belgium was a NATO country that required host-government notification after the recovery of human remains. To comply with all laws and ordinances, Roath presented evidence substantiating that all three sets of remains belonged to U.S. servicemen. After his presentation, the meeting attendees completed documentation for the legal transfer of the remains to American custody. They also arranged for a memorial service similar to the one conducted for Beckwith, Kokotovich, and Read. The local officials, headed by the mayor of Büllingen, scheduled the service for June 29, 2001, at the church in Krinkelt, across the street from the 99th Division monument.

The day before the event, Roath and his subordinate Mark L. Baldwin arrived at the home of Erich Hönen where the remains of the three soldiers had been in storage. A high hedgerow screened part of Hönen's yard, and the two Americans had ample privacy as they donned latex gloves and processed the bones and then secured them inside aluminum transfer cases. The two mortuary men finished by covering each container with a U.S. flag.

At 11:00 A.M. on the big day, a crowd gathered at the small park in Krinkelt, where the 99th Division monument stood. The onlookers included special invitees, townspeople, and a surprise guest—Will Cavanagh. He happened to be in the area that day, leading a group of U.S. Army officers on a battlefield tour. Neither Seel or Speder had seen him in years. After his two children graduated from high school, Cavanagh and his family had moved back to England in 1996, and he reestablished his career there. He worked for a tour operator located in southeast England and was the author of a soon-to-be-published guidebook: *A Tour of the Bulge Battlefield*. Cavanagh had a few gray hairs, but little else about him had changed. Seel and Speder spoke with him, and they reminisced about old friends Byers and Whitehead.

The special invitees that day included the new U.S. ambassador to Belgium, Stephen F. Brauer, and his wife. Standing beside the ambassador, the mayor of Büllingen wore a tricolored sash around his waist. Two flagpoles flanked the monument, one with an American flag and the other with a Belgian flag. Both hung at half-mast. The honor guard consisted of troops from the 82nd Engineer Battalion (1st Infantry Division) stationed at Bamberg, Germany. The ceremony got under way when Erich Hönen stepped front and center and read a brief statement. Afterward, Marc Marique and a member of the 82nd Engineers laid a wreath at the base of the monument, one of three wreaths laid that morning. The entire time, photojournalists darted around, snapping pictures. Television cameras recorded every word and movement.

The entire crowd migrated across the street to the church, walking slowly behind a color guard from the 82nd. David Roath had positioned all three transfer cases in the center aisle of the sanctuary. Thirteen Belgian soldiers wearing powder blue berets stood at attention beside the rectangular containers while the crowd entered the church and filled every pew. The soldiers belonged to the 17ème Bataillon d'Hélicoptères Antichars (17th Antitank Helicopter Battalion) stationed at Bierset, Belgium. The parish priest spoke first, followed by a U.S. Army chaplain. Jean-Philippe Speder then addressed the crowd in French, German, and English:

In the name of the 99th Infantry Division Association and its MIA Project, I would like to welcome you here today for a special ceremony.

We are here today to honor three soldiers of the 99th Infantry Division who were killed in action the first day of the Battle of the Bulge, on December 16, 1944. The three young soldiers were brought to a forward aid station where they laid with other casualties. The next day, under increasing enemy pressure, their outfit was forced to withdraw and abandon their fallen comrades. They were recovered after the battle, all but three who remained in an unmarked grave for fifty-seven years, listed as missing . . . missing but not forgotten.

The MIA Project of the 99th Infantry Division Association started a search for them as early as 1990, but it remained fruitless until recently. The time has finally come to bring the boys back home and give them a decent burial with military honors.

Thank you for joining us today and paying your respects.

The mayor of Büllingen followed with a lengthy oration in German. Ambassador Brauer spoke last, thanking the MIA Project team and forest ranger Hönen. After Brauer finished, the Belgian soldiers marched away from the transfer cases. American soldiers replaced the Belgians and then carried the flag-covered boxes outside to three waiting vehicles, a hearse and two vans. A bugler rendered "Taps," and the vehicles pulled away, escorted by Belgian military police.

Fidler, Larson, and Zimmerman now embarked on a long, silent journey back to their families.

Chapter 10

BUREAUCRATS
AND SCIENTISTS

Vern Swanson's telephone rang on the morning of May 21, 2001. A female voice on the other end claimed to be that of an armed forces television reporter. She had already interviewed Seel and Speder, and now she wanted Swanson's reaction to the discovery on Hill 627. He had anticipated the call, having received e-mail messages from both Belgians. Swanson told the woman about his wartime experiences and his involvement with search efforts on the hill, but he carefully refrained from mentioning the names Beckwith, Kokotovich, and Read. Their families had not yet received notification, and informing them was the army's responsibility. The reporter never asked for the names and understood the need for confidentiality. Seel and Speder had stressed that point to her, and they also stressed it to a correspondent from *Stars and Stripes*.

The *Stars and Stripes* correspondent called Swanson a day after the television reporter. The conversation went much like the previous one, but the newspaperman asked Swanson to identify the three soldiers. He declined to comment. The correspondent baited him by dropping the names Beckwith and Kokotovich. Swanson still declined. The correspondent said he gleaned the names from a book called *Upfront with Charlie Company*, which Swanson published in 1997. The names Beckwith and Kokotovich appeared in the book, as did the name Read.

Anxious for a scoop, the correspondent said he intended to publish the names in the Memorial Day edition of his newspaper. Swanson asked him to reconsider, but the eager journalist turned a deaf ear.

Swanson wasted no time telephoning me and explaining his concern. If the Associated Press or another wire service picked up the *Stars and Stripes* story, the names might appear in newspapers across the country. That would be the worst possible way for the families of those missing soldiers to learn about the recoveries on Hill 627. What could be done to stop the story? During World War II, *Stars and Stripes* operated under the auspices of the Office of War Information, and a censor scrutinized every article. The Department of Defense now owned the newspaper, but its writers and editors operated free from outside influence. Nothing could be done to stop or change the story. That meant the families had to receive notification before the names became public knowledge.

We had provided next-of-kin names, addresses, and telephone numbers to David Roath, and he had transmitted that information to the Casualty and Memorial Affairs Operations Center in Alexandria, Virginia. Had anyone there taken action? That seemed doubtful because we had received no word from any of the families. At least one of them would have called Swanson. They had his phone number, and Kokotovich's sister also had my number. Time ticked by as Swanson and I debated what path to take. We discussed calling Roath's contact in Alexandria and explaining the dilemma, but we had no name or telephone number for that person, and Roath was away from his office on leave. Only one sensible course of action remained. We had to call the families. Our relationship with them dated back ten years, so we would not be talking to strangers. We agreed to wait until Memorial Day weekend to call the families, and we agreed to do the job together on a conference call.

Our first call went to David Read's brother Frank, who lived near me in Ohio. After introducing Swanson and myself, I told Frank that Dick Byers and I had known his late brother, Tommy. Frank recalled that acquaintance and also remembered that his brother Verne traveled to Europe in 1995 and met Seel, Speder, and Swanson. I then asked if anyone from the army had contacted him in recent days. He said no and asked why I inquired. "There's been a development," I said. "Last month, Seel discovered the graves of three GIs, and one of them appears to be David." My answer caught Frank by surprise. He paused, taking a moment to absorb the meaning of my words. He asked a question, then another and another. I had anticipated them and expounded on the search-and-recovery operation. I also described the mechanics of the ongoing identification process and the role of the Casualty and Memorial Affairs Operations Center. He understood me when I explained that nobody had yet positively identified his brother's remains. The status "believed to be" now applied to the remains. As our discussion continued, I mentioned that my Belgian colleagues had e-mailed me digital photos showing the graves area and the fallen-soldier detail held at the Hürtgen cemetery. Frank had no e-mail, but he wanted to see everything in my possession. He asked if he and his wife could visit me later that day. I said yes, and we arranged to meet in the afternoon.

Swanson and I said good-bye to Frank, and we dialed Kokotovich's oldest sister, Mary Maisel, who lived in northern Indiana. She immediately recognized Swanson's voice but had no inkling that our call was anything more than social. Swanson broke the news.

"After all your years of work," she said, "God bless you guys."

"Well, it's not over yet," Swanson said. "The identification process comes next, and that has been known to drag on for more than a year."

"Let's hope it doesn't take too long. I'm not getting any younger."

"That makes two of us, but unfortunately the army bureaucracy doesn't take such things into account. I'll do everything I can to push the process toward closure."

After saying good-bye to Mary Maisel, Swanson and I attempted to contact Beckwith's brother, Sam Ohnstad, who lived in Montana. His wife was the only person home when we called, and we made arrangements to call back the following morning.

In the meantime, I met with Frank and Nancy Read. We spent several hours talking, and I showed them maps, documents, and photographs. Before we parted, I mentioned that in less than a month the 99th Division Association would hold its annual reunion, and all four Belgian diggers planned to attend. Frank and Nancy marked the event on their calendar, and said, "We'll be there."

Swanson and I spoke with Beckwith's brother on Memorial Day morning. He asked all the anticipated questions about the search-and-recovery operation and the identification process. During our conversation, Swanson spoke about the upcoming 99th Division reunion, and Ohnstad said that he and his wife wanted to attend.

Within days, Mary Maisel, her daughter, and son-in-law were also onboard, as were Verne Read, his wife, and their youngest son. The reunion promised to be a memorable occasion.

IT WAS ONE WEEK after Memorial Day when Marique discovered the burial place of Fidler, Larson, and Zimmerman. Amid the flurry of e-mail that followed that startling development, Speder received several messages from David Roath. One of them contained the name and telephone number of his contact at the Casualty and Memorial Affairs Operations Center (CMAOC). Her name was Liz E. Tate, and Speder forwarded that information to Swanson and me.

Tate worked in Alexandria, Virginia, at one of the sprawling office buildings in the Hoffman complex. A career civil servant, she currently held a position at the CMAOC, a component of the U.S. Total Army Personnel Command. She and her co-workers administered worldwide casualty reporting and next-of-kin notification. That delicate mission required communicating with family members of sick, injured, missing, or deceased soldiers. Most of the caseload involved present-day casualties, however she and another staff member handled cases pertaining to past conflicts such as World War II.

Letters from across the country covered her desktop on June 7, 2001, in response to a recent Ann Landers column titled "DNA link can still bring home missing soldiers." While organizing the mail, she grabbed her telephone receiver in response to an incoming call. Vern Swanson introduced himself and asked if anyone from her office had contacted the families of Beckwith, Kokotovich, and Read. She said no, but she had received relevant paperwork. Swanson informed her of recent developments including the *Stars and Stripes* article. He also mentioned the search-and-recovery operation that uncovered the remains of Fidler, Larson, and Zimmerman. She thanked him for the news and promised to contact the first three families without delay. She asked Swanson if he or one of the Belgians had provided Roath with contact information for the other three families. He said yes.

True to her word, Tate placed calls to the families that very day. She said that specialists at Roath's mortuary in Germany had positively identified Read and Kokotovich based on dental anatomy, dog tags, and other evidence. The identification of Beckwith was still pending. Tate qualified her remarks by stating that all the identification work in Germany might be for naught. She said all three sets of remains might still be flown to the Central Identification Laboratory in Hawaii. She had no control over that decision but assured each family that she would keep them abreast of developments.

Two weeks after receiving official notification from Liz Tate, the three families met for the first time. They gathered at Fort Mitchell, Kentucky, site of the fifty-second annual reunion of the 99th Division Association. Besides getting to know each other, they met all four diggers, plus Swanson, Whitmarsh, and me. The group of new and old friends spent many hours together. We talked, laughed, posed for photographs, shared meals, and posed for more photographs. The diggers gave Swanson a memento of the Hill 627 recovery operation. Seel unveiled the American grenade he found just before the fateful moment when he discovered a dog tag bearing the name David Read. Swanson grinned, and said, "Hopefully one of you guys defused this thing." Everyone laughed. "Why don't you pull the pin and find out?"

Despite the levity and good times, it was impossible to escape an awareness of the tragedies that had brought us together. That proved especially true one evening when a small group gathered in Seel and Speder's hotel room. Kokotovich's sister, Mary, and her daughter were among the group. The Belgians had a surprise. They presented Mary with the signet ring found with her brother's remains. It was a moment choked with emotion. She soon produced a scrapbook containing a wedding portrait of her brother and his young bride. Under magnification, I immediately discerned a shiny object on his left ring finger. There was no mistaking it. The precious piece of platinum *had* been a wedding ring. Mary slipped it on a gold chain around her neck and hugged the Belgians, thanking them for having kept possession of the ring. Speder said they kept it because the families of Sito and Holloway never received all the artifacts that he and Seel turned over to the army. Speder told how Sito's oldest brother had tried to obtain a pair of dog tags but eventually gave up in frustration.

The Belgians also retained another item from their recent exhumations, and Speder brought it to the reunion. He fished around in his luggage and produced a narrow carton. He opened it and handed me the contents. "I'm sure you know what comes next," he said. I nodded. We carefully packaged the item in a FedEx box and drove to the Cincinnati–Northern Kentucky airport.

The next day we telephoned Logan, Utah, and Paully Whitehead answered our call. She said her husband had just received a package. Emphysema had a tight grip on his lungs that day, but he wished to speak with us anyhow. His voice resonated no louder than a whisper, and he paused to catch his breath after every sentence. His words nevertheless exuded gratitude and a profound sense of accomplishment. Never before had I heard so much happiness in a voice so feeble. The pen engraved Rex Whitehead was again in the hands of its original owner and had become a symbol of perseverance. He subsequently had the artifact framed with a photograph of Stanley Larson.

WHEN DAVID ROATH'S TEAM excavated the graves on Hill 627, Speder took that opportunity to ask him about the X-9476 case. David said he knew nothing about it, and asked for more details. Speder dug out a copy of my report on the case and gave it to Roath. He promised to investigate the matter and ascertain the current disposition of the commingled remains recovered in July 1992. Dick Byers and I had repeatedly requested that information, but the army always answered our requests with silence.

Within days Roath sleuthed out an answer. The remains were in storage at the Central Identification Laboratory in Hawaii. The only way to identify them was by means of DNA analysis, and the lab gained access to that technology in 1994 through the Armed Forces DNA Identification Laboratory. Examination of X-9476 eventually began in January 1999 when scientists submitted samples from nine bones, but little else had transpired by the time of Roath's inquiry. The case now gained fresh attention, and the army resumed the process of DNA analysis in hopes of identifying the remains.

All humans possess two types of DNA: nuclear and mitochondrial. The nuclear variety, known as nDNA, has two sources: a maternal contributor (the mother) and a paternal contributor (the father). The nuclear variety is the hereditary material that defines each person as an individual. Mitochondrial DNA, known as mtDNA, serves a different purpose. It functions as the center of intracellular energy transfer.

Unlike nDNA, the inheritance of mtDNA occurs only on the maternal line, from mother to child, and it passes unchanged or nearly unchanged from one generation to the next. In addition, mtDNA exists in far greater quantity than nDNA, making it easier (but not simple) to extract from bone collagen and dentin. Those factors make mtDNA analysis the tool of choice for the Central Identification Laboratory.

The next step in the analysis of X-9476 was the collection of blood samples from maternal relatives of the missing soldiers. My report provided 1945 addresses for their families. The army opted to begin with John Puckett and Earnest Brown because they were the two soldiers most associated with the case. Liz Tate had little difficulty tracing Brown's relatives because he had a large family and was from a small town in western Virginia. She made one telephone call to someone with the surname Brown, and that led her to Earnest's only surviving sibling, Reverend Paul R. Brown. As a maternal relative, he agreed to provide a blood sample. Tate also contacted Mary Ann Boggs, a granddaughter of Earnest. At the time of his death in 1945, he had a wife and three children, but all of them had since passed away according to Boggs. Only grandchildren remained.

Finding Puckett's family presented a greater challenge for Tate. His widowed mother lived in Wichita, Kansas, at the time of his death. One of his two sisters lived there, too. Tate found no trace of them in Wichita after the passage of so many years. She turned to a seasoned genealogist for help. Linda Abrams, a retired air force sergeant, lived with her husband in Springfield, Massachusetts, and had helped the army locate hundreds of military relatives since her first case in 1990. The job of finding Puckett's family fell to her. It took a week of Internet searching and long-distance phone calls before she succeeded.

Puckett's mother remarried after the war and moved to California, following his youngest sister who had already moved there. His mother had died in 1988, but the sister still lived there, and Linda contacted her and made an unusual request. Joann Bowman found the request difficult to fathom at first. Having an absolute stranger telephone and without warning ask for blood was hardly an everyday occurrence. Yet there was something sincere about Linda's voice, and her story, though incredible, had the ring of truth. Bowman agreed to cooperate and soon received a call from Tate, who made arrangements to collect fifteen milliliters of blood. Tate also asked Bowman if she had any surviving siblings. No, her older sister, Barbara, died in 1994, and that made Bowman the only surviving sibling.

Soon after Tate's call, a medical technician from a local laboratory arrived at Bowman's condominium and drew two samples. Hours later the samples were aboard a cargo jet and bound for the Armed Forces DNA Identification Library in Rockville, Maryland. Several weeks later, Bowman received a letter of acknowledgment that stated, "On 7/5/01 the Department of Defense DNA Registry received your whole blood sample. It will be processed and your mitochondrial DNA sequence added to the family reference database and used in the future, if needed, in the remains identification process." The letter continued:

"To obtain a copy of your mtDNA Sequence Report, please return the attached form to the address shown. When your sample has been sequenced and reported, we will forward a copy of the report to you. Unless your case has been designated a priority by the United States Army Central Identification Laboratory, Hawaii, reference samples are processed in the order they are received. Due to the high volume of blood samples received, it may take up to one year to complete sequencing of your blood sample."

Bowman waited and wondered. Was her brother's case a priority? She had inferred that somebody in Hawaii felt it was important, but six months passed without any news from the army. Bowman remained patient.

DAVID ROATH GREW UP in Fargo, North Dakota, as the son of a Methodist minister. He graduated from high school in 1978 and enlisted in the army, serving six years on active duty as a radio repairman. After receiving a discharge, he matriculated to the ROTC program at Augusta College in Georgia but soon transferred to the University of Minnesota. He earned a degree in mortuary science and returned to active duty as a second lieutenant. The newly minted officer entered the U.S. Army Quartermaster School at Fort Lee, Virginia. He graduated from the Quartermaster Officer Basic Course and the Mortuary Affairs Officer Course. His first overseas assignment came when he was deployed to Somalia in 1993. Returning to Fort Lee, he became a first lieutenant and chief of the Mortuary Affairs Training Branch. He later attended the Quartermaster Officer Advance Course and attained the rank of captain. But as a captain there was no chance of remaining a mortuary officer. He wanted to continue in the mortuary business, so he resigned his commission in 1995 and accepted a civilian position as deputy director of the Mortuary Affairs Center located at Fort Lee. By that time, he had married, and his wife had given birth to a baby girl. The new father spent four months deployed to Bosnia after which he accepted another civilian position.

He and his family moved to Germany where he became director of the U.S. Army Memorial Affairs Activity–Europe. After his arrival in 1996, the unit moved from its aging facility at Frankfurt to a newly constructed mortuary at the Landstuhl Regional Medical Center. The staff there included forensics professionals capable of conducting medical and legal investigations. The staff also included mortuary affairs specialists who handled duties such as embalming, cosmetics, dressing, and casketing. Roath had the added responsibility of heading up the Disaster Mortuary Affairs Response Team (DMART), which recovered remains from mass-fatality events like aircraft crashes. He also led missions to recover the remains of servicemen missing from World War II, and he even led one mission to reclaim World War I–era remains. His organization served a geographic region including 121 countries. All too often, Roath and his team faced the chore of identifying bodies torn and burnt beyond recognition and sometimes commingled. Those ghastly sights and smells often tested the grit of Roath and his subordinates. "I'm a religious man," he once told a journalist. "In this business, if you don't believe in God you'll go crazy. You really will."

The staff at Landstuhl possessed the technical skills and legal authority to establish positive identification but sometimes had to defer. That happened with the 99th Division soldiers recovered in 2001. Landstuhl had authority over cases in Europe, but the Central Identification Laboratory had authority over cases from past wars. Overlapping jurisdictions existed between the two organizations. Higher headquarters interceded and intra-army politics came into play. The staff at Landstuhl had already begun identifying the soldiers when Roath received instructions to transfer the remains and artifacts to Hawaii. His organization complied. Read, Beckwith, and Kokotovich reached the island on July 13. Fidler, Larson, and Zimmerman arrived on July 25.

Besides identifying remains, the army had to contact the families of Fidler, Larson, and Zimmerman. The Casualty and Memorial Affairs Operations Center received a list of telephone numbers from Roath. Nobody in the news media learned the names of the three soldiers, so Swanson and I rested easy. The army made first contact this time.

On August 2, I received an e-mail from Bill Zimmerman: "Just talked to my nephew Wes Welch in Groveport. If you recall, you made contact with him when you located us years ago. He phoned to tell me the Department of the Army was trying to reach the eldest relative of Fred's to tell us that his remains have been found."

Zimmerman went on to explain that Liz Tate was the person who called his nephew, and she said that searchers recovered a comb marked Goble and a single dog tag. She also said that Roath had forwarded everything to Hawaii. Zimmerman called her in the morning and reported back to me that Tate had also contacted the families of Fidler and Larson.

I conveyed that information to Rex Whitehead. He had been anxious to speak with all three families, and I gave him the go-ahead. He picked a day when his emphysema eased somewhat, and he began placing calls, first speaking with Leon Larson. Whitehead summarized that conversation in two sentences: "Leon expressed his happiness and surprise to hear that Stanley's remains had been recovered after so many years. He became very emotional when he said that his parents so wanted the body recovered after the war."

Whitehead left a message for Zimmerman, and he returned the call. The two had spoken several times a decade earlier and now renewed their acquaintance and began exchanging e-mails. Whitehead also placed a call to Oklahoma and talked with an uncle of Ewing Fidler. The uncle provided contact information for Ewing's brother Chuck who lived in Garland, Texas.

"I had a long telephone chat with Chuck Fidler this evening." Whitehead reported. "Seems I was the first to call since Tate called him, and he was delighted to hear more details. He was born five years after Ewing, and I was shocked to find he [Ewing] was in my ASTP unit at Jonesboro, Arkansas. His family lived in Oklahoma and visited Ewing at Jonesboro and at Maxey. Also, Chuck went to the Ardennes in 1983 and knew California Highway but thought his brother was killed about two miles east of the road. Very sharp guy, a retired engineer." (Whitehead and Ewing Fidler also belonged to the same basic training company at Fort Benning but never knew each other because they bunked in different barracks.)

Whitehead and I regretted that nobody from our group had contacted Chuck Fidler a decade earlier when we first located the Larson and Zimmerman families. Fidler enjoyed doing research and had a strong interest in the Bulge. He would have been an asset to our search, but such was the clarity of hindsight.

LESS THAN A MONTH after the army contacted the families of Fidler, Larson, and Zimmerman, news arrived of another burial site discovery.

The hills around Lützkampen, Germany, yielded the skeletal remains of a 28th Infantry Division soldier who became a casualty on the first day of the Bulge. Manfred Klein and three of his colleagues made the discovery after a Lützkampen resident provided a tip.

Klein had served as David Roath's surveyor and mapmaker on Hill 627 and at the aid station site. The young German and his colleagues had previously located the remains of two American pilots and three Luftwaffe aviators. The German team specialized in pinpointing crash sites and excavating them. Klein had earned a degree in surveying and geomatics engineering from the Fachhochschule Mainz (University of Applied Science in Mainz), and he had also become engaged in archeology while attending the school. His dissertation project involved survey work and archeology at ancient sites in the Republic of Yemen. That experience and others prepared him for the meticulous job of managing the excavation of a crash site, but work of that complexity was sometimes unnecessary. One day Klein received a call from a farmer who said that as a boy he had observed the body of a GI in one of several foxholes in a field north of Lützkampen. The farmer had no recollection of anyone removing the body, and he presently owned the property.

After the farmer pointed out where he saw the dead American, Klein and his colleagues—Peter Drespa, Robert Fuchs, and Lambert Lehnertz—spent three days working in the field. They scanned the area with metal detectors and excavated foxholes filled in after the war. On the surface, Drespa found a tiny aluminum badge displaying the greyhound insignia of the 116.Panzer-Division. Klein found an identification bracelet belonging to a soldier of the 112th Infantry Regiment (28th Division). American hand grenades also turned up. Excavation work ended on August 29, 2001, when the German diggers uncovered the remains of Staff Sergeant Leonard V. Kacprzak of Detroit, Michigan. He died while serving with Company B, 112th, and his remains rested at the bottom of a foxhole. The farmer had pinpointed the location of the grave within ten meters.

That night, Klein called David Roath at home and found him sick in bed. The ailing mortuary director deferred to his assistant, Mark Baldwin, who brought a recovery team to Lützkampen the following week. Baldwin also arranged for a fallen-soldier detail on September 7 at a civilian cemetery adjacent to the recovery site. The Belgian diggers received an e-mail invitation, and Speder took time off from work to attend. Roath himself was unable to be there. He had begun to feel better but had to catch a flight back to the States for a short stay that included a meeting at the Hoffman complex in Alexandria, Virginia. His trip became far more than routine.

The meeting in Alexandria led him into the path of unforeseen tragedy.

Roath was delivering a briefing on the Disaster Mortuary Affairs Response Team when word arrived that an airliner had slammed into the World Trade Center. News of a second crash caused an evacuation of the Hoffman complex. Outdoors, Roath and his colleagues heard sirens and saw smoke rising from the Pentagon. His short stay turned into a three-week operation to help recover and identify victims of the Pentagon attack. The tragedy touched him personally when he learned that a buddy from ROTC and Fort Lee perished in the attack.

While winging his way back to Germany, Roath knew that 9/11 would generate a military response, probably in southwest Asia, and his organization would bear the brunt of processing any U.S. fatalities in that region.

AS ROATH AND HIS STAFF girded for future battle deaths, the staff at the Central Identification Laboratory in Hawaii labored to resolve deaths from past wars. The laboratory had an annual budget of twenty million dollars and a workforce of about two hundred civilian and military personnel. That included the largest staff of forensic anthropologists in the world, all of whom divided their time between lab duties in Hawaii and recovery operations in places like Vietnam, North Korea, and Papua New Guinea. When working in Hawaii, the anthropologists, along with forensic odontologists (dentists), attempted to establish individual identities. The "anthros" visually inspected skeletal morphology for characteristics that pointed toward identity. Bones alone provided insufficient evidence to pinpoint a specific person unless the anthros conducted DNA analysis. Teeth differed in that regard. They often provided sufficient evidence upon visual inspection. The "odonts" had the ability to establish identity depending upon the amount of dental remains present and the quality of records available for comparison.

Unfortunately, World War II dental records tended to be imperfect, and that was the case with those for the 99th Division soldiers recovered in 2001. The odonts discovered inconsistencies when comparing dental remains with tooth charts from 1943 and 1944. The charts showed that Beckwith had two molars extracted, Fidler had three extracted, Read had four extracted, and Larson had four extracted. Yet those supposedly uprooted molars were present in 2001, and the odonts knew why. During the war years, army dental officers often performed oral examinations without the benefit of X-ray photographs. During examinations, the officers recorded unobservable teeth as "missing." That meant dental charts showed impacted molars as missing until they eventually erupted and became visible.

There were also dental discrepancies beyond impacted molars. Beckwith's remains had one tooth with an amalgam filling indicated nowhere on his charts. Zimmerman had two undocumented fillings, Fidler had three, Kokotovich had nine, and Larson had thirteen. These discrepancies sometimes occurred because army dentists annotated only their own restorations and excluded work done by previous dentists. In other cases, the undocumented restorations occurred after the date of the last available dental chart. That was particularly true of restorations made overseas, at least in the case of the 99th Division. The odonts scrutinized all the discrepancies and found nothing inexplicable.

The odonts also found every restoration documented on the dental charts. That helped in identifying Kokotovich and Zimmerman, who both had numerous silicate and amalgam restorations. In a letter home, Zimmerman once mentioned his dental work. "Last night I had to go to the dentist. I went at five o'clock last night, and when I got back it was eleven-thirty. I had five teeth filled, and boy that didn't feel so good. I was in the chair for almost three hours. I thought they never were going to let me go." More than five decades later, abundant dental work permitted a "good match" in his case. By contrast, David Read had perfect teeth and was the only one of the six 99th Division soldiers so distinguished, but that perfection had a downside. It offered less evidence to help establish identity. (Read did have one tooth lost postmortem. The other soldiers also had teeth posthumously missing, but the odonts had no difficulty discerning them from teeth pulled before death.)

The odonts completed their work by preparing written reports illustrated with photographs. These reports, one for each soldier, ended with an opinion. The statement regarding Kokotovich was typical: "Given the provenance in this case combined with the correlated findings in Pfc. Kokotovich's antemortem dental record, the dental remains designated CILHI 2001-126-I-01 are probably those of: Private First Class Saul Kokotovich, 35094839, U.S.A."

The forensic anthropologists also prepared reports, and those documents provided a biological profile for each soldier. The documents included determinations regarding age, race, gender, stature, and skeletal injuries. To avoid bias in their work, the anthros approached each case "blind," screened from any knowledge about the decedent or decedents associated with the case.

The first step involved answering a basic question. Did the remains belong to a single individual? The anthros looked for duplication of bones. The anthros also checked to see if opposing left and right bones exhibited equal size and appearance, bilateral symmetry in other words. The principle of articulation also applied to the question. In a living person, certain bones articulate with other bones, and they fit together with mechanical precision. Lack of articulation among skeletal remains signals possible commingling and multiple individuals. After careful study, the anthros discovered no commingling among the remains of Beckwith, Kokotovich, and Read. The opposite was true of Fidler, Larson, and Zimmerman. They had lain in a common grave, and mixing had occurred. Zimmerman's remains included three small bones that belonged to Larson. Fidler's remains included a tooth from Zimmerman, two small bones and several fragments from Zimmerman, and one fragment and four small bones from Larson.

After answering the individuality question, the anthros judged age by examining ossification centers, the areas where bone replaced cartilage during development from infancy to adulthood. When the soldiers were children, each long bone in their arms and legs consisted of a shaft and two end pieces, all connected by cartilage. The cartilage gradually disappeared with age, and the individual pieces fused into one bone, or almost fused into one bone. The men died before every piece had time to fully knit together. Various long bones from the soldiers displayed signs of recent or ongoing fusion. The anthros fixed an age range depending upon the location and degree of fusion. Ribs, skulls, and hipbones also displayed evidence of fusion. Again, the location and degree suggested an age range. Tooth maturity added to the picture. The pattern of molar eruption or lack of eruption suggested a range, as did wisdom teeth with partially formed roots.

Racial determinations primarily resulted from skull examinations. The cranium of each soldier exhibited a narrow nasal opening and a long, high cranial vault. Both features were typical of Caucasians, as were recessive cheekbones that appeared sharp and angular. Palates that were narrow and triangular also hinted at Caucasian ancestry. Drastic erosion of Kokotovich's facial bones exposed his sinus cavities and made assessment of his race less certain, although two of his teeth displayed Carabelli's cusps, a trait linked to Caucasians. The skull of Fidler had suffered less erosion and permitted precise craniometric measurements that pegged him as Caucasian with 98.4 percent certainty. He too had teeth with Carabelli's cusps. The anthros also studied thighbones or femora to gain insights into race. Curvature and twisting were characteristic of Caucasians.

The process of determining gender started with each soldier's pelvis and skull. Female pelvic bones tend to be wider and shallower than those of males, the demands of pregnancy and childbirth necessitating the difference. The anthros scrutinized various anatomical features of the pelvic bones to determine sex, but in some cases the bones offered few clues because of erosion. Masculine skull features included blunt chin structure, prominent mastoid areas, and pronounced ridges above the eye sockets. The anthros also considered the overall size and robusticity of each skeleton. The soldiers all exhibited enough male characteristics to leave little doubt about their gender, although Fidler had an especially slender skeleton that stood out as atypical.

What was each soldier's height? The anthros tackled that question by utilizing regression formulas developed during the late 1940s by a pioneering scientist. Mildred Trotter, a professor of anatomy at a medical school in St. Louis, traveled to Honolulu after World War II and examined the skeletal remains of servicemen perished during combat operations against Japan. The military was preparing the remains for final shipment to cemeteries in the United States. All the men had one thing in common. Medical personnel had measured them when they entered military service. Those measurements enabled Trotter to make correlations between their stature and the lengths of their long bones. She and Goldine Gleser published the results in 1952, and those findings provided the basis for analysis work done on the 99th Division soldiers in 2001.

Staff members at the Central Identification Laboratory carefully measured long bones on a simple apparatus called an osteometric board. It provided accurate numbers unobtainable with a ruler or measuring tape. In the case of Larson's left femur, the board showed a maximum length of 49.2 centimeters. That equated to an estimated stature of 178.5 centimeters or 70.3 inches. The anthros determined that by using Trotter's femur formula ($2.38 \times$ femur length $+ 61.41$ centimeters $=$ height). The margin of error in calculating height using the femur formula was 3.27 centimeters. Trotter produced only one formula with a smaller margin of error. That calculation combined femur length and tibia length, but shell fragments had shattered both of Larson's tibiae, making it impossible to measure their original lengths precisely. There were additional difficulties, too. Several long bones from other soldiers proved troublesome because erosion had caused slight but critical size reductions. Despite the difficulties, the soldiers had enough unspoiled long bones to permit accurate height estimation.

Injuries such as Larson's shattered tibiae were points of interest because all the 99th Division soldiers reportedly died from enemy shellfire. The damaged tibiae corresponded to that cause of death. The remains of Beckwith exhibited trauma to the pelvis and the arms and legs, especially the lower left leg and foot. Shell fragments remained imbedded in some of the bones. Those injuries paralleled Vern Swanson's memory of the wounds he witnessed. Obliterated bone in Zimmerman's right leg squared with the circumstances of his death. The bones of Fidler, Read, and Kokotovich showed no evidence of trauma. Of all the soldiers, only Beckwith's bones displayed signs of an injury sustained well before death. His left femur had a bony lesion that resembled a healed fracture. David Roath first noticed that old break, and Swanson attempted to corroborate it by contacting boyhood and college friends of Beckwith. Nobody remembered such an injury. Fidler's vertebrae exhibited spina bifida occulta, but that birth defect was no aid in identification because it went undiagnosed during his life.

The anthropology report for each soldier ended with an overall conclusion, such as the one written for Kokotovich: "The remains designated CILHI 2001-126-I-01 consist of the nearly complete skeleton of a 17–21-year-old, probable Caucasoid male, who stood approximately 71 to 74 inches tall." The anthro who drew that conclusion had worked blind but subsequently compared her findings with the known physical characteristics of Kokotovich, whose name appeared on the dog tag found with the remains. She prepared an addendum to her report that included a table comparing Kokotovich to the remains she studied:

	CILHI 2001-126-I-01	PFC KOKOTOVICH
Sex:	Male	Male
Age:	17–21 years	20 years 1 month
Race:	Probable Caucasoid	White
Stature:	71–74 inches	71 inches

In addition to anthropology and odontology reports, laboratory staffers prepared material-evidence reports. These documents identified or attempted to identify all artifacts recovered with each set of remains. A casualty-data analyst reported on the historical background surrounding the deaths of all the 99th Division soldiers. The entire collection of reports underwent an external review process. The laboratory selected three consultants from a pool of forensic scientists around the United States. The consultants could agree with the findings they received from Hawaii or request clarification on points of disagreement. No disagreements emerged regarding the 99th soldiers.

The authority for establishing individual identities rested with Dr. Thomas D. Holland, a board-certified forensic anthropologist and the scientific director at the laboratory. He weighed all the evidence and analysis work and approved the identity of each soldier. He rendered his decisions in December 2001.

The entire process in Hawaii took just over six months, fast service for an organization that often required a year or more to complete a case. The quicker-than-usual turnaround resulted because the army had contacted all the families soon after the recoveries occurred. That kept attention focused on all the cases, as did oversight from Vern Swanson's U.S. congressman, Mark S. Kirk, and the congressman's representative, Roy Czajkowski. (None of that happened in the case of Leonard Kacprzak, whose recovery occurred in August 2001. Dr. Holland finally approved his identity in February 2003, and the army took an additional six months to locate and meet with his family.)

Chapter 11
OPERATION FINAL JOURNEY

During World War II, American servicemen rarely left burial instructions with their families. Many servicemen refused to discuss the prospect of dying, even though they considered it possible or even probable. On several occasions, war correspondents polled combat troops on the question, and most respondents said that if they died, they preferred to rest overseas with their comrades. One correspondent on Okinawa found that to be true among 99 percent of soldiers and marines he interviewed. But widows and parents of the dead frequently had a different attitude. It was customary to bury loved ones in a family plot, keeping alive a sense of togetherness.

In May 1946, President Truman signed legislation giving families the option of bringing the dead home at government expense or leaving them overseas in military cemeteries maintained by the government. That option still existed when the army positively identified the remains of the 99th Division soldiers recovered in 2001.

Liz Tate contacted all six families during the first week of 2002 and updated them. She e-mailed Kathleen Winkle, niece of Saul Kokotovich: "I just found out yesterday that the lab has completed the identifications. The cases are on their way to my office for review." Winkle's mother, Mary Maisel, was the oldest surviving sibling of Kokotovich, and she would have to make the burial decision. The army considered her the primary next of kin and therefore the "person authorized to direct disposition" (PADD). Tate informed Winkle that an army representative would personally visit her mother, but there would be a delay. "Unfortunately we are somewhat backlogged right now, so it will be approximately three weeks before we can set a date to meet with your mom and provide a briefing of the details and assist with burial arrangements."

Three weeks eventually became three months, and that was true for all the families. Concerned by the delay, the brother of Ewing Fidler telephoned Tate's office on March 22 and spoke with one of her co-workers Johnny L. Johnson, a mortuary affairs specialist. Chuck Fidler later reported on the conversation:

"Setting up disposition arrangements with next of kin appears to be Johnson's primary function, so he spends most of his time visiting families around the country and is therefore not around the office much. He just returned to the office yesterday after completing visits with the next of kin of an entire WWII B-24 bomber crew whose remains were recovered last year. He told me he hoped to get back with me next week to schedule a visit."

Johnson did get back in touch with Fidler, and they set a date. Johnson also telephoned the other families and set dates. The first visits took place on April 3, 2002, when Johnson flew to Chicago. The families of Kokotovich and Stanley Larson both lived within driving distance. The first stop for Johnson was the home of Leon Larson in DeKalb, Illinois. The day happened to be Leon's eighty-second birthday, and four members of his family sat at his side during the meeting. They listened as Johnson explained how scientists at the Central Identification Laboratory established positive identification. He presented a case file totaling eighty-three pages. The file included a forensic anthropology report, a forensic odontology report, and a material-evidence report. The writing was dense and technical, so Johnson carefully explained everything in simple terms. The file had maps and photographs of the recovery site. There were also color images of the artifacts, dental anatomy, and skeletal remains. The language of the reports may have been difficult to comprehend, but the color pictures required no words of explanation and were an emotional jolt.

The meeting lasted two hours, during which time Johnson elaborated on burial options. Interment could take place overseas at an

ABMC cemetery or in the United States at any national cemetery or at a private cemetery. Leon had already decided on Lawnridge Cemetery in Rochelle, Illinois. His brother Stanley already had a granite headstone there. Their father had purchased it and placed it over an empty grave at the cemetery. In addition, their mother and sister rested in nearby graves. Johnson said the Department of the Army granted a burial allowance of 4,325 dollars for interment at a private cemetery like Lawnridge. The allowance covered flowers, stationery, obituary notices, headstone purchase, cemetery-plot purchase, burial vault purchase, funeral director services, clergy and musical honorariums, opening and closing of the grave, and limousine services on the day of the funeral. The family had to pay all expenses out of pocket and submit receipts for reimbursement. Casket purchase was nonreimbursable because the army furnished a casket. Two options existed: hardwood or eighteen-gauge steel. Leon selected steel after viewing pictures of both types. The army offered to provide an honor guard if Leon desired a military funeral. A chaplain was also available. Johnson requested at least two weeks notice prior to whatever date Leon selected for the funeral. The Larson family knew that all four Belgian diggers planned to visit the United States for the annual 99th Division reunion. After inviting the Belgians to attend the funeral, Leon and his family set the date for July 22, the first Monday after the reunion. To coordinate final arrangements, the army appointed a casualty assistance officer. That person also had responsibility for assisting with postfuneral details like obtaining reimbursement for expenses.

Johnson had a tight schedule on April 3. After leaving the Larson family, he hurried through the greater Chicago area to make his appointment with Mary Maisel in Portage, Indiana. That evening, he presented her with a case file regarding the identification of her brother's remains. Johnson reviewed all the interment options, but she had already made a decision. Maisel selected the Henri-Chapelle American Cemetery in Belgium. That ABMC cemetery had the most 99th Division burials, including five members of her brother's company. She requested Saturday, June 22, for the funeral.

The choice of an ABMC cemetery carried with it special compensation for overseas travel. Recent legislation permitted the army to defray those expenses. That had been impossible in previous years, and it discouraged some families from selecting an ABMC cemetery.

The cost of overseas travel was simply prohibitive. Johnson said the army would pay for three family members to attend the funeral. All expenses related to the burial would also be paid.

Meetings with the remaining 99th Division families were on Johnson's docket for later in April. In the meantime he had other visits to make, including one with relatives of a serviceman who had died in Oregon during a 1944 plane crash. The army had recently uncovered his remains.

On April 16, Johnson finally reached the home of Chuck Fidler. He selected Rosedale Cemetery in Ada, Oklahoma, and he picked Saturday, June 8, for the funeral. Unfortunately that date was too late for his sister Thelma. Her death occurred in April at age seventy-four. "She had been in poor health for several years," Fidler told me in an e-mail, but the previous autumn he informed her about the discovery in Belgium. "She was in a nursing home and couldn't speak, but she understood everything I was saying," Fidler recalled. "When I told her, she cried for two hours. She and Mom both suffered from broken hearts after Sonny was killed. Mom just withered away. She never got over his death." Fidler's grieving mother died of cancer in 1958, and his father eventually remarried but died from a heart attack in 1971. The couple rested side by side at Rosedale Cemetery. Fidler's decision in 2002 to inter his brother there was easy. The fallen soldier already had a piece of ground reserved at the cemetery. His father purchased a plot and a granite headstone several years after the war, firmly convinced his son would eventually find his way home. Before the old man died, he left specific instructions with his surviving son: "Someday they'll find your brother . . . Bring him home."

The day after visiting Fidler, Johnson called on Bill Zimmerman. He chose Henri-Chapelle and June 22. The following day, Verne Read opted to bury his brother at Arlington National Cemetery on July 18, which allowed the Belgians to attend. Johnson's final stop came when he journeyed west to confer with Sam Ohnstad, half brother of Jack Beckwith. Ohnstad had yet to make a decision and asked if he could have additional time. He favored Henri-Chapelle, but his younger sister preferred a private cemetery in North Dakota where their mother rested.

Because family members sometimes disagreed about funeral arrangements, the army vested all decision-making authority in one person (the PADD, in military jargon). Ohnstad had that authority. He never reached agreement with his sister, and ultimately selected Henri-Chapelle after much consternation. He wanted his brother to rest alongside Saul Kokotovich and other soldiers from their unit. Ohnstad also had another thought on his mind. Before his mother passed away, she made it known that her fallen son should remain overseas if anyone found his remains. He belonged to the land he helped liberate. Ohnstad honored the wish of his mother. He also agreed to the June 22 date that Maisel and Zimmerman selected. Henri-Chapelle would have a triple funeral.

BEFORE ANY OF THE CEREMONIES took place, Chuck Fidler journeyed to Europe to see for himself the place where his brother died and the place where he had rested with Larson and Zimmerman. In May 2002 he and his wife joined a group of 99th Division veterans on a tour of battlegrounds where the division fought. Seel and Speder led the group, and they guided everyone to Henri-Chapelle, where the cemetery superintendent pointed out three burial spots recently selected for Beckwith, Kokotovich, and Zimmerman. The veterans heard from David Roath, who gave a presentation on the history and mission of the U.S. Army Memorial Affairs Activity–Europe. The main event on the tour was a ceremony to unveil a bronze plaque commemorating one of three 99th Division units that earned a Presidential Unit Citation for actions during the Bulge. The group later participated in Memorial Day ceremonies at the Ardennes American Cemetery, and Chuck saw his brother's name inscribed on the Tablets of the Missing. On the final day of the tour, Seel and Speder led Chuck to the site of the log cabin where his brother perished. Only the outline of its foundation remained. They also visited the location where his brother shared a common grave with Larson and Zimmerman.

Chuck was a student of the battle, and his knowledge level impressed the two Belgians. He could have led portions of the tour. Before parting company, they made plans to see each other in July at the annual 99th Division reunion, slated for Pittsburgh.

The week after Chuck returned home, eighteen members of David Read's family traveled to Europe. The diggers guided a small procession of rental vehicles deep into the Schleiden Forest and atop Hill 627. The passengers included two of his surviving brothers, Verne and Doug. It was Verne's second visit to the hill. He had been there in 1995 and walked within yards of his brother's unmarked grave. The Read family congregated around the wooden cross that marked the center of the burial site, and they listened as Seel recounted how he discovered the graves and what had transpired on the hill in December 1944. Afterward, he produced a single dog tag. It was the one that marked David's grave and led to the discovery of the burial site. "This belongs to you," Seel said to Verne. The Belgian handed over the artifact along with a small plastic bag that contained the leather wallet found with David's remains. The diggers had told only David Roath about their decision to maintain possession of the tag and wallet for eventual handover to the eldest family member.

The presentation took Verne by surprise. He just stood there, overwhelmed by the moment as he clutched both items. He eventually let other family members inspect the artifacts. The plastic bag kept the wallet from drying out and prevented shrinkage. Seel counseled Verne to keep the wallet in the bag and to seek advice from a professional conservator, who could make recommendations for long-term preservation. That night at supper, the atmosphere lightened and Verne's wife entertained the Belgians with stories of her travels abroad. She spoke French and Italian and had seen Hitler and Mussolini in 1938 while attending a girls' school in Florence. The following day, the diggers guided the Read family on a tour of battle areas outside the 99th Division sector and later escorted everyone to a Bulge museum in Diekirch, Luxembourg. (Verne eventually had the wallet freeze-dried after seeking professional advice.)

THE FUNERAL OF EWING FIDLER took place on the same day as the museum tour in Luxembourg. The local newspaper in Ada, Oklahoma, had recently published a story about the young soldier's life and death and the recovery of his remains. The story included an announcement: "Everyone is invited to attend the burial of Ewing Fidler at 11:30 A.M., June 8, at Rosedale Cemetery." The announcement brought friends and townsfolk, and they gathered around a funeral tent erected at the graveside. The entire group numbered nearly one hundred and included five veterans of the 99th Division, among them Ewing's boyhood pal Billy Hoipkemeir. The Fidler family occupied folding chairs under the tent. Outfitted in black, Chuck and his wife sat alongside their two daughters and one son-in-law. Chuck's four-year-old grandson climbed atop his mother's lap and wore an American-flag pin on his little sweater. Thelma's son and daughter and their spouses sat in the second row.

Half a dozen soldiers from Fort Sill performed honor-guard duties during the ceremony, which lasted some forty-five minutes. The soldiers carried a flag-covered casket to the tent, and then they marched away to pick up M16 rifles and double as the firing party. Major Johnny Messer, an army chaplain, eulogized PFC Fidler and recounted the search for his remains. After the chaplain finished speaking, the soldiers fired three volleys and a bugler rendered "Taps." Two of the soldiers returned to the tent and folded the casket flag and presented it to Chuck. That concluded the ceremony.

Chuck eventually had a new line engraved on his brother's headstone: Buried Here on June 8, 2002.

FEW PEOPLE WHO VISITED the Henri-Chapelle American Cemetery realized that an underground system of concrete beams on piles connected all 7,989 marble headstones. The system kept the headstones level and perfectly aligned in broad sweeping rows, and nothing short of an earthquake could alter that harmony. The triple funeral for Beckwith, Kokotovich, and Zimmerman created the need for three new headstones and an extension of one underground beam. The beam required extension because the American Battle Monuments Commission never anticipated additional interments at Henri-Chapelle. After completing construction of its World War II cemeteries in Europe, the ABMC closed all but one of them for burials. Only the Ardennes Cemetery remained open, but that changed decades later, when the ABMC opened all its cemeteries for remains recovered on battlefields.

When the three 99th Division families selected Henri-Chapelle, no burials had taken place at the cemetery since 1954, and its staff had no experience with interments. David Roath was a licensed funeral director and had purview over all U.S. military funerals conducted in Europe. The ABMC welcomed his services. Before he arrived at the cemetery, the superintendent and his staff selected three burial spots just past the end of row 7, plot C. Workers dug a narrow trench, laid batten boards and steel reinforcing, and poured concrete to extend the beam underlying the row. The extension included attachment points for three marble crosses.

The ABMC supplied the crosses at a cost of more than one thousand dollars apiece. Stoneworkers in northern Italy had quarried them from pure white Lasa marble and cut them to U.S. government specifications. The ABMC kept a stockpile of the headstones at its Meuse-Argonne Cemetery in France and had an engraving machine at the cemetery. The army consulted with each of the three families to ascertain if a Latin cross or Star of David was appropriate, and each requested a cross. The staff at Meuse-Argonne fulfilled the requests and sent the finished products to Henri-Chapelle.

While workers installed the crosses, I flew to Belgium and rendezvoused with Vern Swanson and Byron Whitmarsh at the airport in Brussels on the morning of June 18. We shared a rental car, which Swanson drove to our hotel in Waimes, Belgium. Whitmarsh had attended Fidler's funeral, and he gave a firsthand account of the recent event as we rode to the hotel. Suffering from jet lag, all three of us sacked out until suppertime when the diggers arrived at the hotel to welcome us. The next day we had a noon meeting scheduled with Roath at Henri-Chapelle. The families of Beckwith, Kokotovich, and Zimmerman had yet to arrive from the United States.

I had visited Henri-Chapelle several times before, as had Swanson and Whitmarsh. All of us recognized the towering limestone pylons at the cemetery entrance, each with a giant-sized eagle perched atop. Roath met us outside the visitors' room and introduced us to the cemetery superintendent, Gerald V. Arseneault, and his assistant superintendent. Roath reviewed the entire funeral program, which had the name Operation Final Journey, and he showed us three flag-draped caskets positioned inside the cemetery chapel, along with a cornucopia of floral arrangements.

I wandered out into the graves area, where I spotted a backhoe hauling up scoops of earth. Roath had a four-man team digging graves. The gravediggers included two enlisted men from his organization, SFC James Doster and PFC Lucas Moore, as well as Manfred Klein and Peter Drespa. The two Germans participated because Klein worked as an engineer for a construction company, and Roath subcontracted the company to provide labor and excavation equipment. Rocky soil at

Henri-Chapelle necessitated the use of a jackhammer and a backhoe. The soil in places approached the hardness of concrete. As I watched Klein operate his Zeppelin backhoe, I remembered that during World War II the burial ground was the largest American military cemetery in Europe, and German prisoners of war dug many of its graves. After more than a half century, Germans were once again digging graves at Henri-Chapelle. During the war, the Germans had only picks and shovels, and their work must have been backbreaking. Roath's team required over two days to dig three graves using power equipment. The last step was to insert burial vaults made of heavy black vinyl and to cover each hole temporarily with plywood.

After the gravediggers completed their chore, U.S. Army soldiers from Headquarters and Headquarters Company, V Corps, gathered at the burial site. The group of eighteen soldiers were members of an honor guard and had volunteered for special duty as casket bearers during the funeral. One of Roath's subordinates briefed them on the operation ahead. Hundreds of eyes and cameras would be on them. Another subordinate positioned the soldiers according to height, lest there be uneven weight distribution and an unforgivable catastrophe. The soldiers drilled with an empty transfer case and practiced folding an American flag into a perfect triangle. On the day of the funeral, the V Corps honor guard planned to augment the casket bearers with a bugler, rifle team, and a color guard.

Three other soldiers also had duties vital to the success of Operation Final Journey. Roath obtained a trio of seasoned noncoms to act as casualty assistance officers: Sergeants First Class Michael A. Johnson, Joseph A. Harbolt, and James A. Campbell. They served with the 39th Signal Battalion at Chièvres, Belgium, and their work began on June 20 when the three families arrived at the Brussels airport. Each sergeant had a rental van and transported his assigned family to the hotel in Waimes, where all the travelers spent the day recuperating from jet lag. Mary Maisel's contingent included her daughter, Kathy, and son-in-law, Larry, and their youngest daughter, Sheli. Bill Zimmerman brought his wife, Mary Ann, and two of their children, Fred and Jeramy. Sam Ohnstad brought his wife, Joan. The next morning the sergeants drove the families to Henri-Chapelle. None of them had ever visited the cemetery before.

Like all ABMC cemeteries, Henri-Chapelle had a commanding view of the countryside, unblemished by power lines and obtrusive buildings.

Flowering trees and shrubs kept the grounds in a succession of bloom from spring through autumn. Roses added delicate explosions of color. Emerald lawns overspread the graves area, and every blade of grass appeared cut to a uniform height. The architects who designed the cemetery avoided the tradition of setting headstones in straight rows, which created a dreary feeling of sameness. The rows of marble crosses and Stars of David stood in gentle arcs that fanned out from a bronze sculpture called the Angel of Peace. Birch trees interrupted the rows at random intervals. Sunlight beamed down on the array of headstones, and each marker glowed bright white thanks to the fastidious care of cemetery workers. The superintendent had fourteen maintenance employees, and several times a year they washed each headstone by hand and treated it with a chemical agent to eliminate moss. They gently rubbed away stains with pumice stone. Workmen occasionally performed cosmetic surgery to repair minor cracks and chips. No detail was too small to escape attention. Each headstone symbolized American pride and commitment—commitment to the peoples of Europe and an ideal called freedom. The achingly beautiful vista caused Sam Ohnstad to remark, "After seeing this place, I know that I made the right decision to bring my brother here."

Roath greeted the families outside the chapel doorway and welcomed everyone to Belgium. He explained the details of his role as funeral director. Afterward, he offered the families a chance to view inside the caskets. Ohnstad and Maisel accepted, and Roath escorted them into the chapel one at a time and opened the appropriate casket. The staff at the laboratory in Hawaii had neatly arranged each set of remains on an olive-drab blanket and tightly folded the bones inside. An appropriately decorated uniform lay on top and provided the finishing touch. The families had already seen color photographs of the remains, so there was no need to undo anything. Ohnstad and his wife inspected the uniform inside his brother's casket and took a photograph. Maisel placed her hand on the uniform in her brother's casket. Afterward, she and her family and Roath held hands and recited the Lord's Prayer.

Roath and the three families opened the chapel to the public, and visitors began entering, all adhering to a code of silence and respect. U.S. Army soldiers guarded either side of the chapel doorway. Adjacent to the chapel, a limestone colonnade carried the names of 450 missing servicemen. The name Jack Beckwith now had a bronze rosette next to it, indicating that he was no longer missing. Rosettes decorated several other names on the colonnade and were a new feature at ABMC cemeteries. (The name Frederick Zimmerman appeared among the missing commemorated at the Ardennes Cemetery, and the name Saul Kokotovich appeared at the Netherlands Cemetery.)

The families strolled out onto the cemetery grounds and gravitated toward a pair of funeral tents standing over three freshly dug graves. After inspecting the burial site, everyone adjourned to the nearby town of Aubel for lunch and to see St. Hubert Eglise, an enormous neo-Gothic church near the center of town. The cemetery superintendent had made arrangements for a religious service there as part of the funeral. He and Roath had designed an elaborate and dignified event, which, by permission of the families, local news media had announced as open to the public. That guaranteed a strong turnout. The time for planning and preparations had ended. The ceremony was less than twenty-four hours away.

Like a bright yellow bulb, the sun lingered over the cemetery on the morning of the funeral. Three hearses parked at the curb in front of the burial ground. The casket teams entered the chapel and hoisted the steel boxes. Exiting the chapel, the teams turned onto a broad walkway leading to the curb. The families followed. Sam Ohnstad looked up and noticed Old Glory hanging at half-mast on the flagpole that towered over the parking area. "That's when it really hit me," he later recalled. The trip to Belgium had been like a vacation until that moment. Now the past weighed heavy, the death of his brother no longer a faraway memory.

Headlights burned as the funeral cortege rolled along the road to Aubel. In the town, Belgian and American flags fluttered from windowsills, and pedestrians stopped to watch the cortege as it passed. The column of vehicles pulled into the church parking lot where the casket teams unloaded the three hearses. The teams led the way into St. Hubert Eglise, and the families followed. I trailed behind as did Swanson, Whitmarsh, and the four diggers. It was noontime. We paused outside the main entrance to the church, waiting for someone to usher us to our assigned pew. There was no way to see into the sanctuary, and the building sounded empty. We finally walked into the great room and discovered over one thousand people packed inside.

The size of the crowd impressed me, but the absolute silence impressed me even more. I listened carefully but never heard so much as a cough or a whisper. The Belgians in that church had come out of respect, not curiosity. More than a few of them were old enough to remember the Nazi occupation.

The parish priests of Aubel and Henri-Chapelle wore white robes and purple stoles, and both men addressed the crowd. One delivered an invocation in French, and the other did the same in English. After they spoke, U.S. Army Chaplain Stephen Cook read from Scripture. The St. Cécile Choir followed with two selections in French. Roy Czajkowski spoke on behalf of Swanson's U.S. congressman. The crowd then heard eulogies from Mary Maisel, Sam Ohnstad, and Bill Zimmerman. Maisel wore a watch brooch on her dress, and she told listeners about the delicately crafted timepiece. Her brother presented it to their mom as a Mother's Day gift, and she wore it until her death. Maisel also spoke about her brother's musical talent and the young bride he left behind. He had been a newlywed, as had Fred Zimmerman. When Ohnstad spoke, he recounted his near fatal bout with appendicitis, which occurred the same month his brother died in combat. "Mom nearly lost both her boys," he said. Ohnstad went on to describe a blue Schwinn bicycle his brother handed down before leaving in 1944. There was also another gift. "His insurance money paid for my education," Ohnstad said, "so I'm forever grateful." Bill Zimmerman talked about his brother, and repeated a question his family had often wondered. "Fred, where are you? We love you." Zimmerman said that his brother and soldiers like Beckwith and Kokotovich had answered every day: "Here we are, in your hearts, your memories and your daily living. It's called love." Chaplain Cook and the choir concluded the ceremony.

The cortege retraced its route from Henri-Chapelle and entered the cemetery on a service road that cut around its perimeter. Onlookers thronged the funeral site, and that included Belgian veterans, who unfurled an assemblage of colorful flags decorated with unit names and battle honors. The hearses halted at the edge of the burial ground, and the casket teams carried the three fallen soldiers into that vast garden blossoming with white marble. TV reporters and photojournalists captured the scene. The families sat in front-row chairs under the funeral tent, and I sat directly behind them, as did the four diggers,

Swanson and Whitmarsh. An embroidered checkerboard on Swanson's blazer made it clear he was a 99th Division veteran. One by one, the casket teams positioned the silver burial cases on three catafalques erected over the graves. The team members stood at attention beside the caskets as Chaplain Cook began the graveside service by reading Bible verses. Jean-Philippe Speder contributed the most memorable words when he recited the poem "Bury Me with Soldiers." As he spoke, Swanson and Whitmarsh looked on silently. I could only wonder what thoughts ran through their minds. They had four Purple Hearts between them, and only by some special dispensation had they survived. The shell that killed Beckwith might easily have taken Swanson instead. The might-have-beens were numerous.

Swanson flinched a little when he heard the first sudden crack of three rifle volleys. After several seconds of silence, a lone bugler sounded the mournful melody of "Taps," and it carried across the countryside with nary a broken note. The casket bearers lifted the three flags. The soldiers folded Kokotovich's flag, and an army captain presented it to his sister. Another captain presented Beckwith's flag, and yet another captain presented Zimmerman's flag, concluding the graveside service.

Hundreds of attendees queued up in a receiving line and offered words of sympathy and appreciation to the families. Most of the crowd had dispersed by 3:30 P.M., when Roath and two of his colleagues began lowering the caskets. The families gathered around and placed roses on the caskets and watched as they slowly sank into the earth. One final ritual concluded the day's events. The families shoveled a few lumps of earth into the open graves. Roath and the four diggers did the same. I took my turn last, dropping a shovelful into each grave. The soil landed with a hollow thud.

The funeral party vacated the cemetery, leaving several of Roath's crew to disassemble the catafalques, cap the burial vaults, and backfill the remaining soil.

Over the next two days, Seel and Speder acted as tour guides, leading the families and their casualty assistance officers on terrain walks over former battlegrounds of the 99th Division. Speder wore his trademark New York Yankees baseball cap and did much of the talking, although Seel took over on Hill 627 and at the former grave of Fidler, Larson, and Zimmerman.

While visiting the hill, the families gathered around the wooden cross that marked the former burial ground, and camcorders rolled as Seel and Swanson spoke. When Seel pointed to the spot where medics buried Kokotovich, Joan Ohnstad put her arm around Mary Maisel as tears welled up in Mary's eyes. I took a few photographs and then stood in the background with Speder and his wife. I glanced over at Swanson, who was now quiet. He had taken a seat on a tree stump, clutching a wooden cane in one hand and staring off into the distance at the hushed beauty of the forest. Yet that beauty belied a nightmarish past, and in his mind's eye, it was all still there, the shattered tree limbs, the black shell holes, and the haggard faces of combat infantrymen. For Whitmarsh, too, the fires of war burned on his memories, but the two old soldiers could now take comfort in the knowledge that none of their fallen comrades remained forsaken on that lonely hilltop.

I REVISITED HENRI-CHAPELLE before departing Europe and took a long, last look at the graves. Cemetery workers had resodded them and decorated each with flowers.

Mary Maisel also revisited the cemetery. She and I took the same transatlantic flight home, and she mentioned having collected a small amount of earth from her brother's grave. She planned to spread the soil over her parents' graves. She also planned to attend the upcoming 99th Division reunion and would be there with her daughter and son-in-law. I expected to see all of them there, but first I had to attend David Read's funeral at Arlington National Cemetery.

The day of the burial, I met up with Seel and Speder at the cemetery administration building. They were in a waiting room overflowing with members of the Read family. Speder's wife was also there, but I saw no sign of Marique or Menestrey. Seel explained that Marique had to bow out due to a family problem, and Menestrey discovered at the last minute he had an expired passport. It would be years before Menestrey lived down the passport slipup.

While chatting with the Belgians, I asked if they had toured the cemetery. Yes, they said, but during a previous trip to the States. As we talked about Arlington, they wondered why it appeared less well kept than ABMC cemeteries. Money, I explained. Arlington was a colossus with many more graves than all ABMC cemeteries combined, and it had a lower maintenance budget on a per-grave basis. The Belgians nodded with understanding. They had observed marble headstones severely stained, slumped out of alignment, and eroded almost to the point of illegibility. Lawn care also fell below ABMC standards. Apart from observing those shortcomings, the Belgians noticed that Arlington had one point of unparalleled excellence—the 3rd Infantry Regiment "Old Guard." That venerable unit performed all army burials at Arlington and represented the gold standard of military precision. Soldiers from Company C had the job of handling David Read's graveside service, one of twenty-five interments on the schedule that day at Arlington.

It was a day of wilting temperatures and humidity at the hallowed burial ground. The Read family and guests departed the air-conditioned comfort of the administration building and climbed into vehicles. Amid shimmering waves of heat, a silver hearse rolled along Eisenhower Drive. The vehicle carried PFC David A. Read's flag-shrouded casket. The funeral party followed in a pair of black limousines and more than a dozen other automobiles. Read's three surviving brothers rode in the limousines. I rode with the Belgians in their rental car. As we passed section 12, I glanced toward a grave I visited years earlier. It belonged to PFC Dean W. Sword, the second member of Read's company to die in combat. His family had interred him at Arlington in 1947.

After driving less than five minutes, the motorcade stopped at section 66, and everyone emerged from the vehicles. Six soldiers in dress blue uniforms—the casket team—waited at attention beside the road. They marched forward to the hearse and carefully removed the burial case. They carried it to a steel catafalque erected over Read's final resting spot. The soldiers bent at the knees and, in slow motion, set down the hardwood box. Their white-gloved hands lifted the flag, then pulled it taut and level. Despite the overwhelming heat, none of the casket men shed a bead of sweat, a testament to their physical condition. The men stood frozen with the flag while an army chaplain read the Twenty-third Psalm and spoke about Read's service as a combat infantryman. The clergyman also read from John 14 and he recited verses from "America the Beautiful."

Then a firing party raised its rifles skyward. The throaty voice of a sergeant commanded, "Aim! Fire!"

A seven-shot volley cracked the calm. Two more volleys followed.

In the distance, a bugler lifted a silver trumpet to his lips. He blew "Taps," crisp and impeccable. After his last note faded into the trees, the casket bearers folded the flag into a neat triangle and passed it to their sergeant. He turned and placed it in the chaplain's hands. The chaplain approached the Read family and knelt.

He gently conveyed the flag to Verne Read.

"Sir, I present this flag to you and your family on behalf of a grateful nation as an expression of our appreciation for the service and sacrifice that David gave to our country. I hope the flag will serve as a reminder to all that freedom is not free. It often costs us the lives of young soldiers like David." The chaplain rose, snapped a salute, and stepped away. The service took thirteen minutes.

The last member of the army contingent to leave the graveside was a single soldier—the "vigil." He watched over the casket until the funeral party departed. Afterward, cemetery workers lowered the wooden box into the earth.

VERNE READ INVITED EVERYONE to lunch at his hotel. My Belgian friends and I accepted the offer, and after eating and socializing we departed for Pittsburgh, site of the annual 99th Division reunion. The event was in full swing when we arrived, and we quickly located Chuck Fidler and Mary Maisel as well as Swanson and Whitmarsh. Fidler expressed disappointment when he learned that Marc Marique was unable to attend. Fidler had received his brother's dog tag from the army, and he wanted to present it personally to Marique, the digger who had found the artifact. Seel accepted the tag on behalf of his absent colleague. (Marique later had it framed with a wartime photo of Ewing Fidler.)

By this time, Seel and Speder had something akin to celebrity status at 99th reunions. Everyone seemed to know the Belgians, and they constantly had veterans tugging them in different directions and were guests of honor at the Saturday night banquet. The reunion became a blur of events. It ended the morning after the banquet when everyone except the Belgians and me departed for home. We had an engagement in Rochelle, Illinois. My calendar had Larson Funeral penciled in for July 22, 2002. The Belgians headed there via the Pittsburgh airport, and I began a long road trip.

The funeral was also on Rex Whitehead's calendar. He had never made plans to attend the Henri-Chapelle funeral because his emphysema precluded overseas travel, but he considered a flight to Illinois within the bounds of possibility. He hoped to be there with his oldest daughter, Robyn, and her husband. The ailing veteran wrote a eulogy that he intended to deliver in person. He clung to that ambition until a week before the funeral when I received an e-mail from him: "I was just faking myself out, for no way could I hack the trip to Illinois. I am sending my three daughters with their husbands, with Robyn and hers taking my place as a speaker. It is the best decision, but how I hate to give up." Whitehead asked me to digitally photograph the funeral and send him a CD-R with pictures. I promised to oblige.

My road trip to Rochelle ended the night before the funeral. The next morning, I visited Lawnridge Cemetery, about an hour before the church portion of the ceremony. The weather was hot and humid as it had been at Arlington. I spotted two vehicles parked in the sun, a dump truck heaped with earth and a flatbed carrying a burial vault. Near the vehicles, a solitary figure labored in the shade of a maple tree. He wrestled metal scaffolding into position over an open grave. The man spoke to me as I approached, and we chatted. During our conversation, I knelt down and brushed dirt off a pink-granite stone at the foot of the grave. The stone had Stanley E. Larson engraved on it as well as an American flag and a 99th Division checkerboard. At the head of the grave stood a large granite marker with the surname Larson. Inside the hole, I noticed the left side of a concrete box that held the casket of Larson's mother. The workman jockeyed the burial vault off the flatbed and over to the scaffolding. He scratched his chin. The hole was too small for the vault, but he said, "I'll find a way to squeeze her in there." I took a few pictures, knowing that Whitehead always had an interest in behind-the-scenes details. My time ran short, and I left the workman to reason out a solution to his problem.

I motored ten blocks along streets straight out of a Norman Rockwell painting until I reached Rochelle United Methodist Church, where I found a parking lot quickly filling with cars. Inside an annex to the church I found Seel, who guided me through the crowd and introduced me to Robyn Daines, the eldest Whitehead daughter. She introduced me to her sisters, Lane and Carolyn. She also introduced me to Leon Larson. As we shook hands, a newspaper photographer captured the moment. Within minutes, everyone began filing into the church sanctuary. Cloaked by a U.S. flag, Stanley Larson's casket sat at the top of the center aisle. Belgian and American flags graced either side of the altar. Seel and Speder looked on from a second-row pew, as did Speder's wife and Vern Swanson. I positioned myself above in a balcony where I had a good camera angle. The church organist played "Amazing Grace" as VFW members marched past the casket, each man stopping to render a hand salute.

The church service began after the VFW men took their seats. One speaker after another addressed the congregation, most of them born after the death of the teenage soldier whose memory they honored. Ron and Robyn Daines were two of the speakers, and Ron quoted words written by Rex Whitehead: "I have lived a long, happy life, enjoying family, business, trips, and good times. For Stan and the others, and many of them were just kids, there was nothing during that time— nothing." Ron said that a sense of debt and guilt motivated Whitehead to join the search for missing 99th Division soldiers. The search was a way of keeping faith with fallen comrades and requiting some of the prosperity he had enjoyed in life. After Ron and Robyn spoke, Speder addressed the congregation, and he described the search, which he likened to a persistent little flame flickering in the dark. "They're not forgotten," he said of the missing soldiers. All eyes and ears concentrated on the speakers. The words of 99th Division veteran Roger Foehringer caught the moment when he spoke on behalf of Stanley Larson: "It's great to be home, home where I belong."

The church pastor led the funeral party outdoors, and a hearse carrying Larson's casket soon led a train of cars, trucks, and vans. At Lawnridge Cemetery, soldiers from Fort Leonard Wood conducted the graveside service. Afterward, the crowd withdrew to the air-conditioned comfort of VFW Post 3878 in downtown Rochelle, where a buffet-style feast waited. Besides eating, everyone viewed the fountain pen recovered with Stanley Larson's remains. Ron and Robyn had brought the incredible artifact for all to see. There were also Larson family photos and mementos including Stanley's varsity letter. A picture of his mother sat on a table that commemorated her service as the first president of the Ladies Auxiliary at Post 3878.

That afternoon I had an opportunity to meet Maralyn Brennan-Guthrie, Stanley's high school sweetheart. She married in 1952 and had two children but had since divorced her husband. Among the Larson family photos, I noticed a cracked and faded snapshot of her standing arm in arm with Stanley. The smiling soldier had a suntan and wore summer khakis. I asked Maralyn if she remembered anything about the date or place of the photo, but she drew a blank. Someone sitting nearby had an answer. The picture was taken during Stanley's final visit home when he stayed with his sister and brother-in-law at their farm.

Out of curiosity, I later traced the dates of that visit. The morning reports of his company showed that he received a fourteen-day furlough beginning July 9, 1944. His mother remembered the furlough as a "happy time and one we will cherish." She saw him off at the local train station, and he spent July 22 riding the rails back to Camp Maxey, Texas. After his death, she wrote a poem about him and recalled his departure from home:

> *You said that morning as you stood there*
> *All dressed and ready to go*
> *"Mother it's going to be years*
> *Before I'll return to you."*

Stanley Larson returned to his mother fifty-eight years later on July 22.

Chapter 12

FRIENDLY FIRE

Vern Swanson had two goals in mind when he became involved in the search for missing servicemen. He wanted to find the graves of his comrades killed on Hill 627, and he wanted to see them buried in a manner befitting the measure of their sacrifice. After the funerals in 2002, he could have retired to some quiet corner, satisfied with having achieved his goals. Instead he felt a sense of loss. A driving force in his life had faded. It hit him after returning home to find he no longer had incoming e-mail. There had been a continuous stream of correspondence stretching back to the day Seel discovered the first dog tag on Hill 627. Swanson commented to me, "It's a shock to check the computer in the morning and find no e-mail."

The Belgian diggers and I felt a sense of loss, too. After more than a year standing on the pinnacle of success, we were now back at the bottom of the hill, pushing the boulder up again. We had many more cases to solve, enough to keep us working for decades. Swanson wasted no time in lending a hand and never considered doing otherwise. The Belgians resumed searching in fields and forests of the Ostkantone, while Swanson and I focused on a long-standing issue: X-9476.

Before the funerals, Swanson had several conversations with Liz Tate, and during one of them he mentioned X-9476 and dropped the names Earnest Brown and John Puckett. To his amazement, she knew the names and had contacted their families. She said that maternal relatives had donated blood samples for mtDNA analysis. Swanson and I knew that David Roath had made inquires about the case in 2001, but we had no idea what, if anything, occurred afterward. His inquiries had resuscitated the case, whereupon Tate took an active role. I sent her an e-mail expressing my appreciation for her help. I also made her aware of a complicating circumstance regarding Puckett. Besides his connection with X-9476, a link existed with another set of unidentified remains: X-3144.

ON MARCH 26, 1946, Graves Registration troops recovered X-3144 from a mass grave near the Elsenbüchel forest. Investigators learned that civilians had established the grave in the spring of 1945. The burial place contained the remains of seven Americans. The army eventually identified six of them: five infantrymen from the 99th Division and one airman from the 332nd Bomb Squadron.

Despite an exhaustive effort, army technicians failed to identify the seventh man. They designated him as X-3144. The remains were crushed and largely decomposed, weighing a mere sixty pounds. The lower jaw was the only portion of the head recovered. One dog tag accompanied the remains, but it belonged to a 99th soldier who survived the war and died in 1990. Ample remnants of GI clothing existed: cotton socks, wool scarf, wool undershirt, cotton undershirt, wool drawers (size 30), OD sweater, OD wool shirt, OD wool trousers, herringbone-twill jacket, web waist belt (size 36), and an M41 field jacket (size 36). Additional artifacts included an M1 rifle (serial #3090422) and an entrenching tool. There was also a helmet, which had the mark P-2911 in two places. The mark corresponded to John T. Puckett, 17082911.

Technicians compared Puckett's known height and the estimated height of X-3144. The two measurements matched. An odontologist compared Puckett's dental records with the lower jaw of X-3144. The comparison showed similarities but no exact match. The link between Puckett and X-3144 was clear, but insufficient to establish positive identification.

The army permanently interred the remains as an unknown soldier at the Ardennes American Cemetery: plot A, row 40, grave 32.

TATE THANKED ME for bringing X-3144 to her attention, and she forwarded my information to Hawaii. Months passed, and soon after the 2002 funerals I received an unexpected e-mail from Christopher M. McDermott, who introduced himself as "a historian working on European missing for the U.S. Army Central Identification Laboratory, Hawaii." He wanted to speak with me about X-3144 and X-9476. I provided my phone number, and he called several weeks later. During our discussion, I referenced my 1992 report on X-9476. He knew nothing about the report. None of the copies I had provided the army ever reached Hawaii, or if they had, no longer existed there. McDermott asked me to e-mail it to him. After promising to do that, I inquired about the mtDNA samples collected from the families of Brown and Puckett. I wondered if army scientists had compared the samples to mtDNA extracted from X-9476. McDermott said yes, and there was a match for one soldier but not the other. He declined to be more specific.

I asked if the army planned to locate the families of William Cooper and Harold Dechon. I had associated both missing soldiers with X-9476, despite a lack of information about the circumstances of their deaths. McDermott said the army intended to collect mtDNA from both families. We then discussed X-3144 and its tenuous link with Puckett. I suggested that Brown, Cooper, and Dechon might also be associated. McDermott agreed.

Together, X-3144 and X-9476 represented the remains of four soldiers, and we had four names. Analysis of mtDNA had already connected either Brown or Puckett to X-9476. After a decade of dawdling, the army appeared to be moving toward resolution.

I had always refrained from contacting the families of Brown and Puckett because I feared the army might never seek resolution. I imagined the emotional distress that knowledge might cause. The situation had thankfully changed. I decided to locate both families, and Swanson offered to help. Privacy Act restrictions prevented anyone in the army from disclosing the present whereabouts of family members, leaving us without access to Liz Tate's information. That meant that Swanson and I had to work through unofficial channels.

According to a 1946 document in my possession, Earnest Brown's wife and three children lived in Clintwood, Virginia, and his parents lived in nearby Bristol, Virginia. I searched the Internet and prepared a list of persons with the surname Brown currently living in those two Appalachian Mountain communities. Swanson selected nine people on the list and sent them letters of introduction. He also sent letters to the Bristol library and to five postmasters in the region. After allowing time for all the letters to reach their destinations, he followed up with phone calls. Within minutes he had someone who knew the right family. That came as no surprise since Appalachian communities tended to be insular places where family roots ran deep. Swanson then spoke with Reverend Paul Brown, the youngest brother of Earnest. As they talked, Paul said he had supplied a blood sample in 2001 and had occasional contact with Liz Tate until she left the army in 2002. Paul then had contact with Johnny Johnson, among others. Paul also mentioned that Tate had contacted Earnest's granddaughter in Clintwood.

Swanson kept in touch with Paul and Mary Ann until January 2003. That month the laboratory in Hawaii advised Johnson that mtDNA analysis showed no match for Earnest Brown. Johnson passed that information to the dead soldier's family.

With Brown no longer in the picture, the need to find John Puckett's family became paramount. I had already initiated a search, and Swanson lent a hand. According to Puckett's life insurance application, he had a mother and sister—Marie and Helen—living at 619 North Terrace Drive in Wichita, Kansas. Nobody named Puckett still resided at that address, but I found eleven people with that name living in Wichita. Swanson and I contacted each of them, but the search proved fruitless because none of them were relatives. I spent countless hours searching through census records in hopes of tracing John Puckett's family. The records yielded nothing. I presumed the mother had long since died and the sister probably married and no longer used her maiden name. Perhaps she still survived, but how could I locate her?

While searching the Internet, I found an e-mail address for Bill Pennington, a genealogist living in Wichita. I sent him a request for assistance. He replied the next day. Pennington had city directories and an abundance of other records at his fingertips. Those materials showed what Liz Tate had learned through Linda Abrams, that John Puckett had two sisters, Helen and Barbara, and his mother was a widow. According to the Social Security Death Index, her second husband died in 1977, and she passed away eleven years later. I thanked Pennington for his help. The following week, I wrote to the county registrar's office in Los Angeles, California, where Puckett's mother died, and requested a copy of her death certificate. It arrived several weeks later and provided the address of a daughter named Joann Bowman. The address on the certificate was still current, and I soon had a telephone conversation with Bowman.

She told me her full name was Helen Joann, but nobody ever called her Helen, including her parents. We talked for an hour and discussed her brother's life. I learned that he had become the man of the family at an early age when their father died in 1937. Jack Puckett graduated from Wichita High School and later attended the business school at the University of Kansas. He joined the Phi Gamma Delta fraternity and stayed in college until he voluntarily enlisted in March 1943. Several months later, he transferred to the ASTP and began attending Manhattan College in New York City. He remained there until the ASTP ended. and he received orders to Camp Shelby, Mississippi, where he joined the 69th Infantry Division.

Joann and I also discussed X-3144 and X-9476. She filled me in on the two letters she received in response to the blood sample she had provided in 2001. Around the time of the last letter, Liz Tate quit her job with the army, and thereafter Bowman found it difficult to get assistance. She always had to initiate contact and each time received the same vague response regarding her brother's case: "It's still being worked on in Hawaii." By the time I spoke with her, more than a year had passed since she had received the last letter. "I feel totally out of the loop," she told me. "I can't find anyone who knows what's going on with the DNA."

She asked what I knew about the situation. I said that in addition to her, the army had collected blood from Paul Brown. She had never heard of him. I told her that mtDNA from one of the blood samples matched mtDNA from X-9476. I then added that Brown had recently received word his sample was not a match.

"So my sample matched?" she said.

"Apparently," I said.

"How can I confirm that?"

She decided to continue calling her contacts in the army, none of whom were familiar to me. Swanson offered to help by asking his U.S. congressman to make an official inquiry.

Representative Mark Kirk belonged to the Armed Services Subcommittee, and he wrote to a colonel at the U.S. Total Army

Personnel Command to ask for a status report. Kirk received a response within three weeks but not from the colonel. The reply came from Mr. Johnie E. Webb Jr., deputy commander of the Central Identification Laboratory. He wrote a letter verifying that X-9476 represented the remains of three individuals. He also explained, "To date four bone fragments have been identified, using mitochondrial DNA analysis, as being those of Sgt Puckett." Webb went on to write, "No identification can be made for Pvt. Brown at this time, nor in the foreseeable future given the remains currently under analysis."

The letter confirmed what Swanson and I already knew. It also raised a new question. What bones did the four fragments come from? Maybe they represented some of the missing portions of X-3144. That possibility begged another question. Did the army plan to exhume X-3144 from the Ardennes Cemetery? Circumstantial evidence suggested a connection between X-3144 and X-9476. Both sets of remains may have shared a common burial site in the Elsenbüchel forest and may have become separated when Belgian civilians hastily removed X-3144 without realizing the site contained additional remains.

Webb's letter provided no timeline for resolving the X-9476 case and made no mention of X-3144. Two weeks after the letter arrived, an unexpected discovery in Belgium temporarily diverted attention from the case.

AFTER THE FUNERALS IN 2002, the Belgian diggers resumed work in the fields and forests that had become their primary search area. The list of missing soldiers in that area totaled forty-five names, half from units other than the 99th Division. Since I first began working with the diggers, we gradually expanded our scope of work to encompass units that fought alongside the 99th. We even added two fighter pilots from the Ninth Air Force. Yet our efforts centered on the 99th for one reason. Veterans of the division were the only ones who came forward with eyewitness information. We received no such response from veterans of other units, despite numerous attempts.

Clues provided by 99ers kept the diggers busy, as did my archival research. The diggers rotated between locations where missing soldiers died or where eyewitnesses last saw them. The search was like fly-fishing. The Belgians kept casting their lines in hopes of making a catch.

Their success in 2001 had earned them recognition throughout the region and carte blanche to operate almost anywhere. Gone were the days of surreptitious missions. They had support from forest rangers and other government officials. Seel never again had to worry about handcuffs. Digging was different for him in another respect, too. In recent years, he sometimes had the company of his older son, who loved to go digging with Dad.

In 1992, Seel had married an artist and esthetician named Marie-France Viroux, and they had two sons, Julien born in 1994 and Antoine born in 1999. At age eight, Julien began asking to accompany his father into the Ardennes. His papa consented and gave him a shovel. Julien entertained himself digging small targets his father pinpointed with the detector. The boy unearthed shell fragments and cartridge casings. Speder's two sons, both now teenagers, had also accompanied their father into the forest. The older one went digging once, but his interests lay elsewhere, mainly girls and soccer. The younger one, Roman, assisted his father on numerous digs and expressed a desire to own a metal detector someday. Marique had a son, his only child, and the two went digging together once. The youngster found a grenade, and his mother forbade any future outings. Menestrey had a daughter, and the idea of digging never entered her mind. She and her mother had equestrian interests. They owned a horse and a pair of ponies. Julien and Roman were the only ones who showed any signs of becoming diggers, although little Antoine was too young to have a leaning either way.

One of the places that Seel took Julien was a section of forest where a significant discovery had occurred in 1989. Relic hunter Jean-Michel Roth found a stainless-steel dog tag belonging to Manuel B. Wince of Pike, West Virginia. The soldier had died during the first two days of the Bulge, and the army never recovered or identified his remains. After discovering the dog tag, Roth traded it to Seel for a Luftwaffe dagger. Four years later, I located an eyewitness who reported that Wince fell mortally wounded in the area where Roth found the tag. I passed that information to the diggers, and they routinely searched the area in hopes of finding Wince's grave. They made several visits immediately after the 2002 funerals. Menestrey found a pair of service shoes belonging to a man from Wince's company. Nothing else special turned up there until the following summer when Marique found half of a German dog tag made from zinc. He surmised that it belonged to a soldier killed in action. German identification tags had a perforation so they could be snapped in half if the wearer died. The upper portion stayed with the corpse, and the lower portion served as a record of death. Unfortunately the tag that Marique found had serious corrosion, making it illegible except for the letter S. He also found two GI mess kits, one marked "A-1510" and another engraved with a name and serial number: BEAUDIN 6918829.

Seel dutifully recorded when and where every artifact turned up. He kept a journal of digging activities and also maintained a database of artifacts identified with individual soldiers. He occasionally sent me extracts from the database, and during the summer of 2003 I noticed a surprising statistic. None of the diggers had found an American dog tag in over two years. Prior to that time, they had steadily accumulated dog tags every year for well over a decade. The sudden change had a simple explanation. The diggers no longer trekked into the forest searching for artifacts. Their hobby had turned into a passionate search for specific missing servicemen. The shift in goals sharply reduced the number of areas where they spent time, and those places no longer had low-hanging fruit.

SEEL HAD A DAY OFF FROM WORK on September 16, 2003, and he planned to search a remote sector northwest of Rocherath. He and the other diggers frequently visited the area in hopes of finding two graves. As he drove through Rocherath, he approached an electronic signboard at the north edge of town. Most often the sign was dark, but that day its lights beamed a warning in two languages:

SCHIESSUBUNG
Gespertt nach 2 Km
TIR EN COURS
Route barrée à 2 Km

Seel cursed his timing when he saw the lights. The Belgian Army had the road blocked ahead because of firing exercises at Camp Elsenborn. Stray shells occasionally flew in the direction of the road, and that ruined his plans for the day. He had no way to reach his destination, and the destination itself was in the live-fire zone.

"Hmmm, what to do?" he said to himself. There were no other suspected grave sites anywhere close to his present location. While continuing in the direction of the roadblock, he detoured onto a slender asphalt road that cut through pastureland. An idea entered his mind. He remembered a nearby hole that he and Speder had partially excavated years earlier. It contained GI gas masks and cattle bones. Why not check the hole again? He had always wondered what else it had to offer. Seel veered onto a winding road that descended into a shady hollow. Hardwood trees of the Lichtenbret woods surrounded him. He pulled over along the road, and walked a few paces to the hole. It was much bigger than he remembered and too large for him to handle alone. The day seemed like a total bust, but serendipity had a surprise for Seel.

Acting on impulse, he decided to poke around in a dried-up creekbed on the other side of the road. His metal detector immediately led him to the tailfin of a German 12-cm mortar shell. He also found an American canteen cup made of stainless steel and a handful of 20-mm and .50-caliber brass casings. The cup had no markings that identified its owner but made a good holder for the casings. Farther down the creekbed, Seel collected one MKIIA1 fragmentation grenade and an expended M48 trip flare that he hacked free from tree roots. The bed also yielded the bottom half of an aluminum mess kit engraved Lt. Harris and an American entrenching tool with a thumb-sized hole punctured by shrapnel. As Seel continued moving along the bed, his detector indicated a sizable target just below the surface. He turned the soil with his mattock and found over two dozen 60-mm mortar shells. Among the pile of shells, he discovered the top portion of the carrying container for an American cooking stove. The artifact had the mark S-3050.

The south bank of the creekbed sloped uphill at a sharp angle. Seel began climbing upward while operating his detector. He picked up more GI material: another grenade, an aluminum canteen cup, and two M9A1 rifle grenades. Near the top, he came upon a kind of natural terrace. Standing there, he looked over the top of the bank. Several meters away stood a hunting lodge built after the war. It resembled a Swiss chalet and seemed vacant, all its windows tightly shuttered. He eyeballed a fine collection of stag skulls nailed to the back gable of the lodge. But something more interesting lay at his feet. The terrace had three shallow depressions. Foxholes, he thought. Glancing around, he realized the terrace would have made a perfect machine-gun position. It had a commanding view of the entire hollow and offered a superb field of fire.

He ran his detector over one of the depressions and found a grenade. The same thing happened in the next depression—another grenade. The third depression also held a grenade, but that one had fabric clinging to it. His detector indicated more metal targets below. He kept digging and found a packet of powdered lemon juice from a K-ration. On the left side of his hole, he struck something hard with the blade of his mattock. He noticed what looked like a tree root. There was a silver birch standing nearby, but as he studied the root closer he recognized it as something else—a human tibia. "My blood pressure was high in a second," he later recalled. He wiggled the leg bone out of the ground and noticed shreds of cloth around the spot where he removed it. As he examined the bone, he discovered that he had inadvertently cleaved off a long sliver of it with his mattock. Glancing at his watch, he saw the time was 1:00 P.M.

Seel cleaned the area of twigs, branches, and dead leaves. After resuming work in the hole, he pulled out four packets of instant coffee and a plastic comb. His detector had indicated something else metal in the hole, and he soon found the object, a spare bolt for a Browning M1917A1 heavy machine gun. As he enlarged the hole, another tibia and two femurs emerged, as did an American belt buckle and an M3 trench knife in its scabbard. Realizing he had found the grave of an American, a dread thought crossed his mind. What if there were no dog tags? Please, not another X-9476! Moments later, he brushed away soil and caught sight of a stainless-steel tag. It had a rubber silencer stretched around its rim, and that completely obscured the name of the soldier. The tag was on a chain, so he dug around for a second tag. Within seconds he had it, along with a corroded religious medal. The tag had a partially intact silencer, and he could read the name Odell. After more than a decade of searching for missing 99th Division soldiers, Seel had all their names and units memorized. The grave belonged to Odell Sharpe of Company H, 393rd Infantry. None of the diggers had ever searched for him because they had no information about the place and circumstances of his death.

The time was 2:40 P.M., and Seel dashed to his car and fetched his cell phone. No signal. He drove a short distance out of the forest and within range of a cell tower. The excited digger placed calls to his colleagues. He caught Speder at work, and Speder blasted out an e-mail stateside before heading to the recovery site. Within an hour, Speder and Menestrey rendezvoused with their lucky comrade. Only Marique had to remain at work. Speder brought a sifter, plastic bags, and digging implements. Menestrey brought a digital camera and began documenting the operation. Seel also had a camera and had already taken some photographs.

Tree and plant roots permeated the earth more than any other grave the diggers had hitherto encountered. Abundant moisture in the soil supported the vegetation. The water, combined with corrosive elements in the soil, had degraded the bones. All showed evidence of erosion. Riddled with holes, many bones looked like cork. Most of the small bones from the hands and feet had completely disintegrated. The hardest part of the excavation was removing the skull, which lay pinned under a thick root. Over a period of decades, the root had slowly crushed the facial bones. Afraid of doing more damage, the diggers gently loosened and removed the earth around the skull until it came free. Underneath the skull, they found a Bakelite box that contained a shaving razor and spare blades. The ribs and vertebrae were the last bones out. Traces of a shelter half also turned up in the hole. The dead soldier had perhaps lain on the waterproof canvas or someone had covered him with it. Seel ran his detector over the hole one last time and located a brass spoon.

The team finished at 6:15 P.M. and drove to the home of Erich Hönen. They informed the forest ranger of the discovery and turned over the remains to him. That night, Seel called David Roath at home, and he promised to dispatch personnel from his office the following week.

The next day, Speder and Menestrey took time off from work and met at Hönen's home. They cleaned the remains and did a skeletal reconstruction to determine which bones were missing. They also inventoried the artifacts. Sharpe wore a winter combat uniform typical for the Bulge: OD flannel shirt, OD wool trousers, OD wool sweater, and an M43 field jacket. He had no footwear, which suggested that German soldiers had discovered his body and removed his boots. He also had no watch or billfold, two other items the Germans might have removed.

All four diggers planned to take a vacation day and re-excavate the site on Friday, September 19. They hoped to uncover missing bones. Meanwhile, Speder and I began researching the circumstances of Sharpe's death. During previous years, neither of us had requested his IDPF because we never expected to find his remains. Not a single 99th Division veteran had ever come forward with eyewitness information. I had only one document pertaining to his death: the Company H morning report for December 28, 1944. The document listed Sharpe as missing on December 19 while occupying a "defensive position." Somebody in the company later penciled out the date 19 and wrote 25 above it. No reason given. The amendment changed Sharpe's official date of loss to December 25, which puzzled Speder and me. On that date, Sharpe's unit held defensive positions over two miles from the location of his grave. German troops controlled the terrain surrounding the grave at the time. The enemy soldiers took over the area after nightfall on December 19 when American units pulled out of defensive positions there. Sharpe belonged to one of those units.

Before pulling out that day, the men of Company H suffered dead and wounded during a "friendly fire" incident. Was Sharpe one of the dead men? I began contacting survivors of the company in an effort to learn the truth. Swanson helped me. Neither of us found a veteran who had witnessed Sharpe's death, but we found men who recalled the friendly fire and its human toll.

DECEMBER 18, 1944. The machine-gun crews of Company H used their steel helmets and entrenching tools to carve out fighting positions in the chilly, wet earth. Nearby riflemen did the same. The entire 2nd Battalion, 393rd, burrowed into the Lichtenbret woods and adjacent pastures. The soldiers heard the rattle of small-arms fire and the thump of big shells. Mayhem raged about a mile away in the twin villages of Krinkelt and Rocherath.

It was the third morning of the Bulge, and the previous day everyone in the battalion had retreated across miles of hilly timberland. The men now had orders to defend the Lichtenbret and tie in with units on both flanks. Enemy bullets and shells began nipping at the defenders, but the Germans made no serious push toward the woods. Some of the Americans kept watch, others catnapped in their holes, and others munched on K-rations, trying to fuel their exhausted bodies. During the late afternoon, the battalion received a radio signal ordering a retreat to Elsenborn Ridge. The battalion moved out after dark and made slow progress toward the ridge. The men tramped forward in long files. Their weaponry and ammunition hung on them like a ton of weights, as did their sodden overcoats. Many soldiers ditched these coats and wore only field jackets. Gas masks and other unnecessaries went by the wayside, too. While on the march, the unit received urgent instructions: "Get back! Turn around and get back!" The retreat signal had been a mistake. The men hung their heads in resignation, their spirits at low ebb. Nobody wanted to go back. The battalion completed the return trip by midnight, but many troops had difficulty finding their original positions in the darkness. When dawn broke, soldiers from one rifle company found their former holes occupied by enemy infantrymen. The Americans killed five Germans at bayonet point and reoccupied the area.

Elsewhere in the Lichtenbret, PFCs Milo V. Price and Lester Miller saw no sign of the enemy as they hunted for their original position. Price was a Serbian immigrant and a former ASTP man from Baylor University. Miller had grown up in the mountains of Kentucky and had no education beyond grammar school. The two men were ammunition bearers with the First Heavy Machine Gun Platoon of Company H, but that day neither man carried ammunition. It was their turn to lug the water-cooled machine gun and its tripod. Miller had the gun, and Price had the tripod. After finding their position, they shucked their loads onto the forest floor and began hanging their personal gear on a tree limb. Each man had a haversack, pistol belt, and a holstered .45 automatic.

Suddenly there was a noise in the air. They looked around searchingly. The noise increased from a whistle to a thunderous howl. Incoming shells filled the air. One round burst in front of Miller and Price. Another shell detonated behind them. The men fled to a nearby depression in the ground and flung themselves in. As they dove, a shell landed on their machine gun and blasted it to bits. The gear on the tree limb vanished. Geysers of smoke and dirt shot up in the woods. Incoming projectiles also burst in the treetops. Shell fragments whined through the air. Some of them careened into the mud and hissed until they cooled. Splinters from one shell reached Miller and Price despite their attempt to hide. One fragment ripped into the left pocket of Price's field jacket and struck a magazine for his pistol. The metal-on-metal collision diverted the fragment into his left thigh. The hunk of steel burrowed along his femur, cutting muscle but never breaking the bone. Miller fared worse. He took a hit to his lumbar vertebrae and lay paralyzed.

The bombardment lasted half an hour. During the shellacking, anguish seized the leader of the machine-gun platoon. First Lieutenant Francis A. Fariday Jr. was in tears when Price caught sight of him. The distraught lieutenant raced around, shouting and gesticulating for medics to attend to this or that man. He felt angry and impotent, powerless to make an iota of difference as he watched his men sliced down. Although unhit himself, the shelling irreparably injured the lieutenant. He crossed over some peculiar line that day and stopped being the person that he had been.

Litter bearers eventually got to Price and hauled him to a jeep. Still able to stand up, Price hopped around on one leg as medics helped him into the jeep. Several other wounded men boarded the vehicle, which was the only available transportation. Medics also retrieved Miller, and he survived the war. The Company H morning reports, notwithstanding the error regarding Sharpe, showed a total of ten casualties: one missing, two killed, and seven injured. The missing man was Sharpe, an ammunition bearer. The two killed were Sergeant Orleen S. Downing, a squad leader, and PFC Ernest T. Parker, a heavy machine gunner. Besides the Company H losses, another company reportedly suffered five wounded and seven killed.

Before Price departed the battlefield, he heard talk that American guns caused the causalities. Years later, James C. Revell of Company H explained what had happened: "A tank destroyer unit supporting us was misinformed as to our forward positions. Their shells exploded right above our machine gunners. They might as well have killed Lieutenant Fariday. He was never the same after that." (Medical personnel evacuated Fariday for combat exhaustion. He returned to Company H on January 12, 1945, but soon received a transfer to battalion headquarters, his nerves too shaky for front-line duty.)

As the morning wore on, the Germans began pressing the 2nd Battalion defenders, hitting their flanks with patrols. American mortar shells scattered the enemy, but more patrols ventured forward. Gun battles erupted. During the afternoon, the battalion commander received an order to pull back to Elsenborn Ridge. This time the order was genuine. After dark, the battalion abandoned the Lichtenbret. The overland route to the ridge was too treacherous for vehicles, so the men carried the remaining wounded and left the dead behind. The troops plodded westward with sagging shoulders and stony expressions on their faces. Mud clung to their boots in great globs and made each step a test of endurance. Fatigue seeped into their muscles and brains. Turning to look back, the weary troops saw German tanks in the distance. Behind the enemy machines, Krinkelt and Rocherath blazed away in the winter night.

THE DISCOVERY OF SHARPE'S GRAVE came almost six decades after the friendly-fire incident and at a time when his country was again fighting a war. David Roath knew the human cost of the latest war all too well. As of September 2003, he had personally spent four months in Iraq and Kuwait. His organization operated a mortuary at Baghdad International Airport and also had casualty-collection points throughout the country. The organization handled the daily flow of dead U.S. soldiers, airmen, and marines. There were other bodies, too: dead government contractors, journalists killed while accompanying U.S. forces, and the corpses of Saddam Hussein's two sons and grandson. In August 2003, Roath oversaw the recovery of remains after insurgents bombed the United Nations headquarters in Baghdad. He also had spent several weeks in Pakistan and Afghanistan. Combat operations in southwest Asia were the focus of Roath's activities, and he no longer had time for World War II recoveries and related research. He delegated that work to his colleague and subordinate Mark Baldwin, a white-bearded funeral director from Oklahoma whom Roath had hired in 2000. In addition to working on World War II recoveries, he had become a board-certified medicolegal death investigator (a credential also held by Roath).

The Sharpe case fell to Baldwin. He and Seel made arrangements to meet at Erich Hönen's home at 3:00 P.M. on September 22. Before the mortuary specialist arrived, the Belgian diggers returned to the grave site on September 19 and reworked the location. Alongside the grave, they found a shrapnel-riddled ammunition can of the type that Sharpe carried. In the hole itself, they uncovered assorted buttons, bits of clothing, and several small bones. Hönen observed the work and took possession of the newly found items.

The rendezvous with Baldwin took place at the prescribed time and place. He examined all the artifacts and human remains. He accompanied the diggers to the Lichtenbret woods, photographed the recovery area, and took longitude and latitude coordinates with a GPS device. While surveying the site, he and the diggers talked shop. Baldwin mentioned that he had recently acquired ground-penetrating radar. The equipment had its limitations, but the diggers knew of at least one 99th Division case where radar might prove useful. Before leaving Belgium that day, Baldwin made arrangements to return with a recovery team and comb the site one last time. In advance of his return, the diggers searched a wide area around the site and uncovered more American material, including rifle grenades, fragmentation grenades, and two bayonets. The diggers also found a German grenade and several Sturmgewehr magazines.

Baldwin and two enlisted men from his organization showed up on the morning of October 2 and started work at the burial place. Three of the Belgian diggers wandered below and searched for artifacts in and around the creekbed. Speder stayed above with the Americans. Late that morning, he saw a BMW station wagon arrive at the hunting lodge. Thinking it was the lodge owner, Speder strode over for a chat. To his surprise, Hönen climbed out of the vehicle, as did a gentleman clad in leather hunting apparel. Hönen introduced the man, but he was not the lodge owner. Earlier in the day, he had shot a deer in the Dreiherrenwald and attempted to field dress the animal but discovered his knife was missing from its sheath. He later encountered Hönen and explained the situation. The blade was as big as a bayonet and expensive. The forest ranger had an idea.

Upon hearing the story, Speder agreed to help. He grabbed his metal detector and jumped in the BMW. The hunter thought he lost the knife in an area that Speder recognized as the location where Captain Stephen Plume surrendered on the first day of the Bulge. High grass covered the ground. Speder immediately had a large echo near a tree stump. He pawed through the grass but found no knife. The target was underground and definitely not the missing knife. Probably a big shell fragment, he reasoned. Despite a sweep of the entire area, the knife remained lost. The hunter thanked him for an honest effort. Before leaving the forest, curiosity got to Speder and he checked the underground target. He had no shovel or mattock, so he dug with his bare hands until he felt something plastic and granular. It was the knurled grip of a Model 1911A1 .45-caliber pistol. Speder had searched in the Ardennes for twenty-four years and had never found one of these prized weapons. Ironically, he discovered this one after giving up relic hunting to search for missing GIs. While examining the weapon, he noticed that its safety lock was in the off position, and the weapon had one round chambered. Speder wondered if Plume had tossed it away before surrendering.

After being gone over an hour, the search party returned to the burial place. Seel asked if the knife turned up. "No," the hunter said. "Well, you didn't use the good detector," Seel said facetiously. Speder was getting out of the BMW and heard the remark. "My detector was good enough to find this!" He held up the pistol. Everyone gathered and listened to his tale of incredible luck.

Speder had the only success story that day. Baldwin's team enlarged the hole but discovered nothing more. So ended the recovery operation. The next step was to arrange for the legal transfer of the remains to U.S. custody. As part of that procedure, Baldwin had to answer one question with reasonable certainty. Were the remains actually those of an American? In order to provide an answer, he needed Sharpe's IDPF. It presumably contained medical records and other documents to support the material evidence gathered on-site. The dog tags constituted the best evidence, but they were only circumstantial in a legal sense. Biological evidence was paramount. Neither the Belgian diggers nor I had ever requested the IDPF, so Baldwin requested it himself. He anticipated a three-month delay in getting it. Staffers at the Hoffman complex in Alexandria had to have the IDPF pulled from a storage area deep in the underground recesses of the Washington National Records Center at Suitland, Maryland. During the delay and until legal transfer occurred, Hönen kept the remains and artifacts under lock and key.

Even though the recovery operation had ended, the diggers continued to visit the area looking for any bit of evidence that may have gone unnoticed. About one hundred yards from the site, Seel located an unexploded three-inch shell of U.S. manufacture. Rifling marks on its brass driving band indicated that it had traveled down a gun tube.

American M10 tank destroyers used ammunition of that type. Was the shell one of those unleashed during the friendly-fire incident? There was no way to know for certain. Seel photographed the item and reported it to Hönen. He in turn gave it to Belgian Army explosive-ordnance specialists at Camp Elsenborn, who disposed of the shell along with all other live munitions found in the Lichtenbret woods.

Speder too uncovered something, but not in the woods. He searched for the original owner of the mess kit that Seel found with Lt. Harris engraved on it. Speder queried his database of 99th Division soldiers and found First Lieutenant Paul D. Harris, leader of the Company H mortar platoon.

LIKE ME, REX WHITEHEAD RECEIVED e-mail notification about the Sharpe discovery on the day it happened. I expected to see a response from him. He loved to write e-mail, one of the few things he could still do despite his worsening emphysema. No response came. I then realized there had been no word from him in almost a month. The lack of communication suggested that the disease had finally reached its climax. That was indeed true. Hospice nurses had begun making daily visits to his home.

Whitehead's eight-year battle with emphysema ended on November 24, 2003. He was seventy-eight years old. He requested cremation, and his daughters honored his wishes. They planned to inter his ashes at a nearby cemetery in the spring, on his birthday.

DECLINING HEALTH ALSO BECAME a concern for Joann Bowman, John Puckett's sister. Her memory faltered with increasing regularity, and she often had difficulty completing sentences and finding words. Frustration mounted, as did worry. She began contemplating the possibility of Alzheimer's disease. Fear of that led to another worry. Would she still be alive and mentally competent when the army finally got around to resolving the X-9476 case?

Over two years had passed since she had provided a blood sample, and all she knew for certain was that army scientists had attributed four bone fragments to her brother. She longed for more information. Unexpectedly, an opportunity to learn more came about. She received a

Department of Defense flyer announcing a "family member update" meeting on February 21, 2004, in Woodland Hills, California. She immediately registered to attend. The meeting was one of nine scheduled at various locations around the United States during 2004. A letter from the Pentagon explained, "At the family update, you'll have the opportunity to meet with others who have lost a family member in one of our nation's conflicts. You'll also be able to meet with approximately twenty-five civilian and military representatives of the Department of Defense whose expertise includes: foreign government negotiations, policy, remains recovery and identification, DNA science, archival research, and intelligence analysis." The letter concluded by saying, "We will be prepared to discuss the latest developments in our efforts to resolve your loved one's case."

On the day of the meeting, Bowman navigated through a relentless downpour to reach the Marriott Hotel in Woodland Hills. She hustled inside out of the rain, and an army casualty officer welcomed her at the front door. Despite the inclement weather, there were only a handful of no-shows among the 120 family members registered to attend. Everyone spent the morning listening to briefings that included an audiovisual presentation on worldwide operations to recover and identify the remains of missing servicemen. Following a lunch break, Bowman had a one-on-one meeting with Johnie Webb. She pulled out a list of questions. As the two spoke, the casualty officer sat with them and took notes. Bowman's most important question was simple:

"What's the time frame for resolving my brother's case?"

"Within a year," Webb said.

Chapter 13
THE LONG SHADOW
OF WAR

The remains of Odell Sharpe stayed locked in a cabinet at the forest ranger's home throughout the winter. The delay resulted because the army had difficulty locating the IDPF for Sharpe. Mark Baldwin made four requests for the file, and it finally arrived after a six-month wait, twice as long as he had anticipated.

The file contained dental records and other information necessary to show a credible link between Sharpe and the remains recovered in the Lichtenbret woods. Baldwin contacted the European Regional Dental Command and arranged for a review of the records and the dental anatomy found with the remains. Anticipating a favorable comparison, he also arranged for a transfer of the remains from Belgian control to U.S. government custody. He made plans for the transfer to include a fallen-soldier detail as with previous transfers.

The dental review took place on April 28, 2004, at the home of Erich Hönen. Baldwin and a staff sergeant from his organization traveled there with Dr. Maria L. Freyfogle, a U.S. Army colonel and odontologist. She created a postmortem dental chart and compared it with the wartime records in the IDPF. Those records showed no dental restorations and no missing teeth. Freyfogle's chart showed no dental restorations and three teeth extracted before death. The differences were reconcilable, although there was insufficient evidence to make positive identification based solely on dental remains. Yet enough similarities existed to warrant the transfer to U.S. custody. Baldwin and the staff sergeant placed the remains inside a transfer case and covered it with an American flag. Afterward, all three Americans drove to the town hall in Büllingen, where they explained their findings to Jean-Pierre Kever, chief of the registry office for the local municipality. The meeting also included Seel and Hönen. The evidence presented during the meeting entailed more than dental records. Baldwin showed similarities regarding age, race, stature, and gender. He also provided IDPF documents that established the time period and geographic area where the 99th Division reported Sharpe missing. Kever accepted the evidence and completed the paperwork necessary to legally transfer the remains to American hands. The formal transfer took place the following day at the church in Krinkelt.

The 80th Area Support Group, headquartered at Chièvres, Belgium, provided U.S. troops for the event. They received the transfer case from Belgian Army soldiers while a crowd looked on. The highest-ranking American attendee was the chargé d'affaires from the U.S. embassy in Brussels. (There was currently no U.S. ambassador to Belgium. Stephen Brauer had resigned and his replacement had unexpectedly resigned before ever taking his post in Brussels.) Although on a smaller scale, the event followed the same pattern as the fallen-soldier detail conducted for Fidler, Larson, and Zimmerman. Following the solemn ceremony, Baldwin transported the remains back to the Landstuhl mortuary, where they stayed in storage pending shipment to Hawaii.

SWANSON AND WHITMARSH DECIDED to visit Belgium in June 2003. They also had a wartime buddy who wanted to return for the first time since the Bulge. Harold Wright had lost contact with the 99th Division until he read a newspaper article that I wrote about the recoveries on Hill 627. He recognized the names Swanson and Whitmarsh as well as Beckwith and Kokotovich. My article mentioned Swanson's place of residence, so Wright gave him a call and reestablished contact for the first time since December 1944. He began attending 99th reunions and inquired about joining a tour group of veterans heading to the Bulge area. Swanson and Whitmarsh told him to forget the tour group. "Come with us," Swanson said. "We're planning to go over so

Whitmarsh can show his two daughters and sons-in-law where he fought during the war." Wright eagerly accepted. He especially hoped to see the location of the aid station where he last saw Beckwith. Swanson said the Belgian diggers knew the spot and would take everyone there. Wright also wanted to visit Henri-Chapelle to see the graves of Beckwith and Kokotovich and those of other fallen comrades.

The day after the three 99th veterans left home for Europe, Seel received an unanticipated phone call from a man with a British accent. He introduced himself as Dr. Mark Leney, an anthropologist from the Central Identification Laboratory. He and several colleagues from Hawaii were at the Landstuhl mortuary reviewing files relating to unresolved casualty cases from World War II. Leney said the laboratory had recently become part of the newly created Joint POW/MIA Accounting Command, which he referred to as JPAC (pronounced "Jay-Pack"). Earlier in the year, he accepted a permanent position at the laboratory and was the first non-American anthropologist to work there. He had special expertise in mtDNA analysis and held the title of DNA manager at the lab. Leney hoped to find cases in Europe that his organization could pursue, such as aircraft-crash sites that still required excavation. The staff at Landstuhl had little time to handle those cases due to ongoing combat operations in Iraq and the constant flow of fatalities. While looking for new cases, he arranged to take charge of Odell Sharpe's remains and transport them to Hawaii. He also obtained Seel's phone number and called him with the intent of arranging a meeting. Leney and his colleagues wanted to see the recovery site and photograph it. He and Seel agreed to rendezvous in three days at Henri-Chapelle.

Swanson and his fellow travelers touched down at the Brussels airport, rented a van, and motored to the Ardennes. They soon learned about the upcoming meeting with Leney and adjusted their itinerary to include it. Beforehand, they squeezed in visits to Henri-Chapelle, Hill 627, and the aid station location. Speder acted as tour guide.

Seel kept his appointment with Leney. They met on June 16 at Henri-Chapelle (after Swanson, Wright, and Whitmarsh had already been there). Leney had three colleagues from Hawaii with him. The group of five drove to Stembert, where they picked up Marique and Menestrey. The next stop was the 99th Division monument at Krinkelt, where they rendezvoused with Swanson, the other two veterans, and

Speder. After a round of introductions, the group caravaned to the Lichtenbret, where Seel pointed out the burial place. The crew from Hawaii took measurements and shot photographs. Downhill from the area, Marique discovered another artifact. While kicking through dirt and leaves, he found a leather wallet that looked American, at least judging by its size and shape. Did it belong to Odell Sharpe? The wallet was old enough, but it contained nothing that identified its owner.

The meeting that day gave Swanson an opportunity to ask about the X-9476 case. Leney knew about it because it involved mtDNA analysis. The two men did more than discuss the case. They and everyone else departed the Lichtenbret and drove a short distance to Elsenbüchel forest. The Belgian diggers guided the group to the recovery site of X-9476, and Seel described how the discovery took place. The conversation turned to X-3144, and the diggers led the way to the spot outside the forest where that recovery took place. Leney said he and his colleagues had visited the Ardennes Cemetery to see the graves of several unknown soldiers, including X-3144. One of his colleagues was still at the cemetery checking records. The unknowns were candidates for disinterment and mtDNA analysis. Swanson asked when an exhumation might take place. Leney had no exact date. Red tape abounded. Swanson mentioned that Johnie Webb had recently assured Joann Bowman her brother's case would reach closure within one year. Leney seemed hesitant to endorse that assurance. "Was that an empty promise?" Swanson said. He went on to complain, "The army has piddled around for twelve years now. Somebody needs a kick in the ass!" Leney replied that he planned to personally oversee the identification process and that JPAC would operate within the time frame given by Webb. Leney also planned to oversee the identification of the remains believed to be those of Odell Sharpe. Swanson expressed satisfaction, and Leney promised to stay in contact with him. The two exchanged e-mail addresses.

The team from Hawaii departed, and Swanson focused on sightseeing plans. He and his group had reservations at an ornate Victorian-era hotel on the Rhine River. The vanload of Americans visited the remains of the Remagen Bridge where the 99th Division had crossed the Rhine in March 1945. They also stopped at Steinshardt, Germany, a village where Swanson's company suffered its heaviest casualties of the war. Six men died there and many more sustained wounds, including Whitmarsh. All the sights in Germany were new to

Wright, whose war had ended with trench foot in December 1944. At Steinshardt, he accompanied Whitmarsh and his family to foxholes in a nearby forest. Shortly after returning to town, Wright collapsed. He had suffered a massive heart attack. German paramedics arrived within minutes and managed to restart his heart and rushed him to a hospital in the city of Linz. The eighty-one-year-old veteran was brain dead, and three days later, his family gave permission via telephone for his removal from life support. Steinshardt had claimed another man from the ranks of Company C, 395th Infantry.

"It was a big shock losing him near the end of our trip." Whitmarsh later wrote. "However, I suppose it shouldn't be a big surprise when one of us age 80+ folks comes to the end of the line." Swanson echoed those sentiments, and commented, "I feel like I'm in good health, but who knows? Any given morning I could wake up dead. That's just the way it goes for us World War II folks. The clock is definitely ticking."

Joann Bowman still heard the clock ticking even after Alzheimer's testing showed no sign of the disease. Her memory difficulties had most likely resulted from her history of transient-ischemic attacks or mini-strokes, but the exact pathology behind her condition remained a mystery. All she could do was take a prescription blood thinner to reduce the possibility of a major stroke. If none occurred, she expected that she would be able to attend her brother's funeral. Then the bottom fell out of her hopes, and not because of her medical condition. Six months had passed since her meeting with Webb, and nobody from the army had provided her with a progress report. Her contact in Alexandria had no news and passed her request for an update to Captain Paul D. Madrid, chief of the World War II Branch, Repatriation and Family Affairs Division. He sent her an e-mail stating that none of her brother's remains had been identified. With regard to X-9476, he wrote "only Brown matches the mtDNA profile for some of those remains."

Madrid's words contradicted what Webb had told Bowman and had put in writing to Congressman Kirk. She immediately sent Madrid an e-mail asking for clarification. Why had the army done an about-face on her brother's case? She never received a reply from Madrid.

MARK LENEY ESCORTED Sharpe's remains to Hawaii. The laboratory took possession of them on July 21, 2004, and designated them as CIL

2004-103-I-01. The scientists who conducted the identification process worked blind according to standard procedure. None of them knew Sharpe's name. Since Leney knew the name, he took no part in the analysis work. He did, however, manage the process so as to ensure no undue delays.

The forensic odontologist completed his work in September and reached the same conclusion as Dr. Maria Freyfogle. Insufficient evidence existed to establish positive identification, but the odont found "no inexplicable discrepancies." He recommended the dental remains "be identified as possibly those of Private Odell Sharpe." The forensic anthropologist assigned to the case completed his work in October. He found no evidence of trauma before or at the time of death. All the bones required delicate handling on his part lest they fracture or crumble. In the anthro's expert opinion, the poor state of preservation resulted from decades of interment in a wet environment. He concluded that the remains represented "a Caucasoid male who was 16-20 years of age at death and who stood between 63.7 and 68.9 inches tall." After completing his initial analysis, he became privy to the name on the dog tags found with the remains. Given that information, he found "overall biological agreement between the skeletal remains designated CIL 2004-103-I-01 and the physical characteristics of Pvt. Odell Sharpe."

Two other anthros studied the artifacts found with the remains and prepared a material-evidence report. During the preparation of that report, the anthros made use of a twenty-page document titled "Recovery of Pvt. Odell Sharpe," which Speder authored the previous autumn. His document also served as a source of information during the preparation of a historical report, the one nonscientific report generated as part of the identification process. Historian Chris McDermott created the report.

Copies of all the reports went to the desk of Dr. Holland, scientific director at the laboratory. He studied them and rendered a verdict: "In my opinion, the results of laboratory analysis and the totality of the circumstantial evidence made available to me establish the remains designated CIL 2004-103-I-01 as those of: Pvt. Odell (NMI) Sharpe, 34834475, U.S. Army."

Holland forwarded his opinion and the reports to an independent consultant in upstate New York. The outside analyst studied the material presented and agreed with Holland's identification. On

November 8, the commanding general of JPAC forwarded copies of all the reports to the commander of Human Resources Command (formerly U.S. Total Army Personnel Command). The JPAC commander requested "disposition instructions" for the remains. The army now had to contact Sharpe's family.

THE PREVIOUS SPRING, I had tracked down Sharpe's next of kin in the rural town of Uvalda, Georgia. My search began after Mark Baldwin received the IDPF. One document in the file provided the first names of the dead soldier's parents. Baldwin faxed the document to Seel, who e-mailed me the names. My search for family members went no further than a genealogy Web site where one of them had posted a family tree. Odell Sharpe had three brothers and two sisters, and three of them still survived. The oldest, George Sharpe, resided in Uvalda. When Baldwin took custody of the remains, Speder provided a copy of his twenty-page report, and he also provided George's address and telephone number.

After Mark Leney transported the remains to Hawaii, Swanson decided to contact the family. He wrote a letter of introduction to George and told him about the ongoing search for missing 99th Division soldiers. The letter mentioned nothing about the recovery of his brother's remains because the identification process was ongoing. Swanson had several brief telephone conversations, and George mailed a couple of wartime pictures of his brother.

When the army positively identified the remains, Leney advised Swanson that someone from the Casualty and Memorial Affairs Operations Center would notify the family. Nothing happened. Swanson knew several people who worked there and placed a call to one of them. He reported to Leney in an e-mail, "I have a contact at CMAOC, so I called her about the notification. She received information about Odell Sharpe on November 12 but no call had been made because they had no information about the next of kin!!!!! I faxed the information to her. She asked me some more questions about other siblings and then assured me she would call George Sharpe immediately."

Leney had provided contact information, but somehow it never reached the woman responsible for making the call. After receiving Swanson's fax, she called George on November 24 and broke the news.

The following month, mortuary affairs specialist Johnny Johnson traveled to Uvalda and met with George and other family members, including his sister Mary Miller. During the meeting, Johnson presented copies of all the reports prepared in Hawaii, and George signed a document approving the identification of his brother's remains. Burial arrangements were also a subject of discussion. After the meeting, George decided on Sunday, January 30, 2005, for the funeral. He and his sister maintained contact with Swanson, who decided to attend the event, as did Seel and I.

During the week prior to the burial, the laboratory released Odell Sharpe's remains. As with every fallen soldier, the military provided a uniformed escort to ensure the remains reached their final destination safely and received dignified handling along the way. On this occasion, Johnny Johnson arranged for something special. The escort was Michael Cason, a great-nephew of the deceased and a marine staff sergeant assigned to a recruiting office in Alabama. After receiving travel orders, he flew to Hawaii, where he signed for a casket containing his great-uncle's remains and accompanied them to Savannah/Hilton Head International Airport in Georgia. The reception party at the airport included Mary Miller. "I thought my heart was going to burst out of my chest," she recalled after seeing her brother's casket. "It really, really hit me that he was home."

The day before the funeral, Seel, Swanson, and I caught flights to Atlanta, and together we drove south to a funeral home on the outskirts of Vidalia, Georgia. It was the nearest large town to the tiny community of Uvalda. The funeral home had a large chapel where the Sharpe family and friends had gathered that evening. Framed photographs of the teenage soldier sat on pedestals next to the flag-covered casket. One of the pictures showed his full head of curly, black hair. "It was pure ringlets, like a little girl's hair," Mary said to me. "He'd comb, and he'd comb, trying to straighten that stuff." She also told me that he took great umbrage when several of his childhood peers started calling him Kinkyhead. According to Mary, "That made him so mad, but he wasn't really a high-strung person. He'd just pout at them." She then added, "He had sky blue eyes like my mother. I always thought he was such a handsome brother."

Even though sixty years had passed since his death, the sense of loss and sorrow among his family was as strong as if he had perished only days before. World War II had cast a long shadow. The following afternoon, the chapel held over 250 people who turned out for the funeral. They listened to a tenor who strummed a guitar and sang. The preacher from one of numerous local Baptist churches presided over the service. Seel and Swanson addressed the crowd and told of past and present efforts to locate missing 99th Division soldiers.

The most striking part of the funeral was entirely unrehearsed. During the twenty-mile drive to Dead River Cemetery, all oncoming traffic—every single car and truck—pulled off the road and waited for the mile-long cortege to pass. Swanson commented, "They definitely have respect for the dead here. You'd never see this in other parts of the country." Seel nodded, and said, "And you'd never see it in Belgium, either." Along the route, policemen blocked intersections. One officer after another removed his hat as the cortege passed. Some lowered their heads, and others saluted.

Eight soldiers from nearby Fort Stewart conducted the graveside service. All wore the shoulder patch of the 3rd Infantry Division, and half of them wore it on both shoulders, indicating they had served in combat with the unit in Iraq. The soldiers followed the prescribed drill for rendering military honors. After the sergeant in charge presented the casket flag to George Sharpe, the funeral turned into an impromptu family reunion. It was shirt-sleeves weather, and much of the crowd socialized for nearly an hour. Seel and I chatted with friends and family, and we wandered around looking at headstones. The cemetery was the final resting place for veterans of every American war dating back to the revolution. It was also the resting place of Odell Sharpe's parents, Make and Lizzie. His mother died of cancer in 1967, and his father passed away in 1996 at age ninety-five. At the foot of their graves stood a weather-beaten cenotaph with Odell's name on it. The marble stone had come free of charge from the Veterans Administration. But due to the morning-report error, the stone had the wrong date of death: December 25, 1944. Sadly, the error also tainted every Christmas thereafter, bringing tears to his mother's eyes each year.

There was also another cenotaph, a homemade one (temporarily removed for the funeral). The grieving parents had memorialized their dead boy by casting a marker made out of concrete. Unable to read and write, Make had relied upon Lizzie to engrave words into the still-wet material. She used her finger. He later brushed on a coat of white paint.

Six decades later, their simple but lovingly made creation became a headstone.

AFTER ODELL'S FUNERAL, his three surviving siblings—George, Mary, and Joe—led my colleagues and me on a tour of land where their family once lived and worked. During the 1920s and the Great Depression, the Sharpe family had resided a few miles from the cemetery. Make and Lizzie labored as sharecroppers, a story as southern as Spanish moss and Stonewall Jackson. The family lived in a tin-roofed home provided by a local landlord, and their most valuable possessions were four mules. Both parents tended fields owned by the landlord, and they grew three cash crops: cotton, peanuts, and tobacco. Work in the fields stretched from sunup to sundown, or as Joe put it, "Everyone worked from can-to-cain't: just can see in the morning until cain't see in the evening." That schedule went on every day except Sunday. According to Mary, "After harvesttime, Daddy usually found employment rafting timber on a nearby river." When planting season arrived, he spent most of his waking hours bent over a plow under the Georgia sun. His wife often toiled at his side, and Odell stayed at home minding the younger children. On occasions when she worked at home, Odell and his brother Alex worked in the fields with their father. The boys spent innumerable hours stooped over cotton plants, pulling out their fluffy white bolls. The boys also "cropped off" tobacco leaves and helped their father thresh harvested peanut plants. Both brothers attended a one-room schoolhouse where they learned to read and write, but work in the fields eventually took priority. Odell went as far as the sixth grade. Like his forebears, he expected to spend his life sharecropping on some other man's dirt, earning just enough to survive. World War II altered his outlook.

The Sharpe family lived one hundred miles from the ocean and the port city of Brunswick, Georgia. Its population tripled during the war years after the J. A. Jones Construction Company took over a local shipyard and began building troop transports known as liberty ships. Much of the workforce flooded in from farming communities in Georgia and other southern states. The promise of high wages enticed Odell to join the migration to Brunswick. He became a welder at the shipyard and lived in a boardinghouse where three workers shared each bed and slept in shifts around the clock. Hot-bedding they called it. His father and brother Alex soon followed, and they eventually secured government housing whereupon the entire family moved to Brunswick. His mother joined the workforce, too, becoming a welder. Odell continued living at the boardinghouse and courted a dark-haired girl named Viola Wiggins, who came from a well-to-do family in town. He had come a long way from the barefoot boy in overalls picking cotton, but his brush with prosperity ended in January 1944. His hometown draft board sent him an induction notice.

He reported to Fort McPherson in Atlanta and then to Camp Wolters, Texas, where he received basic training. The fledgling soldier transferred to an infantry training battalion at Fort Meade, Maryland. He and the other men in his unit received orders to Europe but not as part of a fighting formation like the 99th Division. The men were merely privates destined to join combat units as individual replacements. Before shipping out, Odell received a furlough and returned to Brunswick. He asked Viola for her hand in marriage, but she declined under the present circumstances. She said, "I love you enough to wait until you return."

In Europe, a network of replacement depots, or "repple depples," replenished losses among front-line units. After landing in the United Kingdom, Private Sharpe bounced from one depot to the next and reached France in late July 1944. The next month, he became part of the newly established 3rd Replacement Depot, which served the First U.S. Army. The repple-depple network (part of the Ground Force Replacement System) had developed a notorious reputation for inefficiency and callousness. Treated like stockyard animals, men amounted to little more than commodities. When the demand for replacements ran high, soldiers who joined the 3rd moved quickly to one of several replacement battalions and then to the front. By the time Sharpe arrived, the demand had slackened, creating an overstock of replacements. He became stranded at the depot and moved with it across France and Belgium in the wake of the rapid Allied advance.

Seemingly lost in the system, his mail never caught up with him, even though his mother and others wrote to him almost daily. Like most GIs, letters from home were his only connection to everything he held dear. Loneliness and melancholy grew with each passing mail call. "Four months now and no mail," he lamented in a letter dated

November 10. "If I could just get some mail, it sure would make me feel a lot better," he wrote the following week. By the time he inked those words, casualties in First Army had begun climbing, and his state of limbo neared an end. On November 24, he and four other privates joined Company H, 393rd Infantry by way of the 41st Replacement Battalion. The privates, all ammunition handlers, replaced soldiers evacuated because of trench foot. The company was in regimental reserve at the time and two days later relieved front-line troops along the German border.

During the first days of December, he related good news to his parents. "Just a few lines to let you know I got your letter. Sure was glad to hear from you. I think I will get mail now that I am in a regular outfit. I sure hope so anyway."

A fortnight later, Odell Sharpe was gone, killed by friendly fire. He had spent less than a month with his company, and few people in the unit had ever learned his name or remembered his correct date of death. The very fact of his death had even been a matter of confusion at first.

The War Department initially sent his mother a telegram reporting him "missing in action since twenty-five December in Belgium." Another telegram reached her in July 1945, and it changed his status to "killed in action." According to Mary Miller, "Mama lost her mind" after the second telegram arrived. "She went totally crazy for a couple months, and then she finally came back to her senses."

As the war drew to a close, the construction of liberty ships at Brunswick ended, and the Sharpe family returned to Uvalda. The ex-shipbuilders sharecropped for a short period but soon purchased their own farm. They had saved enough money working for J. A. Jones to become landowners. The war brought Make and Lizzie Sharpe a piece of the American dream but at a heavy price—the loss of a son.

Chapter 14
CASE CLOSED

During the months leading up to Sharpe's burial, Vern Swanson kept in contact with Mark Leney, DNA manager at the laboratory in Hawaii. The aging 99th Division veteran advised Leney of distressing news. Joann Bowman, Puckett's sister, had received an e-mail from Captain Madrid of the Repatriation and Family Affairs Division. He stated that only Private Brown matched the mtDNA profile for the remains. Flabbergasted by that sudden reversal, Swanson appealed for clarification. Leney immediately calmed his nerves. Madrid had disseminated false information. There was indeed a match for Puckett, no doubt about it. Swanson immediately phoned Bowman. She breathed a sigh of relief and thanked him for his continued assistance.

Behind the scenes at the laboratory, Leney and other staff members considered exhuming unknown soldier X-3144 from the Ardennes Cemetery. Circumstantial evidence suggested the remains might belong to Puckett and should be consolidated with the remains already identified in Hawaii. DNA analysis offered a potential answer to the mystery, but there was a hitch. Leney knew it might be impossible to extract mtDNA from X-3144. During the 1940s and '50s, army morticians routinely sprinkled formaldehyde powder on decomposed remains. Intended as a preservative, the powder degraded mtDNA.

Leney had encountered the problem while conducting DNA analysis on unknown soldiers from the Korean War. The practice had thwarted the analysis process, and Leney had spent countless hours working on a scientific breakthrough to alleviate the impediment. Success still lay beyond his grasp, and he hoped X-3144 was formaldehyde-free.

Before an exhumation could take place, the laboratory staff needed the IDPF for X-3144, but the file had proven difficult to locate at the Washington National Records Center. During a conversation with Swanson, Leney learned that I had obtained a copy of the file years earlier. At his request, I mailed a copy to Hawaii and e-mailed scanned images of a tooth chart and skeletal diagram. The instant Leney saw the diagram, he knew that X-3144 was not Puckett.

The mtDNA supplied by Joann Bowman had compared well with X-9476, matching six teeth attached to a maxillary fragment as well as six long bones. The long bones included a left clavicle, left and right humeri (upper bone in each arm), a right ulna (lower arm bone), a 90-percent intact right fibula (smaller of the two long bones in the shin), and a 30-percent intact right femur. Each of those bones also appeared on the skeletal diagram for X-3144. The duplication of bones meant that X-3144 was somebody other than John Puckett. But who?

The likely X-3144 candidates were Earnest Brown, Harold Dechon, and William Cooper. Leney soon scratched Brown's name off the list after making an unanticipated discovery. Brown's mtDNA type matched three bones from X-9476: a right ulna, a left tibia, and a left hipbone. All three of those bones were present on the skeletal diagram for X-3144, so the unknown soldier had to be someone other than Brown or Puckett.

The positive match between Brown and X-9476 had gone unnoticed for months, and Leney figured out why. The staff in Hawaii had initially taken mtDNA samples from nine bones and submitted the samples to the Armed Forces DNA Identification Laboratory. Those samples had shown positive for Puckett and negative for Brown. In September 2003, the staff in Hawaii submitted samples from an additional six bones and two teeth. That sampling resulted in the positive match for Brown. It went undetected because the laboratory's computer software still showed Brown as negative based on the initial sampling. The first result should have been cleared prior to the second sampling.

The remains known as X-9476 represented Brown, Puckett, and a third person whose mtDNA type still had to be matched to a reference sample supplied by the family of a missing serviceman.

Maternal relatives of Dechon and Cooper had yet to submit mtDNA samples, so Swanson spearheaded an effort to find them. He hired a professional genealogist and quickly located maternal relatives willing to submit samples. Incredibly, a private corporation working for the army had contacted Dechon's family several years earlier with the goal of obtaining a blood sample. Somehow that contact never resulted in the submission of a sample. Acting on Swanson's information, Leney sent collection kits to both families, and they sent him vials of blood by way of an overnight courier. He forwarded the vials to the Armed Forces DNA Identification Laboratory.

Besides collecting the samples, Leney aimed to finally wrap up the Brown and Puckett cases. By November 2004, they were among the top ten cases awaiting closure at the laboratory. On average, its staff completed one case per week. Leney hoped to have Brown and Puckett resolved by the end of January 2005, but a sudden calamity ended that hope. During the final days of 2004, a magnitude 9.3 earthquake struck the eastern edge of the Indian Ocean, resulting in a tsunami that killed a quarter of a million people. The laboratory and JPAC dispatched forensic specialists to Phuket, Thailand, as part of Operation Unified Assistance. The specialists formed teams that helped identify human remains. Leney stayed behind in Hawaii, but other scientists working on the Brown and Puckett cases deployed to Thailand. At the end of January, the teams returned home.

The completion of scientific reports for Brown and Puckett took place shortly after the teams returned. During the final week of March, Dr. Holland, scientific director at the laboratory, approved the two identifications.

TWO MONTHS AFTER HOLLAND CLOSED THE BROWN AND PUCKETT CASES, the Armed Forces DNA Identification Laboratory attained a positive match between the hitherto unidentified portions of X-9476 and mtDNA obtained from the family of Harold Dechon. The identified bones and teeth included a left femur, right clavicle, right humerus, two fibulae, and four teeth attached to segments of maxillary bone.

After nearly thirteen years of delays and question marks, the X-9476 investigation had accounted for the remains of three servicemen, yet mysteries still lingered. Who was X-3144? The most likely candidate was now William Cooper, but the army had yet to make a decision whether to exhume the remains for mtDNA analysis. There was also another mystery. When and how did Dechon die? No eyewitness had ever stepped forward. The only information came from a document contained in the dead soldier's IDPF:

"Private Dechon was a member of a combat patrol whose mission on 23 January 1945 was to contact the enemy, capture prisoners, and locate enemy installations in a wooded area east of Elsenborn, Belgium. Private Dechon was last seen pinned down by intense enemy machine gun and mortar fire. Enemy activity was too strong to permit a search."

There was just one problem with that account. It bore no resemblance to actual combat operations on January 23 as recorded in the unit journal of the 394th Infantry Regiment. Dechon's outfit conducted only one patrol that day. All eight members of the patrol returned safely to friendly territory. Chest-deep snowdrifts were a bigger problem than the enemy.

So when did Dechon die? One plausible explanation came from John P. Scaglione of Woodside, New York. He and Dechon had served together in the 69th Infantry Division and had transferred to the 394th as replacements. The two became separated after joining different companies on Elsenborn Ridge. During the summer of 1945, Scaglione was traveling to Paris when he met a private who had served in combat with Dechon. The private told Scaglione, "I was next to Dechon when he got shot through the head." The private also said that he thought Dechon died on the ill-fated patrol that Company B launched on January 15.

One survivor of the patrol offered additional evidence. Cliff Selwood recounted seeing a BAR gunner drop to his stomach just as the patrol entered the forest. The man lay frozen with fear, never firing a shot. As the patrol began retreating under galling enemy fire, Selwood saw the man suddenly rise. "He jumped up from the snow and started firing his BAR and yelling at the same time." Crazy with courage, the man hollered like a marauding Apache as he cut loose with his weapon. The Germans ended his show of valor and madness. "They picked him off, hitting him a couple times in the head. The bullets tore away half of his face." Sixty years later, Selwood still retained a vivid memory of that BAR man screaming away the final seconds of his life. Who was he? Eyewitness testimony established that Brown and Puckett died under different circumstances. Dechon seemed to be the only possibility.

As THE FAMILIES OF BROWN AND PUCKETT went about planning funerals, Dechon's relatives knew nothing about the recent mtDNA results because the Central Identification Laboratory had yet to complete work on his case. The laboratory staff had no time to finish the job until well after the burial ceremonies for the other two soldiers.

During the first week of April 2005, the laboratory had forwarded the case files for Brown and Puckett to the Casualty and Memorial Affairs Operations Center. Someone at the center then telephoned both families on April 26 and informed them of the positive identifications. Joann Bowman expected the news, but it stunned Reverend Paul Brown. His sense of shock was little wonder. The army had previously told him that his mtDNA did not match any portion of X-9476.

The army now deemed Bowman and Reverend Brown as the persons authorized to direct disposition. On May 23, Johnny Johnson flew to Los Angeles and visited Bowman at her home in Pasadena. He presented her with a copy of the case file pertaining to her brother. She signed paperwork accepting the identification and specifying her preference for a place of final interment. Months earlier, she had decided to bury him at the Ardennes American Cemetery. She felt her brother should rest with other fallen soldiers in the land he helped liberate.

The following day, Johnson visited Reverend Brown in Bristol, Tennessee. During their meeting, Johnson explained that army scientists had identified three bones using mtDNA analysis. One of them was a left hipbone, and it allowed the scientists to identify another twenty bones using the principal of articulation. The left hipbone articulated with a sacrum and a right hipbone, and the sacrum articulated with eighteen vertebrae. After reviewing the science associated with the identification process, Johnson explained interment options. The Baptist minister decided to bury his brother alongside their parents at Sharrett Cemetery in Bristol, Virginia. (The city of Bristol lies astride the Virginia-Tennessee border.)

After completing the two visits, Johnson transmitted disposition instructions to the Central Identification Laboratory. Staff members at the lab coordinated with mortuary personnel at nearby Schofield Barracks. Those personnel took possession of the remains for casketing at a local funeral home and subsequent shipment on commercial flights departing from Honolulu International Airport.

AN AIRCRAFT CARRYING EARNEST BROWN'S REMAINS touched down in Knoxville, Tennessee, where a hearse driver from a Bristol funeral parlor took possession of the casket from a uniformed soldier who had escorted the remains all the way from Hawaii. During the subsequent trip to Bristol, eight motorcycles escorted the hearse. The riders all belonged to Rolling Thunder, a Vietnam MIA/POW advocacy group. They turned out as a show of respect.

Four days later, on June 15, 2005, well over a hundred people attended Brown's funeral, but only one of them had actually known the soldier. His wife and children had all passed away, the last one in 1998. All his brothers and sisters were gone, except seventy-four-year-old Reverend Brown. The elderly clergyman and his immediate family walked silently behind the casket. Earnest's granddaughters Mary Ann Boggs and Donna Johnston walked behind, too. Soldiers from Fort Lee, Virginia, carried the metal box to a catafalque set up over an open grave. Representatives of the Disabled American Veterans and Veterans of Foreign Wars accompanied the Brown family to the cemetery, as did countless local residents and police officers and bikers from Rolling Thunder. Following the graveside service, Paul Brown told a local newspaper reporter, "I know it's a sad day today, but there's also peace and joy to know that he's laying up there now with Mom and Dad, back home where he belongs. It's kind of a relief knowing I don't have to go through missing him anymore. I can visit when I want now."

VERN SWANSON AND I WANTED TO ATTEND THE BROWN FUNERAL, but we were in Belgium when it took place. Both of us traveled there to participate in Puckett's final interment. His sister Joann also made the journey, accompanied by her son Derek Bowman of Reno, Nevada, and her niece Sharon "Sherry" Hughes of Brampton, Ontario. All three made the trip at government expense, but they were not the first of their family to visit a U.S. military cemetery in Belgium. More than a half century earlier, Joann's mother had done the same during a vacation in Europe.

When I met Joann at our hotel in Belgium, she had a black-and-white snapshot of her mother kneeling beside a wooden cross with "UNKNOWN" stenciled on it. The Gold Star Mother had presumed her son rested in such a grave. Joann had believed the same. During her civil-service career with the Southern California Rapid Transit District, she attended a conference in Washington, D.C., and had an opportunity to visit Arlington National Cemetery, including the Tomb of the Unknowns. Joann gazed at the tomb with a faraway look in her eyes. Did her brother rest there? She never imagined that one day she would have an answer to that question.

On June 18, 2005, Joann entered the memorial chapel at the Ardennes American Cemetery for her brother's funeral. The building had an austere boxlike shape and an enormous American eagle sculpted in relief above the entrance doors. Inside the huge limestone structure, the flag-covered casket containing her brother's remains rested at the head of the center aisle. A framed photograph of the dead soldier sat on a wooden stand nearby. Nearly a hundred people packed the one-room building while many more waited outside. Joann took a front-row seat beside her son and niece. The four diggers, Swanson, and I had front-row seats across the aisle. The six of us were honorary pallbearers. Mark Baldwin of U.S. Army Memorial Affairs Activity–Europe served as funeral director and organized the event along with the cemetery superintendent, Hans H. Hooker. The funeral was the first interment at the cemetery since the burial of an unknown soldier in 1988. (David Roath had hoped to be at the funeral but was Stateside attending Army Management Staff School. The previous year, he had moved from Memorial Affairs to become chief of field services for the 21st Theater Support Command in Germany.)

The funeral service for Sergeant John Thomas Puckett began at 11 A.M. sharp and moved outdoors thirty minutes later. U.S. Army soldiers from the 80th Area Support Group carried the casket to a waiting hearse. The three family members rode in the hearse while the soldiers marched alongside. Following an asphalt pathway, the vehicle slowly moved through the burial ground. The honorary pallbearers walked just behind the hearse, and behind them followed all the other attendees, hundreds of them. Sunlight poured over the cemetery, and three colors predominated: blue of the summer sky, green of the pampered lawns and trees, and white of the marble crosses and Stars of David. It was a place of deep, quiet beauty, enough to make one jealous of the dead.

At the western edge of Plot B, the entire mass of people gathered around a blue canopy erected over an open grave. Mark Baldwin spoke a few words, and the chaplain, Lieutenant Colonel Byron Simmons, read from the Old Testament. After Joann received the casket flag, Hans Hooker addressed the crowd in English and French. He invited everyone to return to the memorial chapel for a short ceremony.

Twelve granite tablets flanked the chapel. They lay horizontally and had engraved on them the names of 462 missing servicemen. Here and there, bronze rosettes marked the names of men whose remains were no longer missing. Earnest Brown had a shiny new rosette, but John Puckett had none. His sister accepted the honor of putting one beside his name. She knelt down and threaded the rosette into a tiny metal sleeve recently set into the stone. That simple act brought closure to the Puckett case but only in an official sense.

JOANN BOWMAN CAME TO BELGIUM to do more than lay her brother to rest. She wanted to view the places where he spent the last days of his life. Her first stop was the brick factory at Welkenraedt where her brother initially set foot on Belgian soil after traveling by train from France. The factory complex had been abandoned for several years and had begun to crumble. She and her son and niece walked the factory floor, their shoes crunching bits of broken glass. They tried to picture the long-ago days when a river of replacement soldiers flowed through the collection of buildings. How many of those replacements never left Belgium alive?

After Welkenraedt, the three members of Puckett's family followed the route he had taken by truck in 1945 to the village of Elsenborn. The three rode in a van driven by Sergeant Anthony Maddox, a former Humvee driver with the 1st Armored Division in Iraq. At his side was Sergeant First Class Arlene S. Popp, the casualty assistance officer assigned to the family for the duration of their stay in Europe. More than 1,100 kilometers of roadway passed beneath the van as the two noncommissioned officers escorted the family over a six-day period.

Maddox normally served as a driver with the NATO Support Activity in Brussels. He had chauffeured many brass hats in his time, but in his mind, none of that compared with the privilege of accompanying Joann, Derek, and Sherry. In addition to Welkenraedt and Elsenborn, he took them to the 99th Division monument in Krinkelt, where they joined all four diggers and Erich Hönen. Swanson and I were there, too. With Hönen leading the way, the group drove out onto the open terrain of Elsenborn Ridge. It was a Sunday, so the area was free of Belgian Army troops who often trained there.

Moor grass and broom weed tufted the ridge, and a few tall bushes stood out against a sky swept clean of clouds. The ridge had remnants of World War II foxholes incised into its rocky soil. Derek, Sherry, and I hiked a short distance to the area where their uncle had once lived in a log-covered hole. I told them that he and his buddy Eugene Lett had insulated the hole with their woolen overcoats. Like most GIs on the ridge, they had spent day and night underground, seeking shelter from enemy shells and the icy breath of winter. Their only source of heat and light had been an old ration can filled with a lump of gasoline-soaked earth.

Derek was a "baby boomer," born after the war, and he never knew Uncle Jack. Sherry had seen him once but was only five months old. She told me that her father was an air force officer stationed at Langley Field, Virginia. One day, in November 1944, her mother and father bundled her in blankets and smuggled her aboard a military transport aircraft. They flew to an airfield in the New York City area where they met Jack. He and his regiment were at nearby Camp Kilmer, preparing to ship out for Europe. He later mentioned the meeting in a letter home, "I think of you all a lot and am certainly glad I got to see Sherry. I am really proud of my little niece." He never would have believed that one day she would stand on the wind-swept expanses of Elsenborn Ridge.

The final stop that Sunday afternoon was the Elsenbüchel forest, where a wooden cross marked the former burial site of Brown, Dechon, and Puckett. Around us, slanting beams of sunlight streamed in between the spruce boughs. Everybody listened as Seel and Hönen described the 1992 discovery. Seel spoke about the person or persons who had pilfered the site and presumably removed artifacts, maybe even dog tags, acts which might have thwarted the identification process.

The edge of the forest was a couple hundred yards away, and it was there that Jack Puckett found a bullet with his name on it. The group gathered at the location where the sergeant and his comrades entered the forest on January 15, 1945. I recounted what transpired that day as well as two weeks later when 99th Division soldiers finally captured the forest after a bitter struggle. German dead choked the woods, their bodies lying twisted and stiff. There were American casualties, too. But all that was difficult to envision six decades later as we stood there in the cathedral-like silence of the forest. My words and the place itself lacked the gravity to adequately convey the cold cruelty of war or the howling hurricane of combat.

After thirteen years, the Puckett story reached an end that day in the very forest where it had begun. My colleagues and I had never grappled with a tougher case than X-9476. We felt a sense of accomplishment but no sense of ultimate victory. The funeral of Harold Dechon still lay ahead as did resolution of the Cooper case, but even those events promised no end to our work.

For us there would always be one more lead to pursue, one more battleground to search, and one more missing man to find.

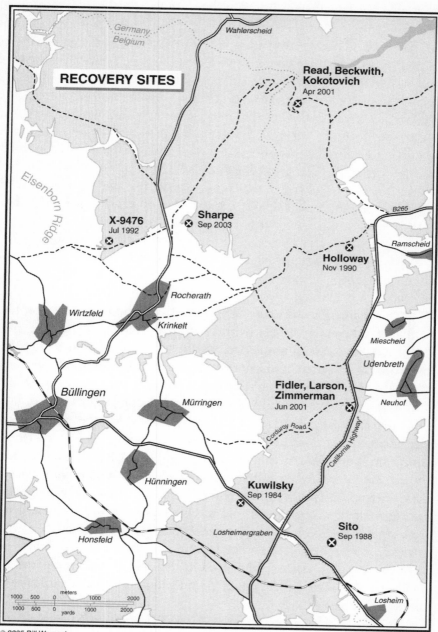

RECOVERY SITES

Germany
Belgium

Wahlerscheid

Read, Beckwith,
Kokotovich
Apr 2001

Elsenborn Ridge

X-9476
Jul 1992

Sharpe
Sep 2003

B265

Ramscheid

Holloway
Nov 1990

Rocherath

Wirtzfeld

Krinkelt

Miescheid

Udenbreth

Büllingen

Mürringen

Fidler, Larson,
Zimmerman
Jun 2001

Neuhof

Corduroy Road

"California Highway"

Hünningen

Kuwilsky
Sep 1984

Honsfeld

Losheimergraben

Sito
Sep 1988

meters
1000 500   0   1000   2000
1000 500   0   1000   2000
yards

Losheim

© 2005 Bill Warnock

Appendix A
ACCOUNTING FOR THE DEAD

The wartime graves registration process in the European Theater of Operations began with battlefield collection. Because the Graves Registration Service (GRS) did not engage in battlefield collection, the task fell upon combat units. Litter bearers usually carried the body of a fallen soldier to a battalion collecting point, normally near a battalion aid station. Procedures at collecting points varied, but generally medical personnel checked each body for the presence of identification. The medics also slipped each body inside a mattress cover, the World War II equivalent of a body bag. Regimental service troops then evacuated each body to a division collecting point serviced by GRS troops. The collecting points usually occupied advantageous positions along major supply routes. One platoon (twenty-three men) from the 606th Graves Registration Company serviced the 99th Division. Operating under the assumption that the possibility of identification diminishes as bodies change hands, the GRS men held all bodies at the division collecting points until positive identification could be established.

Normally, the presence of two identification tags sufficed to establish positive identification. But soldiers in combat sometimes exchanged tags, and it became customary to check a man's tags against his driver's license, personal letters, and identification cards. If no discrepancies arose, the body had clearance for delivery to a temporary cemetery operated by GRS personnel. But the absence of identification tags meant the beginning of a wider search. After studying all papers on the body, examiners checked the time and place of death against operational records to determine which unit had been in the area. The likeliest parent unit received a request to report the names of all persons missing on the specified day and to send someone to the collecting point to examine the unidentified body. Prompt identification of as many bodies as possible at division collecting points reduced the number of unidentified bodies delivered to cemeteries.

The final phase in the wartime graves registration process involved burying the dead in accessible and well-maintained cemeteries. The 99th Division had a plot within the First U.S. Army temporary cemetery at Henri-Chapelle, Belgium. If both identification tags were present, cemetery workers left one on the body and nailed the other to the back of a wooden grave marker. If only one tag was present, workers secured an embossed metal plate to the back. The front had a stenciled name and serial number. In each case, the workers placed a copy of the interment report in a sealed waterproof container and deposited it in the grave. The report contained a complete history of the decedent, including all details regarding the manner and place of death, objects found with the body, and other pertinent data. The GRS seldom performed embalming or used caskets at its cemeteries. The incredible volume of casualties precluded such niceties. Dead soldiers went into the ground encased in nothing more than a mattress cover. Decomposition occurred quickly. (After the war, the army disinterred all the dead and placed their remains in steel caskets. The family of each fallen serviceman had the option of having his remains "repatriated" to the United States or interred at a permanent military cemetery overseas.)

All phases of the wartime graves registration process depended in large part upon prompt and efficient execution of the initial phase of the process at battalion level among fighting units. Yet these units, because of their preoccupation with combat at the very times when casualty rates ran the highest, were least able to meet their responsibility with respect to the dead. The weakest link in the process was the one that anchored it to the battlefront. That was never truer than during the Battle of the Bulge when numerous fighting units left bodies behind as German troops overran large swaths of territory. The bodies became recoverable only after U.S. forces threw back the enemy advance. But the possibility of recovery and identification diminished when a long delay like that occurred. (After the Bulge, one platoon from the 606th Graves Registration Company and one platoon from the 3060th Graves Registration Company swept the First U.S. Army area, which included the 99th Division battleground. Many 99ers participated in the grim work. Recovered bodies went to Henri-Chapelle.)

V-E Day brought an end to hostilities in Europe and a need for the GRS to shift its emphasis from the collection and evacuation of battlefield fatalities to the search and recovery of isolated remains and the final disposition of war dead. This shift occurred in accordance with the European Casualty Clearance Plan approved by the War Department on July 12, 1945. Unfortunately, downsizing and reorganization of U.S. forces in Europe hampered the shift. It became imperative for the GRS to restructure itself as a self-sufficient, theater-level command. On October 1, 1945, the War Department established the American Graves Registration Command (AGRC). The introductory paragraph of its plan for "Operation and Organization" stated:

"In resolving the undetermined casualty status of military personnel in connection with the European Casualty Clearance Plan, it is considered, as a basic premise, that all otherwise undetermined cases are those of potential death. Therefore, it becomes an accepted responsibility of the American Graves Registration Command to undertake the location, not only of recorded or reported burials of United States military deceased, but the searching out of all probable locations of graves for those in an unsolved casualty status who, under the basic premise, will be presumed to have become deceased."

This in part resulted in a twofold search-and-recovery operation: 1) the implementation of area sweeps to locate, identify, and evacuate isolated burials and unburied remains; 2) the coordination of activities aimed at resolving unsolved casualty cases (e.g., "unknown soldiers").

The task of search and recovery normally began with an AGRC search team usually consisting of three persons—a team leader, a driver, and an interpreter. Within the bounds of an area designated for a sweep, the search team traveled by jeep to communities in an effort to solicit information regarding the whereabouts of American dead. In particular, the team contacted prominent members of the community, including the mayor, police, parish priest, and other persons thought to have pertinent information. Sometimes a publicity team placed bilingual posters on billboards and distributed report forms. Newspaper announcements and radio broadcasts further increased public awareness. Upon completion of a search, the team leader prepared detailed reports on all discovered isolated graves and unburied remains. Each report went to an AGRC recovery team.

In most instances, a recovery team consisted of five persons—a medical technician, clerk-driver, and at least three laborers. Arriving in a community with information gathered by a search team, the recovery team journeyed to the grave site or unburied remains and recovered the remains. The team always endeavored to obtain one or more of the following items: 1) an identification tag worn around the neck; 2) a paybook found in the clothing; 3) an emergency medical tag—U.S. Army Medical Department Form No. 52b—signed by a medical officer and fastened to the body; 4) an identification bracelet worn around the wrist; 5) an official military identification card found on the person.

Recovery teams operating throughout Europe transferred all recovered remains to military cemeteries in the liberated countries where identification teams processed all remains. After August 1, 1946, all remains went directly to the newly established Central Identification Point (CIP) at Strasbourg, France.

Among the most important functions of the CIP were "the thorough processing of all remains recovered by the search teams, and the recording of all information gathered; preparation of remains for reburial in a temporary U.S. military cemetery; the reprocessing of unknowns currently buried in temporary U.S. military cemeteries and of special cases as directed, and the conduct of research in the field of identification processing for the purpose of developing new and better techniques and improving those currently employed."

Thorough processing of remains involved a complete anatomical examination to determine age, race, and stature as well as any physical abnormalities that might aid in identification. Evidence of criminal violence required examination by specialists from the War Crimes Commission. Radiologists at the CIP used a fluoroscope to detect foreign objects like jewelry and identification tags embedded in the remains. Technicians scrutinized all clothing and equipment and recorded color, design, fabric, and size measurements. If necessary, the clothing underwent a special cleaning process designed to bring out faded laundry marks. Clothing and equipment also provided clues as to nationality and branch of service. Personal effects provided clues, too. At the CIP's chemical laboratory, faded writing on paper documents was often made decipherable by treating the paper with a solution of ammonium sulfide. Infrared lamps and ultraviolet lamps also helped decipher faded writing and laundry marks. Laboratory staff members examined hair, jewelry, bloodstains, and anything else that could provide a clue. In all cases, technicians made tooth charts and, whenever possible, took fingerprints. Beyond the scientific means employed at the CIP, researchers consulted documents such as battle maps, morning reports, after-action reports, missing-aircrew reports, and individual service records.

Standard procedure at the CIP required two or more of the following items to establish identity: 1) identification tags, when found elsewhere than on the person of the deceased, but in the immediate vicinity; 2) a motor vehicle operating permit, government or civilian; 3) personal papers, including a social security card, marriage certificate, wills, letters addressed to the decedent, money orders, unofficial identification cards and similar papers; 4) engraved jewelry; 5) laundry marks containing the first letter of the last name and the last four digits of the decedent's serial number; 6) favorable comparison of tooth charts obtained from the remains and the last known tooth chart of the deceased.

After processing a set of remains, CIP workers wrapped it in a clean sheet and blanket and then placed it in a casket. When two identification tags were available, the workers fastened one tag to the blanket near the head and tacked the other one to the head of the casket in the upper-right corner. In cases where only one tag existed, an embossed metal plate went on the head of the casket.

In the late spring of 1947, budget cuts forced the CIP to transfer its operation to the AGRC Depot at Fontainebleau, France, and the U.S. cemetery at Neuville-en-Condroz, Belgium (future site of the Ardennes American Cemetery). By the end of 1947, the unit at Fontainebleau moved to Neuville-en-Condroz where the CIP remained until 1950, when it moved a short distance to the outskirts of Liège. When the AGRC officially terminated operations on December 31, 1951, statistics showed a total of over 148,000 recovered dead in the European Theater. Of that number, slightly over 1,700 remained unidentified. The small percentage of "unknowns" reflected great credit upon the AGRC and the CIP in particular.

After the AGRC disbanded, recovery and identification of World War II remains became the responsibility of the 7770th European Quartermaster Mortuary Service and various descendent organizations finally emerging in its current configuration as the U.S. Army Memorial Affairs Activity–Europe. The mission of those organizations centered on current casualties, service members and their dependents who died on assignment in Europe and neighboring areas. World War II cases were an add-on to the mission, and no money or personnel existed to conduct search operations as the AGRC had done. The recovery of remains occurred primarily as the result of accidental discoveries. The identification process took place at an army mortuary in Frankfurt, Germany.

In 1982, the identification process shifted to the Central Identification Laboratory, Hawaii. The laboratory had already been in existence for six years but had focused on cases related to the recent war in southeast Asia. The first European casualties identified in Hawaii were three soldiers of the 63rd Infantry Division killed in Germany during the final months of World War II. Mortuary affairs specialists from USAMAA–E recovered the remains and shipped them to Hawaii. That arrangement became standard procedure thereafter. USAMAA–E continued to carry out recovery operations, but it began sharing the work in 1996 when CILHI started dispatching staff members to Europe. They made several trips each year, sometimes working alongside USAMAA–E personnel. However, the greatest number of World War II recoveries undertaken by CILHI took place elsewhere, especially at aircraft-crash sites in China and on Pacific islands.

"There is an unprecedented need for additional WWII recovery teams," CILHI reported in a fiscal year 2000 report to Congress. "Not only has the advancement of communications and technology facilitated the increase in potential WWII resolutions but the collapse of communism in Eastern Europe will undoubtedly continue to yield the discovery of more WWII sites." The report explained that CILHI had teams operating at "full capacity" in Southeast Asia and North Korea. According to the report, "It must be said that CILHI is currently executing WWII investigations and recoveries by exception. Congressional interest is a primary reason that current cases are investigated and subsequently excavated. The organization has not been equipped with enough personnel and resources to complete more extensive operations."

As of this writing, the lack of personnel and resources still exists with respect to World War II recoveries in Europe. After the war in Iraq began, USAMAA–E transferred much of its responsibility for World War II cases to CILHI—now called JPAC. The men and women of USAMAA–E still conduct recoveries but only when JPAC lacks the ability to respond in a timely manner after a discovery occurs.

In the near future, the Department of Defense plans to restructure and decrease its presence in Europe, and USAMAA–E will downsize accordingly. JPAC may soon be the only organization capable of conducting recoveries in Europe.

Appendix B
U.S. ARMY DOG TAGS
IN WORLD WAR II

The War Department introduced a new identification tag in December 1940, and it became known as the M1940 (Quartermaster Stock No. 74-T-60). The new tag was rectangular with rounded corners and measured 2 inches x 1⅛ inches. It had a thickness of .025 inches and a smooth, rolled edge. (The previous type had been circular and about the size and thickness of a half-dollar coin.) The M1940 also had a "locating notch" on its left edge, and that notch permitted proper alignment of the tag in Graphotype or Addressograph embossing machines. The M1940 tag was the first embossed tag worn by U.S. Army personnel.

The War Department originally specified a silver-colored nickel alloy called Monel as the only authorized metal. It contained 65–70 percent nickel, 20–29 percent copper, and small amounts of iron, carbon, silicon, and manganese. That composition gave it resistance to corrosion, but nickel became a critical material during the war years and the army frequently used brass as a substitute. Brass also became critical, and 18/8 stainless steel (18 percent chromium, 8 percent nickel) eventually replaced Monel and brass. Stainless steel proved far superior to either metal in terms of corrosion resistance.

Seel and Speder have recovered many stainless-steel tags since 1980, and each tag came out of the ground without a trace of corrosion. The two diggers have also found numerous brass and Monel tags. The brass ones always showed the effects of corrosion, ranging from red-and-green patina to severe pitting and erosion. The Monel tags often exhibited corrosion, ranging from reddish purple patina to pitting and erosion. Monel tags sometimes had green patina because the metal contained copper. The diggers occasionally found Monel tags in pristine condition. They looked exactly like stainless-steel tags, but a simple way existed to tell them apart. Monel and stainless steel made distinctly different sounds when dropped on a hard surface like stone.

Embossing Formats

Each M1940 had room for five lines of type with eighteen spaces per line. Changes to army regulations yielded four embossing formats that appeared on identification tags during World War II. Other formats existed but had no official basis.

First format, authorized 12 December 1940
Line 1: Name of wearer (1–18)
Line 2: Army serial number (1–8)
Line 3: Next-of-kin name (1–18)
Line 4: Next-of-kin street address (1–18)
Line 5: Next-of-kin city and state (1–18)

Second format, authorized 10 November 1941
Line 1: Name of wearer (1–18)
Line 2: Army serial number (1–8), tetanus immunization year (10–12), tetanus booster year (14–15), blood group (17–18)
Line 3: Next-of-kin name (1–18)
Line 4: Next-of-kin street address (1–18)
Line 5: Next-of-kin city and state (1–18), religion in space 18 if vacant, otherwise in space 18 of Line 4

Third format, authorized 20 July 1943
Line 1: Name of wearer (1–18)
Line 2: Army serial number (1–8), tetanus immunization year (10–12), tetanus booster year (14–15), blood group (17–18)
Line 3: Blank
Line 4: Blank

Line 5: Religion (18)

FOURTH FORMAT, AUTHORIZED 31 MARCH 1944
Line 1: Last name, first name, middle initial (1–18)
Line 2: Army serial number (1–8), tetanus immunization year
(10–12), tetanus booster year (14–15), blood group (17–18)
Line 3: Blank
Line 4: Blank
Line 5: Religion (18)

NAME OF WEARER: Prior to March 1944, no rule existed regarding word order, but one problem remained despite the creation of a rule. The first line sometimes lacked enough space for individuals with long names. The War Department resolved the problem in April 1946 with a change: "In those cases in which the space provided on the first line is insufficient to emboss the name ... the first line will contain the last name only. The first name and middle initial will be placed on the second line." That format sometimes appeared during the war but on an unofficial basis. Another unofficial format appeared, too. The first line had eighteen spaces according to army regulations but the line could actually accommodate twenty spaces. The two extra spaces sometimes provided enough room for a long name. Other unofficial formats during the war also solved the long-name problem.

TETANUS IMMUNIZATION: The letter T and the last two numerals of a year reflected a serviceman's first tetanus immunization, e.g., T43. That injection usually occurred when he entered active duty or soon thereafter. He usually received a tetanus booster during his second year of duty, but occasionally the booster came during the latter part of his first year. Sometimes he had the last two numerals of the booster year embossed on previously issued tags, but often that never happened because he received new tags instead.

BLOOD GROUP: A, B, AB, or O were the only authorized symbols. They lacked Rh status, i.e., Rh positive or Rh negative (blood group + Rh status = blood type). Army regulations during World War II referred to blood group as blood type because Rh status was not fully understood at that time.

NEXT-OF-KIN INFORMATION: For security reasons, NOK names and addresses disappeared beginning in July 1943, thus revealing only minimal information about servicemen who fell into enemy hands, dead or alive.

RELIGION: The only authorized abbreviations were C for Catholic, H for Hebrew, and P for Protestant. No convention existed for servicemen who declared another preference, e.g., atheist, agnostic, Hindu, Muslim, or Buddhist. Such a person typically had no preference embossed on his tags, but sometimes P was used as a matter of expediency. Jewish servicemen occasionally declared no preference as a means of protection in the event of capture by Nazi forces.

SOURCE DOCUMENTS

The documents below provided the basis for embossing formats used during World War II.

CIRCULAR   WAR DEPARTMENT,
No. 151   WASHINGTON, December 12, 1940.

* * * * *

I—Changes in AR 600-40.—Pending the revision of AR 600-40, June 22, 1931, paragraph 35 of those regulations is rescinded and the following substituted therefore:

35. Tags, identification.—a. Two identification tags of monel metal, each approximately 2 inches long by $1^1/_8$ inches wide, and about 0.025 inch thick, the corners rounded and the edges smooth, will be worn by each member of the Army when in the field, when traveling on transports, and when the field kit is worn in garrison; one tag to be suspended from the neck underneath the clothing by a cord or tape, 40 inches in length, passed through a small hole in the tag, the second to be suspended about $2^1/_2$ inches above the first one, on the same cord or tape, both held securely in place by knots.

b. Each tag has a capacity of five lines of type, and will be embossed, by a machine provided for that purpose, as follows:

First line:	Name of wearer.
Second line:	Army serial number.
Third line:	Name of person to be notified in case of emergency.
Fourth line:	Street address of person to be notified in case of emergency.
Fifth line:	City and State address of person to be notified in case of emergency.

c. Identification tags are prescribed as a part of the uniform, and will be habitually kept in the possession of the owner. The tags embossed as herein provided will be issued to each member of the Army as soon as practicable after entry in the service.

(A.G. 421 (12-3-40).)

ARMY REGULATIONS   WAR DEPARTMENT,
No. 600-35   WASHINGTON, November 10, 1941.

* * * * *

62. Tag, identification.—a. Of monel metal, approximately 2 inches long by 1⅛ inches wide, and about 0.025 inch thick, the corners rounded and the edges smooth.

b. Each tag has a capacity of five lines of type, 18 spaces to the line, and will be embossed by a machine provided for that purpose as follows:

First line: Name of wearer.

Second line: First eight spaces, Army serial number; ninth space vacant; tenth, eleventh, and twelfth spaces, record of tetanus immunization (date completed) (letter T and the last two numerals of the year); thirteenth space vacant; fourteenth and fifteenth spaces, the last two numerals of the year in which the immunity stimulating injection of the tetanus toxoid is completed; sixteenth space vacant; seventeenth space, the letter signifying the blood type; eighteenth space vacant unless the blood type is indicated by two letters. For example:

30611333 space T41 space 42 space A or

30611333 space 41 space 42 space AB

(Blood types are indicated by the symbols "A," "B," "AB," "O.")

Third line: Name of person to be notified in case of emergency.

Fourth line: Street address of person to be notified in case of emergency.

Fifth line: City and State address of person to be notified in case of emergency.

The religion of the wearer, when stated, will be stamped in space 18 of the fifth line if that space is vacant, otherwise in space 18 of the fourth, and will be indicated by a capital letter as follows: C for Catholic; H for Hebrew; and P for Protestant.

After completion of the initial tetanus immunization and the blood typing test, additional records of these data will be made by inserting the identification tag in the model 70 addressograph and adjusting it so that it will print only the first two lines of the identification tag. A record will then be made by operating this machine so that the information contained in the first two lines is printed on the individual's Service Record (W.D., A. G. O. Form No. 24) under "Other vaccinations," and on the Immunization Register (W.D. , M. D. Form No. 81) under "Tetanus Toxoid" as indicated. Upon the completion of the immunity stimulating injection of the tetanus toxoid, the last two numerals of the year in which it occurred will be entered on the forms by writing them into the spaces corresponding to spaces 14 and 15 of the printed record, and embossing them on the tag in spaces 14 and 15.

CHANGES
No. 25

WAR DEPARTMENT,
WASHINGTON 25, D.C., 20 July 1943.

AR 600-35, 10 November 1941, is changed as follows:

* * * * *

62. Tag, identification.

* * * * *

b. Each tag has a capacity of five lines of type, 18 spaces to the line, and will be embossed by a machine provided for that purpose as follows:

First line: Name of wearer.

Second line: First eight spaces, Army serial number; ninth space vacant; tenth, eleventh, and twelfth spaces, record of tetanus immunization (date completed) (letter T and the last two numerals of the year); thirteenth space vacant; fourteenth and fifteenth spaces, the last two numerals of the year in which the immunity stimulating injection of the tetanus toxoid is completed; sixteenth space vacant; seventeenth space, the letter signifying the blood type; eighteenth space vacant unless the blood type is indicated by two letters. For example:

30611333 space T41 space 42 space A or
30611333 space 41 space 42 space AB

(Blood types are indicated by the symbols "A," "B," "AB," or "O.")

The religion of the wearer, when stated, will be stamped in space 18 of the fifth line if that space is vacant, otherwise in space 18 of the fourth line, and will be indicated by a capital letter as follows: C for Catholic; H for Hebrew; and P for Protestant.

ARMY REGULATIONS   WAR DEPARTMENT,
No. 600-35   WASHINGTON 25, D.C., 31 March 1944.
                    * * * * *

85. Tag, identification.—*a.* Of monel or other adopted metal, approximately 2 inches long by 1⅛ inches wide, and about 0.025 inch thick, the corners rounded and the edges smooth.

b. Each tag has a capacity of five lines of type, 18 spaces to the line, and will be embossed by a machine provided for that purpose as follows:

(1) *(a) First line.*—Name of wearer as follows:
Last name, first name, middle initial.
Example:
    Doe, John C.

(b) Existing identification tags in possession of individuals will not be reembossed to change the order of the name as indicated above. Identification tags embossed from this date on will follow the order prescribed above.

(2) *Second line.*—First eight spaces, Army serial number; ninth space vacant; tenth, eleventh, and twelfth spaces, record of tetanus immunization (date completed) (letter T and the last two numerals of the year); thirteenth space vacant; fourteenth and fifteenth spaces, the last two numerals of the year in which the immunity stimulating injection of the tetanus toxoid is completed; sixteenth space vacant; seventeenth space, the letter signifying the blood type; eighteenth space vacant unless the blood type is indicated by two letters. For example:
    30611333 space T41 space 42 space A or
    30611333 space 41 space 42 space AB
(Blood types are indicated by the symbols "A," "B," "AB," or "O.")

(3) The religion of the wearer, when stated, will be stamped in space 18 of the fifth line if that space is vacant, otherwise in space 18 of the fourth line, and will be indicated by a capital letter as follows: C for Catholic; H for Hebrew; and P for Protestant.

(4) After completion of the initial tetanus immunization and the

blood typing test, additional records of these data will be made by inserting the identification tag in the model 70 addressograph and adjusting it so that it will print only the first two lines of the identification tag. A record will then be made by operating this machine so that the information contained in the first two lines is printed on the individual's Service Record (W.D., A. G. O. Form No. 24) under "Other vaccinations," and on the Immunization Register (W.D., M. D. Form No. 81) under "Tetanus Toxoid" as indicated. Upon the completion of the immunity stimulating injection of the tetanus toxoid, the last two numerals of the year in which it occurred will be entered on the forms by writing them into the spaces corresponding to spaces 14 and 15 of the printed record, and embossing them on the tag in spaces 14 and 15.

NOTES

Chapter 1: Creepy Corner

"C'est occupé!" (p. 3), e-mail from Jean-Louis Seel to the author, 8:45 A.M., July 18, 2003.

"He asked me" (p. 4), letter from Jean-Philippe Speder to Richard Byers, December 1, 1990.

"Find anything?" and following quotation (p. 6), author's interview with Jean-Louis Seel, Waterside Marriott, Norfolk, Virginia, July 5, 2003.

For "unforgettable restaurant" (p. 8), letter from Jean-Philippe Speder to Richard Byers, December 1, 1990.

"We were very touched" and following quotations (p. 8), author's interview with Jean-Philippe Speder, Waterside Marriott, Norfolk, Virginia, July 5, 2003.

"For me, the billfold was a private thing." (p. 9), author's interview with Jean-Louis Seel, Waterside Marriott, Norfolk, Virginia, July 5, 2003.

"The first time I read George Ballinger's story" (p. 11), letter from Jean-Philippe Speder to Richard Byers, December 1, 1990.

For "Creepy Corner" (p. 11), eleven-page letter from George Ballinger to Jean-Philippe Speder, undated but postmarked October 18, 1989.

"When one exploded" (p. 12), four-page letter from George Ballinger to Jean-Philippe Speder, undated but postmarked January 31, 1990.

The mortally wounded platoon leader was Second Lieutenant Charles E. Butler. He died while hospitalized on December 18, 1944. (p. 12)

"The Germans, who had moved up quite close" and following quotations (p. 13), eleven-page letter from George Ballinger to Jean-Philippe Speder, undated but postmarked October 18, 1989.

The II. Bataillon of Grenadier-Regiment 48 carried out the German attack against Ballinger's company. Major Gerhard Kruse commanded the enemy battalion. He was a highly decorated officer, holding the Knights Cross with oak leaf cluster, the German Cross in Gold, and the Honor Roll Clasp. (p. 13)

"I wasn't more than three or four meters away" and following quotation (p. 14), letter from Robert Muyres to Jean-Louis Seel, October 25, 1988.

In his letter of October 25, 1988, Muyres stated that he shared a foxhole with an "assistant squad leader named Davidson," who was killed during the German attack. But in a subsequent letter dated February 27, 1989, , Muyres corrected himself and said, "I told you his name was

Davidson, but I now remember it was Davis." That was Staff Sergeant Robert W. Davis of El Cerrito, California, but he survived the war. Like many members of his company, Davis was a prisoner at Stalag XIIID. In May 2002, he and his wife visited Losheimergraben and met Seel. Davis confirmed that he shared a foxhole with Muyres. The man who died was Staff Sergeant Ernest F. Davidson of Alabama.

"It seemed as if all their firepower" and following quotations (p. 14), eleven-page letter from George Ballinger to Jean-Philippe Speder, undated but postmarked October 18, 1989.

Ballinger died of cancer on September 15, 1999 at age eighty-five. His son and daughter interred him at Highland Cemetery in South Bend, Indiana.

The B/394 morning report for December 15, 1944, recorded 159 officers and enlisted men present for duty. Subsequent morning reports recorded 101 officers and enlisted men missing in action. Of that number, 7 were dead (including Sito), and 94 were prisoners of war.

"When I regained consciousness" and following quotation (p. 15), letter from Robert Muyres to Jean-Louis Seel, October 25, 1988.

The Germans evacuated Muyres to Bad Neuenahr and a military hospital that had been a luxury hotel in peaceful times. He remained there until February 1945, when he was transferred to another hospital at Olpe, about twenty-five kilometers east of Cologne. Troops of the U.S. 8th Infantry Division liberated him there on April 9, 1945. After the war, Muyres traveled to Olpe six times to visit a German doctor and a Catholic nun who had treated his injuries. Muyres passed away at age sixty-six on December 26, 1991.

"They disliked the military" (p. 16), author's interview with Richard Sito, August 27, 2003. (similar quotation found in a letter from Richard Sito to Rex Whitehead, October 10, 1990.)

Stanley Sito died of heart failure on October 24, 2001, at age eighty-one. His brother John died on July 14, 1991, at age fifty-eight, and his brother Frank died on September 17, 1994, at age seventy-two.

Chapter 2: Digging into History

"Yeeees, another rifle!" and following quotation (p. 20), e-mail from Jean-Philippe Speder to the author, 4:50 P.M., December 12, 2003.

EC blank powder was a proprietary compound first manufactured by the Explosive Company in England, hence the designation EC. The powder consisted of 80.4 percent nitrocellulose, 8.0 percent potassium nitrate, 8.0 percent barium nitrate, 3.0 percent starch, 0.6 percent diphenylalamine.

"The guy came out" (p. 23), e-mail from Jean-Louis Seel to the author, 10:32:13, September 17, 2004.

"*Chocolat* for Mama?" and following quotation (p. 24), Jean-Louis Seel, MIA Project presentation, 99th Infantry Division Association Reunion, Biloxi, Mississippi, August 4, 2004 (videotape by Kathy Winkle).

"I'd sooner have you break a leg" (p. 24), author's interview with Jean-Louis Seel, Waterside Marriott, Norfolk, Virginia, July 5, 2003.

"Then, like in slow motion" (p. 26), e-mail from Jean-Philippe Speder to the author, 22:07:53, September 15, 2004.

Franz Kuwilsky rests in block 57, grave 24 at the Lommel Soldatenfriedhof in northern Belgium.

"We stopped in Verviers" and following quotation (p. 31), author's interview with Jean-Philippe Speder, Waterside Marriott, Norfolk, Virginia, July 5, 2003.

"The dog tags found in a forest" and following quotation (p. 31), letter from Mary Wisnieski to William Cavanagh, September 16, 1984.

"No, no, not in my car!" and following quotations (p. 33), author's interview with Jean-Louis Seel, Waterside Marriott, Norfolk, Virginia, July 5, 2003. Dialogue between Seel and Mrs. Haulotte extracted from author's interview with Seel, November 21, 2004.

The *Nebelwerfer* projectile was a 15-centimeter Wurfgranate 41 Spreng.

The 105-mm antitank shell that killed Rahier contained 2.5 kilograms of Pentolite, an explosive made from TNT and Penthrite. By comparison, a standard 105-mm high-explosive round packed a heavier punch, containing 4 kilograms of TNT. If Rahier had set off one of those, the deadly blast would have ripped into neighboring homes.

"He was on the front page" (p. 38), author's interview with Jean-Louis Seel, December 24, 2004.

For "What's next?" and following quotations (p. 38), author's interview with Jean-Louis Seel, Waterside Marriott, Norfolk, Virginia, July 5, 2003.

"Hand me your identification cards" and following quotations (p. 39), author's interview with Jean-Louis Seel, August 29, 2004.

For "thick as a dictionary" and following quotations (p. 39), author's interview with Jean-Louis Seel, Waterside Marriott, Norfolk, Virginia, July 5, 2003.

"We came face-to-face" and following quotations (p. 41), author's interview with Jean-Louis Seel, August 29, 2004.

Herbert Meister died while serving with the 8. Kompanie of Fallschirmjäger-Regiment 5.

"School was mainly a place" (p. 43), e-mail from Jean-Louis Seel to the author, 10:03 A.M., August 27, 2003.

Chapter 3: "Can You Help Find Them?"

"500 German dead" (p. 45), Crookenden, *Battle of the Bulge* 1944, p. 25.

"One for you" (p. 47), author's recollection, corroborated by William Cavanagh.

"My uncle had a truck" (p. 49), author's interview with William Cavanagh, October 18, 2004.

"We could hear rifles" (p. 50), Howard I. Bowers, *Memories of World War II*, p. 17. (unpublished manuscript, revised June 1, 2004).

"The Association has a number of Associate Members" (p. 51), letter from Walt Schroeder to the author, undated but October or November 1985.

In the Ostkantone, the so-called Heimattreue Front opposed Belgian control after World War I and aligned itself with the NSDAP (Nazi party). Between 1940 and 1945, 8,700 German-speaking Belgians served in the Wehrmacht and Waffen-SS. About two thousand died in combat and sixteen hundred came home as invalids. An unknown number of Ostkantone residents joined anti-Nazi resistance movements. The two main (noncommunist) armed resistance groups were the Armée Secrète and the Front de l'Indépendence.

"Belgian Makes Big Discovery" (p. 54), *Checkerboard: Official Publication of the 99th Infantry Division Association*, March 1988, volume 41, number 2, p. 12.

"It may be six months" (p. 55), *Checkerboard*, February 1989, volume 42, number 1, p. 2.

"Artilleryman's recollections of Bulge" (p. 55), *Checkerboard*, December 1988, volume 41, number 6, pp. 3–9.

"On the way out" and following quotations (p. 56), *Checkerboard*, December 1988, volume 41, number 6, p. 5.

"Christ, I hope it doesn't tear my trench coat!" (p. 57), *Checkerboard*, December 1988, volume 41, number 6, p. 7.

"Unfortunately it was unusable" and following quotation (p. 59), *Checkerboard*, December 1988, volume 41, number 6, p. 4.

"W. of Missing" (p. 59), *Checkerboard*, February 1987, volume 40, number 1, pp. 8-9.

"MIA, Still Missing After 45 Years" (p. 61), *Checkerboard*, March 1990, volume 43, number 1, p. 3.

Chapter 4: The Triumph of Teamwork

The first member of Company K to die in combat was PFC Buefird T. Bowman, a twenty-two-year-old machine gunner from Coolville, Ohio. The mortar shell that killed him November 18, 1944, also wounded Sergeant Gilbert B. Northcott and PFC James W. Phillips. The three casualties served with the Second LMG Squad of Holloway's platoon.

For "incompetence" (p. 63), letter from Joseph Dougherty to the author, December 15, 1988.

For "severe alcoholic" and following quotation (p. 63), letter from Joseph Dougherty to the author, January 7, 1986.

"He was locked up" and following quotation (p. 64), letter from Joseph Dougherty to the author, September 15, 1986.

Stephen Kellogg Plume Jr., from Watertown, Connecticut, spent five years at the United States Military Academy: July 1, 1936, to June 11, 1941. (Plume's maternal grandfather, John Spry Parke Jr., graduated with the class of 1879 and retired as a colonel before his death in 1927.) After graduating from the academy, Plume attended the basic infantry officers' course at Fort Benning, Georgia and then became a member of the 1st Infantry Regiment (6th Infantry Division) at Fort Leonard Wood, Missouri. In February 1942, he moved to the Infantry Replacement Training Center at Camp Croft, South Carolina, where he served as an instructor and later commanded an OCS preparatory school. While at Camp Croft, he attained the rank of first lieutenant on June 12, 1942 and the rank of captain on March 22, 1943. He returned to Fort Benning in June 1943 and completed the advanced infantry officers' course. Afterward, he joined the 393rd Infantry Regiment in Louisiana and had short-lived assignments to Headquarters Company, 1st Battalion and then Headquarters Company, 2nd Battalion. By the time the 393rd embarked overseas, he had become the munition officer for Service Company. According to company morning reports, he went AWOL in Belgium at 07:00 hours on November 6, 1944, and returned the following day at 15:30 hours. He found himself under arrest and confined to quarters under the provisions of Article of War 104 (disciplinary powers of commanding officers). He spent three days under arrest. Plume was relieved of his duties as munition officer and transferred to Company I, where he became leader of its Weapons Platoon. The transfer took place on November 13, and Plume remained there until December 1, when he received command of Company K. He became a prisoner of war just over two weeks later. After being liberated from German captivity in April 1945, he became a patient at Moore General Hospital in North Carolina. The former POW returned to duty at Fort McClellan, Alabama, and received an overseas assignment to Germany, where he spent three years with a constabulary unit. In 1949 he entered the Armored School at Fort Knox, Kentucky. While a student there, he appeared before an elimination board, which questioned his fitness to remain in the military. He survived the proceedings and stayed at Fort Knox until 1951, when he transferred to the 5th Cavalry Regiment (1st Cavalry Division) in Korea. After that unit moved to Japan in 1952, he remained in Korea and became a ground liaison officer assigned to the 474th Fighter Bomber Group at K-8 Airbase. Repeatedly passed over for promotion, his military career ended on June 1, 1953, after a court-martial convicted him of "dereliction of duties" and "drunk and disorderly conduct."

"Fisher, the company executive officer" (p. 64), letter from Joseph Dougherty to the author, August 15, 1986.

"I went to battalion" (p. 64), letter from Joseph Dougherty to the author, January 7, 1986.

"He once told me" (p. 65), author's interview with Dwight Bishop, October 21, 2004.

"He liked to walk alone" (p. 67), letter from Joseph Dougherty to the author, January 7, 1986.

For "getting along swell" and following quotation (p. 67), letter from Holloway to family, December 15, 1944. Holloway's sister had the original letter framed and donated it to the 99th Infantry Division Collection at the Soldiers and Sailors Memorial Hall in Pittsburgh, Pennsylvania.

"Bart, here's a pair of binoculars" (p. 68), author's interview with Nello Bartolozzi, March 1, 1992.

The Company K morning report for December 16, 1944 listed 172 soldiers as present for duty. That included six officers.

"I knew what they meant to do" (p. 70), author's interview with Dwight Bishop, October 21, 2004.

"He apparently had been in his sleeping bag" and following quotations (p. 70), *Kapers*, second quarter, 1999 ("Bazooka team gets back to battalion despite Capt. Plume" by Donald Rader and edited by Byron Wilkins).

"Lou Gainey came to me" (p. 70), letter from Thomas Price to Richard Byers, May 28, 1990.

"Okay, well, come on in here" (p. 71), author's interview with Thomas Price, February 29, 1992.

"The M1 rifle sings" and following quotations (p. 71), author's interview with Nello Bartolozzi, March 1, 1992.

"The Germans attacked us" and following quotations (p. 72), author's interview with Arthur Hicks, June 14, 1991.

The I.Bataillon of SS-Panzer-Grenadier-Regiment 25 operated in the Dreiherrenwald on the first day of the Bulge. SS-Hauptsturmführer Alfons Ott (b. September 30, 1917) commanded the battalion.

"We only had morphine" (p. 74), letter from Curtis Amuedo to William Cavanagh, November 29, 1990.

The Company K morning report for December 25, 1944, named most of the eighty-seven MIAs and listed them as missing on December 17, 1944. Confusion during the first two days of the Bulge made it impossible to determine which men became casualties on which day. For administrative reasons, the report simply listed everyone as missing on the second day. That resulted in Holloway's official date of death being December 17 rather than the actual date, December 16. A similar situation happened with Alphonse Sito, resulting in his official date of death being December 18 rather than December 16.

For "statement" (p. 75), statement written by First Lieutenant Joseph Dougherty, Headquarters, Infantry Training Replacement Center, Fort McClellan, Alabama, October 25, 1945. Dougherty provided the author with a related letter indorsement dated March 4, 1946, which references the 201 file of Stephen K. Plume, Jr. (army service records were known as 201 files).

For "no leadership" (p. 75), letter from Joseph Dougherty to the author, January 7, 1986.

For "he made the decision to surrender" (p. 75), statement by First Lieutenant Joseph Dougherty, Headquarters, Infantry Training Replacement Center, Fort McClellan, Alabama, October 25, 1945.

"I regret having surrendered" and following quotation (p. 75), letter from Joseph Dougherty to the author, January 7, 1986.

"I saw no one run" (p. 75), letter from Joseph Dougherty to the author, August 15, 1986.

For "Board of Investigation" and following quotation (p. 75), letter from Joseph Dougherty to the author, January 7, 1986.

For "dereliction of duties" and following quotations (p. 75), *Court-Martial Reports: The Judge Advocates General of the Armed Forces and the United States Court of Military Appeals 1952–1953*, vol. 8, pp. 352–355 (CM 357802, *United States v. Captain Stephen K. Plume Jr.*, O-24054). The court convicted Plume of offenses stemming from three incidents at K-8 Airbase, Korea: drunk and disorderly conduct at the 3rd Bomb Wing officers open mess on the evening of August 25, 1952; dereliction in the performance of duties by failure to appear for work on August 26, 1952; drunk and disorderly conduct on the evening of August 26, 1952, at Barracks 371.

"I was a journeyman in the trade" (p. 75), letter from Joseph Dougherty to the author, January 7, 1986. Dougherty served as commander of Company A, 27th Infantry Regiment during the Korean War.

"Lt. Holloway was dead" (p. 77), letter from Curtis Amuedo to Richard Byers, March 30, 1990.

"Certainly someone else" (p. 77), letter from Curtis Amuedo to Jerry Pittaway and Bill Craven, April 3, 1990. Gerald "Jerry" Pittaway published the Company K newsletter *Kapers*. William F. Craven was the company clerk.

"He had the courage" (p. 78), letter from Thomas Price to Richard Byers, May 28, 1990.

Alois Adelmann rests in block 57, grave 18 at the Lommel Soldatenfriedhof in northern Belgium.

"He asked me to dig" (p. 82), letter from Jean-Louis Seel to the author, July 31, 1991.

"Well, well, after all these years" and following quotation (p. 83), Amuedo's transcription of a telephone conversation between him and William Cavanagh, November 22, 1990.

"I had mixed feelings" and following quotation (p. 84), *Corpus Christi Caller Times*, August 26, 1991, p. A1.

"All of this is so incredible" (p. 85), Curtis Amuedo's transcription of a telephone conversation between him and Sarah Holland, November 27, 1990.

Holloway's casualty status remained MIA until the War Department issued a death report on July 26, 1945. The report resulted from eyewitness testimony provided by Second Lieutenant Herman Dickman, who led the Second Platoon of Company K. He became separated from his platoon during the German attack and stopped at Holloway's mortar position. Dickman briefly inspected the dead lieutenant's body before retreating to the rear. After the survivors of Company K regrouped, he remained with them until January 10, 1945, when he permanently departed the unit, suffering from "osteoarthritis chronic" (according to a morning report). Dickman later stated he had a hernia. Whatever the case, the army tracked him down and inquired about Holloway. Dickman later met Holloway's parents and told them he saw their son's body, but he had little more information.

For "Male, Caucasian" and following quotation (p. 85), case file for CILHI 0251-90 and USAMAA-E Search and Recovery 5172 (X-9472). Jean-Louis Seel corroborated the quotations during author's interview with him, Waterside Marriott, Norfolk, Virginia, July 5, 2003.

"The convention was absolutely fantastic" (p. 86), *Checkerboard*, September 1991, volume 44, number 6, p. 1.

"The service and burial" (p. 86), letter from Curtis Amuedo to Jean-Philippe Speder, September 11, 1991.

"She, her daughters and friends" (p. 87), *Kapers*, fourth quarter, 1991, p. 2.

ABC News included an interview with Sarah Holland during a broadcast of the television newsmagazine *Turning Point*: "A Christmas to Remember: The Battle of the Bulge," narrator David Brinkley, producer Susan Lested, aired December 15, 1994.

Chapter 5: Unknown Soldiers

Public Law 490, section 5, change 828 (December 24, 1942) stipulated the following: "When the twelve months' period from date of commencement of absence is about to expire in any case of a person missing or missing in action and no official report of death or of being a prisoner or of being interned has been received, the head of the department concerned shall cause a full review of the case to be made. Following such review and when the twelve months' absence shall have expired, or following any subsequent review of the case which shall be made whenever warranted by information received or other circumstances, the head of the department concerned is authorized to direct the continuance of the person's missing status, if the person may reasonably be presumed to be living, or is authorized to make a finding of death. When a finding of death is made it shall include the date upon which death shall be presumed to have occurred for the purposes of termination of crediting pay and allowances, settlements of accounts, and payments of death gratuities and such date shall be the day following the day of expiration of an absence of twelve months, or in cases in which the missing status shall have been continued as hereinbefore authorized, a day to be determined by the head of the department."

"We don't know" (p. 91), faxed letter from Jean-Louis Seel to Richard Byers, July 6, 1992.

Dick Byers and I had contact with several B/394 veterans before visiting the National Archives in August 1992, but the contact only concerned Puckett.

In this chapter, I used portions of my 1992 report *X-9476: A Historical Analysis*. Cavanagh excerpted portions of that report in his 1994 book *Dauntless: A History of the 99th Infantry Division*, although those portions appeared without quotation marks and without reference to their source.

After having spent almost three weeks occupying front-line foxholes and dugouts, B/394 moved to a battalion-reserve position on January 8, 1945. The reserve position was slightly behind the front line, and it was from there that B/394 launched its raiding patrol on January 15, 1945.

First Lieutenant Roger C. Lenihan joined B/394 on December 29, 1944 after transferring from headquarters, 1/394.

"I thought he had been killed" (p. 97), *Checkerboard*, fifth Issue 1996, volume 49, number 5, p. 9.

For "Topper" (p. 97), Report on "Topper" Raid, Headquarters, 1st Battalion, 394th Infantry, January 15, 1945; 399-INF(394)0.3, box 14195, National Archives.

Roger Lenihan and George Speace each received the Bronze Star Medal for "heroic action" on January 15, 1945. Speace suffered a minor wound to his right leg but refused medical evacuation. He received a battlefield commission on February 25, 1945, and became a second lieutenant. Thomas Cornett received the Silver Star Medal for "gallantry in action" on January 15, 1945. According to his award citation, he used a rocket launcher to destroy an enemy machine-gun nest. Robert Doebler lost his left foot while returning from the raiding patrol. He detonated an antipersonnel mine. The medic, Guerrina Prola, also received the Silver Star, and he was responsible for rescuing Doebler from the minefield.

"This patrol was made up of a few old hands" (p. 98), letter from Carl Combs to Richard Byers, July 24, 1992.

"I was assigned a BAR man" (p. 98), letter from Carl Combs to the author, October 9, 1992.

"A sergeant came up" and following quotations (p. 99), Checkerboard, fifth Issue 1996, volume 49, number 5, p. 9.

For "receiving no enemy fire as yet" (p. 99), entry number 33, Unit Journal, 394th Infantry, 0001 to 2400, January 15, 1945; 399-INF(394)0.3, box 14195, National Archives.

"The effectiveness of the 4.2 mortars" and following quotation (p. 99), Report on "Topper" Raid, Headquarters, 1st Battalion, 394th Infantry, January 15, 1945; 399-INF(394)0.3, box 14195, National Archives.

"Keep your damn head down!" and following quotation (p. 100), author's interview with Clifford Selwood, April 23, 2005.

"We gotta rush 'em" and following quotations (p. 100), author's interview with Eugene Lett, May 7, 2005.

"He's done for" (p. 101), author's interview with Carl Combs, September 13, 1992.

"He asked if we could hold" (p. 102), letter from Carl Combs to the author, October 9, 1992.

"I found all the clips" (p. 102), Checkerboard, fifth Issue 1996, volume 49, number 5, p. 10.

"I used one clip" (p. 102), letter from Carl Combs to Richard Byers, July 24, 1992.

Private Leonard E. Waterman from Massachusetts was the rifleman with the injured ankle. He suffered a compound fracture of his right ankle, and medical personnel transported him to the 128th Evacuation Hospital.

"Can we help you" and following quotations (p. 103), Checkerboard, fifth Issue 1996, volume 49, number 5, p. 10.

"I'm dying anyway" (p. 104), author's interview with Emanuel Rind, July 28, 1992.

"There's one that's still kicking" and following quotations (p. 104), Checkerboard, fifth Issue 1996, volume 49, number 5, p. 10.

"Every time he asked" (p. 105), author's interview with Emanuel Rind, July 28, 1992.

Chapter 6: In Shallow Graves

"My brother's been killed in Europe" and following quotation (p. 108), author's interview with Frank Read, October 19, 2001.

"It is with deep regret" (p. 108), letter from Colonel James B. Clearwater to Mr. and Mrs. Verne Read, December 10, 1951.

For "conscientious, hard worker" (p. 109), WRA Archives, Hudson, Ohio: Information Sheet, W.R.A. boys killed, lost, or prisoners in service, David Read.

"We earned a dime" (p. 109), author's interview with Frank Read, March 15, 2003.

"David was a great 'big brother'" (p. 110), e-mail from Doug Read to the author, 12:14 A.M., October 25, 2001.

The name Savo appeared on Kokotovich's birth certificate and was a misspelling of the popular Serbian name Sava (spelled Сава in Cyrillic). St. Sava was the patron saint of the Serbs.

"When we went to school" (p. 111), author's interview with Mary Maisel, January 4, 2003.

"Pop, if he worked" (p. 111), author's interview with George Kokotovich, January 18, 2003.

For "intellectual capacity" (p. 113), Palmer, Wiley, and Keast, The Procurement and Training of Ground Combat Troops, p. 6.

"If a town had a water tower" and following quotations (p. 113), author's interview with Jerome Gleesing, February 16, 2003.

Gleesing served with the USAAF as the copilot of a B-24 assigned to the 757th

Bombardment Squadron (459th BG). He and his crew were shot down on January 15, 1945, while flying their second combat mission. Gleesing was interned at Stalag XIIID then Stalag VIIA, where he was liberated by U.S. troops.

"I intend to make it" (p. 116), Byers, *Charley Battery Blues*, p. 111.

"Many former ASTP men" (p. 116), *Checkerboard*, Wednesday, March 15, 1944, p. 3.

"Do you know" (p. 116), letter from Saul Kokotovich to his mother, March 25, 1944.

"But your name is Saul" and following quotations (p. 117), letter from Mike Gracenin to Mary Maisel, November 21, 1991.

"Dear Mom" (p. 117), telegram from Saul and Martha Kokotovich to Mrs. George Kokotovich, July 9, 1944. Saul and Martha married at Camp Maxey Chapel #7, the chapel assigned to the 395th Infantry.

"He had a daughter" (p. 118), eulogy delivered by Warren Thomas, July 17, 2002. Warren served in combat with Company K, 395th Infantry.

"Each morning" (p. 118), e-mail from Vern Swanson to the author, 1:18 P.M., April 25, 2003.

"Whatever you do" and following quotation (p. 119), letter from Jack Beckwith to Mom, undated but written at sea.

"My tent buddy" (p. 119), e-mail from Vern Swanson to the author, 1:45 P.M., April 29, 2003.

For "big Swede from Chicago" and following quotation (p. 120), letter from Beckwith to Mom, Dad, Norma, and kids, November 8, 1944.

"Today I imagine" (p. 120), letter from David Read to Verne Read, November 23, 1944. The two dead BAR gunners from C/395 were PFC Robert S. Vose (KIA November 23, 1944) and PFC Dean H. Olson (KIA November 26, 1944).

"Just ending my last day" and following quotation (p. 121), letter from Jack Beckwith to Mom, Dad, Norma, and kids, December 3, 1944.

"Same ol' place" and following quotation (p. 121), letter from Saul Kokotovich to Mom, December 6, 1944.

"You all have been" (p.122), letter from David Read to Mother, Dad and family, December 8, 1944.

For "one of the toughest" (p. 122), letter from George Kennedy to Mr. and Mrs. Read, August 21, 1945. David Read and George were born ten days apart in 1925: February 8 and February 18 respectively.

"It hit me hard" (p. 123), author's interview with Harold Smith, May 16, 2001.

"Mike, Koke wants you." and following quotations (p. 124), letter from Mike Gracenin to Mary Maisel, November 21, 1991.

"The medic told me" and following quotations (p. 124), author's interview with Harold Wright, December 17, 2002.

Wright was taken to the 44th Evacuation Hospital in Malmédy, then to hospitals in Verviers and Paris. His final hospital stay was in Cardiff, Wales. He never returned to the 99th Division after his recuperation.

"How'd ya make out?" and following quotations (p. 125), author's interview with Vern Swanson, April 21, 2001.

Aileen Read died on December 18, 1936 along with Carolyn Smith, eighteen, and Walter G. Shull, nineteen. The only survivor in their car was Aileen's brother Tommy, seventeen. Aileen's remains were cremated and her ashes spread in Silver Lake. More than six decades later, the ashes of Tommy and his wife were also spread in the lake.

"Their grief and sorrow" (p. 126), e-mail from Doug Read to the author, 12:14 A.M., October 25, 2001.

"We were just dumbfounded" (p. 127), author's interview with Mary Maisel, January 4, 2003.

"All he wanted" (p. 127), Porter County Post-Tribune, July 4, 2001, p. A4.

"They examined me" (p. 127), author's interview with Sam Ohnstad, January 18, 2003.

Chapter 7: Chasing the Past

"I went there half expecting" (p. 129), e-mail from Vern Swanson to the author, 1:10 A.M., January 18, 2003.

"MIA, Still Missing After 45 Years, Can You Help find Them?" (p. 129), *Checkerboard*, March 1990, volume 43, number 1, p. 3.

"The territory was familiar" (p. 131), e-mail from Vern Swanson to the author, 5:37 P.M., January 18, 2003.

"We wanted to see" and following quotation (p. 131), *Checkerboard*, December 1990, volume 43, number 5, p. 20.

"Vern Swanson advised me" (p. 132), letter from the author to Mary Maisel, April 29, 1991.

Charles P. Biggio located the aerial photograph of Hill 627. He spent countless hours at the National Archives searching for aerials of the 99th Division zone of operations during the Bulge. He served as an artillery officer with the 372nd Field Artillery Battalion (99th Division).

"The shell that killed him" and following quotation (p. 133), author's notes from the forty-second annual reunion of the 99th Infantry Division, June 11-16, 1991.

"I was hit in the throat" (p. 133), Swanson, *Upfront with Charlie Company*, p. 35.

"Davis and I put him on a stretcher" (p. 133), letter from Mike Gracenin to Mary Maisel, November 21, 1991.

Gracenin died at age seventy-three on November 5, 1995. He was a resident of Hermitage, Pennsylvania, and worked as a shop steward with Westinghouse Electric Corporation for over forty years prior to his retirement.

"He's alive and well" (p. 134), letter from Vern Swanson to the author, May 21, 1992.

"We have to forget Saul and Jack for a couple months" (p. 134), letter from Jean-Philippe Speder to the author, November 11, 1991.

Woolf died from emphysema on April 29, 1992, at his home in Indianapolis, Indiana. He was age sixty-six and a retired chemist for Eli Lilly and Company.

"It was a great moment" (p. 135), letter from Jean-Louis Seel to the author, March 13, 1992.

List of foxhole contents came from Seel's letter to the author, April 17, 1992, and enclosed photographs.

"I found two M1 rifles" (p. 135), letter from Jean-Philippe Speder to the author, April 10, 1992.

"I don't remember losing it" and following quotation (p. 136), *Johnson City Press*, August 23, 1992, p. 1.

"It's on my desk" and following quotation (p. 136), e-mail from Vern Swanson to the author, 12:25 A.M., January 24, 2003.

"That dugout over there" and following quotation (p. 137), narrative and annotated map from Jean-Philippe Speder, undated but autumn 1992.

For "near Hellenthal, Germany" and following quotation (p. 138), extract from Battle Casualty Report #31, Headquarters 395th Infantry, 21 December 1944.

"Burial services were conducted" (p. 139), letter from Captain William R. Feaster to Mrs. Margret Sims, 24 December 1944.

"I personally saw him" (p. 139), letter from Chaplain James L. Neighbours to John Sims's next of kin, February 12, 1945.

For "typical army bullshit" (p. 139), handwritten note from Vern Swanson to the author, undated.

On May 30, 1945, Captain Feaster responded to a letter he received from Brigadier General Leonard H. Sims (John's uncle). The captain wrote, "Burial took place at Henri-Chapelle Number 1, Belgium."

"I have no personnel file" (p. 139), letter from William R. Feaster to the Quartermaster General, 8 August 1946.

"It was impossible" (p. 139), letter from Major James L. Neighbours to the Memorial Division, Quartermaster General, September 18, 1946.

"I did see him" (p. 140), letter from Major James L. Neighbours to Mrs. Sims, September 18, 1946.

For "isolated grave" (p. 140), Report of Burial, Sword, Dean W., 33630779, March 27, 1945. Sword is interred at Arlington National Cemetery, section 12, grave 2720.

"To this day" and following quotations (p. 141), "Battle of the Bulge," narrator Patricia Kelly, CNN Brussels bureau chief and correspondent, aired December 15, 1994.

For "law enforcement investigators" (p. 142), trifold brochure produced by NecroSearch International, 2886 Robb Circle, Lakewood, CO 80215, undated.

Verne Read's friend was John Dahlberg, a Bulge veteran who served with the 28th Infantry Division.

"*Grabungen sollen Gewißheit*" (p. 143), *Grenz-Echo: Die Deutschsprachige Tageszeitung in Ostbelgien,* August 23, 1997, p. 9.

Roger Lane served with the 53rd Fighter Squadron (36th FG) and was shot down by Leutnant Carl Resch of 15./JG 54 who was himself killed on January 14, 1945. Lane's aircraft crashed just east of Prüm, about seven hundred meters south of the Siedlung Schwirzheim-Gondelsheim. His sole surviving relative, a half niece, buried his remains at Ledge Cemetery, Yarmouth, Maine.

Erickson was a pilot with the 38th Fighter Squadron (55th FG) and was lost on December 1, 1943, while flying his first combat mission. His aircraft struck ground adjacent to a small stream, and the impact crater soon filled with water, although ammunition and aviation fuel still burned nearby. Close to the hole, residents of Lanzerath found a strip of human scalp with dark blond hair. In the stream, they found a human foot, still laced into a leather boot. These and other small pieces of the pilot were buried several days later in a civilian cemetery at Manderfeld, Belgium. Thirteen months later, amid the Battle of the Bulge, the Royal Air Force hit the cemetery during a bombing raid. This unfortunate incident obliterated whatever headstone or wooden marker identified the pilot's burial spot. The entire episode remained forgotten until Manfred Klein learned about the crash site from a gray-haired gentleman who, as a fifteen-year-old boy, observed the impact crater on the day of the crash. One autumn day in 1996, Klein and Drespa probed the area with shovels and picks. Imbedded in the clay, they found 20-mm shells and a supercharger from an Allison V-1710 engine. These items indicated the aircraft was a P-38. But there was something else. They discovered remnants of a vertical stabilizer with the number 3 stenciled in yellow paint, undoubtedly part of a six-digit tail number. Klein sifted through German wartime records pertaining to crash sites, and he examined USAAF missing aircrew reports. That research allowed him to narrow down the aircraft to one flown by Lieutenant Erickson, who died while flying a P-38 with the tail number 267033. That triggered plans for an excavation of the entire site. News of the impending excavation reached Erickson's family in Ohio and California. His two younger brothers and their spouses put their lives on hold and flew to Belgium. A television reporter and cameraman accompanied them from a Cleveland TV station. The recovery operation began on August 18, 1997, and lasted nine days. Besides aircraft wreckage, the diggers found personal effects, among them an identification bracelet engraved Wilton G. Erickson. Traces of the pilot included over 150 bone fragments, tufts of hair, one wisdom tooth, two fingernails, and numerous pieces of skin and muscle. Oil, antifreeze, and aviation fuel had saturated the soil and preserved the tissue in a diminished-oxygen (anaerobic) environment. The remains found in 1997 were interred at Russell Township Cemetery, Novelty, Ohio. The German pilot credited with downing Erickson's P-38 was Unteroffizier Hans Fritz of 3./JG 3. While examining the P-38 wreckage, Manfred Klein reported finding a "bullet hole near the radio equipment" that seemed to be "German 13-mm caliber."

Klein's team also assisted with the recovery of another P-38 pilot—First Lieutenant James O. Baxter of the 394th Fighter Squadron (367th FG). His aircraft was lost over Trier, Germany, on December 24, 1944. Jack T. Curtis and Guy Coquillat found the crash site in 1990, however, the location was not excavated by CILHI until 1999. The impetus for this recovery operation came when Klein's team unearthed human remains at the site. Prior to this, CILHI had refused involvement with the case. (Curtis, a former P-38 pilot, was one of Baxter's wartime buddies.)

Lemuel Herbert, 33023842, died on November 7, 1944, while serving with Company B, 112th Infantry. His remains were found in the garden behind Nr. 140 Kommerscheidt, the home of Hans-Dieter Naas and his son, Thomas. Herbert is interred at Arlington National Cemetery, section 59, grave 1034.

Robert Cahow, 36206366, died on December 13, 1944, while serving with Company K,

311th Infantry. His remains lay near the village of Simonskall in the Ochsenkopf forest area and fifty feet from German bunker 111. The ordnance-disposal team that recovered Cahow was from the firm Röhll GmbH, a government contractor specializing in munitions removal and destruction. The recovery took place on April 14, 2000.

"I read the name" (p. 146), e-mail from Jean-Louis Seel to the author, 5:08 A.M., June 4, 2001.

"Jack Beckwith, Saul Kokotovich, and David Read" (p. 146), e-mail from Jean-Philippe Speder to Vern Swanson, Rex Whitehead, Byron Whitmarsh, and the author, 17:04:56, April 17, 2001.

For "positive signal" (p. 146), e-mail from Jean-Louis Seel to the author, June 4, 2001.

Status of forces agreements (known as SOFAs) define the legal status of U.S. military personnel and property in foreign countries. These agreements establish the rights and responsibilities of the U.S. and host governments on a wide range of issues including criminal and civil jurisdiction as well as entry and exit of personnel and property. The U.S. has a multilateral agreement in place with all NATO countries. In many instances, individual countries have negotiated supplemental agreements. This is particularly true of countries that have a significant American military presence. The original NATO agreement was signed in 1951, and the German government has since negotiated several supplements, the first one signed in 1963.

"During the ceremony" (p. 149), press release by Specialist Christy Johnstone (PAO, 1st Infantry Division), July 4, 2001, USAREUR Public Affairs.

"It's a way to thank them" (p. 150), "Three Remains Returned," narrator Mary L. Doyle, producer and director, V Corps Tv5, May 2001.

Chapter 8: On the Devil's Anvil

"I always disliked the fact" (p. 153), e-mail from Rex Whitehead to the author, 2:52 P.M., January 18, 2003.

For "shovel leaners" (p. 154), author's interview with William L. Zimmerman, January 15, 2004.

"My mother's relatives" and following quotations (p. 154), author's interview with William L. Zimmerman, June 26, 2003.

For "colder than a well-digger's butt" and following quotation (p. 157), author's interview with Lyle F. Kunde, December 3, 2003.

"Mike worked in the canning end of it" (p. 157), author's interview with Lyle F. Kunde, June 14, 2004.

"He had the mind" and following quotations (p. 157), author's interview with Lyle F. Kunde, December 3, 2003.

"The Rochelle boys are here!" (p. 158), *Rockford Register Star*, July 7, 2002, p. 2B.

"He was born at the Fidler farm" and following quotation (p. 159), author's interview with Charles E. Fidler, October 13, 2003.

"He was always the most brilliant student" (p. 161), letter from Mickie Bigham-Nelson to Charles Fidler, June 9, 2002.

"We all went down to the courthouse" (p. 161), author's interview with Charles E. Fidler, October 13, 2003.

"We have some young college kids" (p. 162), Daines, *Let's Go to Belgium!* p. 24.

"Fred came home on leave" (p. 163), author's interview with William L. Zimmerman, June 26, 2003.

"I recall it took a telegram" (p. 163), author's interview with William B. Williams Jr., May 17, 2003.

"Occasionally he hitchhiked home" (p. 163), author's interview with Charles E. Fidler, October 13, 2003.

"I liked Stan from the moment I met him" and following quotation (p. 163), eulogy presented by Ron Daines on behalf of Rex Whitehead, Stanley Larson funeral, July 2002.

"I had never played with anyone as good" (p. 164), e-mail from Rex Whitehead to Jean-Philippe Speder, 17:48:21, June 2, 2001.

"We're still underway" (p. 164), v-mail letter from Ewing Fidler to his mother, undated but probably October 6, 1944.

"The green rolling hills" (p. 164), Rex Whitehead, unpublished manuscript, December 1945, Camp Butner, North Carolina, p. 2.

For "goddamn Jew" and following quotations (p. 165), author's interview with William B. Williams Jr., May 17, 2003.

"Letters are going to be something rare" (p. 165), letter from Stanley Larson to his mother, November 10, 1944.

"Tonite finds me writing you from a foxhole" (p. 165), v-mail letter from Ewing Fidler to his parents, undated but written "somewhere in Germany" during November 1944.

"I just hope and pray" (p. 166), v-mail letter from Frederick Zimmerman to his parents and brother, November 13, 1944.

"Just a few lines to let you know" (p. 167), v-mail letter from Frederick Zimmerman to his mother, November 28, 1944.

"He seemed cheerful" (p. 167), author's interview with William B. Williams Jr., May 17, 2003.

"Tonite, from candlelight" (p. 168), letter from Ewing Fidler to his parents, December 3, 1944.

"The date on this letter" (p. 168), letter from Ewing Fidler to his mother, December 7, 1944.

"I was hit in the right hand" (p. 170), letter from William B. Williams Jr. to Richard Byers, March 30, 1990.

"I tried to hold him down" (p. 170), author's interview with William B. Williams Jr., May 17, 2003.

"I was with Larson" (p. 170), Rex Whitehead's telephone interview with Andrew Woods, April 14, 1992. Reported in a letter from Whitehead to William Cavanagh, Pierre Dullier, Jean-Philippe Speder, and Jean-Louis Seel, April 15, 1992.

"Let's carry Larson" (p. 170), oral history by James S. Dickey, undated but sometime in 1990.

"We just put the litter down and left" (p. 171), Rex Whitehead's interview with Warren Wenner, June 6, 2001.

"The shelling stopped" (p. 171), letter from William B. Williams Jr. to Richard Byers, March 30, 1990.

"Get the hell in here!" (p. 171), Rex Whitehead, unpublished manuscript, December 1945, Camp Butner, North Carolina, p. 5.

"I was raised in Grace, Idaho" (p. 172), author's conversations with Rex Whitehead, undated. Quotation also paraphrased in Rex's obituary written by Ron Daines, November 2003.

Chapter 9: The Lost Aid Station

Besides Western Union, the War Department and Navy Department employed the services of the Postal Telegraph & Cable Corporation to send telegrams, but only Western Union used blue stars to denote messages with casualty information. Sometimes the stars appeared on the envelope rather than the telegram itself. (Stars on a telegram envelope created a dramatic moment in the 1944 movie *Since You Went Away*.) Postal Telegraph and Western Union were competitors until the two companies merged in 1945.

For "missing" and following quotation (p. 173), telegram from Brigadier General Robert H. Dunlop, Acting the Adjutant General, to Mrs. Artie E. Fidler, 3:20 P.M., January 4, 1945.

"She walked in the door" (p. 174), author's interview with Lyle F. Kunde, December 7, 2003.

"We were outside my parents' home" (p. 174), author's interview with William L. Zimmerman, June 26, 2003.

"Correct report now received" (p. 174), telegram from Major General James A. Ulio, the Adjutant General, to Mrs. Martha J. Zimmerman, 7:58 A.M., February 9, 1945.

"Martha Jane lived across the street" (p. 174), author's interview with William L. Zimmerman, June 26, 2003.

"My brother Bill" (p. 174), author's interview with Esta Morrow, April 15, 1991.

For "killed in action" (p. 175), poem titled "My Son" by Ella Larson, September 22, 1945.

For "white as a sheet" (p. 175), author's interview with Angelo Spinato, September 19, 1992.

For "combat exhaustion" (p. 175), morning report, Company E, 394th Infantry Regiment, December 16, 1944, p. 4.

"We have tried to locate his grave" (p. 175), letter from Artie Fidler to the Quartermaster General, July 12, 1946.

"It is with deep regret" (p. 175), letter from Major James L. Prenn, Quartermaster Corps, August 14, 1946.

"The thing I remember best" (p. 176), letter from Rex Whitehead to Jean-Louis Seel, Jean-Philippe Speder, and William Cavanagh, March 24, 1991.

"The happiest day of my life" (p. 176), letter from Rex Whitehead to Roger Foehringer, January 15, 1993.

"After the visit" (p. 176), Daines, *Let's Go to Belgium!* p. 48.

"One girl said she would scream" (p. 177), letter from Rex Whitehead to Roger Foehringer, January 15, 1993.

"It is hard for me to understand" (p. 178), letter from Jerome G. Nelson to Richard Byers, undated but March or April 1990.

"Sometimes I think I should go back to golf" (p. 179), memorandum from Rex Whitehead to the author, March 31, 1991.

"That was my uncle" (p. 180), author's letter to Rex Whitehead, March 26, 1991.

"I have pictures" (p. 180), author's notes, Zimmerman file.

"You will never know" (p. 181), letter from Esta Morrow to the author, April 16, 1991.

"You need somebody like that" (p. 181), Daines, *Let's Go to Belgium!* p. 19.

German forces held the junction of Corduroy Road and California Highway until the morning of February 2, 1945, when troops of the 325th Glider Infantry Regiment (82nd A/B Division) recaptured the area and pushed into the villages of Neuhof and Udenbreth. The troops remained in the villages until the night of February 4–5 when the 393rd Infantry Regiment (99th Division) took charge of the area. The 393rd remained there until February 12 when the 273rd Infantry Regiment (69th Division) came on line and took over the area. The 273rd was the last American unit to hold that sector before it became a rear area.

"The highlight for this old dogface" (p. 182), letter from Rex Whitehead to Jean-Louis Seel, Jean-Philippe Speder, and William Cavanagh, March 24, 1991.

"I talked to Warren Wenner" (p. 182), memorandum from Rex Whitehead to the author, April 25, 1991.

"I recall seeing his body myself" (p. 183), author's interview with Angelo Spinato, September 19, 1992.

"Unknown X-287" (p. 183), Statement of Investigation, written by A. Kennedy, undated, contained in the Individual Deceased Personnel File for Frederick F. Zimmerman.

"I feel overwhelmed" (p. 186), letter from Rex Whitehead to the author, February 12, 1993.

"Dick could only whisper" and following quotations (p. 187), e-mail from Rex Whitehead to the author, February 8, 2001.

"You have caused a lot of excitement" (p. 187), e-mail from Rex Whitehead to Jean-Philippe Speder and Jean-Louis Seel, 23:17:30, April 17, 2001.

"Find myself waiting for another e-mail" and following quotation (p. 188), e-mail from Rex Whitehead to the author, Vernon Swanson, Byron Whitmarsh, Jean-Philippe Speder, and Jean-Louis Seel, 18:08:51, April 19, 2001.

"Check it. This one may belong to Fred Zimmerman" and following quotation (p. 189), report from Jean-Louis Seel, created August 7, 2001, p. 2.

"Hey, guys, come see." And following quotation (p. 189), e-mail from Jean-Philippe Speder to the author, 23:12:26, June 1, 2001.

"He handed it to me" and following quotation (p. 192), e-mail from Jean-Philippe Speder to the author, Vernon Swanson, and Byron Whitmarsh, 18:18:46, June 2, 2001.

"What are you trying to do" and following quotations (p. 192), e-mail from Rex Whitehead to the "diggers," 17:48:21, June 2, 2001.

"In the name of the 99th Infantry Division Association" (p. 195), e-mail from Rex Whitehead to the author et al., 2:05 P.M., July 5, 2001.

Chapter 10: Bureaucrats and Scientists

On Memorial Day 2001, the *Stars and Stripes* story appeared in print and on the Internet. The correspondent revealed the names Beckwith and Kokotovich but not Read. The latter name apparently escaped him while thumbing through *Upfront with Charlie Company*. The correspondent claimed that stories on the 99th Division Association's Web site had already disclosed the two names he mentioned. That was untrue. Anyone who checked the Web site saw that it contained no such information. At that time, the association's Web master had no knowledge of the recoveries on Hill 627. (Forest ranger Erich Hönen owned a copy of *Upfront with Charlie Company*, and he unwittingly allowed the correspondent to peruse the book.)

"There's been a development" and following quotations (p. 198), author's notes, May 26, 2001.

"DNA link can still bring home missing soldiers" (p. 200), *Chicago Tribune*, June 4, 2001, section 5, p. 3.

"Hopefully one of you guys" and following quotation (p. 201), author's notes, June 21, 2001.

In 1992 the Department of Defense began collecting blood and saliva samples from military personnel as a means of establishing identification.

"On 7/5/01 the Department of Defense" (p. 204), letter from Nicol R. Jimerson (supervisor, Database Team, DoD DNA Registry) to Joan Bowman, July 10, 2001.

"I'm a religious man" (p. 205), *The Forum* (Fargo, ND), July 7, 2002.

"Just talked to my nephew" (p. 206), e-mail from William L. Zimmerman to the author, 7:55 P.M., August 2, 2001.

"Leon expressed his happiness" (p. 206), e-mail from Rex Whitehead to the author, Vernon Swanson, Byron Whitmarsh, Jean-Philippe Speder, Jean-Louis Seel, William Cavanagh, and Marc Marique, 3:38 P.M., August 8, 2001.

"I had a long telephone chat" (p. 206), e-mail from Rex Whitehead to the author, 10:35 P.M., August 8, 2001.

Manfred Klein and his colleagues recovered the remains of three Luftwaffe aviators:

- Heinrich Zinnen (11./JG 1) crashed on December 25, 1944, near Olzheim, Germany, while piloting an Me109 G-14/AS, Werk-Nr. 784111.
- Joachim Selpin (3./JG 2) crashed on December 17, 1944, near Krewinkel, Belgium, while piloting an FW 190 A8, Werk-Nr. 750154.
- Unidentified remains of an aircrew member recovered from a Junker 52 crash site near Großlangenfeld, Germany.

The identification bracelet found near Leonard Kacprzak's grave belonged to Richard (NMI) Thompson, 37678888. He entered the army in 1943 from Marshall County, Iowa, and he died in 1983.

On April 30, 2004, Kacprzak's final interment took place at Arlington National Cemetery, section 66, grave 2935-A.

"Last night I had to go the dentist." (p. 209), letter from Frederick Zimmerman to his mother and family, 10:30 P.M., May 9, 1944.

For "good match" (p. 210), Memorandum for Commander, USACILHI, Subject: Identification of CILHI 2001-133-I-01, CILHI 2001-134-I-01, CILHI 2001-135-I-01, Thomas D. Holland (Scientific Director), December 17, 2001, p. 3.

"Given the provenance in this case" (p. 210), Forensic Odontology Report: CILHI 2001-126-I-01, LTC Christopher G. Fielding (Odontologist), July 20, 2001, p. 6.

Trotter and Gleser recognized a discrepancy in the way U.S. Army personnel took height measurements. In October 1942 the War Department published a regulation that provided detailed instructions for taking measurements, but the regulation overlooked an important point. The War Department amended the regulation in April 1944 and added the following sentence: "The shoes should be removed when the height is taken." (Trotter and Gleser, pp. 469–470)

"The remains designated CILHI 2001-126-I-01" (p. 213), Forensic Anthropology Report: CILHI 2001-126-I-01, Ann W. Bunch (Senior Anthropologist), November 2, 2001, p. 5.

Comparison between CILHI 2001-126-I-01 and Pfc. Kokotovich (p. 213), Addendum to Forensic Anthropology Report: CILHI 2001-126-I-01, Ann W. Bunch (Senior Anthropologist), November 6, 2001.

Chapter 11: Operation Final Journey

"I just found out yesterday" and following quotation (p. 215), e-mail from Liz Tate to Kathy Winkle, 06:59:50, January 4, 2002.

"Setting up disposition arrangement" (p. 216), e-mail from Charles Fidler to Vernon Swanson, 1:15 P.M., March 22, 2002.

"She had been in poor health" (p. 218), e-mail from Charles Fidler to the author, 4:00 P.M., April 20, 2002.

"She was in a nursing home" (p. 218), *Daily Oklahoman*, June 8, 2002, p. 7A.

"Someday they'll find your brother" (p. 218), author's interview with Charles Fidler, October 13, 2003.

"This belongs to you" (p. 220), author's interview with Jean-Louis Seel, Waterside Marriott, Norfolk, Virginia, July 5, 2003.

"Everyone is invited" (p. 220), *Ada Evening News*, May 26, 2002, p. 1C.

ABMC cemeteries only permitted burial of servicemen killed during World War I and World War II, but a special exception occurred in the case of Captain Thomas R. Caldwell. The U.S.A.F. pilot died in October 1990 when his F-111 crashed on the Arabian Peninsula during Operation Desert Shield. His home base had been RAF Lakenheath, England, and his widow requested burial at the Cambridge American Cemetery in England, but the ABMC denied the request. The U.S. Congress ultimately reversed the decision and cleared the way for Caldwell's interment at Cambridge alongside a legion of airmen killed during World War II.

"After seeing this place" and following quotations (p. 224), author's notes from funerals of Beckwith, Kokotovich, Zimmerman, Read, and Larson, June–July 2002.

"His insurance money" and following quotations (p. 226), press release by Tom Larscheid, USAREUR Public Affairs, June 26, 2002.

"Bury Me with Soldiers" (p. 227), poem by Father Charles R. Fink of Hewlett, New York, who served as an infantryman with the 199th Light Infantry Brigade in Vietnam.

"Aim! Fire!" and following quotation (p. 229), Jim Lampe's video recording of David Read's funeral, July 18, 2002.

"I was just faking" (p. 231), e-mail from Rex Whitehead to the author, 12:17 A.M., July 13, 2002.

"I'll find a way" (p. 231), author's notes from funerals of Beckwith, Kokotovich, Zimmerman, Read, and Larson, June–July 2002.

"I have lived a long, happy life" (p. 232), e-mail from Rex Whitehead to the author, 5:08 P.M., July 21, 2002.

"They're not forgotten" and following quotation (p. 232), video recording of Stanley Larson's funeral, July 22, 2002.

For "happy time and one we will cherish" and following quotation (p. 233), poem titled "My Son" by Ella Larson, September 22, 1945.

Stanley Larson returned to duty on July 23, 1944. He presumably departed his hometown on July 21 or July 22.

Chapter 12: Friendly Fire

"It's a shock" (p. 234), e-mail from Vern Swanson to the author, 11:37 A.M., July 31, 2002.

For "a historian working on European missing" (p. 236), e-mail from Chris McDermott to the author, 7:45 P.M., August 1, 2002.

"It's still being worked on" and following quotations (p. 238), author's interview with Joann Bowman, April 25, 2003.

"To date four bone fragments have been identified" and following quotation (p. 239), letter from Johnie E. Webb to Mark S. Kirk, August 29, 2003.

"Hmmm, what to do?" (p. 242), author's interview with Jean-Louis Seel while visiting Odell Sharpe's grave site, August 27, 2004.

"My blood pressure was high in a second" (p. 243), 2003 digging-activity report, Jean-Louis Seel, e-mailed to the author, 10:55 A.M., January 4, 2004.

"Get back! Turn around and get back!" (p. 246), Arnold, *Easy Memories*, p. 41.

"A tank destroyer unit supporting us was misinformed" (p. 247), Cavanagh, *Dauntless*, p. 173.

Francis A. Fariday Jr. was born on May 13, 1911, in Iowa. He died on December 2, 1966, and his wife interred him at Oak Hill Cemetery in Lakeland, Florida (block 679, lot 3, space 2).

Captain William Fox's "combat interview" pertaining to the 2nd Battalion, 393rd Infantry describes the friendly-fire incident: "On the morning of the 19th, very early, the Battalion was hit with a barrage from what appeared to be friendly TD's, since they reported that the shells were all high velocity. They suffered casualties in E, G and H companies, with the firing lasting ¹/₂ hour. Several people were sent out to Division and to Regiment in effort to stop the fire and, finally, the barrage was called off. However, it had been a costly action, with G Co having 7 KIA, 5 WIA, H Co 12 WIA and 2 KIA and several others having casualties. There was no aid station because of the difficulty of getting supplies up and this made the treatment and evacuation of the wounded very difficult. It also caused a great state of confusion." (The Company H casualty figures provided by Fox do not jibe with the Company H morning reports.)

"Well, you didn't use the good detector" and preceding quotation (p. 250), 2003 digging-activity report, Jean-Louis Seel, e-mailed to the author, 10:55 A.M., January 4, 2004.

"At the family update" (p. 252), letter from Jerry D. Jennings, deputy assistant secretary of Defense, to family members, February 4, 2004.

"What's the time frame" and following quotation (p. 252), author's interview with Joann Bowman, February 23, 2004.

Chapter 13: The Long Shadow of War

Brenda B. Schoonover was the chargé d'affaires from the U.S. embassy in Brussels.

"Come with us" and following quotations (p. 254), author's interview with Vern Swanson, June 23, 2004.

"It was a big shock" and following quotation (p. 257), e-mail from Byron Whitmarsh to the author, 21:49:32, July 1, 2004.

"I feel like I'm in good health" (p. 257), author's interview with Vern Swanson, June 23, 2004.

For "only Brown matches the mtDNA profile" (p. 257), e-mail from Captain Paul D. Madrid to Joann Bowman, 14:50:51, July 14, 2004.

For "no inexplicable discrepancies" and following quotation (p. 258), Forensic Odontology Report: CIL 2004-103-I-01, CDR Kevin R. Torske (Odontologist), September 21, 2004, p. 2.

For "a Caucasoid male" (p. 258), Forensic Anthropology Report: CIL 2004-103-I-01, Alexander F. Christensen (Anthropologist), October 12, 2004, p. 4.

For "overall biological agreement" (p. 258), Addendum to Forensic Anthropology Report: CIL 2004-103-I-01, Alexander F. Christensen (Anthropologist), October 12, 2004, p. 4.

"In my opinion" (p. 258), Identification of CIL 2004-103-I-01, Thomas D. Holland (Scientific Director), November 8, 2004, p. 3.

For "disposition instructions" (p. 259), First Endorsement to Identification of CIL 2004-103-I-01, Major General W. Montague Winfield (Commander, JPAC) to Commander, Human Resources Command, November 8, 2004.

"I have a contact at CMAOC" (p. 259), e-mail from Vern Swanson to Mark Leney, 2:20 P.M., November 22, 2004.

"I thought my heart was going to burst" (p. 260), Chuck Mobley, "A soldier's family reunited," *Savannah Morning News*, Internet posted, January 30, 2005.

"It was pure ringlets" and following quotations (p. 260), author's interview with Mary Miller and Joe Sharpe, January 30, 2005.

"They definitely have respect for the dead" and following quotation (p. 261), author's notes from Odell Sharpe's funeral, January 30, 2005.

"Everyone worked from can-to-cain't" and following quotation (p. 262), author's interview with Mary Miller and Joe Sharpe, January 30, 2005.

"I love you enough to wait" (p. 263), author's interview with Mary Miller, January 23, 2005.

"Four months now and no mail" (p. 263), v-mail letter from Odell Sharpe to Alex Sharpe, November 10, 1944.

"If I could just get some mail" (p. 264=), v-mail letter from Odell Sharpe to mother and father, November 14, 1944.

"Just a few lines" (p. 264), v-mail letter from Odell Sharpe to mother and father, December 3, 1944.

For "missing in action" (p. 264), telegram from Brigadier General Robert H. Dunlop, Acting the Adjutant General, to Mrs. Lizzie C. Sharpe, 9:19 P.M., January 19, 1945.

"Mama lost her mind" and following quotation (p. 264), author's interview with Mary Miller and Joe Sharpe, January 30, 2005.

Odell Sharpe's girlfriend, Viola Wiggins, died five days before the army telephoned his brother George with news of the recovery and subsequent identification. She was born on July 17, 1926, in Brunswick, Georgia, and she passed away in Phoenix, Arizona, on November 19, 2004. When she died, her daughter, Sandy, and her husband, Robert C. Esterbrooks, were at her side. Interment later took place in San Diego, California.

Chapter 14: Case Closed

"Private Dechon was a member" (p. 268), Memorandum for Record, written by James A. Frix, September 23, 1949, contained in the Individual Deceased Personnel File for Harold E. Dechon.

"I was next to Dechon" (p. 268), author's interview with John Scaglione, September 27, 1992.

"He jumped up from the snow" and following quotation (p. 268), author's interview with Cliff Selwood, April 23, 2005.

"I know it's a sad day today" (p. 270), *Bristol Herald Courier*, June 15, 2005, p. A1.

Manfred Klein dug John Puckett's grave at the Ardennes American Cemetery. Klein found the soil much less rocky and easier to excavate than at Henri-Chapelle three years earlier. After attending Puckett's funeral, Klein helped backfill the grave.

"I think of you all a lot" (p. 273), v-mail letter from John Puckett to his sister Barbara Bockstanz, November 30, 1944.

Appendix A: Accounting for the Dead

Field Manual 10–63 and the writings of Thayer Boardman and Edward Steere were key sources for this Appendix.

Appendix B: U.S. Army Dog Tags in World War II

The U.S. Army Military History Institute at Carlisle, Pennsylvania, maintains a complete collection of original documents pertaining to Army Regulations 600–35 and 600–40.

SELECTED BIBLIOGRAPHY

BOOKS AND JOURNAL ARTICLES

Arnold, Harry S., *Easy Memories: The Way it Was* (Roper, NC: self-published, 1985).

Ash, Major M. Jr. and Stanley J. Nelson, *Wheeler's Dental Anatomy, Physiology, and Occlusion, 8th edition* (Philadelphia, PA: W. B. Saunders Company, 2003).

Bass, William M., *Human Osteology: A Laboratory and Field Manual, 4th edition* (Columbia, MO: Missouri Archeological Society, 1995).

Bellanger, Yves J., *U.S. Army Infantry Divisions 1943–45, vol. 1— Organization, Doctrine and Equipment* (Solihull, England: Helion & Company, 2002).

Boardman, Thayer M. and Edward Steere, *Final Disposition of World War II Dead 1945–51, QMC Historical Studies, series II, no. 4* (Washington, D.C.: Historical Branch, Office of the Quartermaster General, 1957).

Brothwell, Don R., *Digging Up Bones: The Excavation, Treatment, and Study of Human Skeletal Remains, 3rd edition* (Ithaca, NY: Cornell University Press, 1981).

Byers, Richard H., *Charley Battery Blues: The Prelude to "The Battle of the Bulge"* (Mentor-on-the-Lake, OH: self-published, 1996).

Cavanagh, William C. C., *A Tour of the Bulge Battlefield* (Barnsley, England: Pen & Sword Books Limited, 2001).

Cavanagh, William C. C., *Dauntless: A History of the 99th Infantry Division* (Dallas, TX: Taylor Publishing Company, 1994).

Cavanagh, William C. C., *Krinkelt-Rocherath: The Battle for the Twin Villages* (Norwell, MA: Christopher Publishing House, 1986).

Cole, Hugh M., *The Ardennes: Battle of the Bulge, U.S. Army in World War II* (Washington, D.C.: United States Government Printing Office, 1965).

Crookenden, Napier, *Battle of the Bulge 1944* (New York, NY: Charles Scribner's Sons, 1980).

Daines, Ronald J., *Let's Go to Belgium!* (Logan, UT: self-published, 2001).

Donnelly, John, "No One Left Behind," *Reader's Digest*, June 2003, pp. 113–117.

Enjames, Henri-Paul, *Government Issue: U.S. Army European Theater of Operations Collector's Guide* (Paris, France: Histoire & Collections, 2003).

Hemphill, W. Edwin, ed., *Gold Star Honor Roll of Virginians in the Second World War* (Charlottesville, VA: Virginia World War II History Commission, 1947).

Joyce, Christopher and Eric Stover, *Witnesses from the Grave: The Stories Bones Tell* (Boston, MA: Little Brown & Co., 1991).

Keefer, Louis E., *Scholars in Foxholes: The Story of the ASTP in World War II* (Jefferson, NC: McFarland & Company, 1988).

Lewis, Kenneth, *Doughboy to GI: US Army Clothing and Equipment 1900–1945* (Warley Woods, England: Norman D. Landing Publishing, 1993).

Linet, Louis and Günther Gillot, *Yank's 1944: Matériel, Equipement et Armement du G.I. sur le Théâtre Européen d'Opération en 1944* (Liège, Belgium: Editions du Perron, 1984).

Lüttgens, Karl J., *Kriegsjahre, Kriegsende und Erste Neuanfänge im Kreis Schleiden 1939–1946, 2 vols.* (Gemünd, Germany: Wallraf Druck + Design, 1997).

MacDonald, Charles B., *The Siegfried Line Campaign, U.S. Army in World War II* (Washington, D.C.: United States Government Printing Office, 1963).

———, *The Mighty Endeavor: American Armed Forces in the European Theater in World War II* (New York, NY: Oxford University Press, 1969).

Mays, Simon, *The Archaeology of Human Bones* (New York, NY: Routledge, 1998).

Meunier, Pierre, ed., *Revue Trimestrielle, Etude No. 7: Dog Tags* (Verviers, Belgium: Imprim' Express, 1983).

Meyer, Hubert, *Kriegsgeschichte der 12.SS-Panzerdivision „Hitlerjugend,"* band II (Osnabrück: Munin Verlag GmbH, 1982).

O'Donnell, Michael J. and Stephen W. Sylvia, *Uniforms, Weapons and Equipment of the World War II G.I.* (Orange, VA: Moss Publications, 1982).

Palmer, Robert R., Bell I. Wiley, and William R. Keast, *The Procurement and Training of Ground Combat Troops, U.S. Army in World War II* (Washington, D.C.: United States Government Printing Office, 1948).

Piekutowski, Lynna, ed., *Remembering the Boys: A Collection of Letters, A Gathering of Memories* (Kent, OH: Kent State University Press, 2000).

Ross, William F. and Charles F. Romanus, *The Quartermaster Corps: Operations in the War Against Germany, U.S. Army in World War II* (Washington, D.C.: United States Government Printing Office, 1965).

Scherer, Wingolf, *Die 277.Volksgrenadierdivision in der Ardennenoffensive und im Untergang am Rhein 1944/45* (Düsseldorf: 1987).

Schwartz, Jeffrey H., *Skeleton Keys: An Introduction to Human Skeletal Morphology, Development, and Analysis* (New York, NY: Oxford University Press, 1995).

Shomon, Joseph J., *Crosses in the Wind* (New York, NY: Stratford House Inc., 1947).

Steadman, Dawnie Wolfe, *Hard Evidence: Case Studies in Forensic Anthropology* (Englewood, NJ: Prentice Hall, 2002).

Steere, Edward, *The Graves Registration Service in World War II, QMC Historical Studies, no. 21* (Washington, D.C.: United States Government Printing Office, 1951).

Stanton, Shelby L., *Order of Battle: U.S. Army, World War II* (Novato, CA: Presidio Press, 1984).

Swanson, Vernon E., ed., *Upfront with Charlie Company: A Combat History of Company C, 395th Infantry Regiment, 99th Infantry Division* (Deerfield, IL: Red Danube Publishing Company, 1997).

Tessin, Georg, *Verbände und Truppen der deutschen Wehrmacht und Waffen-SS im Zweiten Weltkrieg 1939–1945, vols. 1–14* (Frankfurt/Main: Verlag E. S. Mittler & Sohn).

Tillotson, Lee S., *The Articles of War Annotated* (Harrisburg, PA: The Military Service Publishing Company, 1943).

Trotter, Mildred and Goldine C. Gleser, "Estimation of Stature from Long Bones of American Whites and Negroes," *American Journal of Physical Anthropology 10* (1952), pp. 463–514

———, "A re-evaluation of Estimation Based on measurements of Stature Taken During Life and of Long Bones After Death," *American Journal of Physical Anthropology 16* (1958), pp. 79–123.

Warnock, William, *X-9476: A Historical Analysis* (Columbus, OH: self-published, October 8, 1992).

Weber, Horst, *Zielpunkt Südeifel: Ein Tagebuch über die Luftkriegsereignisse in den Kreisen Bitburg und Prüm 1939–45, band 2: August 1944–Mai 1945* (Bitburg, Germany: Geschichtlicher Arbeitskreis Bitburger-Land, 2003).

Wilkinson, Stephan, "Homecoming," *Air & Space Magazine*, October/November 1995, pp. 34–39.

BOOKS AND JOURNAL ARTICLES WITHOUT ACKNOWLEDGED AUTHORS

Army Battle Casualties and Nonbattle Deaths in World War II, 7 December 1941–31 December 1946, Final Report (Washington, D.C.: Statistical and Accounting Branch, Office of the Adjutant General, 1 June 1953).

Combat History of the Second Infantry Division in World War II (Baton Rouge, LA: Army & Navy Publishing Company, 1946).

Court-Martial Reports: The Judge Advocates General of the Armed Forces and the United States Court of Military Appeals 1952–1953, vol. 8 (Washington, D.C.: Departments of the Treasury, the Army, the Navy, and the Air Force, 15 May 1953).

First United States Army: Report of Operations, vols. 1–4, 20 October 1943–1 August 1944 (First U.S. Army, 1944).

———, *vols. 5–8, 1 August 1944–22 February 1945* (First U.S. Army, 1945).

———, *vols. 9–11, 23 February 1945–8 May 1945* (First U.S. Army, 1945).

German and Japanese Solid-Fuel Rocket Weapons (Washington, D.C.: Military Intelligence Division, War Department, October 1, 1945).

Handbook on German Military Forces (Washington, D.C.: United States Government Printing Office, 1945).

History, V Corps: Operations in the ETO 6 January 1942–9 May 1945 (U.S. Army, 1945).

Idyllisches Alt-Büllingen: Eine Bilddokumentation über den Zeitabschnitt 1900–1950 (Geschäftsstelle des Gemeindekredit von Belgien in Büllingen, 1980). Forward by Rudi Lejeune.

Official Army Register, 1945 edition (Washington, D.C.: United States Government Printing Office, January 1, 1945).

Register of Graduates and Former Cadets of the United States Military Academy West Point, New York, 2000 decennial edition (West Point, NY: Association of Graduates, United States Military Academy, 1999).

"War Cemetery: Crosses in a Belgian field honor the men who died to win the Rhine" *Life*, April 2, 1945 (vol. 18, no. 14), pp. 26–27.

COMBAT INTERVIEWS

After major combat operations, U.S. Army historians visited the units involved and interviewed key officers and enlisted men. The historians subsequently produced narratives in rough typescript format. These documents, known as combat interviews, are presently part of Record Group 407 at the National Archives and Records Administration.

The German Breakthrough—V Corps Sector: 2nd Battalion, 393rd Infantry, 99th Division; interview with Capt. Carl S. Swisher (S-1, 2nd Bn.), 1st Lt. George E. Ridel (FO, Battery B, 370th FA Bn.); interviewer Capt. William J. Fox; January 29, 1945.

The German Breakthrough—V Corps Sector: 3rd Battalion, 393rd Infantry, 99th Division; interview with Capt. Raymond C. McElroy (S-3, 3rd Bn.); interviewer Capt. William J. Fox; January 27, 1945.

The German Breakthrough—V Corps Sector: 1st Battalion, 394th Infantry, 99th Division; interview with Lt. Col. Robert H. Douglas (CO, 1st Bn.), Capt. John S. Sandiland (Ex O, 1st Bn.), 1st Lt. Leon A. Courath (CO, Co. C); interviewer Capt. John S. Howe; January 29, 1945.

The German Breakthrough—V Corps Sector: 2nd Battalion, 394th Infantry, 99th Division; interview with Capt. Robert R. McGee Jr. (S-3, 3rd Bn.); interviewer Capt. William J. Fox; undated, but January 1945.

The German Breakthrough—V Corps Sector: 2nd Battalion, 394th Infantry, 99th Division; interview with Capt. Ben W. Leagrae (Bn. Ex. O.); interviewer Capt. William J. Fox; January 30, 1945.

The German Breakthrough (13–22 Dec. '44): 1st Battalion, 395th Infantry, 99th Division; interview with Lt. Col. Charles J. Hendricks (CO, 1st Bn.), Capt. William H. Pearce (S-3, 1st Bn.), Capt. Virgil E. Smith (CO, Co. B), Capt. Joseph J. Budinsky (CO, Co. C), Capt. Robert L. Gano (CO, Co. D); interviewers M/Sgt. Forrest C. Pogue and S/Sgt. Jose M. Topete; January 28, 1945.

MICROFICHE

Rosters WW-II Dead (All Services) World War II (Ref. No. 601-07) 268 fiche sheets

FIELD MANUALS

War Department Field Manual 7-10: Rifle Company, Infantry Regiment (Washington, D.C.: United States Government Printing Office, March 18, 1944).

War Department Field Manual 7-15: Heavy Weapons Company, Rifle Regiment (Washington, D.C.: United States Government Printing Office, May 19, 1942).

War Department Field Manual 10-63: Graves Registration (Washington, D.C.: United States Government Printing Office, January 15, 1945).

War Department Field Manual 21-26: Advanced Map and Aerial Photograph Reading (Washington, D.C.: United States Government Printing Office, 23 December 1944).

War Department Field Manual 21-75: Scouting, Patrolling, and Sniping (Washington, D.C.: United States Government Printing Office, February 6, 1944).

War Department Basic Field Manual 23-15: Browning Automatic Rifle Caliber .30, M1918A2 (Washington, D.C.: United States Government Printing Office, June 30, 1943).

War Department Basic Field Manual 23-30: Hand and Rifle Grenades; Rocket, AT, HE, 2.36-inch (Washington, D.C.: United States Government Printing Office, February 14, 1944).

War Department Basic Field Manual 23-55: Browning Machine Gun Caliber .30, M1917 (Washington, D.C.: United States Government Printing Office, June 20, 1940).

War Department Basic Field Manual 23-85: 60-mm Mortar M2 (Washington, D.C.: United States Government Printing Office, November 28, 1942).

TABLES OF ORGANIZATION AND EQUIPMENT

T/O & E 7-14, Infantry Cannon Company (Washington, D.C.: War Department, February 26, 1944).

T/O & E 7-17, Infantry Rifle Company (Washington, D.C.: War Department, February 26, 1944).

T/O & E 7-18, Infantry Heavy Weapons Company (Washington, D.C.: War Department, February 26, 1944).

T/O & E 10-297, Quartermaster Graves Registration Company (Washington, D.C.: War Department, November 6, 1943).

ACKNOWLEDGMENTS

I would like to thank my fellow team members: Richard H. Byers, Marc Marique, Jean-Luc Menestrey, Jean-Louis Seel, Jean-Philippe Speder, Vernon E. Swanson, Rex Whitehead, Byron A. Whitmarsh.

Family members of recovered servicemen: Joann Bowman, Cathy Conner-Buchanan, Charles E. Fidler, Denise W. Holland, Sarah J. Holland, Sharon L. Hughes, George Kokotovich, Leon D. Larson, Mary S. Larson, Mary K. Maisel, Mary Miller, Esta W. Morrow, Samuel J. Ohnstad, Verlie B. Ohnstad, Douglas B. Read, Frank A. Read, Thomas R. Read, Verne R. Read, George Sharpe, Joe M. Sharpe, Madeleine M. Sito, Richard S. Sito, Kathleen Winkle, William L. Zimmerman.

99th Division veterans: Curtis L. Amuedo, Nello Bartolozzi, Dwight C. Bishop, Howard I. Bowers, William A. Bray, Wayne L. Cleveland, Carl W. Combs, Thomas J. Cornett, Herman Dickman, Joseph F. Dougherty, Roger V. Foehringer, Raymond F. Gottsacker, Arthur E. Hicks, Oscar F. Hillring, Milton G. Kitchens, Roger C. Lenihan, Eugene A. Lett, James R. McIlroy, Joseph H. Palmer, Milo V. Price, Thomas D. Price, Emanuel Rind, John P. Scaglione, Harold F. Schaefer, Clifford B. Selwood Jr., William L. Shawver, Harold S. Smith, Warren F. Thomas, Byron O. Wilkins Jr., William Braxton Williams Jr., Harold B. Wright.

Mark L. Baldwin, Mark A. Bando, Richard L. Boylan, Bert Caloud, William C. C. Cavanagh, Roy Czajkowski, Robyn W. Daines, Ronald

J. Daines, Carol A. Erickson, Clark K. Frazier, Joe Geraghty, Grant Gerlich, Jerome V. Gleesing, Maralyn A. Guthrie, Erich Hönen, Jett Johnson, Vincent Joris, Manfred Klein, Lyle F. Kunde, James F. Lampe, Mark D. Leney, Wallace Muir, Lillian A. Pfluke, David B. Roath, Lynna Piekutowski, Edgard Pots, Barbara M. Stricklin, Thomas L. Vince, Horst Weber.

The late Lea Leever-Oldham and the Writers of the Western Reserve: Deanna R. Adams, Aileen M. Gilmour, Cheryl Laufer, Karen Peterson, Nancy E. Piazza, Diane M. Taylor, and Janis C. Thompson. They provided constant encouragement, proofreading assistance, and innumerable suggestions that improved the manuscript.

Nancy Piazza and Timothy Wager provided editing expertise and critiqued the manuscript. My attorney, Stephen L. Grant, provided legal advice.

Special thanks to my agent, Andrew H. Zack, and my editor at Penguin Group USA, Ron Martirano.